McGRAW-HILL

Computing Essentials

Annual Edition 1998-1999

Timothy J. O'Leary
Arizona State University

Linda I. O'Leary

Irwin McGraw-Hill

Boston Burr Ridge, IL Dubuque, IA Madison, WI New York San Francisco St. Louis
Bangkok Bogotá Caracas Lisbon London Madrid
Mexico City Milan New Delhi Seoul Singapore Sydney Taipei Toronto

Irwin/McGraw-Hill

A Division of The **McGraw-Hill** *Companies*

Computing Essentials 1998–1999

This book is printed on acid-free paper.

domestic 1 2 3 4 5 6 7 8 9 0 BAN BAN 9 0 0 9 8 7
international 1 2 3 4 5 6 7 8 9 0 BAN BAN 9 0 0 9 8 7

ISBN 0-07-561040-X

Editorial director: Michael Junior
Sponsoring editor: Rhonda Sands
Developmental editor: Kyle Thomes
Marketing manager: James Rogers
Project manager: Michelle Lyon
Production supervisor: Richard DeVitto
Text designer: Christy Butterfield
Cover designer: Lorna Lo
Photo research coordinator: Nicole Widmyer
Illustrations: Brian Jensen, Wayne Clark; Accurate Art
Editorial assistant: Steve Fahringer
Compositor: GTS Graphics, Inc.
Typeface: Garamond Light Condensed
Printer: Banta Company

International Edition

When ordering this title, use ISBN 0-07-115484-1

http://www.mhhe.com

About the Authors

Timothy J. O'Leary is a professor in the School of Accountancy and Information Systems at Arizona State University. He has written several books and articles on computers and information systems.

Linda I. O'Leary is a professional trainer in the area of computers. She has developed computer training manuals for corporations and presented seminars on a wide variety of application programs.

Dedication

To Dan. Thanks for your youthful perspective, dedication, and hard work. Your help this summer made this edition truly a family project—Mom and Dad

Contents in Brief

Contents

Preface to the Instructor

We have truly entered the Information Age.

No matter what career you choose, information technology will affect your life. Knowledge of information technology and the effective use of information technology can make the difference between whether those effects are positive or negative. Our goal is to give students a basic understanding of computing concepts and to build the skills necessary to ensure that information technology is an advantage in whatever path they choose in life.

The 1998–1999 Edition is truly a Multimedia Annual Edition.

Computer Technology Research (CTR) reports that people retain only 20% of what they see and 30% of what they hear. But they remember 50% of what they see *and* hear and as much as 80% of what they see, hear, and do *simultaneously.* In this edition, the multimedia component has been enhanced and expanded to increase student retention of materials. In addition to the quality text that you've come to expect from us, this edition includes a revised CD-ROM containing graphics, video, sound, animations, and experiential cases that bring the harder-to-grasp concepts.

Unlike many other textbooks with a multimedia component, ours has a CD-ROM designed and developed by the authors specifically to complement the text. Organization, philosophy, and terminology are the same for both components. The CD-ROM adds an important dimension to the textbook with carefully selected videos that grab student interest. Animations show conceptual relationships. Numerous demonstrations show cutting-edge application software used for multimedia, virtual reality, image editing, and many other things. The CD-ROM presents numerous detailed Interactive Cases in which your students can participate in real-world applications of many of the most powerful and widely used software tools.

Computing Essentials features a unique visual orientation.

Because we believe that students learn better and retain more when concepts are reinforced visually, we feature a unique visual orientation. Accordingly, *Computing Essentials* balances text with full-color graphics. Our Visual Summaries capture "in a nutshell" the key concepts covered in each chapter. The text contains numerous color illustrations, photos, and charts. Adopters have long held that the visual orientation enhances their students' interest and comprehension.

Distinguishing Features

A Look at the Future Each chapter has a completely revised section that is titled A Look at the Future. Topics are selected based on their expected near-term impact, interest, and relevance. Presented in a light-hearted manner, this forward looking section is designed to be informative and thought provoking.

On the Web This new end of chapter element visually presents thought provoking questions that can be answered using Web resources. Students either visit our Web Site for links to appropriate resources or use Web search tools to locate information.

Guide to the Internet and the World Wide Web The Internet Guide has been updated and expanded to accommodate the increasing importance of the World Wide Web. This comprehensive guide covers sending and receiving e-mail, joining and participating in newsgroups and chat groups, finding Internet services, browsers, Web pages, search tools, and Web utilities. Additionally, Internet and Web concepts have been woven into the text.

Hands-on-Orientation Each chapter in *Computing Essentials* concludes with a short Project requiring students' use of the Internet to research selected topics; Review Questions; and Discussion Questions designed to reinforce the chapter materials and encourage students to apply the concepts learned to solve real-life problems.

Lab Modules

- Microsoft Office 97 and Netscape Communicator have been added to our extensive list of software applications tutorials.
- New design and layout features include bulleted and colored text that clearly identify the steps students are to perform.
- We've added new art throughout and more descriptive screen callouts.
- The very popular ***concept boxes*** and ***visual concept summaries*** make it easy for students to identify and understand the basic concepts while solving the case problem.
- Extensive use of marginal notes provide procedural tips, menu equivalents and keyboard short-cuts, references back to previous discussions and additional information related to the concept.
- The end-of-chapter hands-on practice exercises are clearly ranked in difficulty level using out ***star rating system.*** Further, they are divided into guided step-by-step problems and on your own open-ended problems that emphasize the concepts learned while promoting critical thinking.

The lab modules follow the "learn by doing" approach by combining conceptual coverage with detailed software instructions. A realistic case study based on real-world use of software in a business situation runs throughout each module and leads the student step-by-step from *problem* to *solution*.

Each lab module includes:

- ***Competencies***—clearly state the desired outcome of each lesson.
- ***Concept boxes***—a concept overview box that provides introduction to all the concepts covered in each lab (chapter). This is followed by individual concept boxes throughout the lab that describe in detail the concepts they will be applying.
- ***Case Study***—students follow one business through the use of word processing, spreadsheet, database, and presentation software to address realistic situations that arise in everyday business.
- ***Numerous Screen Displays*** throughout keep the student on track.
- ***Summaries of Key Terms*** and ***Commands.***
- ***Lab Review***—Matching, Fill-in-the-blank, a Discussion Questions.
- ***Hands-on Practice Exercises***—ranked ***Step-by-Step*** and ***On Your Own*** problems.
- ***Visual Concept Summaries***—exciting graphics that reinforce key concepts of each lesson.
- ***Case Project***—provides students with an opportunity to integrate knowledge gained in preceding lessons, and reinforces conceptual understanding of integrating applications to solve more complex problems.
- ***Glossary of Key Terms.***
- ***Summary of Commands.***
- ***Index.***

The Support Package Comprehensive Teaching Material Sets are available for *Computing Essentials* as well as for each of the lab modules. Ancillaries are also available via our Web site at http://www.magpie.org/essentials/.

Each packaged set includes:

- Instructor's Manual—contains objectives, sample schedules, procedural requirements, teaching tips, answers to end-of-chapter problems, solutions to case project, command summary, answers to practice exercises, a printed test bank, and student data files.
- PowerPoint Presentations—present key figures from the text in an interactive and customizable format.

Also available:

- A Windows-based computerized test bank makes it easy to pick and choose from our text-specific test items or to add your own—tests are deliverable via a Lan or Web site.
- Lecture Launcher Videos: Ten 10-minute segments from PCTV®'s acclaimed series *The Computer Chronicles* on today's hottest topics in computing help you inspire students and grab their attention.

For information on how to obtain any of the supplements described, please contact your McGraw-Hill representative.

Acknowledgments

We are, as always, deeply indebted to our reviewers both past and present: David Anderson, Fort Peck Community College; Dr. John Anderson, VPI—Pamplin College of Business; Gary Armstrong, Shippensburg University; Larry Baker, College of Marin; Bill Barth, Cayuga Community College; Prof. Paula Bell, Lock Haven University; Prof. Bill Boroski, Trident Technical College; Frederick Bounds, DeKalb College; Prof. Rich Bright, Moberly Area CC; Prof. Bruce Brown, Salt Lake City CC; Don Brown, Antelope Valley College; Janice Burke, South Suburban College; C.T. Cadenhead, Richland College; Stephanie Chenault, College of Charleston; Earline Cocke, Northwest Mississippi Community College; Prof. Jan Collins, Lamar University-Port Arthur; Barbara Comfort, J. Sergeant Reynolds CC; Terry Cooper, Medicine Hat College; Sharon Cotman, Thomas Nelson CC; Frank Coyle, Southern Methodist University; Jack Cundiff, Horry-Georgetown Tech; Jim Davies, DeAnza College; Michael Dixon, Sacramento City College; Paul Duchow, Pasadena City College; Orlynn R. Evans, Stephen F. Austin State University; William Ferns, Baruch College; Eleanor Flanigan, Montclair State University; Kathleen Geletko, Community College of Allegheny County; Patrick Gilbert, University of Hawaii; Tanya Goette, Kennesaw State College; Thomas Gorecki, Charles County Community College; Timothy Gottleber, North Lake College; Prof. Tim Hall, Mid-Plains CC Area; William Hix, Motlow State University; Daris Howard, Ricks College; Prof. Colin Ikea, Long Beach CC; Peter Irwin, Richland College; Usha Jindal, Washtenaw Community College; N. Jurkovich, Palo Alto College; Tom Kane, Centennial College; Debbie Kramer, Rowan College; Linda Kridelbaugh, Southwestern Oregon Community College; Elizabeth Langan, Community College of Allegheny County; Albert Leary, St. Charles County Community College; Sue Lister, independent development reviewer; Martha Long, North Essex County CC; Jean Lutt, Wayne State; Prof. Barbara Maccarone, Northshore CC; Dr. Gary Margot, Ashland University; Donna Matherly, Tallahassee Community College; Prof. Vicki McCullough; Curtis Meadow, Valdosta State; George Meghabghab, University of Maine; Josephine Mendoza, California State University, San Bernardino; Grazina Metter, Catonsville Community College; Pam Milstead, Louisiana Tech University; Jeff Mock, Diablo Valley College; Owen Murphy, California State University, San Bernardino; Sonia Nayle, Los Angeles City College; Pamela Nelson, Panhandle State University; Brenda Nielson, Mesa Community College; Jeretta Nord, Oklahoma State; Paul Northrup, University of Colorado; Carl Penzuil, Corning CC; Scott Persky, McHenry County College; Nicholas Picioccio, Middlesex County College; Winfred Pikelis, United States Military Academy; Jerry Ralya, independent development reviewer; Linda L. Rice, Saddleback College; Colleen Rinard, Frostburg State University; Lisa Rosner, Stockton State College; Marion Sackson, DePaul University; LoriLee Sadler, Pace University; Joe Sallis, University of Mississippi; Peg Saragina, Santa Rosa Junior College; Judith Scheeren, Westmoreland County CC; Kay Sherman, Clark College; Faye Simmons, SUNY Canton; Daniel Simon, Northampton CC; Elizabeth Swope, Louisiana State University; Danver S. Tomer, University of Central Arkansas; Suzanne Tomlinson, Iowa State University; Charles Walker, Harding University; Edmund Weihrauch, Community College of Allegheny County; Barbara Wertz, Clackamas CC; Karen Wilson, Leeward Community College; Mark Workman, Frank Phillips College; and James Worley, East Tennessee University.

In addition, we are very appreciative of all the efforts of the Irwin/McGraw-Hill staff and others who worked on this book: Mike Junior, Garrett Glanz, and Rhonda Sands for their support of this edition; Richard DeVitto for production supervision; Michelle Lyon for project management; Lorna Lo for her design instincts; Karen Jackson, Eric Munson, Erika Berg, Steve Mitchell, Roger Howell, Kris Johnson, and Greg Hubit for their past editorial, marketing, and managerial support.

We are also grateful for the contributions of those outside Irwin/McGraw-Hill: Dan O'Leary for his youthful perspective, dedication, and hard work; Colleen Hayes for her hard work and continued dedication to the project; Laurel Anderson for photo research; Susan DeMar for her developmental support; Carol Dean for her reviews and ongoing contributions to the project; Christy Butterfield for her innovative design work; Marianne Virgili of Glenwood Springs Chamber of Commerce and Jim Price of the Sports Authority for their contributions toward the development of case materials; GTS Graphics for line illustrations, composition, and prepress work.

Your Future and Computer Competency

COMPETENCIES

After you have read this chapter, you should be able to:

1. **Explain computer competency.**
2. **Distinguish four kinds of computers: microcomputer, minicomputer, mainframe, and supercomputer.**
3. **Explain the five parts of an information system: people, procedures, software, hardware, and data.**
4. **Distinguish application software from system software.**
5. **Describe hardware devices for input, processing, storage, output, and communications.**
6. **Describe document, worksheet, and database files.**
7. **Explain computer connectivity, the Internet, and the World Wide Web.**

Computer competency: **This notion may not be familiar to you, but it's easy to understand. The purpose of this book is to help you become *competent* in computer-related skills. Specifically, we want to help you walk into a job and immediately be valuable to an employer. In this chapter, we first describe why learning about the computer is important to your future. We then present an *overview* of what makes up an information system: people, procedures, software, hardware, and data. In subsequent chapters, we will describe these parts in detail.**

1

Fifteen years ago, most people had little to do with computers, at least directly. Of course, they filled out computerized forms, took computerized tests, and paid computerized bills. But the real work with computers was handled by specialists—programmers, data-entry clerks, and computer operators.

Then microcomputers came along and changed everything. Today it is easy for nearly everybody to use a computer. People who use microcomputers today are called "end users." (See Figure 1-1.) Today:

- Microcomputers are common tools in all areas of life. Writers write, artists draw, engineers and scientists calculate—all on microcomputers. Businesspeople do all three.
- New forms of learning have developed. People who are homebound, who work odd hours, or who travel frequently may take courses by telephone-linked home computers. A college course need not fit within the usual time of a quarter or a semester.
- New ways to communicate and to find people with similar interests are available. All kinds of people are using electronic mail and the Internet to meet and to share ideas.

What about you? How can microcomputers enhance *your* life?

End Users and Computer Competency

By gaining computer competency, end users can use microcomputers to improve their productivity and their value in the workplace.

End users are people who use microcomputers or have access to larger computers. If you are not an end user already, you will probably become one in the near future. That is, you will learn to use packaged computer programs to meet your unique needs for information. Let us point out two things here.

- By "packaged programs," we mean programs that you can buy rather than those you have to write yourself. Examples of packaged programs include video games and work-related programs, such as word processing for typing documents and electronic spreadsheets for analysis.
- By "needs," we mean various organizing, managing, or business needs. That is, they are *information-related* or *decision-making* needs. Becoming **computer competent**—learning how to use the computer to meet your information needs—will improve your productivity. It will also make you a more valuable employee.

How much do you have to know to be computer competent? Clearly, in today's fast-changing technological world, you cannot learn everything—but very few people need to. You don't have to be a computer scientist to make good use of a microcomputer. Indeed, that is precisely the point of this book. Our goal is not to teach you everything there is to know, but only what you *need* to know to get started. Thus, we present only what we think you will find most useful—both now and in the future.

FIGURE 1-1
End users: People are using microcomputers to meet their informational needs.

Four Kinds of Computers

Computers are of four types: microcomputers, minicomputers, mainframes, and supercomputers.

This book focuses principally on microcomputers. However, it is almost certain that you will come in contact, at least indirectly, with other kinds of computers. Thus, we describe many features that are common to these larger machines.

Computers are electronic devices that can follow instructions to accept input, process that input, and produce information. There are four types of computers: *microcomputers, minicomputers, mainframe computers,* and *supercomputers.*

Microcomputers

The most widely used and the fastest-growing type of computer is the **microcomputer.** (See Figure 1-2.) There are two categories of microcomputers—*desktop* and *portable.*

- **Desktop computers** are small enough to fit on top or along the side of a desk and yet are too big to carry around. (See Figure 1-3.) **Personal computers** are one type of desktop. These machines run comparatively easy-to-use application software. They are used by a wide range of individuals, from clerical people to managers. **Workstations** are another type of desktop computer. Generally, these machines are more powerful. They are designed to run more advanced application software. Workstations are used by engineers, scientists, and others who process lots of data. The distinction between personal computers and workstations is now blurring. The principal reason is that personal computers are now nearly as powerful as workstations and are able to run many of the same programs.

FIGURE 1-2
Microcomputers in use—past, present, and future.

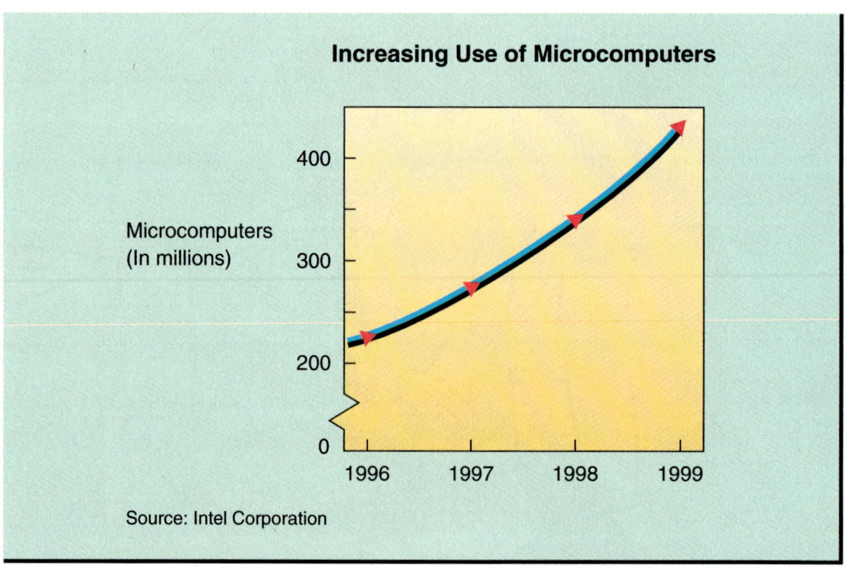

FIGURE 1-3
Desktop computer (Gateway 2000).

- **Portable computers** are microcomputers that are small enough and light enough to move easily from one place to another. There are four categories of portable computers—*laptops, notebooks, subnotebooks,* and *personal digital assistants.*

Laptops, which weigh between 10 and 16 pounds, may be either AC-powered, battery-powered, or both. The AC-powered laptop weighs 12 to 16 pounds. The battery-powered laptop weighs 10 to 15 pounds, batteries included, and can be carried on a shoulder strap. The user of a laptop might be an accountant or financial person who needs to work on a computer away from the desk.

Notebooks are a smaller version of the laptop. (See Figure 1-4.) They weigh between 5 and 10 pounds and can fit into most briefcases. The user of a

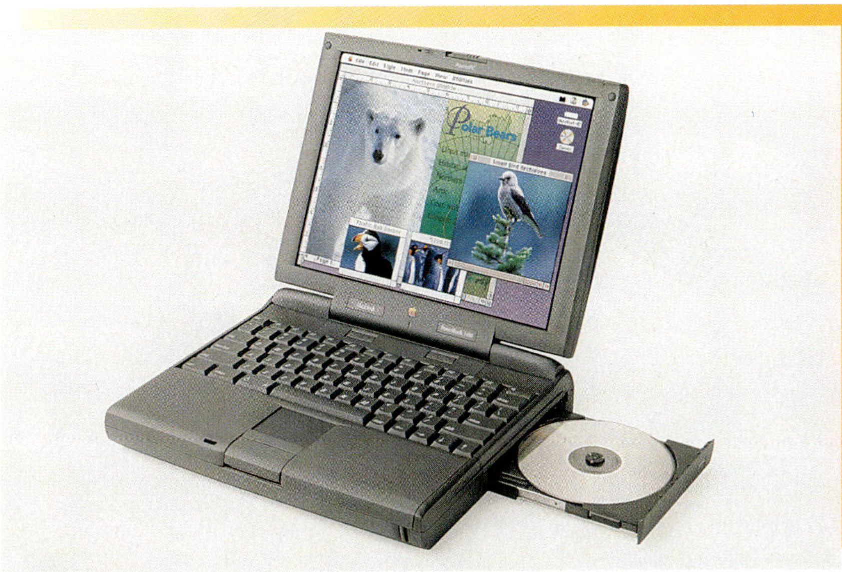

FIGURE 1-4
Notebook computer (IBM ThinkPad 750).

FIGURE 1-5
Subnotebook (Toshiba Portege 300CT).

notebook PC might be a student, salesperson, or journalist who uses the computer for note-taking. It is especially valuable in locations where electrical connections are not available. Notebook computers are the most popular portable computer today.

Subnotebooks, also known as **ultra portables,** are for frequent flyers and life-on-the-road types. Subnotebook users give up a full-size display screen and keyboard in exchange for less weight. Weighing between 2 and 6 pounds, these computers fit easily into a briefcase. (See Figure 1-5.)

Personal Digital Assistants (PDA) are much smaller than even the subnotebooks. Also known as **palmtop computers** and **handheld PCs,** these devices combine pen input, writing recognition, personal organizational tools, and communications capabilities in a very small package. A PDA user might be a worker at a warehouse who records changes in inventory or a busy executive handling daily communications. (See Figure 1-6.)

FIGURE 1-6
Personal digital assistant (Apple Newton Message Pad 2000.)

Minicomputers

Also known as **midrange computers, minicomputers** are desk-sized machines. They fall between microcomputers and mainframes in their processing speeds and data-storing capacities. Medium-size companies or departments of large companies typically use them for specific purposes. For example, they might use them to do research or to monitor a particular manufacturing process. Smaller-size companies typically use minicomputers for their general data processing needs, such as accounting.

Mainframe Computers

Mainframes are large computers occupying specially wired, air-conditioned rooms. They are capable of great processing speeds and data storage. (See Figure 1-7.) They are used by large organizations—businesses, banks, universities, and government agencies—to handle millions of transactions. For example, insurance companies use mainframes to process information about millions of policyholders.

FIGURE 1-7
Mainframe computer (IBM ES/9000).

Supercomputers

The most powerful type of computer is the **supercomputer.** These machines are special, high-capacity computers used by very large organizations. For example, NASA uses supercomputers to track and control space explorations. Supercomputers are also used for oil exploration, simulations, and worldwide weather forecasting. (See Figure 1-8.)

Let us now get started on the road to computer competency. We begin by describing the role of the microcomputer in an information system.

The Five Parts of an Information System

An information system has five parts: people, procedures, software, hardware, and data.

When you think of a microcomputer, perhaps you think of just the equipment itself. That is, you think of the monitor or the keyboard. There is more to it than that. The way to think about a microcomputer is as part of an information system. An **information system** has five parts: *people, procedures, software, hardware,* and *data.* (See Figure 1-9.)

- **People:** It is easy to overlook people as one of the five parts of a microcomputer system. Yet that is what microcomputers are all about—making people, end users like yourself, more productive.
- **Procedures: Procedures** are rules or guidelines for people to follow when using software, hardware, and data. Typically, these procedures are documented in manuals written by computer specialists. Software and hardware manufacturers provide manuals with their products. An example is the *Excel Reference Manual.*
- **Software: Software** is another name for a program or programs. A **program** is the step-by-step instructions that tell the computer how to do its work. The purpose of software is to convert *data* (unprocessed facts) into *information* (processed facts).

FIGURE 1-8
Supercomputer (Cray Y-MP Computer System).

FIGURE 1-9
The five parts of an information system.

- **Hardware:** The **hardware** consists of the equipment: keyboard, mouse, monitor, system unit, and other devices. Hardware is controlled by software. It actually processes the data to create information. (See Figure 1-10.)
- **Data: Data** consists of the raw, unprocessed facts. Examples of raw facts are hours you worked and your pay rate. After data is processed through the computer, it is usually called **information.** An example of such information is the total wages owed you for a week's work.

In large computer systems, there are specialists who deal with writing procedures, developing software, and capturing data. In microcomputer systems, however, end users often perform these operations. To be a competent end user, you must understand the essentials of software, hardware, and data.

FIGURE 1-10
Two well-known microcomputer hardware systems: the Apple Performa 6400 and the Toshiba Infinia 7260.

- *Windows 98,* a new operating system with extensive Internet and multimedia support
- *Windows NT,* a powerful operating system designed for powerful microcomputers
- *OS/2 Warp,* the operating system developed by IBM for powerful microcomputers
- *Macintosh operating system,* the standard operating system for Apple Corporation's Macintosh computers
- *Unix,* an operating system originally developed for minicomputers that can run on many of the more powerful microcomputers

Hardware

Microcomputer hardware consists of devices for input, processing, storage, output, and communications.

Microcomputer hardware—the physical equipment—falls into five categories. They are *input devices, the system unit, secondary storage, output devices,* and *communications devices.* Because we discuss hardware in detail later in the book, we will present just a quick overview here.

Input Devices

Input devices translate data and programs that humans can understand into a form that the computer can process. The most common input devices for microcomputers are the keyboard and the mouse. (See Figure 1-12.) The **keyboard** on a computer looks like a typewriter keyboard, but it has additional specialized keys. A **mouse** is a device that typically rolls on the desktop. It directs the **insertion point,** or cursor, on the display screen. A mouse has one or more buttons for selecting commands. It is also used to draw figures.

FIGURE 1-12
Keyboard and mouse.

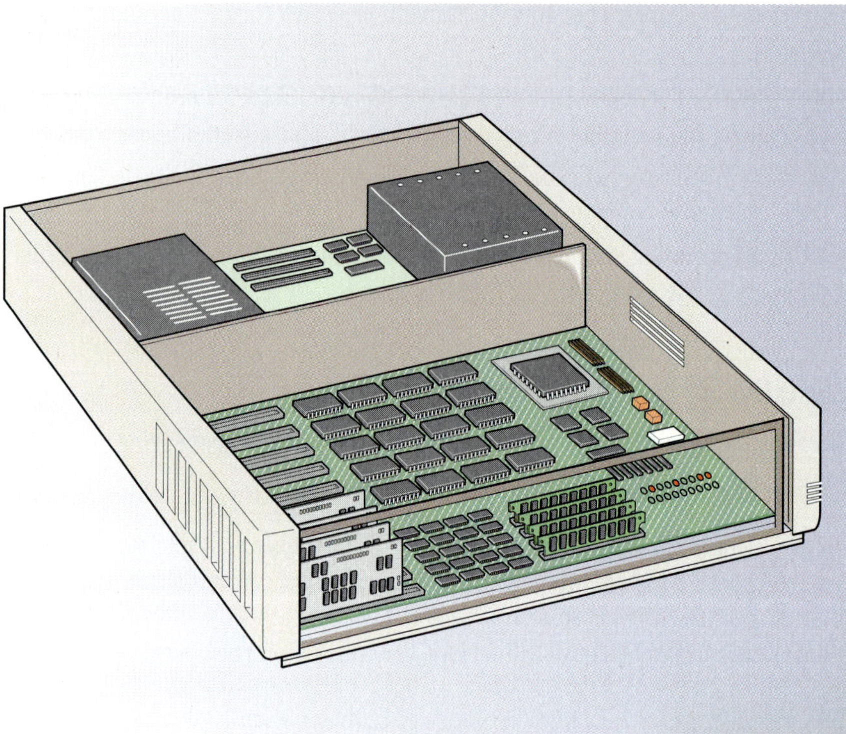

FIGURE 1-13
System unit.

FIGURE 1-14
Intel Pentium microprocessor chip.

The System Unit

The **system unit** is electronic circuitry housed within the computer cabinet. (See Figure 1-13.) The two main parts of the system unit are:

- The **central processing unit (CPU)** controls and manipulates data to produce information. A microcomputer's CPU is contained on a single integrated circuit or microprocessor chip. These chips are called **microprocessors.** (See Figure 1-14.)
- **Memory,** also known as **primary storage** or **random access memory (RAM),** holds data and program instructions for processing the data. It also holds the processed information before it is output. Memory is sometimes referred to as *temporary* storage because it will be lost if the electrical power to the computer is disrupted or cut off. Data and instructions are held in memory only as long as the electrical power to the computer is on. Memory is located in the system unit on tiny memory chips.

Secondary Storage

Secondary storage also holds data and programs. However, it stores *permanently.* That is, the data and programs remain even after the electrical power is turned off. Secondary storage devices are located outside the central processing unit and are typically built into the system unit cabinet.

For microcomputers, the most important kinds of secondary storage "media" are as follows:

- **Floppy disks** (also called "diskettes") hold data or programs in the form of magnetized spots on plastic platters. The two sizes most commonly used are 3½-inch and 5¼-inch diskettes. The smaller size is more durable, can hold more, and is more widely used.(See Figure 1-15.)

  A floppy disk is inserted into a **disk drive.** (See Figure 1-16.) This mechanism **reads** data from the disk. That is, the magnetized spots on the disk are converted to electronic signals and transmitted to primary storage inside the computer. A disk drive can also **write** data. That is, it can take the electronic information processed by the computer and record it magnetically onto the disk.
- A **hard disk** contains one or more metallic disks encased within a disk drive. Like floppy disks, hard disks hold data or programs in the form of magnetized spots. They also *read* and *write* data in much the same way as do floppy disks. However, the storage capacity of a hard-disk unit is many times that of a floppy disk and much faster.
- Unlike floppy and hard disks, **optical disks** hold data and programs by changing the reflecting surface of the disk. Some types of optical disks can read and write data. Some types can be written to only one time. The best-known type of optical disk, however, can only be read from. These are called **CD-ROM** for compact disk–read only memory and **DVD-ROM** for digital versatile disk—read only memory. (Refer to Figure 1-15.)

Floppy and optical disks are inserted into and removed from their disk drives and are stored separately. The hard disk, by contrast, typically is not removable.

FIGURE 1-15
A 3½-inch floppy disk and a CD-ROM disk.

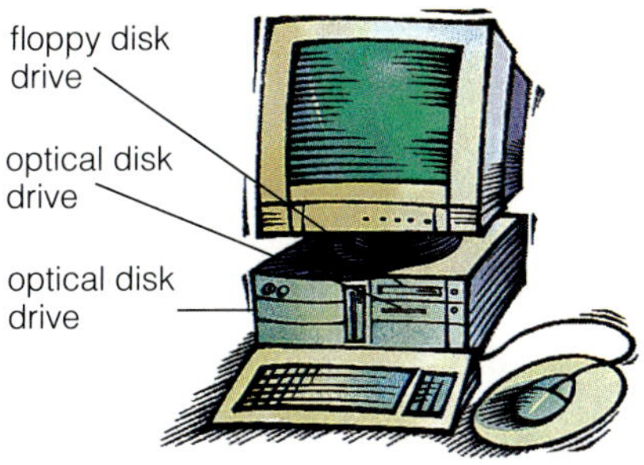

FIGURE 1-16
Three kinds of disk drives: floppy, optical, and hard.

FIGURE 1-17
Newer monitors show sharp images and vibrant colors.

FIGURE 1-18
Some printers can print color images on paper.

Output Devices

Output devices are pieces of equipment that translate the processed information from the CPU into a form that humans can understand. One of the most important output devices is the **monitor,** or **video display screen,** which resembles a television screen. The quality of monitors has improved dramatically. Many monitors now offer crisp images and vivid colors. (See Figure 1-17.) Another important output device is the **printer,** a device that produces printed paper output. (See Figure 1-18.)

Communications Devices

Communications hardware sends and receives data and programs from one computer or secondary storage device to another. Many microcomputers use a **modem.** This device converts the electronic signals from the computer into electronic signals that can travel over a telephone line. A modem at the other end of the line then translates the signals for the receiving computer. A modem may be internal, or located inside a microcomputer's system cabinet. It may also be a separate unit, or external. (See Figure 1-19.)

FIGURE 1-19
An external modem connects a microcomputer and a telephone.

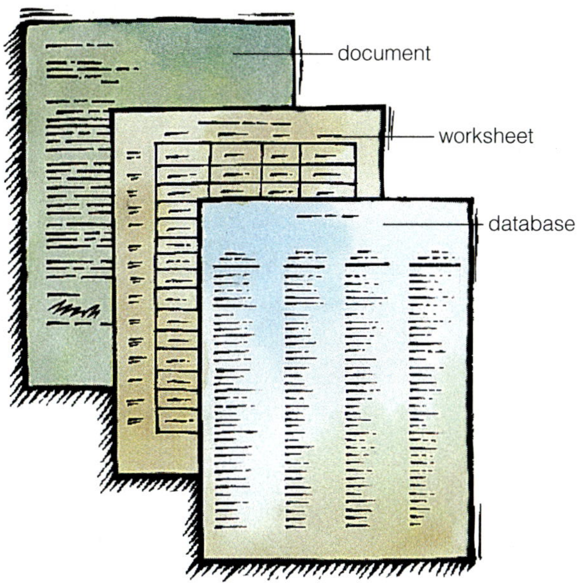

FIGURE 1-20
Three types of files: document, worksheet, and database.

Data

Data is contained in files for documents, worksheets, and databases.

Data is used to describe facts about something. If data is stored electronically in files, it can be used directly as input for the information system.

Three common types of files (see Figure 1-20) are:

- **Document files,** created by word processors to save documents such as memos, term papers, and letters.
- **Worksheet files,** created by electronic spreadsheets like Excel to analyze things like budgets and to predict sales.
- **Database files,** typically created by database management programs to contain highly structured and organized data. For example, an employee database file might contain all the workers' names, social security numbers, job titles, and other related pieces of information.

Connectivity

Connectivity is the microcomputer's ability to communicate with other computers and information sources.

Connectivity is the capability of your microcomputer to share information with other computers. Data and information can be sent over telephone lines or cable and through the air. Thus, your microcomputer can be *connected* to other computers. It can also be connected to many computerized data banks and other sources of information that lie well beyond your desk.

Connectivity is a very significant development, for it expands the uses of the microcomputer severalfold. Central to the concept of connectivity is the **computer network.** A network is a communications system connecting two or more computers. Networks connect people as close as the next office and as far away as halfway around the world.

The **information superhighway** is a term used to describe the future of communication networks and computers. The basis of this highway, also known as the **National Information Infrastructure (NII)** or the **National Information Highway (NIH),** is the **Internet.** The Internet is a huge computer network available to nearly everyone with a microcomputer and a means to connect to it. The **World Wide Web,** also known as **WWW** and the **Web,** is an Internet service that provides access to numerous resources available on the Internet.

A Look at the Future

Computer competency is understanding the rules and the power of microcomputers. Competency lets you take advantage of increasingly productive software, hardware, and the connectivity revolution that are expanding the microcomputer's capabilities.

The purpose of this book is to help you be computer competent not only in the present but also in the future. Having competency requires your having the knowledge and understanding of the rules and the power of the microcomputer. This will enable you to benefit from three important developments: more powerful software, more powerful hardware, and connectivity to outside information resources. It will also help you to remain computer competent and to continue to learn in the future.

Powerful Software

The software now available can do an extraordinary number of tasks and help you in an endless number of ways. More and more employers are expecting the people they hire to be able to use it. Thus, we spend the next three chapters describing basic applications, advanced applications, and system software.

Powerful Hardware

Microcomputers are now much more powerful than they used to be. Indeed, the newer models have the speed and power of room-size computers of only a few years ago. However, despite the rapid change of specific equipment, their essential features remain unchanged. Thus, the competent end user should focus on these features. Chapters 5 through 7 explain what you need to know about hardware: the central processing unit, input/output devices, and secondary storage. A Buyer's Guide is presented at the end of this book for those considering the purchase of a microcomputer system.

Connectivity

No longer are microcomputers and competent end users bound by the surface of the desk. Now they can reach past the desk and link with other computers to share data, programs, and information. Accordingly, we devote Chapters 8 and 9 to discussing connectivity: communications, files, databases, and the Internet. An Internet and World Wide Web Guide describing how to access and use the Internet and the Web is presented at the back of this book.

Changing Times

Are the times changing any faster now than they ever have? Most people think so. Those who were alive when radios, cars, and airplanes were being introduced certainly lived through some dramatic changes. Has technology made our own times even more dynamic? Whatever the answer, it is clear we live in a fast-paced age.

Most businesses have become aware that they must adapt to changing technology or be left behind. Many organizations are now making formal plans to keep track of technology and implement it in their competitive strategies. Nearly every corporation in the world has a presence on the Internet. Delivery services such as Federal Express and UPS provide customers with the ability to personally track the delivery of their packages. Retail stores such as JCPenney and Wal-Mart provide catalog support and sales. Banks such as Wells Fargo and Citibank support home banking and electronic commerce. You can even purchase tickets to concerts, the theatre, and sporting events on the Internet. (See Figure 1-21.)

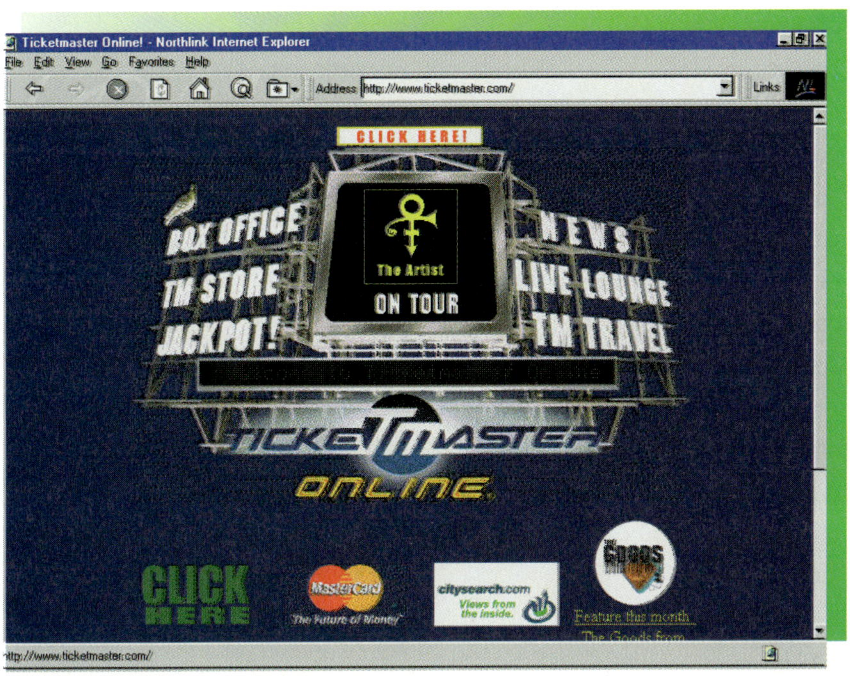

FIGURE 1-21
Ticket Master Web site.

Clearly, such changes do away with some jobs—those of many bank tellers and cashiers, for example. However, they create opportunities for other people. New technology requires people who are truly capable of working with it. These are not the people who think every piece of equipment is so simple they can just turn it on and use it. Nor are they those who think each new machine is a potential disaster. In other words, new technology needs people who are not afraid to learn it and are able to manage it. The real issue, then, is not how to make technology better. Rather, it is how to integrate the technology with people.

After reading this book, you will be in a very favorable position compared with many other people in industry today. You will learn not only the basics of hardware, software, and connectivity. You will also learn the most *current* technology. You will therefore be able to use these tools to your advantage—to be a winner.

KEY TERMS

application software (8)
CD-ROM (13)
central processing unit (CPU) (12)
communications hardware (14)
computer (4)
computer competent (3)
computer network (16)
connectivity (15)
custom program (9)
custom-made software (9)
data (8)
database file (15)
desktop computer (4)
disk drive (13)
document file (15)
DVD-ROM (13)
end user (3)
floppy disk (13)
handheld PC (6)
hard disk (13)
hardware (8)
information (8)
information superhighway (16)
information system (7)
input device (11)
insertion point (11)
Internet (16)
keyboard (11)
laptop (5)
mainframes (6)
memory (12)
microcomputer (4)
microprocessor (12)
midrange computer (6)
minicomputer (6)
modem (14)
monitor (14)
mouse (11)
National Information Highway (NIH) (16)
National Information Infrastructure (NII) (16)
notebook (5)
operating system (10)
optical disk (13)
output device (14)
packaged software (9)
palmtop computer (6)

personal computer (4)
personal digital assistant (PDA) (6)
portable computer (5)
primary storage (12)
printer (14)
procedure (7)
program (7)
random access memory (RAM) (12)
read (13)
secondary storage (13)
software (7)
subnotebook (6)
supercomputer (6)
system software (10)
system unit (12)
video display screen (14)
Web (16)
worksheet file (15)
workstation (4)
World Wide Web (16)
write (13)
WWW (16)

REVIEW QUESTIONS

True/False

1. Microcomputers are common tools in all areas of life.
2. Hardware consists of a monitor, a keyboard, and software.
3. DOS is the standard operating system for Apple Corporation's Macintosh computers.
4. Memory is also known as primary storage.
5. A modem is used to send electronic signals over telephone lines.

Multiple Choice

1. Computers are electronic devices that accept instructions, process input, and produce:
   a. information
   b. prewritten programs
   c. data
   d. end users
   e. system software
2. High-capacity computers used primarily for research purposes are:
   a. microcomputers
   b. minicomputers
   c. mainframes
   d. supercomputers
   e. personal computers
3. The central processing unit (CPU) is located in the:
   a. hard disk
   b. system unit
   c. memory
   d. monitor
   e. keyboard
4. When electrical power is disrupted or cut off, data and programs are lost in:
   a. secondary storage
   b. basic tools
   c. memory
   d. operating system
   e. hard disk

5. Files containing highly structured and organized data are:
   a. documents
   b. worksheets
   c. databases
   d. graphics
   e. communications

Fill in the Blank

1. __________ __________ are people who use microcomputers or have access to larger computers.
2. Also known as midrange computers, __________ are frequently used by departments within larger organizations.
3. Written __________ are guidelines or rules to follow when using software, hardware, and data.
4. Secondary __________ is used to store data and programs permanently.
5. __________ is a service that provides access to numerous Internet resources.

Open Ended

1. What is computer competency?
2. Describe the five parts of an information system.
3. Name the five categories of microcomputer hardware.
4. What is the difference between memory and secondary storage?
5. What are connectivity, the Internet, and the Web?

DISCUSSION QUESTIONS AND PROJECTS

1. *Your reasons for learning computing:* How are you already using computer technology? What's happened in the computer-related world in the last six months that you might have read about or seen on television? How are companies using computers to stay on the cutting edge? These are some questions you might discuss with classmates to see why computers are an exciting part of life.

   You might also consider the reasons why you want to gain computer competency. Imagine your dream career. How do you think microcomputers, from what you already know, can help you do the work you want to do? What kind of after-hours interests do you have? Assuming you could afford it, how could a microcomputer bring new skills or value to those interests?
2. *The Internet and the Web.* The Internet and Web are the most exciting connectivity developments today. If you have used the Internet or the Web, discuss your experiences by describing what you used it for, what you liked about it, and what you did not like. If you have not used the Internet or the Web, describe how you think it will impact your life, how you expect to learn more about it, and what you will likely use it for.

on the web

Exercises and Explorations

1 Virtual Shopping Malls

Like any community, the Internet community has shopping malls. Visit our Web site at http://www.magpie.org/essentials/chapter-1.html to link to one of the most popular malls. Browse through the mall and find a product that you are familiar with, and print out the information provided on that item. Write a paragraph describing how the prices, services, and selection of the virtual mall compare with those of a traditional mall in your community.

2 Virtual Libraries

It might surprise you to learn that you can visit libraries on the Web where you can browse through the stacks, research selected topics, and check out books. Several virtual libraries have *e-texts*, which are entire books on computer, that anyone can download and use. Visit our Web site at http://www.magpie.org/essentials/chapter-1.html to link to one of these libraries. Find a text on a topic that intersts you and print out its first page. Write a paragraph on the benefits and shortfalls of using virtual libraries as a resource for your school papers.

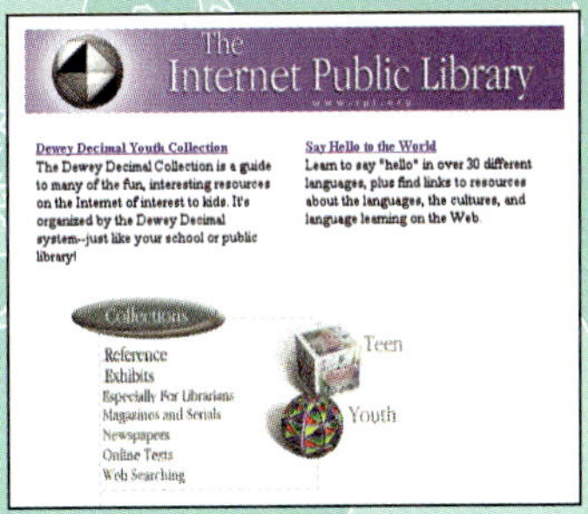

3 Personal Digital Assistants

PDAs are becoming more and more popular with professionals in all areas. They are widely used to store addresses, track appointments, and much more. Learn more about PDAs by connecting to the site Yahoo at http://www.yahoo.com. Look at the subject area "Computers and Intenet: Hardware: PDAs" or search the key words "PDA." Print out the page of search results that you find. Write a paragraph on the abilities of PDAs and how they differ from desktop and portable computers.

4 Ticket Master

Some of the hottest sites on the Web offer the latest music news, present live concerts, and provide updates on your favorite band. Visit our Web site at http://www.magpie.org/essentials/chapter-1.html to link to one the most popular music sites. Once connected to that site, check out your favorite band and print out its tour dates or information about its latest album. Write a paragraph describing how you located the information and discuss how the band could better use the Internet to promote its music.

VISUAL SUMMARY

Your Future and Computer Competency

PEOPLE AND PROCEDURES

People

People are competent end users working to increase their productivity. **End users** use microcomputers and software (such as word processing and spreadsheet programs) to solve information-related or decision-making problems.

Procedures

Procedures are manuals and guidelines that instruct end users on how to use the software and hardware.

SOFTWARE

Software is another name for **programs**—instructions that tell the computer how to process data. Two kinds are application and system software.

Application Software

Application software performs useful functions.

APPLICATION SOFTWARE

BASIC	ADVANCED
Word processors	Graphics programs
Spreadsheet programs	Multimedia
Database managers	Web publishers
Presentation graphics	Groupware
Personal management	Project management
Integrated programs	Artificial intelligence

System Software

System software is "background" software that helps a computer manage its internal resources. An example is the **operating system.** Popular microcomputer operating systems:

SYSTEM SOFTWARE

OPERATING SYSTEM	DESCRIPTION
DOS	The original operating system for IBM and IBM-compatible microcomputers
Windows	Environment that extends capability of DOS
Windows 95	Operating system with built-in Internet support
Windows 98	Operating system with extensive Internet and multimedia support
Windows NT	Operating system for very powerful microcomputers
OS/2 Warp	Developed for very powerful microcomputers
Macintosh operating system	Standard operating system for Apple's Macintosh computers
Unix	Runs on many powerful microcomputers

TYPES OF COMPUTERS

TYPE	DESCRIPTION
Microcomputers	Desktop and portable computers, widely used and number increasing fast
Minicomputers	Medium-sized, also known as midrange, used by medium-sized organizations and departments within larger organizations
Mainframes	Large computers for large organizations
Supercomputers	High-capacity machines for specialized uses like research

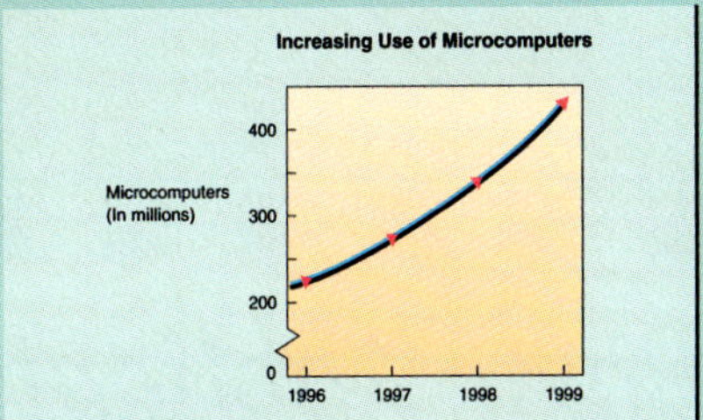

Source: Intel Corporation

HARDWARE

Input Devices

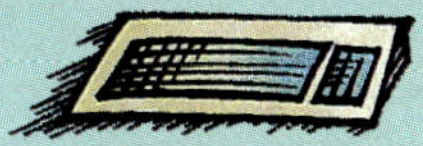

Input devices take data and put it into a form the computer can process. Especially important is the **keyboard,** a typewriter-like keyboard with specialized keys.

The System Unit

The **system unit** consists of electronic circuitry with two parts:

- **The central processing unit (CPU)**—controls and manipulates data to produce information
- **Memory (primary storage)**—temporarily holds data, program instructions, and processed data

Secondary Storage

Secondary storage stores data and programs. Three storage "media":

- **Floppy disk**—removable flexible 3½-inch or 5¼-inch plastic disks
- **Hard disk**—nonremovable, enclosed disk drive
- **Optical disk**—removable, **CD-ROM** and **DVD-ROM** are best known

Output Devices

Output devices output processed information from CPU. Two important output devices:

- **Monitor**—TV screen-like device to display results
- **Printer**—device that prints out images on paper

Communications Devices

These send and receive data and programs from one computer to another. A device that connects a microcomputer to a telephone is a **modem.**

DATA AND CONNECTIVITY

Data

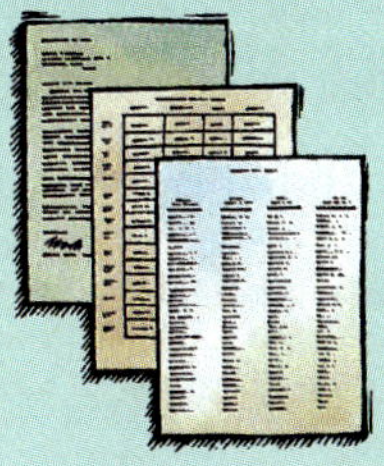

Data describes something and is typically stored electronically in a file. A **file** is a collection of characters organized as a single unit. Common types of files:

- **Document:** letters, research papers, memos
- **Worksheet:** budget analyses, sales projections
- **Database:** structured and organized data

Connectivity

Connectivity is a concept describing the ability of end users to tap into resources well beyond their desktops. Two important aspects of connectivity are:

- **Computer networks**—microcomputers can be linked to other computers to share data and resources.
- **Information superhighway**—is a term used to describe the future of communication networks and computers.
- **World Wide Web** or **Web** is a service to access data and information on the Internet.

Basic Applications

Think of the microcomputer as an *electronic tool.* You may not consider yourself very good at typing, calculating, organizing, presenting, or managing information. A microcomputer, however, can help you to do all these things—and much more. All it takes is the right kind of software—the programs that go into the computer. We describe some of the most important ones in this chapter.

COMPETENCIES

After you have read this chapter, you should be able to:

1. **Explain the features common to all kinds of application software.**
2. **Describe application software for word processing, spreadsheets, database management, presentation graphics, and personal information management.**
3. **Describe integrated software that combines all these tasks.**
4. **Describe software suites that combine separate Windows applications.**

2

Not long ago, trained specialists were required to perform many of the operations you can now perform with a microcomputer. Secretaries used typewriters to create professional-looking business correspondence. Market analysts used calculators to project sales. Graphic artists drew by hand. Data processing clerks created and stored files of records on large computers. Now you can do all these tasks—and much more—with a microcomputer and basic application programs.

General-Purpose Applications

Some features are common to all kinds of applications.

Word processing, electronic spreadsheets, database management, presentation graphics, and personal information management are *general-purpose* applications. That is, they are designed to be used by many people to do the most common kinds of tasks. This is why we call them basic applications. Some well-known software publishers are Microsoft, Lotus, and Corel. They are continually improving and revising their application software to better meet the changing needs of users. When a package first appears, it is assigned the number 1.0. As changes are made to the application software, the number changes. The number before the period refers to the **version,** and the number after the period refers to the **release.** Changes in a version number indicate major changes; changes in releases refer to minor changes.

Most application software (sometimes referred to simply as *software,* a *program,* or an *application*) have common features. The following are the most important.

Menus

Almost all software packages have **menus** to present commands. Typically, the menus are displayed in a menu bar at the top of the screen. When one of the menu items is selected, a pull-down menu appears. This is a list of commands associated with the selected menu. (See Figure 2-1.)

Shortcut Keys

Many applications also have **shortcut keys** for frequently used commands. They make it easier and faster to select certain commands. Many of these shortcuts use the **function keys,** F1, F2, and so on. Other shortcuts use key combinations typically consisting of the Alt, Ctrl, or Shift key used in combination with a letter, number, or function key. For example, in Word 97, the shortcut key F7 starts the spelling tools, and the key combination of shift and F7 starts the Thesaurus tool. (Refer to Figure 2-1.)

Toolbars

Toolbars typically are below the menu bar. They contain **icons** or graphic representations for commonly used commands. This offers the user a graphic approach to selecting commands. It is an example of a **graphical user interface (GUI)** in which graphic objects rather than menus can be used to select commands. (Refer to Figure 2-1.)

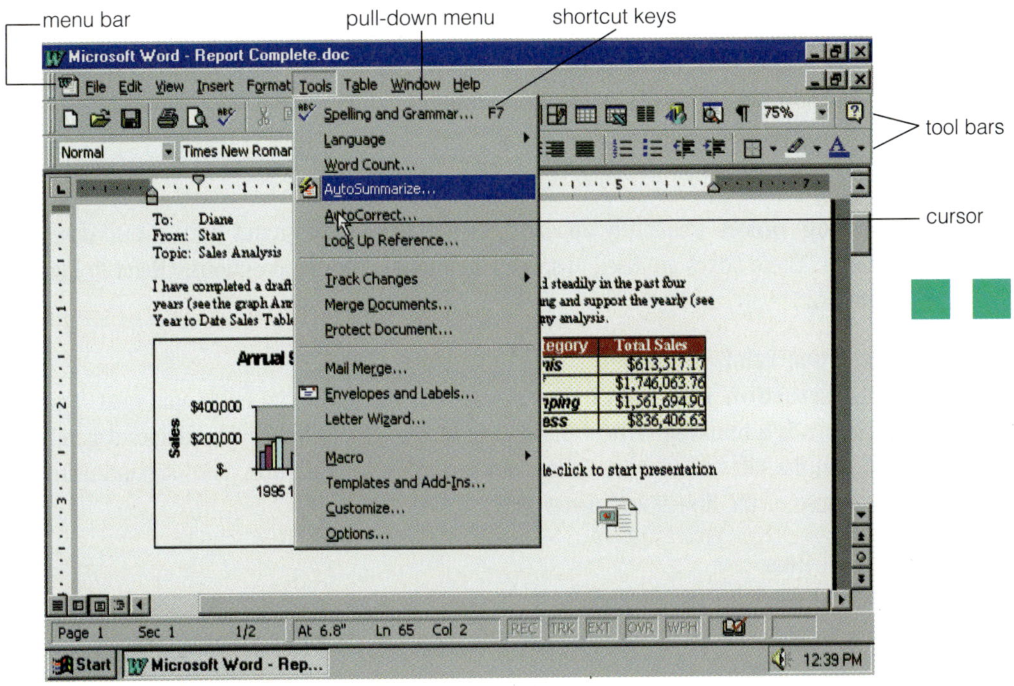

FIGURE 2-1
A menu bar and pull-down menu (Microsoft Word 97).

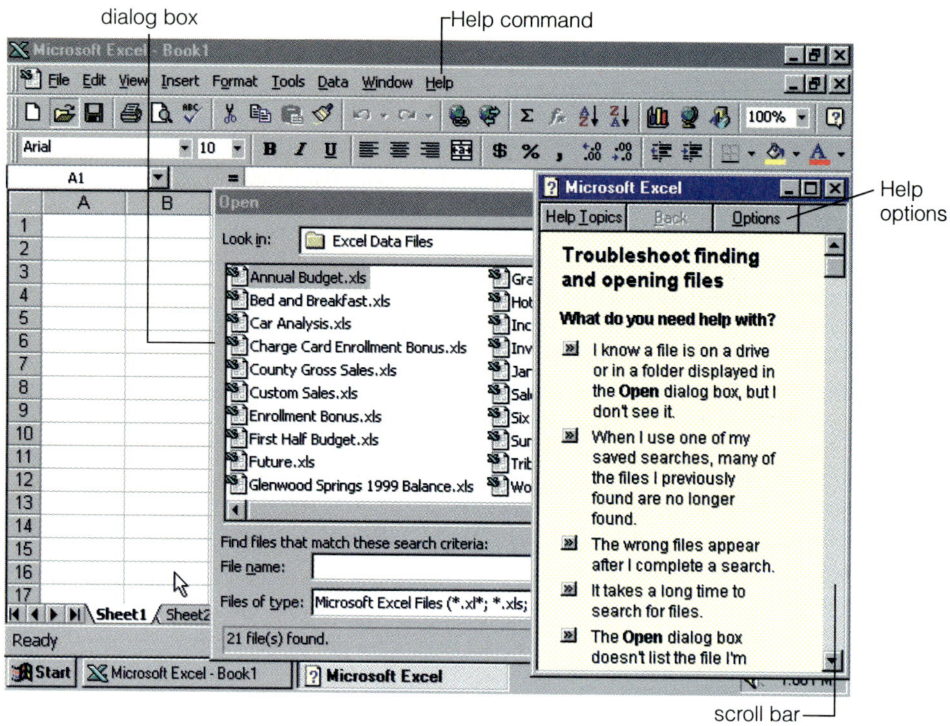

FIGURE 2-2
A Help screen (Microsoft Excel 97).

Help

For most application packages, one of the menus on the menu bar is **Help.** When selected, the help options appear. These options typically include a table of contents, a search feature to locate reference information about specific commands, and access to special learning features such as tutorials and step-by-step instructions. Additionally, most applications have **context-sensitive help.** These help systems locate and display reference information directly related to the task you are performing. (See Figure 2-2.)

Dialog Boxes

Dialog boxes frequently appear after selecting a command from a pull-down menu. These boxes are used to specify additional command options. (Refer to Figure 2-2.)

Insertion Point

The **insertion point** or **cursor** shows you where you can enter data next. Typically, it is a blinking vertical bar on the screen. It can have other shapes depending on the software you are using. You can move the insertion point around using a mouse or the directional arrow keys.

Scroll Bars

Scroll bars are usually located on the right and/or the bottom of the screen. They enable you to display additional information not currently visible on the screen. (Refer to Figure 2-2.)

Edit

Everybody makes mistakes entering data and information. The ability to change or to edit entries is a feature common to almost all applications. The **edit** feature makes revising and updating easy and is one of the most valuable features.

Cut, Copy, and Paste

Perhaps you have entered information that is wrong, or you decide you do not want to include the information at all. Or perhaps you want the same information to appear in multiple locations. You can easily make these changes using **cut, copy,** and **paste.** First, you select the information to be removed or copied by highlighting it. Then you choose the command to cut or to copy. If you select cut, the information simply disappears from your screen. If you select copy, the information remains but a copy is made. Then, by moving the insertion point to another location and selecting the paste command, you can make the selected information appear at the new location. (See Figure 2-3.)

Undo

It is easy to incorrectly select a command. Frequently, these accidently selected commands do things that make changes that are not intended—for example, deleting a paragraph or a formula. No need to panic . . . use **undo.** This feature restores your work to how it was before the last command was selected. Many programs allow you to undo multiple past actions.

Save and Print

Common to all applications is the ability to **save** or store your work as a file on a floppy or hard disk. This allows you to open and use the file at a later time in

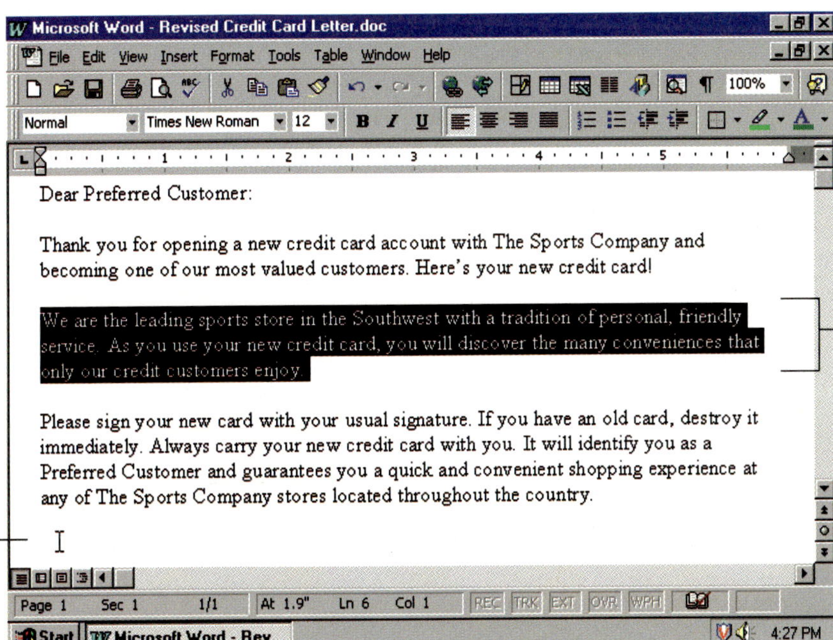

FIGURE 2-3
Cut, Copy, and Paste (Microsoft Word 97).

FIGURE 2-4

Common features of general-purpose applications.

COMMON FEATURES

FEATURE	DESCRIPTION
Menu	Presents commands available for selection
Shortcut Keys	Special-purpose keys for frequently used commands
Toolbar	Presents graphic objects for commands
Help	Presents explanations of various commands
Dialog Box	Used to specify additional command options
Insertion Point	Shows where data can be entered
Scroll Bars	Used to display additional information
Edit	Changes entered information
Cut, Copy, and Paste	Deletes, moves, or copies information
Undo	Restores work prior to last command
Save and Print	Saves work in a file and prints a copy on paper

case you want to add to or modify the document. In addition, all applications allow you to print a copy of your document on paper.

See Figure 2-4 for a summary of the most important common features of general-purpose applications.

Let us now describe the categories of application software that we are calling basic applications.

Word Processors

Word processing software is used to create text-based documents.

Word processing software creates text-based **documents** such as letters, memos, term papers, reports, and contracts. Once it was thought that only secretaries would use word processors. Now they are used extensively in managerial and professional life. Indeed, it has been found that, among the basic software applications, word processors produce the highest gains in productivity.

If you have used a typewriter, then you know what word processing *begins* to feel like. You type in text on the keyboard. However, with word processing, you view the words as you type on a computer monitor instead of on a piece of paper. After you are finished you turn on the printer and print out the results on paper.

The beauty of a word processor is that you can make changes or corrections as you are typing. Want to change a report from double spacing to single spacing? Alter the width of the margins on the left and right? Delete some paragraphs and add some others from yet another document? A word processor allows you to do all these with ease. Indeed, the principal editing activities of *deleting, inserting,* and *replacing* can be done just by selecting text and clicking buttons on the toolbar.

Popular word processing packages include Microsoft Word, Corel WordPerfect, and Lotus Word Pro. (See Figure 2-5.) Some important features shared by most word processors are described in the following sections.

FIGURE 2-5

Word processing software (Microsoft Word 97).

Word Wrap and the Enter Key

One basic word processing feature is **word wrap.** On a typewriter, you must decide when to finish typing a line. You indicate the end of a line by pressing a carriage return key. A word processor automatically moves the insertion point to the next line once the current line is full. As you type, the words "wrap around" to the next line. To begin a new paragraph or leave a blank line, you press the **Enter key.**

Spelling and Grammar Checkers

Spelling can be checked by running a **spelling checker** program. Incorrectly spelled words are identified and alternative spellings suggested. Many word processors include a spelling checker feature that identifies typing errors as you type. For example, Word 97 identifies misspelled words with a red wavy underline. Also commonly included is a feature that will automatically correct many common typing errors as they are made. For example, capitalizing the first letter of a sentence is automatically done.

In a similar manner, **grammar checkers** can be run that will identify poor wording, excessively long sentences, and incorrect grammar. As with spelling checkers, many programs include a feature that checks your grammar as you type. For example, Word 97 identifies possible incorrect grammar with a green wavy underline.

Other Features

- **Alignment:** Text can be **aligned** within the margins in various ways. The most common is left alignment. This means the text is displayed with an even left margin and a ragged right margin. Another common alignment is full justification. This means that the text on both the left and right margins is even.
- **Formatting:** Text can be enhanced in a variety of ways including adding basic **formatting** such as bold, underline, and italics or by applying special effects such as text shadows and colors. Additionally, type font and size can be changed to add emphasis to selected text and to improve the overall appearance of the document.
- **References:** Tables of contents, footnotes, end notes, indexes, page numbers, bulleted lists, and other features found in research papers can be easily created.
- **Search and Replace:** You can quickly locate any character, word, or phrase in your document using the **search** or **find** commands. In addition, you can replace the located text with other text you specify using the **replace** command. For example, you could quickly locate each occurrence of the word *Chicago* and replace it with the word *Denver.* These commands are useful for quickly finding and fixing errors in your document.
- **Tables:** Text documents often include both text and numbers. This type of information can be displayed as a **table** in row-and-column format to make reading and understanding complex information easier.

- **Hypertext links: Hypertext links** can be created to cross-reference information within the current document and between documents. Clicking on a hypertext link jumps your screen display to the specified location in the referenced document. This is most useful for viewing documents online. For example, if you cross-reference another chapter, you can add a hypertext link so the reader can jump to that chapter. Hypertext links can also reference sources on the Web.
- **Thesaurus:** A **thesaurus** enables you to quickly find the right word or an alternative word with a similar meaning.
- **Merge:** A **mail merge** or **form letter** feature allows you to merge different names and addresses. You can mail out the same form letter to different people.
- **Graphics:** Objects such as lines and shapes can be created using a **drawing program.** Additionally, features commonly referred to as **text art** or **word art** can be used to manipulate text into various shapes and colors. You can insert predrawn illustrations such as **clip art** and other types of picture images into a text document. (See Figure 2-6.)
- **Internet publishing:** Many word processors are including features that allow you to create and edit documents to display on the Web.
- **Workgroup:** Group projects that require collaborative efforts in the creation of a document are common in business today. To assist with this need, most word processors include features that allow multiple users to work on a single document at the same time. Each user's changes or contributions are marked in a different color.

FIGURE 2-6
Clip art (Microsoft PowerPoint 97).

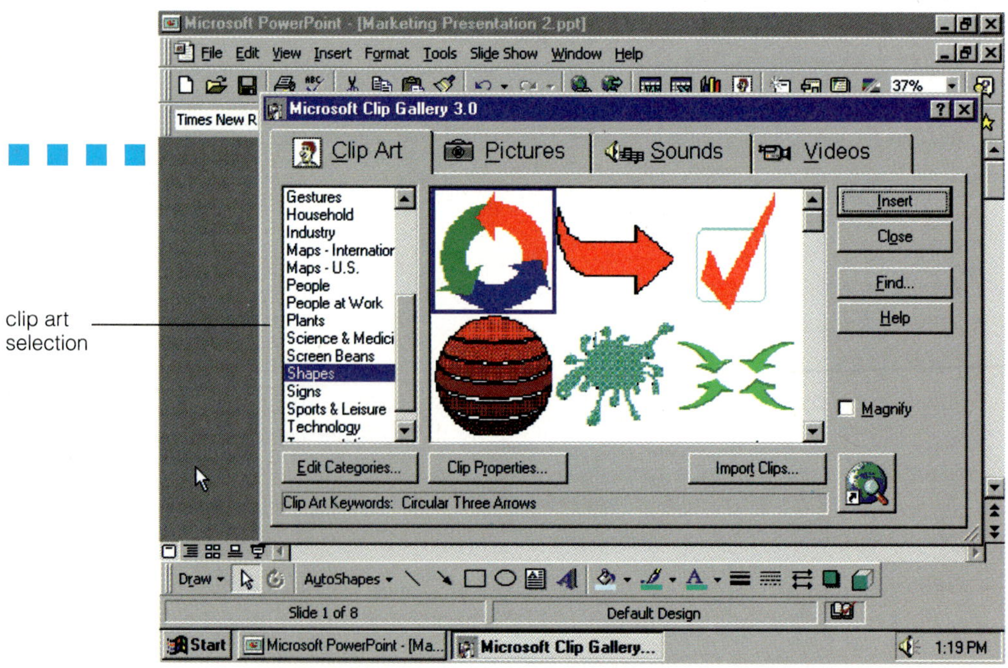

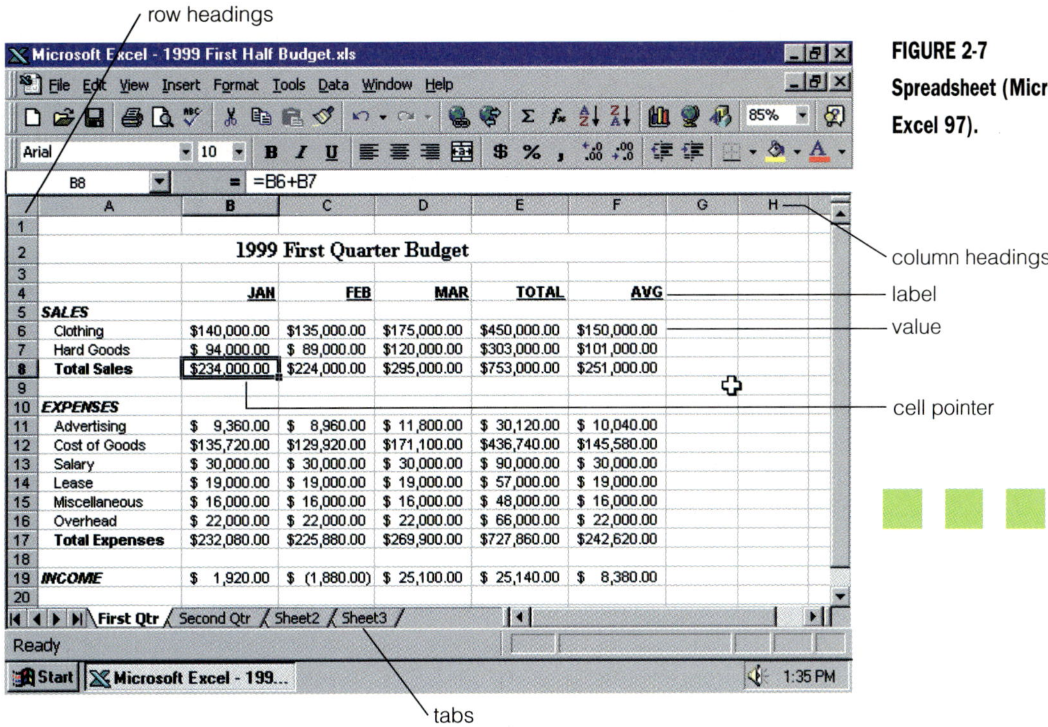

FIGURE 2-7 **Spreadsheet (Microsoft Excel 97).**

Spreadsheets

A spreadsheet is an electronic worksheet used to organize and manipulate numbers and display options for "what-if" analysis.

The electronic **spreadsheet** is based on the traditional accounting worksheet. Paper worksheets have long been used by accountants and managers to work up balance sheets, sales projections, and expense budgets. Spreadsheets are used by financial analysts, accountants, contractors, and others concerned with manipulating numeric data.

A spreadsheet, also known as a **worksheet,** has several parts. (See Figure 2-7.) It consists of a grid of **rows** and **columns.** The rows are numbered down the left side. The columns are identified by letters across the top. The intersection of a column and row is called a **cell.** The cell holds a single unit of information.

The position of a cell is called the **cell address.** For example, "B8" is the address for the cell located in column B and row 8. A **cell pointer**—also known as the **cell selector**—indicates where data is to be entered or changed in the spreadsheet. The cell pointer can be moved around in much the same way that you move the insertion point in a word processing program. In our illustration, the cell pointer is located in position B8.

In addition, most spreadsheet applications include more than one worksheet in a file. This is referred to as a **3-D spreadsheet.** Including multiple worksheets allows you to create smaller and more manageable spreadsheets. For instance, an account representative may maintain separate worksheets for each quarter of the year. **Tabs** are commonly displayed to allow you to move between worksheets. (Refer to Figure 2-7.)

Spreadsheets allow you to try out various "what-if" possibilities. This is a powerful feature. You can manipulate numbers by using stored formulas and calculate different outcomes. For example, a retail store manager can estimate quarterly profits by projecting sales over a three-month period. (Refer to Figure 2-7.) The manager can then subtract expenses from sales. Expenses might include such things as advertising, cost of goods sold, and salaries. If expenses are too high to produce a profit, the manager can experiment on the screen with reducing some expenses and see the results almost instantly. For example, the number of employees, and hence salaries, might be reduced.

Popular spreadsheet packages include Microsoft Excel, Corel Quattro Pro, and Lotus 1-2-3. Some common features of spreadsheet programs include the following:

Format

Labels are often used to identify information in a worksheet. (Refer to Figure 2-7.) Usually a label is a word or symbol, such as a pound sign (#). A number in a cell is called a **value.** Labels and values can be displayed or formatted in different ways. For example, a label can be centered in the cell or positioned to the left or right. A value can be displayed to show decimal places, dollars, or percent (%). The number of decimal positions (if any) can be altered, and the width of columns can be changed.

Formulas and Functions

Formulas are instructions for calculations. They calculate results using the number or numbers in referenced cells. For example, in our illustration, the spreadsheet is concerned with computing total sales. The formula to calculate January's total sales is shown near the top of the screen: +B6+B7. (Refer to Figure 2-7). This means add the value in B6 (clothing sales) to the value of B7 (hard goods sales). The total is displayed in cell B8.

Functions are prewritten formulas that perform calculations automatically. For example, the Lotus function @SUM(B6..E6) adds all the values in the range of cells from B6 to E6.

If you change one or more numbers in your spreadsheet, all related formulas will recalculate automatically. Thus, you can substitute one value for another in a cell and observe the effect on other related cells in the spreadsheet. **Recalculation** is one of the most important features of spreadsheets.

Analysis

The recalculation feature can be used to analyze the effect of changes to the spreadsheet. For example, consider our illustration. If the January-to-March sales are *estimates,* you can change any or all of the values in cells B6 through D7. All of the associated cells including the total in cell E8 and the average in cell F8 will change automatically. (Refer to Figure 2-7.) This is called **what-if analysis.**

Many programs also include built-in analysis tools that help perform complicated what-if analysis. You can use **goal seeking tools** and **solver tools** to find the values needed to achieve a particular end result. **Scenario tools** allow you to test the effect of different combinations of data. For example, a contractor might need to keep the cost of building a house within a budget. The contractor can run cost calculations on various grades of materials and on the going pay rates for labor.

Other Features

Most spreadsheets also include additional capabilities for visually displaying and rearranging data. Among them are the following features:

- **Analytical graphs:** To help visualize the data in your spreadsheets, you can create **analytical graphs** or charts. For example, you could display the numerical data in a worksheet as a pie chart, bar chart, or a line graph. (See Figure 2-8.) The graphs automatically update when the data in the underlying worksheet changes.
- **Workgroup:** One of the newest additions to spreadsheet applications is the **workgroup** program. A workgroup allows multiple users to collaborate electronically on a spreadsheet. The workgroup for a spreadsheet operates much the same as a word processing workgroup, with each user's changes or contributions displayed in a different color.
- **Linked files:** Most spreadsheet programs allow you to **link** cells in one worksheet file to cells in other worksheets in the same file or to other worksheet files. Whenever a change occurs in one file, the linked cells in the other worksheets are automatically updated.

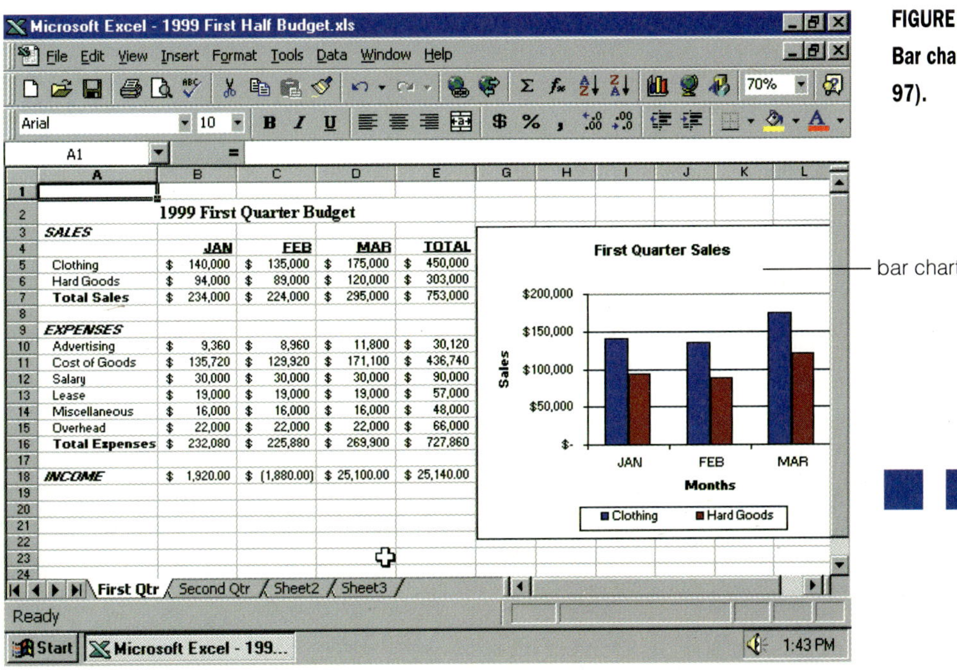

FIGURE 2-8
Bar chart (Microsoft Excel 97).

Database Managers

A database manager organizes a large collection of data so that related information can be retrieved easily.

A *database* is a collection of related data. You come across databases every day at school, at work, and/or in your home. Traditionally, the information in a database was stored in filing cabinets and organized by some category, such as last name. An electronic database serves the same purpose, but it stores the data electronically on a computer.

Database management programs are used by salespeople to keep track of clients. They are also used by purchasing agents to keep track of orders and by inventory managers to monitor products in their warehouses. Database managers are used by many people inside and outside of business, from teachers to police officers. We describe databases in detail in Chapter 9.

A **database manager** or **database management system (DBMS)** is a software package used to set up, or *structure,* a database. It is also used to retrieve information from a database. An example of one database manager is Microsoft Access. (See Figure 2-9.) This database contains address information about employees. The list of employee numbers, names, and addresses is a **table.** Each line of information about one employee is called a **record.** Each column of information within a record is called a **field**—for example, last name.

Another table might contain benefit information. For example, it might include information about each employee's retirement, dental, and medical plans. These two tables are linked or related by a common field called a **key field.** The infor-

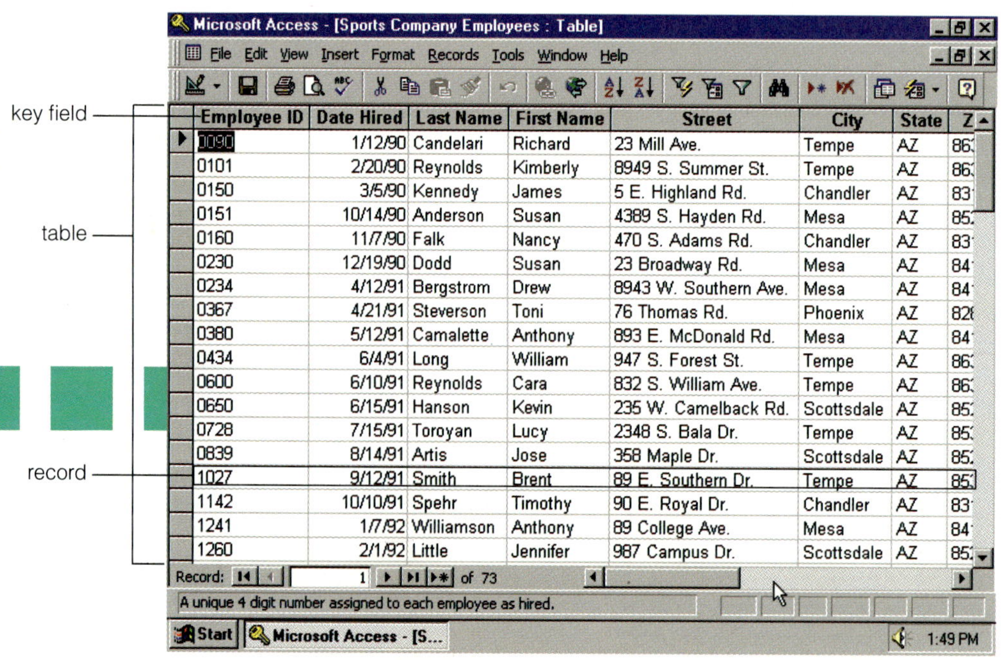

Employee ID	Date Hired	Last Name	First Name	Street	City	State	Z
0090	1/12/90	Candelari	Richard	23 Mill Ave.	Tempe	AZ	86
0101	2/20/90	Reynolds	Kimberly	8949 S. Summer St.	Tempe	AZ	86
0150	3/5/90	Kennedy	James	5 E. Highland Rd.	Chandler	AZ	83
0151	10/14/90	Anderson	Susan	4389 S. Hayden Rd.	Mesa	AZ	85
0160	11/7/90	Falk	Nancy	470 S. Adams Rd.	Chandler	AZ	83
0230	12/19/90	Dodd	Susan	23 Broadway Rd.	Mesa	AZ	84
0234	4/12/91	Bergstrom	Drew	8943 W. Southern Ave.	Mesa	AZ	84
0367	4/21/91	Steverson	Toni	76 Thomas Rd.	Phoenix	AZ	82
0380	5/12/91	Camalette	Anthony	893 E. McDonald Rd.	Mesa	AZ	84
0434	6/4/91	Long	William	947 S. Forest St.	Tempe	AZ	86
0600	6/10/91	Reynolds	Cara	832 S. William Ave.	Tempe	AZ	86
0650	6/15/91	Hanson	Kevin	235 W. Camelback Rd.	Scottsdale	AZ	85
0728	7/15/91	Toroyan	Lucy	2348 S. Bala Dr.	Tempe	AZ	85
0839	8/14/91	Artis	Jose	358 Maple Dr.	Scottsdale	AZ	85
1027	9/12/91	Smith	Brent	89 E. Southern Dr.	Tempe	AZ	85
1142	10/10/91	Spehr	Timothy	90 E. Royal Dr.	Chandler	AZ	83
1241	1/7/92	Williamson	Anthony	89 College Ave.	Mesa	AZ	84
1260	2/1/92	Little	Jennifer	987 Campus Dr.	Scottsdale	AZ	85

FIGURE 2-9
Database (Microsoft Access 97).

mation in a key field must be unique for each record in a table. In this case the key field is the employee number. This is a **relational database.** That is, the address table and the benefits table are related by a key field containing common employee numbers.

To see the value of a relational database, imagine that you are a benefits administrator. You have been asked by your boss to notify all employees using a particular dental plan that rates have changed. If the employee records were stored only on sheets of paper, it might take days or weeks to locate the appropriate names and addresses.

With a database, the names and addresses of all affected employees can be located within moments. The database software first goes to the benefits table to locate all employees who use the dental plan. Then the database software goes to the address table. There, the appropriate employee numbers are used to locate the names and addresses of all employees using that dental plan.

Popular database management programs include Microsoft Access, Corel Paradox, and Lotus Approach. Database managers have different features, depending on their sophistication. A description of the principal features of database manager software for microcomputers follows.

Locate and Display

A basic feature of all database programs is the capability to quickly locate, or find, records in the file. In our example (refer to Figure 2-9), you could instruct the database manager to find all records having a Last Name of Smith. The program finds the first record with the last name of Smith and moves to that record. If more than one record has the last name of Smith, this procedure continues.

Another way to locate information is to apply a **filter** to the database. A filter displays the subset of records that meet certain conditions or criteria. For example, if you were to enter the criteria of Mesa in the City field, only those records would be displayed. A third method of locating information is to create a **query.** A query locates the specified records and displays only selected fields. For instance, you can display only the first and last names of all records meeting the criteria of Mesa in the City field.

Sort

Database managers make it easy to change the order of records in a file. Normally, records are displayed in the order they are entered or by key field, such as by social security number. Although this order may be appropriate for some purposes, it may not be for others. Rearranging or sorting is a common feature of database managers. For example, you might want to print out an entire alphabetical list of employees by last name.

Data Analysis

Many database programs contain built-in math formulas. In the office, for example, you can use this feature to find the highest or lowest commissions earned. You can calculate the average of the commissions earned by the sales force in one part of the country. This information can be organized as a table and printed out in a report format.

Other Features

Among other capabilities offered by some database management programs are the following:

- **Customized data-entry forms:** A person new to the database program may find some of the descriptions for fields confusing. For example, a field name may appear as "CUSTNUM" for "customer number." However, the form on the screen may be customized so that the expression "Enter the customer number" appears in place of "CUSTNUM." Fields may also be rearranged on the screen, and boxes and lines may be added.
- **Professional-looking reports:** A custom-report option enables you to design the elements you want in a report. Examples are the descriptions appearing above columns and the fields you wish to include. You can even add graphic elements, such as boxes or lines, so that the printed report has a professional appearance. Although the database itself may have, say, 10 fields, the report can be customized to display only the five or so important fields.
- **Program control languages:** Most people using a database management program can accomplish everything they need to do by making choices from the menus. Many database management programs include a programming control language so that advanced users can create sophisticated applications. In addition, most allow direct communication to specialized mainframe databases through languages like SQL (Structured Query Language).

Presentation Graphics

Presentation graphics software helps you create professional and exciting presentations. Content development assistance, professional design templates, and support materials are provided.

Research shows that people learn better when information is presented visually. A picture is indeed worth a thousand words or numbers. **Presentation graphics** are used to combine a variety of visual objects to create attractive, visually interesting presentations.

You can use presentation graphics to create class presentations. These programs are excellent tools to communicate a message or to persuade people, such as fellow students, instructors, supervisors, or clients. Presentation graphics programs are often used by marketing or sales people as well as many others. (See Figure 2-10.)

Popular presentation packages include Microsoft PowerPoint, Corel Presentations, and Lotus Freelance. These programs can produce overhead transparencies, 35-mm slides, electronic on-screen presentations, called *slide shows,* and support materials for both the speaker and the audience.

Each page of a presentation, commonly referred to as a *slide,* can include many elements, including text, charts, drawn objects, and shapes, as well as clip art, movies, sounds, and art created in other programs. Features that are common to most presentation graphics programs include the following:

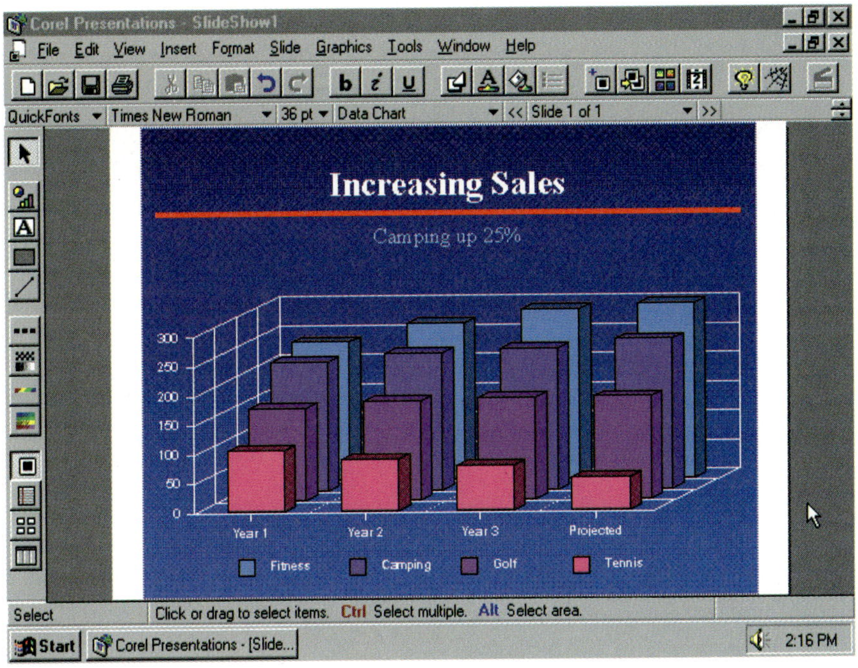

FIGURE 2-10
Presentation (Corel Presentations 7).

Content Development Assistance

Most programs include features that help you organize the content of your presentation. Commonly, an outline feature is included that helps you enter and organize the topics of your talk. Most programs also provide presentation **layout files** that include sample text for many different types of presentations—from selling a product to reporting on progress. You replace the sample text with your own information following the guidelines presented in the sample layout.

Professional Design

Professionally designed **templates** or model presentations are provided. These can help take the worry out of much of the design and layout decisions. They include selected combinations of text layouts with features such as title placement and size. Additionally, various bullet styles, background colors, patterns, borders, and other enhancements are provided. Using these design templates, you can create a professional looking presentation in minutes.

Support Materials

Support materials such as audience handouts and speaker notes are easily created with most presentation graphics programs. These features help the audience follow the presentation as well as helping the speaker keep on track.

Other Features

- **Animations: Animations** include special visual and sound effects. These effects include blinking text, transitions that control how your bulleted points appear when each slide is displayed, and sounds such as applause when a picture is uncovered. These features add interest and keep your audience's attention.

- **Other special effects:** You can put audio and video clips on a slide to play automatically or when selected. You can record your own voice to provide a narration to accompany a slide show. This is convenient for individuals who cannot attend a presentation and for self-running slide shows, such as at a kiosk.
- **Rehearsal:** A **rehearsal** feature lets you practice and time your presentation. The length of time to display each slide can be preset so your entire presentation is completed within the allotted time.

Personal Information Managers

A personal information manager is a program that helps you get organized and keeps you organized. It also helps you communicate with others.

Stop and think for a minute about what you do in a typical day, week, month, and year. Professionals in all kinds of jobs do similar things. They schedule meetings, make to-do lists, and record important names, addresses, and telephone numbers. They jot down notes, make future plans, and record important dates like anniversaries and birthdays.

You may use some of the same tools that many professionals use to keep track of all these things. Such tools include calendars, Rolodex files, address books, index cards, wall charts, notepads, binders, and Post-it notes. **Personal information managers (PIMs)** are programs that provide electronic alternatives for these tools. (See Figure 2-11.)

FIGURE 2-11
Personal information manager (Microsoft Outlook 97).

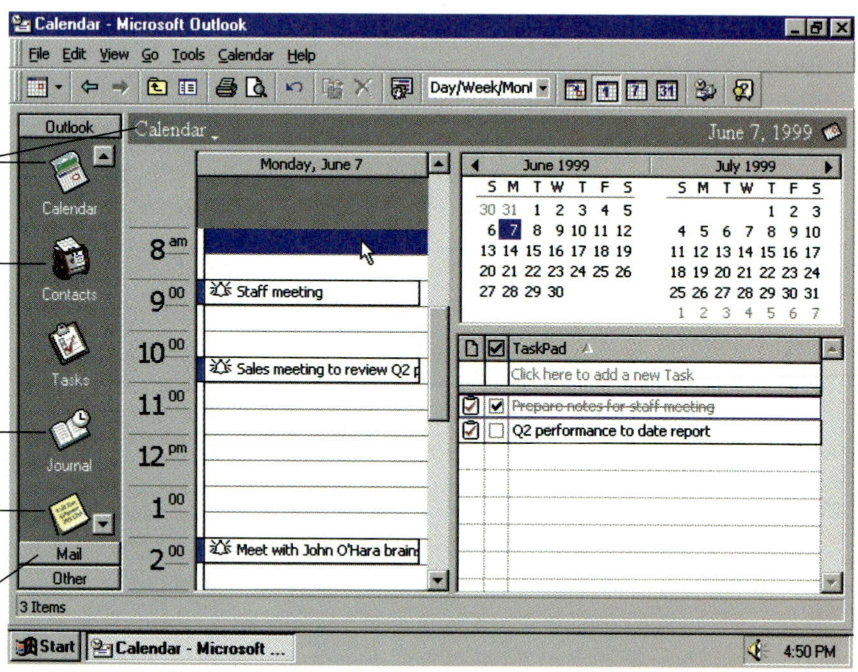

PIMs, also known as **desktop managers,** are designed to get you organized and keep you organized. Most important, they are designed to help maximize your personal productivity. You could join the thousands of managers who review their electronic calendars each morning to see what appointments they have. Later, while you're working on a spreadsheet, say, someone calls to schedule an important business meeting. You switch to the PIM and type in the meeting time on your calendar. You then save the information. With another command, you make the PIM disappear from the screen and return to your spreadsheet.

Examples of PIM software are Microsoft Outlook and Lotus Organizer. Some common features of PIM programs include the following:

Calendar

One of the most important features is the calendar. It operates like an electronic appointment book that keeps track of events, holidays, assignments, and project schedules. Additionally, most provide assistance in scheduling meetings and organizing projects. The **calendar page** looks like a page from a traditional monthly planner. (Refer to Figure 2-11.)

Communication Organizer

For busy people, organization is often the key to success. A basic feature of all PIMs is a communication organizer. It provides two basic functions. First, it works with a variety of email programs for creating, sending, receiving, and organizing your electronic messages. Second, it works with a variety of Internet browsers to provide access to the Internet and to Internet services. (Email programs, Internet browsers, and services are discussed in The Guide to the Internet at the back of this book.)

Address Book

An electronic address book is an essential feature for all PIMs. Like a traditional address book, it is used to record names, addresses, and telephone numbers. In addition, electronic address books are linked to the other parts of a PIM to save you time and energy. For example, when creating an email message to one of your friends, you do not have to look up their address and manually enter the information. Rather, you can automatically copy it from the online address book. Also, most PIMs include the capability to record and provide direct links to Web sites on the Internet.

Other Features

Among other capabilities offered by most PIMs are the following:

- **Notes:** Have you ever used those yellow sticky pads to keep track of meetings and other events? PIMs allow you to create electronic versions of those notes that are displayed on your monitor.
- **Automatic reminders:** We've all forgotten appointments. Have you ever missed an appointment even after writing a reminder note and placing it on your desk or on the dashboard of your car? Many PIMs work with the calendar to keep track of all your appointments and call your attention to an upcoming appointment by flashing a message on your monitor.

- **Journal:** While the communication organizer focuses on keeping track of email communications, the journal does more. It automatically keeps a log of notes, appointments, documents and other events. Later, you can search the log to review old notes and phone calls. You can even search for all the Word or Excel files you worked on in a given week.

Integrated Packages and Software Suites

Integrated software is an all-in-one application package. Software suites are individual windows applications that are sold together.

We have described five important kinds of application software. What happens if you want to take the data in one program and use it in another? Suppose you want to take information stored in the database manager and use it in a spreadsheet. This can be difficult to do with separate application packages. With an integrated package, however, it is easy to share data.

An **integrated package** is a program containing a collection of applications that work together and share information with each other. For example, to create a report on the growth of sales for a sporting goods store, you could use all parts of an integrated package. You could use the database to search and retrieve yearly sales data. The spreadsheet would be used to analyze the data and graphics to visually present the data. You could use the word processor to write the report that includes tables from the spreadsheet and visuals from the graphics program. (See Figure 2-12.)

Finally, you could send the report by electronic mail using the communications capability. Two well-known integrated packages are Lotus Works and Microsoft Works. Packages of this sort are easy to use. They are especially useful for microcomputers that do not have a lot of storage capacity.

FIGURE 2-12
Integrated package (Microsoft Works for Windows 95).

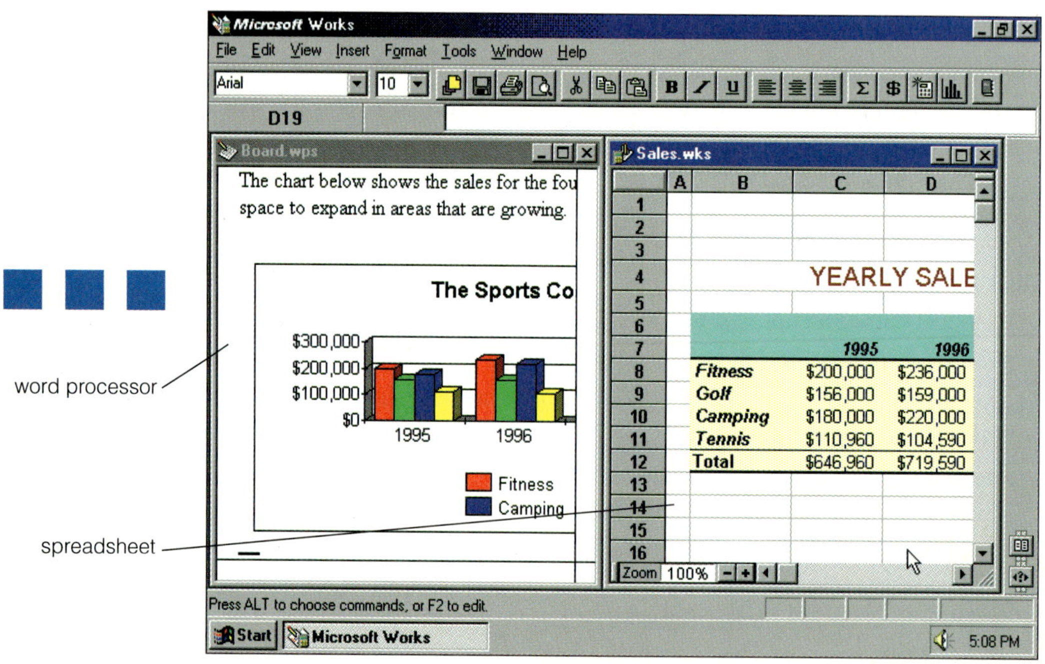

An integrated package has a common structure allowing data to be exchanged easily between the applications within the package. Nevertheless, each application is generally less powerful than separate "stand-alone" application software. The next chapter explains how programs such as Windows allow users to share data between *completely different* stand-alone programs—not just between the applications available within one integrated package.

Some software companies are selling their separate windows application programs as a group—called **software suites.** The most popular software suite is Microsoft Office, which comes in different versions. One—Microsoft Office 97, Professional Edition—includes five individual Windows application packages. (See Figure 2-13.) The word processor is Word, the spreadsheet is Excel, the database is Access, the presentation graphics program is PowerPoint, and the personal information manager is Outlook. Although more expensive than most integrated packages, software suites are much less expensive than purchasing each of the applications separately. Another popular software suite is Corel Office.

For a summary of the basic application software, see Figure 2-14.

FIGURE 2-13
Software suite (Microsoft Office 97 Professional Edition).

BASIC APPLICATIONS

Word processors	Microsoft Word, Lotus Word Pro, Corel WordPerfect
Spreadsheets	Microsoft Excel, Corel Quattro Pro, Lotus 1-2-3
Database managers	Microsoft Access, Corel Paradox, Lotus Approach
Presentation graphics	Microsoft PowerPoint, Corel Presentations, Lotus Freehand
Personal information managers	Microsoft Outlook, Lotus Organizer
Integrated packages	Microsoft Works, Lotus Works
Software suites	Microsoft Office 97, Corel Office 97

FIGURE 2-14
Basic applications.

A Look at the Future

New software versions will offer more capabilities freeing your creativity and enhancing the quality and quantity of your work.

New versions of basic application software are being released all the time. One way these programs change is in the way you interact with them. Another way is in the software's capabilities.

Interacting with them may not be as difficult as you might think. That's because almost all new software today has a similar command and menu structure. When a new version comes out, the basic look and feel is quite similar to the previous version. This frees you to focus on the new capabilities.

Basic applications will continue to become more and more powerful by adding breadth to their capabilities. They are no longer limited by the machines that they were designed to replace. Word processors, for example, do much more than typewriters ever could. Recent versions have added limited desktop publishing and Web page design capabilities.

What does all this mean to you? You will have access to more powerful applications thus freeing your creativity and enhancing the quality and quantity of your work. Additionally, you will be challenged to learn how to use these more powerful tools. Specifically, when and how to apply them. It is for this reason that you need to know more about some of those advanced applications whose capabilities are steadily moving into basic applications. That is the subject of the next chapter.

KEY TERMS

alignment (29)
analytical graphics (33)
animation (37)
calendar page (39)
cell (31)
cell address (31)
cell pointer (31)
cell selector (31)
clip art (30)
column (31)
context-sensitive help (26)
copy (27)
cursor (26)
cut (27)
database management system (DBMS) (34)
database manager (34)
desktop manager (39)
dialog box (26)
document (28)
drawing program (30)
edit (27)
Enter key (29)
field (34)
filter (35)
find (29)
form letter (30)
formatting (29)
formula (32)
function (32)
function key (25)
goal seeking tool (32)
grammar checker (29)
graphical user interface (GUI) (25)
Help (26)
hypertext link (30)
icon (25)
insertion point (26)
integrated package (40)

key field (34)
label (32)
layout files (37)
link (33)
mail merge (30)
menu (25)
paste (27)
personal information manager (PIM) (38)
presentation graphics (36)
query (35)
recalculation (32)
record (34)
rehearsal (38)
relational database (35)
release (24)
replace (29)
row (31)
save (27)
scenario tool (32)
scroll bar (26)
search (29)
shortcut key (25)
software suite (41)
solver tool (32)
spelling checker (29)
spreadsheet (31)
tab (31)
table (in database) (34)
table (in word processing) (29)
templates (37)
text art (30)
thesaurus (30)
3-D spreadsheet (31)
toolbar (25)
undo (27)
value (32)
version (24)
what-if analysis (32)
word art (30)
word processing (28)
word wrap (29)
workgroup (33)
worksheet (31)

REVIEW QUESTIONS

True/False

1. The insertion point or cursor indicates where you may enter data next.
2. Microsoft, Lotus, and Corel are applications.
3. Quattro Pro is a widely used word processor.
4. Spreadsheet programs are typically used to store and retrieve records quickly.
5. With communications programs, you can look up airline reservations and stock quotations.

Multiple Choice

1. The feature common to most application packages that contain icons or graphic representations for commonly used commands:
   a. toolbar
   b. menu
   c. help
   d. WYSIWYG
   e. dialog box
2. The word processing feature that identifies excessively long sentences:
   a. spell checker
   b. paste
   c. copy
   d. merge
   e. grammar checker
3. In spreadsheets, the common feature that specifies instructions for calculation is:
   a. formulas
   b. format
   c. recalculation
   d. consolidation
   e. value
4. A tool used frequently by marketing people to communicate a message or to persuade clients:
   a. word processors
   b. spreadsheets
   c. personal information manager
   d. database managers
   e. presentation graphics
5. A collection of separate Windows applications sold as a group:
   a. combined
   b. suite
   c. communication
   d. integrated
   e. spreadsheet

Fill in the Blank

1. The __________ box is a feature common to many application programs that presents additional command options.
2. The __________ is based on the traditional accounting worksheet.
3. __________ __________ programs are used to keep track of details such as inventory records or client lists.
4. __________ software lets you send data to and receive data from another computer.
5. __________ are used to schedule meetings, make to-do lists, and record addresses.

Open Ended

1. What is context-sensitive help?
2. How do formulas and recalculation work in a spreadsheet?
3. Explain the purpose of presentation graphics.
4. Name three well-known spreadsheet packages.
5. What is the difference between an integrated package and a software suite?

DISCUSSION QUESTIONS AND PROJECTS

1. *Three ways to acquire application software:* The following exercise can be extremely useful. Concentrate on a category of software of personal interest to you—say, word processing or spreadsheets. Go to the library and find information on the following three methods of acquiring software. Which route seems to be the best for you? Why?
   a. *Public domain software* is software you can get for free. Someone writes a program and offers to share it with everyone without charge. Generally, you find these programs by belonging to a microcomputer users group. Or you find them by accessing an electronic bulletin board using your telephone-linked computer. Be aware that the quality of the software can vary widely. Some may be excellent and some may be poor.

   b. *Shareware* is inexpensive. It is distributed free, in the same way as public domain software. After you have used it for a while and decide you like it, you're supposed to pay the author for it. Again, the quality varies. Some shareware is excellent.
   c. *Commercial software* consists of brand-name packages, such as those we mentioned in this chapter. Prices and features vary. Fortunately, there are several periodicals that provide ratings and guides. *PC World* polls its readers to find out the best software brands in various categories. The magazine releases the results in its October issue. Other periodicals (for example, *PC* magazine, *MacWorld, Infoworld*) also have surveys, reviews, and ratings.
2. *New versions and releases:* Software companies seem to be offering new versions and releases of their application packages all the time. For example, in one twelve-month period, Lotus released four variations of its 1-2-3 spreadsheet program.
   a. Take one application package (like Lotus 1-2-3, Microsoft Word, or Corel Paradox) and find out how many variations have been released in the past three years.
   b. If you own one variation of an application package and a new one is released, does yours become obsolete? Discuss and defend your position.
   c. If you own one variation of a software package and a new version is released, should you upgrade to the newer version? What factors should be considered? If you decide to upgrade, how would you go about doing it?
   d. Why do you suppose software manufacturers offer new variations of their software?

on the web

Exercises and Explorations

1 PIMs

Keeping track of due dates for homework assignments, meeting times, and other appointments can become challenging. Personal information management (PIM) software is designed to help you do these and other related tasks. To learn more about PIMs, visit our site at http://www.magpie.org/essentials/chapter-2.html to link to a site providing current articles. Once connected to that site, find an article that reviews the newest PIMs available. Print out the article, and choose the PIM that would best suit your needs. Write a paragraph as to why you chose that PIM.

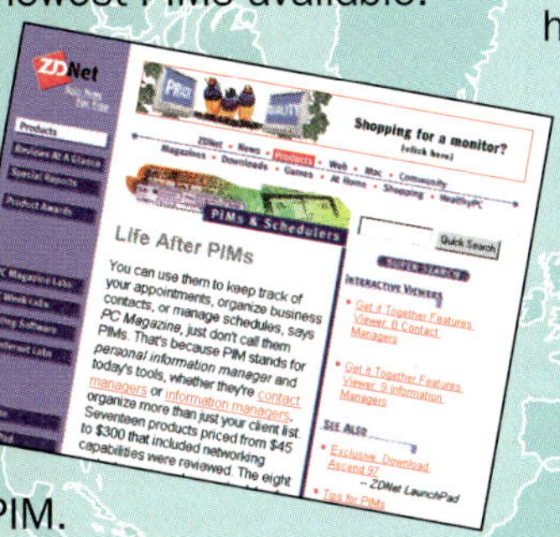

2 Learning Applications

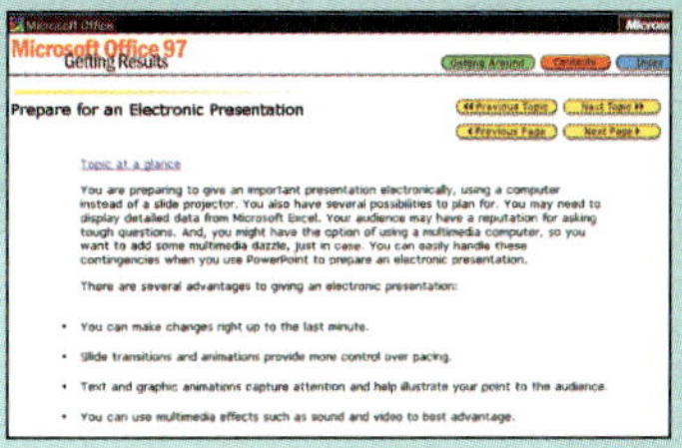

With so many different types of applications available, it can be difficult to know where to begin learning. Visit our site at http://www.magpie.org/essentials/chapter-2.html for a link to a site providing some suggestions. At this site you will find descriptions and tutorials for some of the most widely used basic applications. Select one, read about it, and run its tutorial. Write a paragraph describing the application and the tutorial and what you learned from it.

3 Presentation Software

Microsoft's PowerPoint can help you create effective and professional-looking presentations. Learn more about this basic application by visiting our site at http://www.magpie.org/essentials/chapter-2.html, which provides a link to Microsoft's Web site. Once at the site, read about PowerPoint's capabilities and uses. Write a paragraph summarizing some of PowerPoint's most powerful features, and describe how you could use this program to dramatically convey your ideas to an audience.

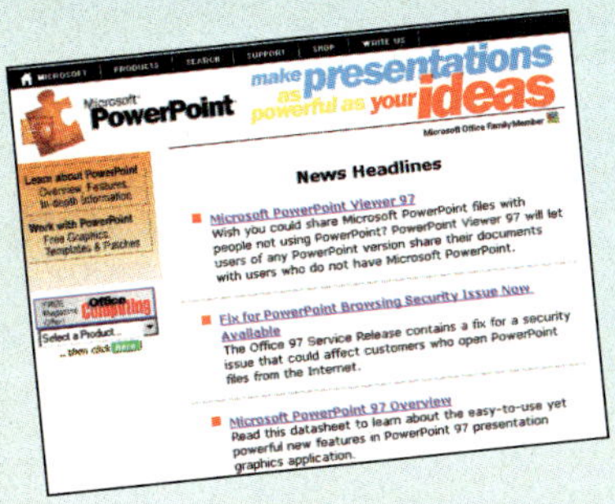

4 Computer Games

Computers are not all work and no fun. Learn more about computer games by visiting our site at http://www.magpie.org/essentials/chapter-2.html, where you'll find a link to a Web site that describes the newest and best games. Check out the demos, or go to the pressroom to read reviews on the latest in computer entertainment. Choose a game, and print out the information presented. Write a summary of the game, describe who will likely use the game, and define the system requirements needed to run the game.

VISUAL SUMMARY

Basic Applications

Applications software does "useful work." The five basic tools or types of general-purpose applications programs are used by many people for different kinds of tasks.

WORD PROCESSING

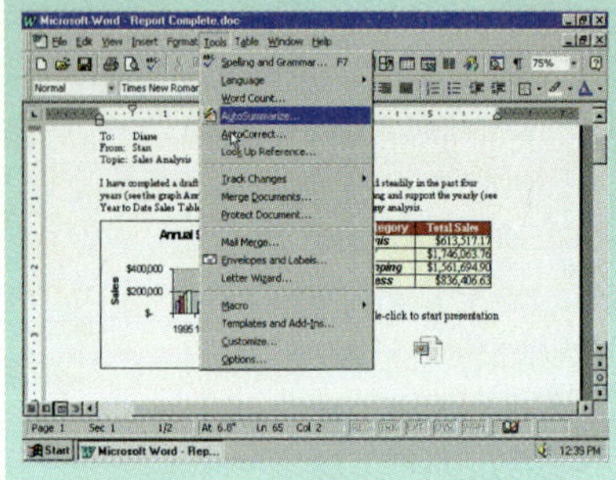

A **word processor** creates, edits, saves, and prints **documents.** Especially useful for deleting, inserting, and replacing. Principal features:

Word Wrap and Enter Key

Word wrap automatically moves insertion point to new line. **Enter key** enters new paragraph or blank line.

Spelling and Grammar Checkers

Spelling checkers identify incorrectly spelled words and present alternative spellings. **Grammar checkers** identify poor wording, grammar, and long sentences.

Other Features

- **Align, format, merge, search, and replace** text
- Create **references, tables,** and **hypertext links**
- Provide **thesaurus, graphic,** and limited **workgroup** capabilities
- Internet publishing to create and edit documents for display on the Web

Examples of Packages

Microsoft Word, Corel WordPerfect, Lotus Approach

SPREADSHEETS

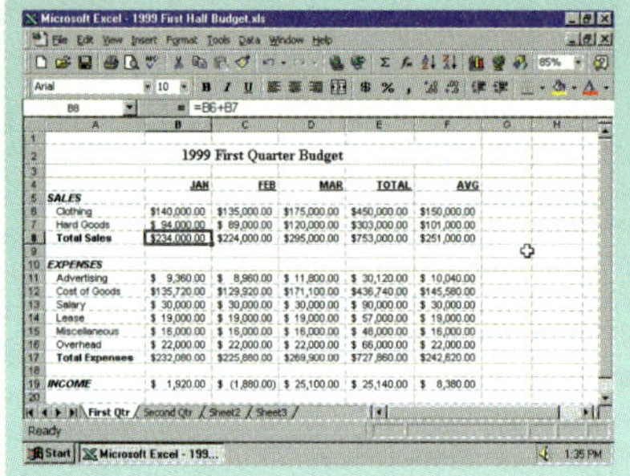

A **spreadsheet** presents and analyzes data. A **cell** is the intersection of column and row. The **cell pointer (cell selector)** indicates where data is to be entered. Principal features:

Format

Labels (column and row headings) and **values** (numbers in cells) can be displayed in different ways.

Formulas and Functions

Formulas are instructions for calculations. **Functions** are built-in formulas. **Recalculation** is automatic recomputation.

Analysis Tools

Built-in tools for **what-if, goal-seeking, solving,** and **scenario** analyses.

Other Features

- Analytical **graphics** to display numerical data from the spreadsheet
- Limited **workgroup** capabilities allowing multiple collaboration on a spreadsheet

Examples of Packages

Microsoft Excel, Corel Quattro Pro, Lotus 1-2-3

DATABASE MANAGERS

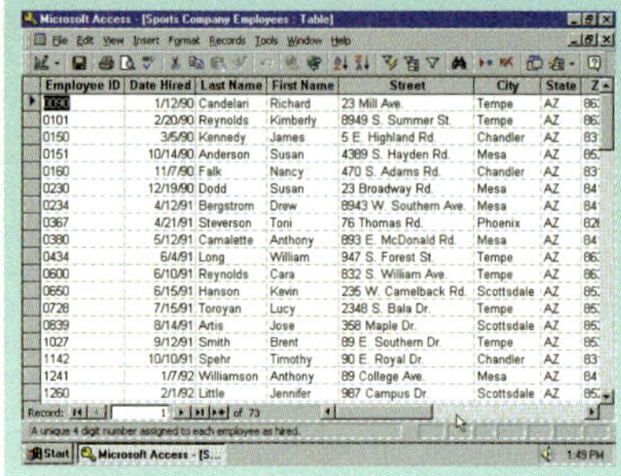

A **database manager** is used to structure a database. **Relational databases** are organized as fields, records, and tables for easy retrieval of selected items. Principal features:

Locate and Display

Information is **located** and then **displayed** either by **finding** records, **filtering** through the records, or **querying** the database.

Sort

Users can sort through records and rearrange them in different ways.

Data Analysis

Built-in math formulas may be used to manipulate data. Data may be printed out in different report formats.

Other Features

- Customized data-entry forms
- Professional-looking reports
- Program control languages, like SQL (Structured Query Language)

Examples of Packages

Microsoft Access, Corel Paradox, Lotus Approach

COMMON FEATURES

FEATURE	DESCRIPTION
Menu	Presents commands available for selection
Shortcut Keys	Special-purpose keys for frequently used commands
Toolbar	Presents graphic objects for commands
Help	Presents explanations of various commands
Dialog Box	Used to specify additional command options
Insertion Point	Shows where data can be entered
Scroll Bars	Used to display additional information
Edit	Changes entered information
Cut, Copy, and Paste	Deletes, moves, or copies information
Undo	Restores work prior to last command
Save and Print	Saves work in a file and prints file

PRESENTATION GRAPHICS

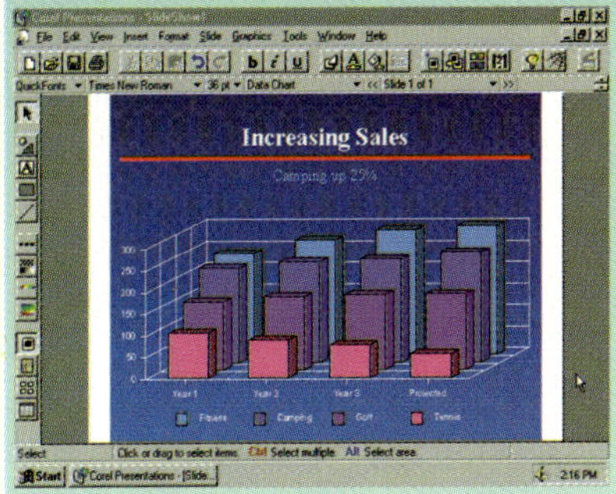

Presentation software is used to create high quality, interesting, and professional presentations.

Content Development Assistance

Outline features help develop a presentation's overall organization. **Layout files** help develop details for individual pages of a presentation.

Professional Design

Professional designed **templates** (model presentations) provide suggestions for text layout, color combinations, backgrounds, and more.

Support Materials

Support materials include audience handouts, speaker notes, and more.

Other Features

Animations, Special effects, Rehearsal

Examples of Packages

Microsoft PowerPoint, Corel Presentation, Lotus Freelance

PERSONAL INFORMATION MANAGERS

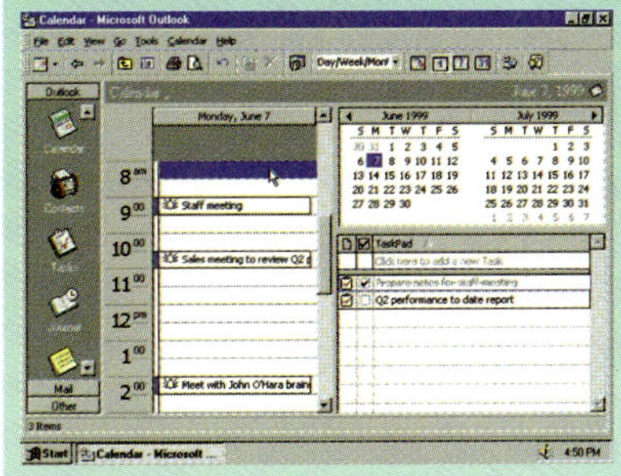

A **personal information manager** (**PIM** or **desktop manager**) helps to organize and increase personal productivity. Principal features:

Calendar

Calendars (electronic appointment books) provide scheduling and organization assistance. A **calendar page** looks like a traditional planner.

Communication organizer

The **communication organizer** works with email and browser programs.

Address book

An electronic **address book** records names, addresses, telephone numbers, and links to Web sites.

Other Features

Notes, Automatic reminders, Journal

Examples of Packages

Microsoft Outlook and Lotus Organizer

PACKAGES AND SUITES

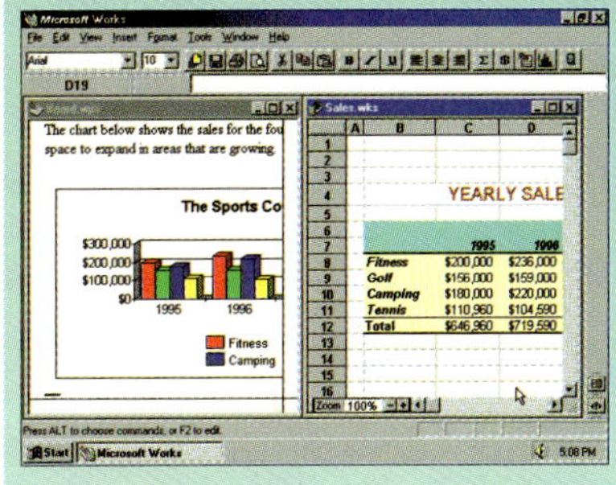

Integrated Packages

An **integrated package** is an all-in-one software program. Some features:

- Common structure for easy data exchange between applications
- Less expensive than software suite
- Each application not as powerful as "stand-alone" application

Examples of Packages

Lotus Works and Microsoft Works

Software Suites

A **software suite** is a collection of individual windows applications packages sold together. Some features:

- Windows (discussed in detail in next chapter) allows sharing of data between completely different applications programs
- Less expensive than buying each individual software package

Examples of Packages

Microsoft Office and Corel Office

Advanced Applications

Expect surprises—exciting ones, positive ones. This is the view to take in achieving computer competency. If at first the surprises worry you, that's normal. Most people wonder how well they can handle something new. But the latest technological developments also offer you new opportunities to vastly extend your range. As we show in this chapter, software that for years was available only for mainframes has recently become available for microcomputers. Here's a chance to join the computer-competent of tomorrow.

COMPETENCIES

After you have read this chapter, you should be able to:

1. **Describe desktop publishers, image editors, and illustrators.**
2. **Describe multimedia.**
3. **Discuss Web publishing software.**
4. **Explain what groupware is.**
5. **Describe project management.**
6. **Explain artificial intelligence: robotics, knowledge-based and expert systems, and virtual reality.**

3

Advanced applications: This is the characterization we have given to a whole new generation of software only recently available for microcomputers. Advanced applications include graphics programs, multimedia, Web publishers, groupware, project managers, and artificial intelligence and virtual reality. Is there really a need to know anything about these new developments? There is if you want to be like those professionals in every area who are at the forefront of their disciplines. They are there because they have found more efficient ways to use their time and talents. You owe it to yourself, therefore, to at least be aware of what this software and hardware can do.

Graphics Programs

Desktop publishers mix text and graphics. Image editors modify bitmap image files. Illustrators modify vector files. Graphic suites bundle separate programs.

In the previous chapter, we discussed analytical and presentation graphics. They are widely used to analyze data and to create professional-looking presentations. Here we focus on more specialized graphics programs used by professionals in the graphic arts profession. These graphics programs are desktop publishing, image editors, and illustration programs. While desktop publishing is used to produce professional publications, image editors and illustration programs are used to modify graphic images.

Desktop Publishing

Desktop publishing programs allow you to mix text and graphics to create publications of professional quality. While *word processors* focus on creating text and have the ability to combine text and graphics, *desktop publishers* focus on page design and layout and provide greater flexibility. Desktop publishing programs are widely used by graphic artists to create brochures, newsletters, newspapers, and textbooks. (See Figure 3-1.) Popular desktop publishing programs include Adobe FrameMaker, Adobe PageMaker, Corel Ventura, and QuarkXPress.

Image Editors

Image editors, also known as **paint programs,** are used to create and to modify bitmap image files. In a **bitmap file,** the image is made up of thousands of dots or pixels—much like how a computer screen displays images. Bitmapped

FIGURE 3-1
Desktop publishing (Adobe PageMaker).

graphic files are very common and are ideally suited to represent realistic images such as photographs. Graphic artists use image editing programs to correct or change colors and to create special effects. One type of special effect called **morphing** allows you to smoothly blend two images so that one image seems to melt into the next, often producing amusing results. Paintbrush for Windows is a low-end image editor. Popular professional image editor programs include Adobe Photoshop, Corel Photo, and Macromedia xRes.

Illustration Programs

Illustration programs, also known as **draw programs,** are used to modify **vector images.** In a vector file, the image is composed of a collection of objects such as lines, rectangles, and ovals. A vector file contains all the shapes, colors, and starting and ending points necessary to recreate the image. Graphic artists use illustration programs to create line art for magazines, books, and special publications. (See Figure 3-2.) Engineers and programmers use them to create 3-D models. One exciting application is to create virtual worlds or virtual reality, as we describe later in this chapter. Popular professional illustration programs include Adobe Illustrator, CorelDraw 7, Macromedia FreeHand, and Micrografx Designer.

Graphics Suites

Some companies are combining or bundling their separate graphics programs as a group called **graphics suites.** The advantage of the graphics suites is that you can buy a larger variety of graphics programs at a lower cost than if purchased separately. The most popular suite is from the Corel Corporation. The suite, called CorelDraw, includes five individual Corel graphics programs plus a large library of clip art, media clips, and fonts. Two other popular suites are Corel's Graphics Pack and Micrografx's ABC Graphics Suite 95.

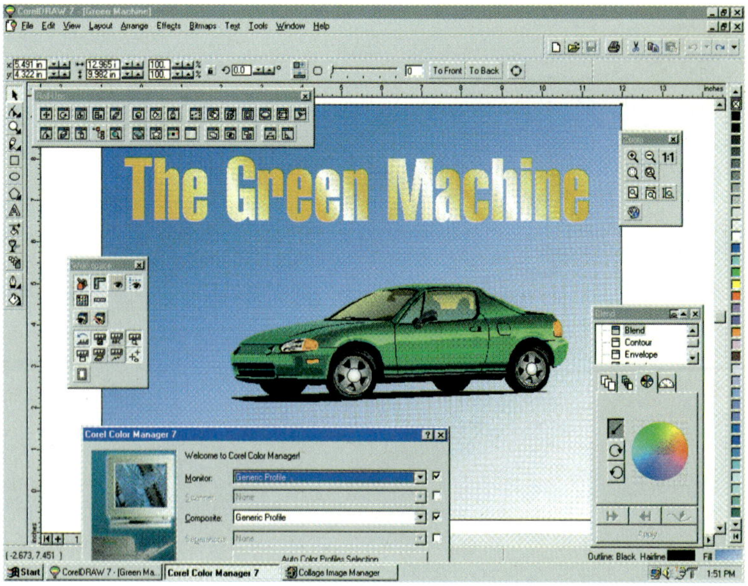

FIGURE 3-2
Illustration program (CorelDraw 7).

Multimedia

Multimedia integrates all kinds of information. Story boards show logic, flow, and structure. Authoring programs create presentations.

Multimedia is one of the fastest-growing computer applications. The majority of microcomputer systems sold today are equipped for multimedia. The trend is expected to continue. (See Figure 3-3.)

Multimedia, also called **hypermedia,** is the integration of all sorts of media into one form of presentation. These media may include video, music, voice, graphics, and text. An essential and unique feature of multimedia is user participation or **interactivity.** When experiencing a multimedia presentation, users typically can control the flow and content. This is done by selecting options that customize the presentation to the users' needs.

Once used almost exclusively for computer games, multimedia is now widely used in business, education, and the home. Business uses include high-quality interactive presentations, product demonstrations, and Web page design. In education, multimedia is used for in-class presentation as well as individual study. In the home, multimedia is primarily used for entertainment. In the very near future, however, higher-end multimedia applications such as interactive home shopping and video-on-demand services are expected.

A multimedia presentation is typically organized as a series of related pages. Each page presents information and provides **links** or connections to related information. These links can be to video, sound, graphics, and text files, to other pages, and to other resources. (See Figure 3-4.)

By clicking special areas called **buttons** on a page, you can make appropriate links and "navigate" through a presentation to locate and discover information.

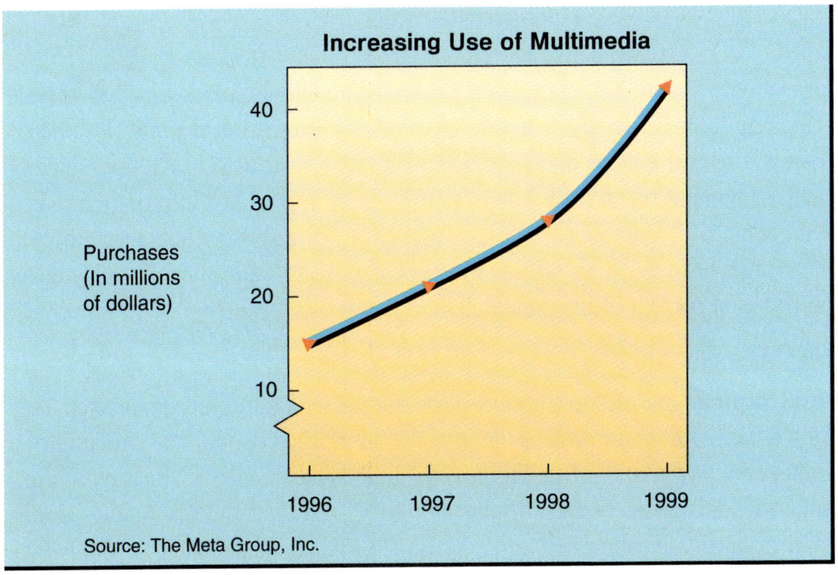

FIGURE 3-3
Multimedia systems in use—past, present, and future.

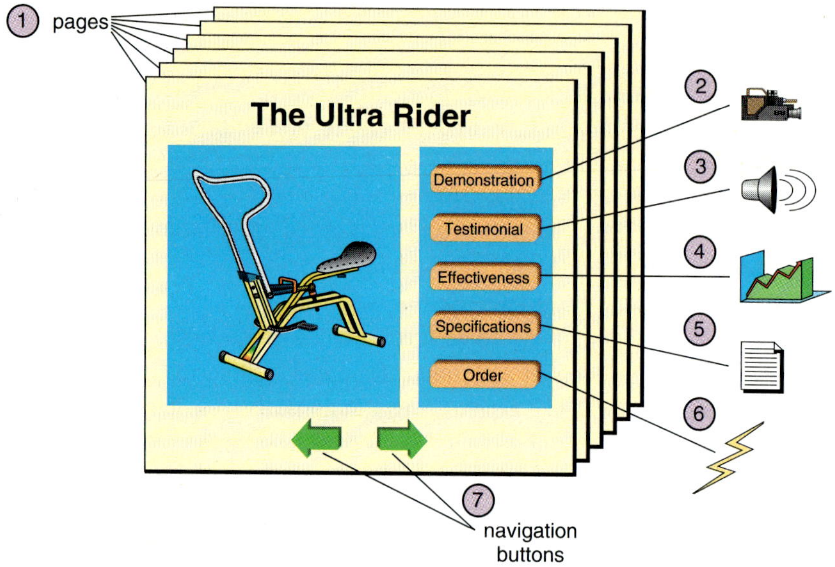

FIGURE 3-4
How multimedia presentations work.

1. This multimedia presentation consists of six pages of related information about The Ultra Rider, a piece of exercise equipment. You navigate through the information by clicking buttons.
2. Clicking the Demonstration button links you to a video clip showing the equipment in operation.
3. Clicking the Testimonial button connects you to an audio or sound clip providing a testimonial on effectiveness of the equipment.
4. Clicking the Effectiveness button links you to a graphic showing actual data relating fa loss to use of The Ultra Rider.
5. Clicking the Specifications button connects you to text providing detailed equipment specifications such as length, width, height, etc.
6. Clicking the Order button provides a direct link to the company's order processing department.
7. Clicking the Navigation buttons connects you to the other pages.

For example, Figure 3-4 represents a multimedia presentation designed to provide marketing information about a piece of exercise equipment called the Ultra Rider. There are several buttons on the page. You can choose to select each one, some of them, or none of them. Each button provides a link to related information. Some of the buttons connect to video, audio, a graphic, or text. Other buttons connect to other pages or to locations outside the presentation. You are in control. You direct the flow and content of the presentation.

Story Boards

Story boards are used in the early planning phase of a multimedia project. They are a design tool used to record the intended overall logic, flow, and structure of a multimedia presentation. (See Figure 3-5.) Individual story boards specify the content, style, and design of each display along with the links to video, audio, graphics, text, or any other media.

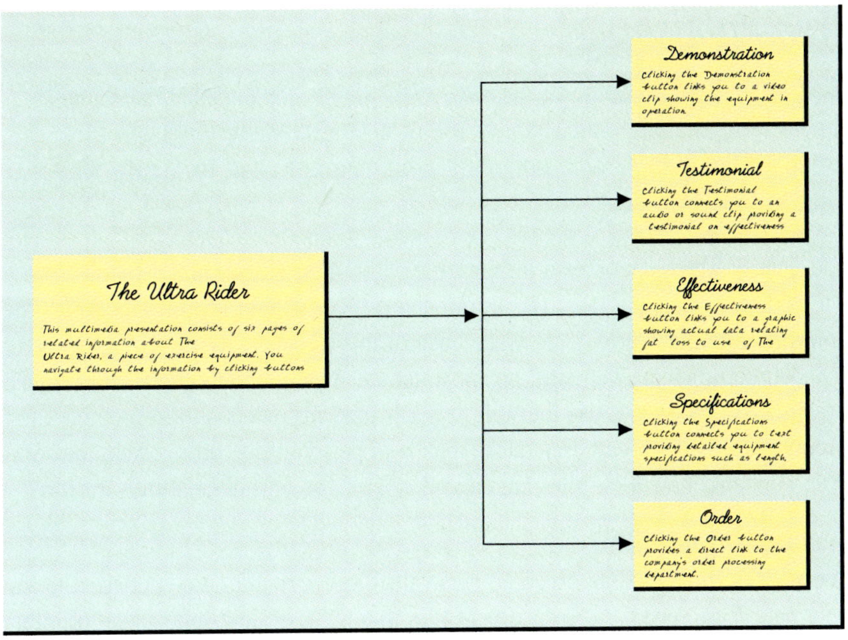

FIGURE 3-5
Partial story board for multimedia project.

Authoring Programs

Authoring programs are special programs used to create multimedia presentations. They bring together all the video, audio, graphics, and text elements into an interactive framework. Widely used authoring programs include Macromedia Director, Authorware, and Toolbook. (See Figure 3-6.)

FIGURE 3-6
Authoring program (Toolbook, version 4.0).

Web Publishing

Web sites are locations on servers. Web pages are an interactive multimedia form of communication. HTML is a programming language to produce Web pages. Web authoring programs are used to create Web sites.

You cannot watch TV or read a magazine without coming across a reference to a site or location on the Web. (For more about the Web and the Internet, see "The Internet and the World Wide Web," beginning on page IG-1.) There are over 300,000 commercial Web sites on the Internet, and hundreds more being added every day. Corporations use the Web to reach new customers and to promote their products. Individuals can even create their own personal sites on the Web. Have you ever wondered how these sites are created or ever thought of creating your own?

Web Site Organization

Web sites are locations on computers called **servers** that are connected to the Internet. These servers store document files that are used to display pages of information. Each site usually consists of many **pages,** with the top-level or opening page called the **home page.**

Before you create the home page or any other page, you should determine the overall content of the site and break it up into related blocks of information. The overall design will be reflected in the home page, and the individual blocks will define the related pages. The overall design is often represented in a block diagram.

Web Pages

What makes the Web so unique is that each page is an interactive multimedia form of communication. A typical Web page presents attractive art, colorful backgrounds, dynamic links to other sites, tables, forms, and scrolling text. (See Figure 3-7.) Many also include audio, video, graphics, and special executable programs called **applets.**

FIGURE 3-7
Web page.

```
<head>
<meta http-equiv="Content-Type"
content="text/html; charset=iso-8859-1">
<meta name="Template"
content="C:\Program Files\Microsoft Office\Office\HTML.DOT">
<meta name="FORMATTER" content="Microsoft FrontPage 2.0">
<meta name="GENERATOR" content="Microsoft FrontPage 2.0">
<title>Sports Company Home Page</title>
</head>

<body background="cream_right.gif">
```

tag

FIGURE 3-8
HTML document.

HTML Documents

The document files that are used to display Web pages are text files containing a special programming language called **HTML (Hypertext Markup Language).** This language consists of statements or **tags** that control how the pages are displayed and provide links to related graphic files and other Web pages. (See Figure 3-8.) You can use a word processor to create HTML documents by entering the appropriate tags.

Web Authoring Programs

Fortunately, you do not need to learn or to know HTML to make Web pages. Some word processing programs have tools for generating pages. Some of these are Corel WordPerfect7, Lotus Word Pro 97, and Microsoft Word 97. More powerful specialized programs are also available. These programs are called **Web authoring programs,** also known as **Web page editors** and **HTML editors.** Some of the best known Web authoring programs are Corel Web Designer, Microsoft FrontPage 97, Netscape Composer, and WebExpress. (See Figure 3-9.)

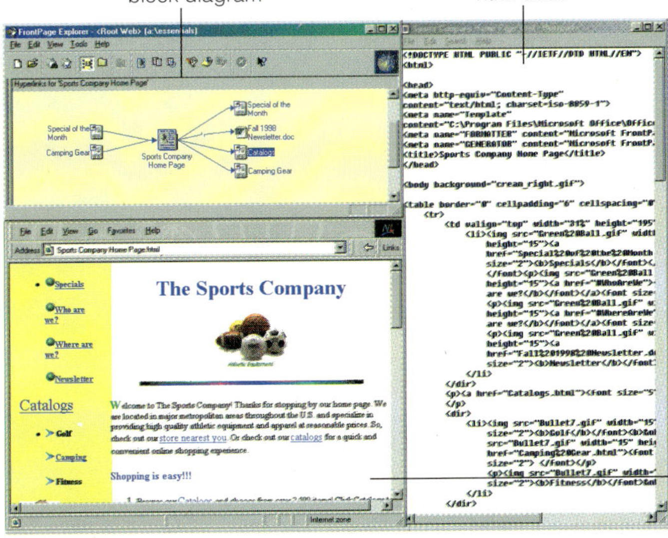

FIGURE 3-9
Web authoring program (Microsoft FrontPage 97).

Groupware

Groupware supports group activities over networks to increase team productivity.

Most application software is designed for individuals working alone. These programs focus on personal or individual productivity. However, in most organizations today, the focus is on teams and team productivity. Team members share information using the organization's computer networks. Many corporations are using recently developed Internet software technologies to create private networks called **intranets.** These intranets are essentially a miniature version of the Internet, completely under the control of the corporation.

Groupware, also known as **collaborative technology,** is software that provides services to support group activities. These include scheduling and holding meetings, communicating, collaborating on ideas, and sharing documents, knowledge, and information. With groupware, two or more people can work on the same information at the same time. This type of software is one of the fastest growing and most widely used network applications. Businesses are investing heavily in groupware to improve group productivity. (See Figure 3-10.)

The most widely used groupware software is Lotus Domino (formerly known as Lotus Notes) with over a million users. Basically, Lotus Domino is a way to share a database over a network so that many users can create and share information. The database is made up of *documents* containing many different kinds of information. They include text, graphics, sounds, images, and even videos. Users can create these documents using so-called *forms.* Users can *view* summaries of the database, share information, collaborate with others, and do many other group activities. Additionally, users can access the Internet as well as the corporate intranet. (See Figure 3-11.)

FIGURE 3-10
Investment in groupware—past, present, and future.

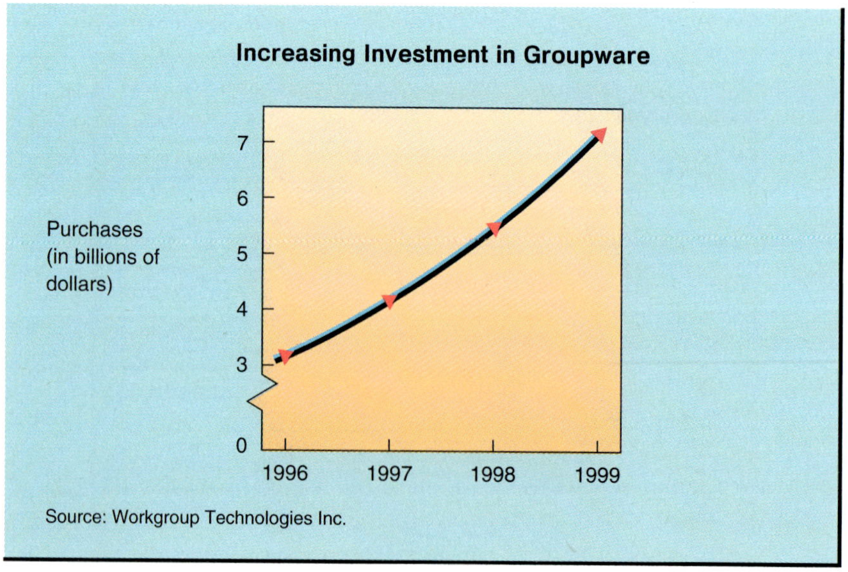

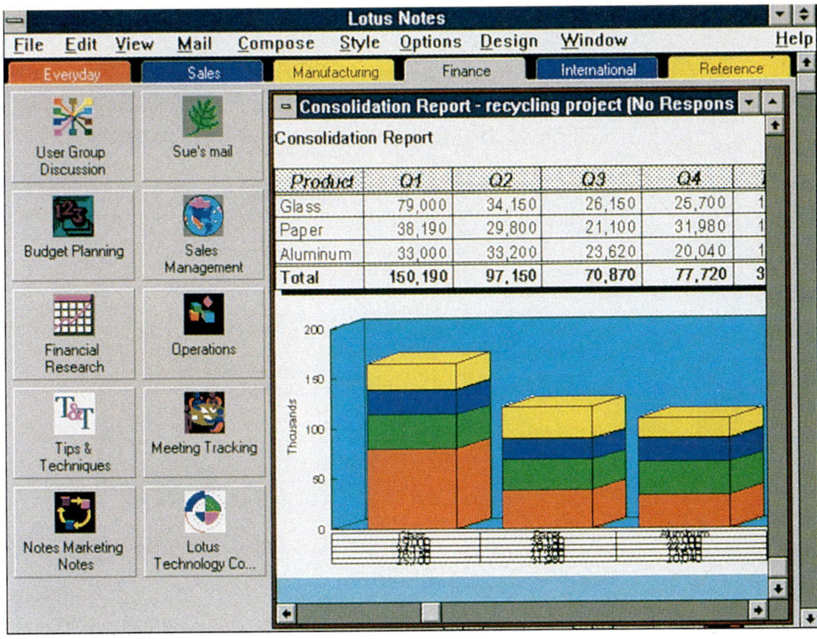

FIGURE 3-11
Groupware software (Lotus Notes).

Project Management

Project management software allows you to plan projects, schedule people, and control resources.

There are many occasions in business where projects need to be watched to avoid delays and cost overruns. A **project** may be defined as a one-time operation composed of several tasks that must be completed during a stated period of time. Examples of large projects are found in construction, aerospace, and political campaigns. Examples of smaller jobs might occur in advertising agencies, corporate marketing departments, and management information systems departments. You may have projects like term papers and lab experiments.

Project management software enables users to plan, schedule, and control the people, resources, and costs needed to complete a project on time. For instance, a contractor building a housing development might use it to keep track of the materials, dollars, and people required for success. Examples of project management software are Harvard Project Manager, Microsoft Project, Project Scheduler, SuperProject, and Time Line.

A typical use of project management software is to show the scheduled beginning and ending dates for each task in order to complete a particular project on time. It then shows the dates when each task was actually completed. Two important tools found in project management software are Gantt charts and PERT charts.

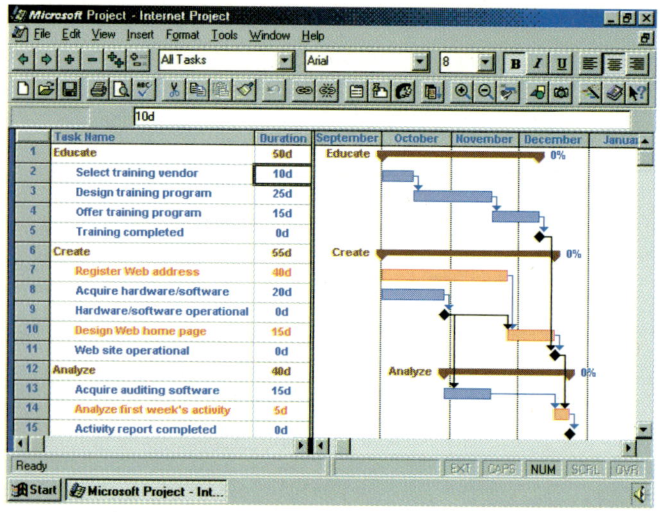

FIGURE 3-12
Gantt chart (Microsoft Project).

Gantt Charts

A **Gantt chart** uses bars and lines to indicate the time scale of a series of tasks. (See Figure 3-12.) You can see whether the tasks are being completed on schedule. The time scale may range from minutes to years.

PERT Charts

A **PERT (Program Evaluation Review Technique) chart** shows not only the timing of a project but also the relationships among its tasks. (See Figure 3-13.) The chart identifies which tasks must be completed before others can begin. The relationships are represented by lines that connect boxes stating the tasks, completion times, and dates. The *critical path,* the sequence of tasks that takes the longest

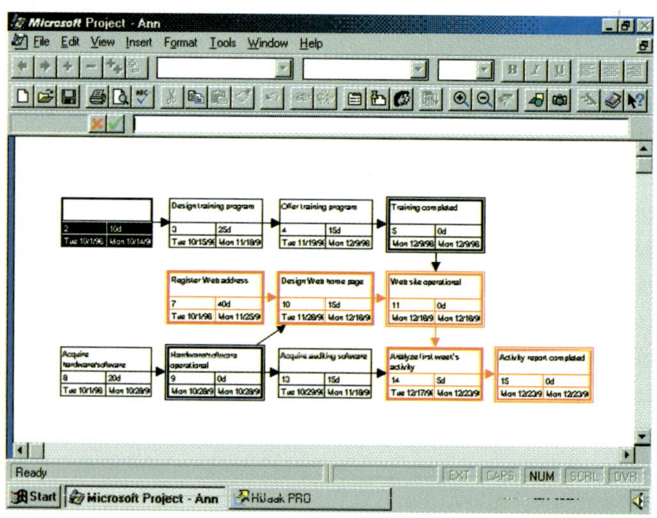

FIGURE 3-13
PERT chart (Microsoft Project).

to complete, is also identified. With project management software, tasks and their completion times can be easily changed to see the effect on the overall schedule.

Artificial Intelligence and Virtual Reality

Artificial intelligence attempts to simulate human thought processes and actions. Three areas are robotics, knowledge-based (expert) systems, and virtual reality.

Does human intelligence really need the presence of "artificial intelligence," whatever that is? Indeed, you might worry, do we need the competition? Actually, the goal of artificial intelligence is not to replace human intelligence, which is probably not replaceable. Rather, it is to help people be more productive. Let us describe how this might work.

In the past, computers used calculating power to solve *structured* problems, the kinds of tasks described throughout this book. People—using intuition, reasoning, and memory—were better at solving *unstructured* problems, whether building a product or approving a loan. Most organizations have been able to computerize the tasks once performed by clerks. However, knowledge-intensive work, such as that performed by many managers, is only beginning to be automated.

Now the field of computer science known as **artificial intelligence (AI)** is moving into the mainstream. AI attempts to develop computer systems that can mimic or simulate human thought processes and actions. These include reasoning, learning from past actions, and simulation of human senses such as vision and touch. True artificial intelligence that corresponds to human intelligence is still a long way off. However, several tools that emulate human problem solving and information processing have been developed. Many of these tools have practical applications for business, medicine, law, and many other fields.

Let us now consider three areas in which human talents and abilities have been enhanced with "computerized intelligence": robotics, knowledge-based systems, and virtual reality.

Robotics

Robotics is the field of study concerned with developing and using robots. **Robots** are computer-controlled machines that mimic the motor activities of humans. Some toylike household robots (such as the Androbots) have been made for entertainment purposes. Most, however, are used in factories and elsewhere. They differ from other assembly-line machines in that they can be reprogrammed to do more than one task. Robots are often used to handle dangerous, repetitive tasks. There are three types of robots:

FIGURE 3-14
Industrial robot: spraying and polishing on car plant production line.

- **Industrial robots:** Industrial robots are used in factories to perform certain assembly-line tasks. Examples are machines used in automobile plants to do painting and polishing. (See Figure 3-14.) In the garment industry, robot pattern cutters create pieces of fabric for clothing. Some types of robots have claws for picking up objects.
- **Perception systems:** Some robots imitate some of the human senses. For example, robots with television-camera vision systems are particularly useful. They can be used for guiding machine tools, for inspecting products, for identifying and sorting parts, and for welding. (See Figure 3-15.) Other kinds of perception systems rely on a sense of touch, such as those used on microcomputer assembly lines to put parts into place.
- **Mobile robots:** Some robots act as transporters, such as "mailmobiles." They carry mail through an office, following a preprogrammed route. Others act as computerized carts to deliver supplies and equipment at medical centers.

Knowledge-Based (Expert) Systems

People who are expert in a particular area—certain kinds of law, medicine, accounting, engineering, and so on—are generally well paid for their specialized knowledge. Unfortunately for their clients and customers, they are expensive, not always available, and hard to replace when they move on.

What if you were to somehow *capture* the knowledge of a human expert and make it accessible to everyone through a computer program? This is exactly what is being done with so-called *knowledge-based* or *expert systems.* **Expert systems** are computer programs that provide advice to decision makers who would otherwise rely on human experts. These expert systems use knowledge bases that contain specific facts, rules to relate these facts, and user input to formulate recommendations and decisions. The rules are used only when needed. The sequence

FIGURE 3-15
Perception system: vision-system robot, used for welding.

of processing is determined by the interaction of the user and the knowledge base. Many expert systems use so-called *fuzzy logic,* which allows users to respond to questions in a very humanlike way. For example, if an expert system asked how your classes were going, you could respond, "great," "OK," "terrible," and so on.

Over the past decade, expert systems have been developed in areas such as medicine, geology, chemistry, military science, and photography. (See Figure 3-16.) There are expert systems with such names as Oil Spill Advisor, Bird Species Identification, and even Midwives Assistant. A system called Grain Marketing Advisor helps farmers select the best way to market their grain. Another, called Senex, shows how to treat breast cancer based on advanced treatment techniques.

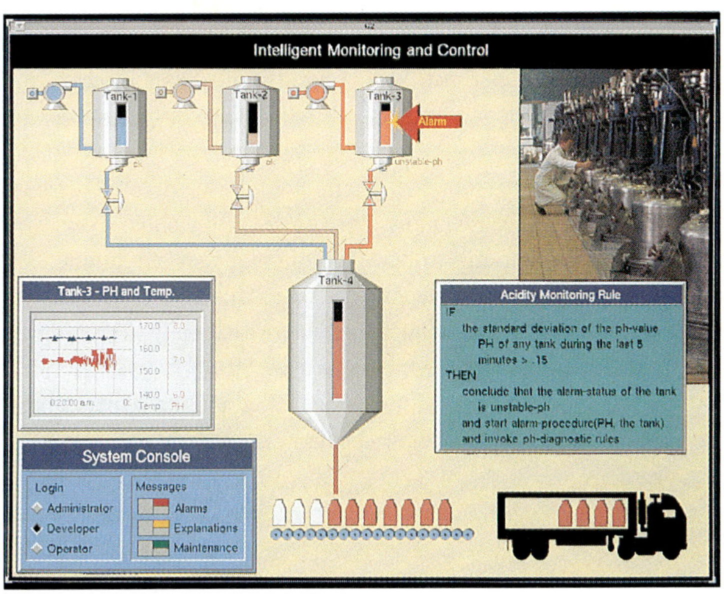

FIGURE 3-16
Expert system: monitoring and controlling chemical acidity.

FIGURE 3-17
Virtual reality: looking inside a molecule.

Virtual Reality

Suppose you could create and virtually experience any new form of reality you wish. You could see the world through the eyes of a child, a robot—or even a lobster. You could explore faraway resorts, the moon, or inside a nuclear waste dump, without leaving your chair. This simulated experience is rapidly becoming possible with a form of AI known as *virtual reality.*

Virtual reality is also known as **artificial reality** or **virtual environments.** Virtual reality hardware includes headgear and gloves. The headgear (one type is called Eyephones) has earphones and three-dimensional stereoscopic screens. The gloves (DataGlove) have sensors that collect data about your hand movements. Coupled with software (such as a program called Body Electric), this interactive sensory equipment lets you immerse yourself into a computer-generated world.

An example of virtual reality is shown in Figure 3-17. In the photo is a person wearing an interactive sensory headset and glove. The rest of the photo shows what the person is actually seeing—in this instance a molecular view of a human cell. When the person moves her head, the stereoscopic views change.

There are any number of possible applications for virtual reality. The ultimate recreational use might be something resembling a giant virtual amusement park. More seriously, we can simulate important experiences or training environments such as flying, surgical operations, spaceship repair, or nuclear disaster cleanup.

A Look at the Future

IPIX, a new immersive photographic technique, may allow you to take virtual tours and exotic vacations.

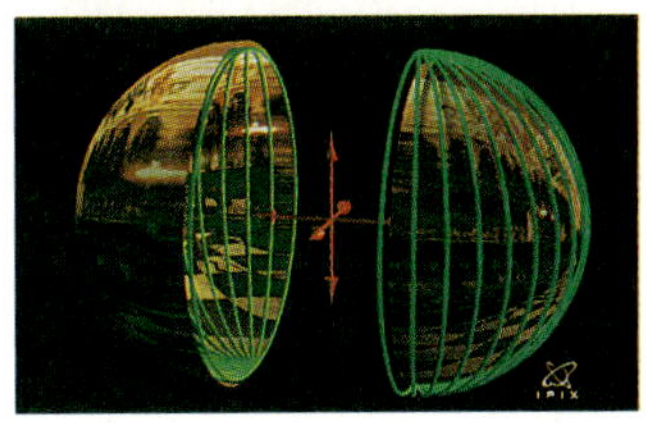

There are few applications with more exciting potential than virtual reality. Although some virtual reality applications do exist, few present lifelike images and fluid motion. This is due in part to the expense and difficulty in capturing 3-D data.

Some experts predict that we will see an explosion of high quality, photo realistic virtual reality applications in the near future. One key is a recently released immersive photographic technique called IPIX. Using a special fish-eye (180-degree) camera, two opposite facing images are recorded digitally and stored in memory. IPIX software takes the two images, corrects for distortion, and joins them into a single image.

Using special software, you can view this image on a computer screen, changing the angle, looking up, down, left, and right. You see almost exactly what you would see if you were standing in one location and looking in every direction. Data for a virtual tour of any environment can be readily captured by taking successive photographs while walking through that environment.

Will we be able to take realistic tours of famous museums, explore classical architecture, or even take exotic vacations without leaving our home? Who knows, but some observers say we will within the next 5 years.

KEY TERMS

applet (56)
artificial intelligence (AI) (61)
artificial reality (64)
authoring program (55)
bitmap file (51)
button (53)
collaborative technology (58)
desktop publishing (51)
draw program (52)
expert system (62)
Gantt chart (60)
graphics suite (52)
groupware (58)
home page (56)
HTML (57)

HTML editor (57)

Hypertext Markup Language (HTML) (57)

hypermedia (53)

illustration program (52)

image editor (51)

interactivity (53)

intranet (58)

link (53)

morphing (52)

multimedia (53)

page (56)

paint program (51)

PERT (Program Evaluation Review Technique) chart (60)

project (59)

project management software (59)

robot (61)

robotics (61)

server (56)

story board (54)

tag (57)

vector images (52)

virtual environment (64)

virtual reality (64)

Web authoring program (57)

Web page editor (57)

Web site (56)

REVIEW QUESTIONS

True/False

1. Desktop publishing programs combine text and graphics to create professional quality publications.
2. Illustrators are used to create HTML code.
3. The opening page of a Web site is called the top page.
4. Groupware is also known as collaborative technology.
5. Expert systems are programs that give advice to individuals who would otherwise rely on human experts.

Multiple Choice

1. The application that can link all sorts of media into one form of presentation:
   a. image editor
   b. word processor
   c. multimedia
   d. spreadsheet
   e. groupware

2. __________ are executable programs on a Web page.
   a. HTML
   b. Bit maps
   c. Vectors
   d. Applets
   e. Tags
3. __________ supports group activities over networks.
   a. Hypermedia
   b. Groupware
   c. AI
   d. Expert system
   e. A knowledge-based system
4. A one-time operation composed of several tasks that must be completed during a stated period:
   a. plan
   b. image editor
   c. manager
   d. schedule
   e. project
5. The __________ chart users bars and lines to indicate time.
   a. Gantt
   b. analytical
   c. PERT
   d. presentational
   e. pie
6. An area of artificial intelligence that simulates certain experiences using special headgear, gloves, and software that translates data into images:
   a. virtual reality
   b. expert system
   c. collaborative technology
   d. hypermedia
   e. shell

Fill in the Blank

1. __________ __________ are used to modify bitmap images.
2. __________ is a programming language used to create Web pages.
3. Linking text, graphics, animation, video, music, and voice into one presentation can be done using __________.
4. Unlike most assembly-line machines, __________ can be reprogrammed to do more than one task.
5. Expert system __________ are special programs that allow a person to custom-build an expert system.

Open Ended

1. Describe desktop publishers, image editors, and illustration programs.
2. Explain how multimedia works.
3. What is groupware? What does it do?
4. Explain what project management software does. Give an example of how one might be used.
5. What are the three areas of artificial intelligence?

DISCUSSION QUESTIONS AND PROJECTS

1. *New areas for expert systems:* There are numerous expert systems designed to pick winning stocks in the stock market. However, not everyone using these systems has become rich. Why? List and discuss three other areas in which you think it would be difficult to devise an expert system.
2. *A picture of things to come:* Over the next 10 to 15 years, say some experts, electronic miniaturization will produce small, portable devices that you can wear like clothing. These devices will do all kinds of wonderful things. For example, they will incorporate display screens, keyboards, CD memories, faxes, telephones, scanners, cameras, and satellite transmitters and will recognize handwriting and voice. What kind of wearable, lightweight "information and entertainment machine" would you design for yourself? What would it do?

on the web

Exercises and Explorations

1 Multimedia

Macromedia Corporation is a leader in multimedia software. Visit our Web site at http://www.magpie.org/essentials/chapter-3.html to link to their site. Once connected to that site, you can preview the latest software and choose one of the multimedia programs. Print out a page from the site that describes the program and write a paragraph discussing how you could use it to enhance or create a multimedia presentation.

2 Creating Web Pages

Nearly every organization today has a Web site and it is very likely that you will be involved with either creating web sites or modifying them. Perhaps you will work with a specialist or work on your own. In either case, it is worthwhile to know what makes a site interesting and attractive. Visit our Web site at http://www.magpie.org/essentials/chapter-3.html to link to a site that provides guidance for web page design, style, and content. Print out the first page of this site, explore the site, and write a paragraph describing some of the programs for creating web pages.

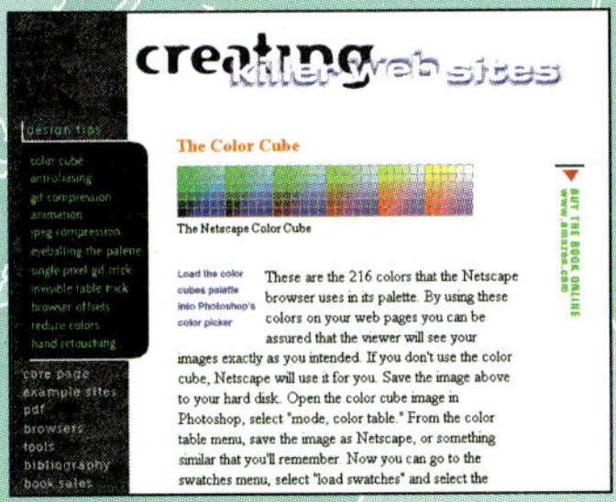

3 Virtual Reality

Everyone looks forward to the day when we can interact with computers in a more natural manner. Many expect virtual reality to make this happen. To get the latest information on virtual reality, connect to the Yahoo site http://www.yahoo.com, and search with key words such as “virtual reality”, “immersive environments technology”, and “VR;” or use categories to look in “Computers and Internet: Multimedia: Virtual Reality” and explore from there. Print out the Web page you find most informative, and write a paragraph listing companies and industries that are using virtual reality and explaining how they use it.

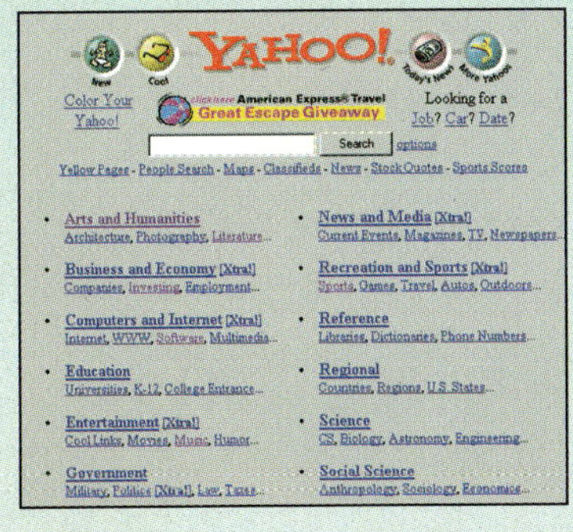

4 Shareware and Freeware

Shareware and freeware are application programs available to the public at little or no cost. Visit our site at http://www.magpie.org/essentials/chapter-3.html for a link to a site providing an extensive list of shareware and freeware that you can download to your computer system. Once connected to this site, find a list of the most popular downloads for your operating system. Print out the list and write a paragraph detailing the three most interesting programs you found at this site.

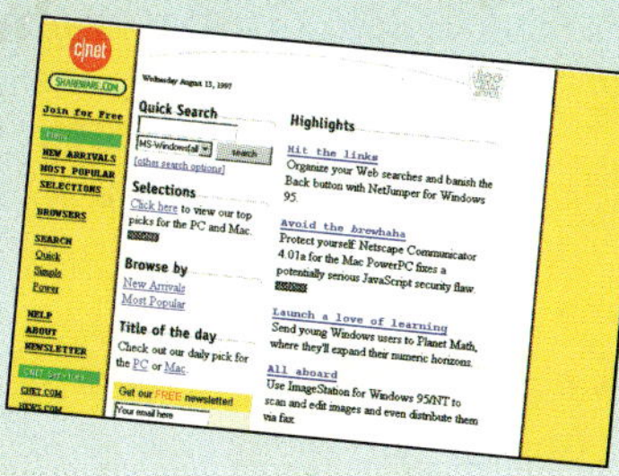

VISUAL SUMMARY

Advanced Applications

Some recent important microcomputer applications are personal information managers, groupware, project management software, desktop publishing, multimedia, and artificial intelligence—robotics, knowledge-based and expert systems, and artificial reality.

GRAPHICS

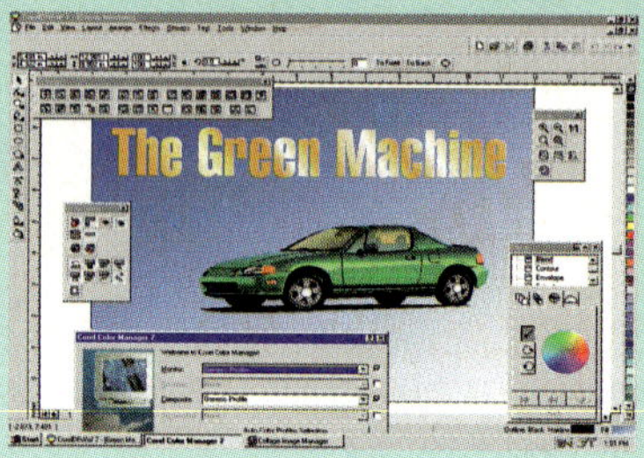

Advanced graphics programs are used by professionals in graphic arts. Three types are desktop publishers, image editors, and illustration programs.

Desktop Publishers

Desktop publishers mix text and graphics to create professional publications.

Image Editors

Image editors (paint programs) create and modify **bitmap images files. Morphing** is a special effect that blends two images into one.

Illustrator Programs

Illustration Programs (draw programs) modify **vector images.**

Examples of Packages

Examples of desktop publishers: FrameMaker, PageMaker, Ventura, QuarkXpress. Examples of image editors: Photoshop, Photo, and xRes. Examples of illustration programs: Illustrator, CorelDraw 7, FreeHand, and Designer

MULTIMEDIA

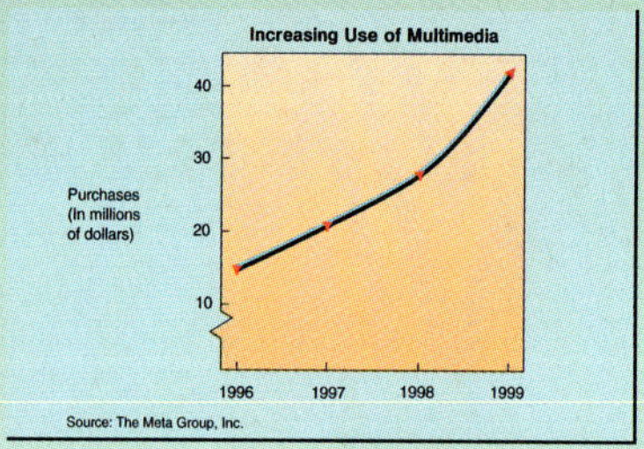

Multimedia or **hypermedia** integrates all sorts of media into an **interactive** presentation. A multimedia presentation is organized by pages of related information. Pages are **linked** or connected by **buttons.**

Story Boards

Story boards are design tools to record the intended overall logic, flow, and structure of a multimedia presentation. Individual story boards specify **links,** content, style, and design of each display.

Authoring Programs

Authoring programs create multimedia presentations. They bring together all the video, audio, graphics, and text elements into an interactive framework. Widely used authoring programs include Macromind Director, Authorware, and Toolbook.

WEB PUBLISHING

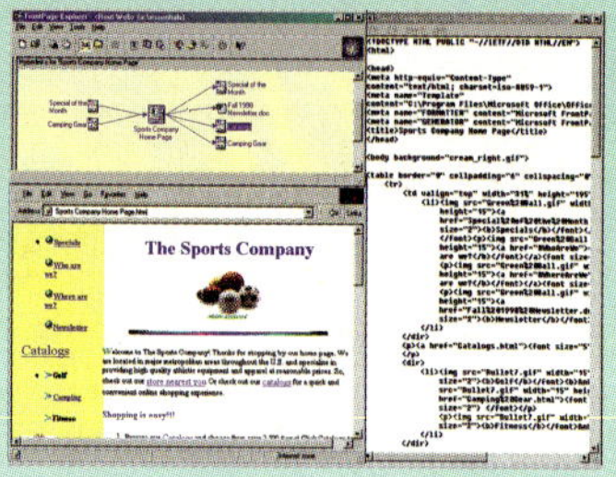

Over 300,000 commercial Web sites exist today. **Web publishing software,** also known as **Web authoring programs,** are typically used to create these sites.

Web Site Organization

Web sites are locations on **servers** (computers) connected to the Internet. Information is presented in **pages** with the first page called the **home page.**

Web Pages

Web pages present information interactively in a multimedia format. Web pages can contain executable programs called **applets.**

HTML Documents

Web pages are displayed from **document files** composed of **HTML** programming code. Program statements are called **tags.**

Examples of Packages

Corel Web Designer, Microsoft FrontPage, Netscape Composer, WebExpress

1. This multimedia presentation consists of six pages of related information about The Ultra Rider, a piece of exercise equipment. You navigate through the information by clicking buttons.
2. Clicking the Demonstration button links you to a video clip showing the equipment in operation.
3. Clicking the Testimonial button connects you to an audio or sound clip providing a testimonial on effectiveness of the equipment.
4. Clicking the Effectiveness button links you to a graphic showing actual data relating fat loss to use of The Ultra Rider.
5. Clicking the Specifications button connects you to text providing detailed equipment specifications such as length, width, height, etc.
6. Clicking the Order button provides a direct link to the company's order processing department.
7. Clicking the Navigation buttons connects you to the other pages.

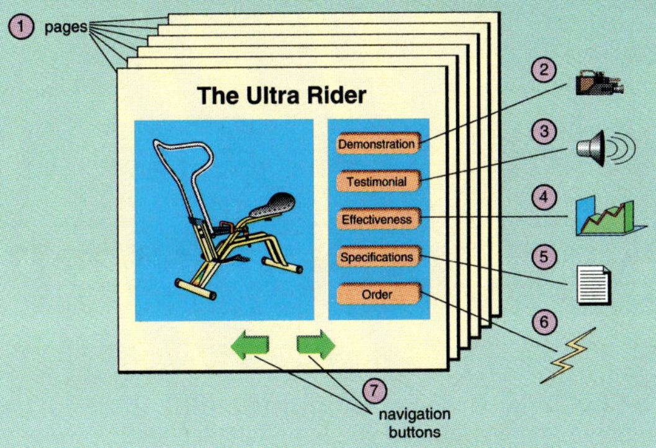

GROUPWARE

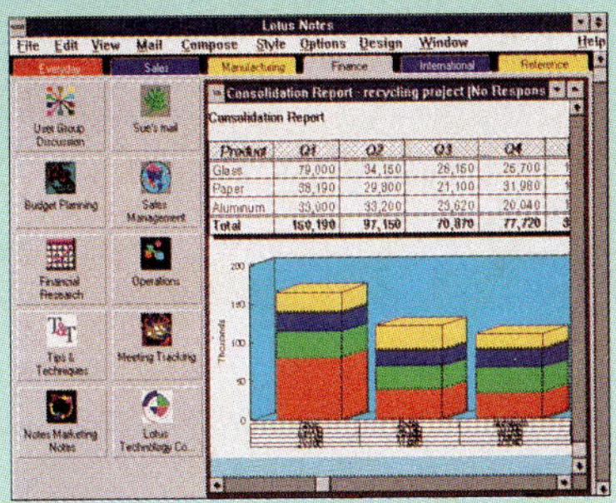

Groupware, also known as **collaborative technology,** allows groups of workers to schedule and hold meetings, communicate, collaborate on ideas, and share documents, knowledge, and information.

Lotus Domino, the most widely used groupware software, shares a database consisting of documents. The documents can contain text, graphics, images, and videos. Users create documents using forms and view summaries of the database.

Intranets are private networks that use Internet software technologies. They are a miniature version of the Internet controlled by a corporation.

Example of Package

Lotus Domino

PROJECT MANAGEMENT

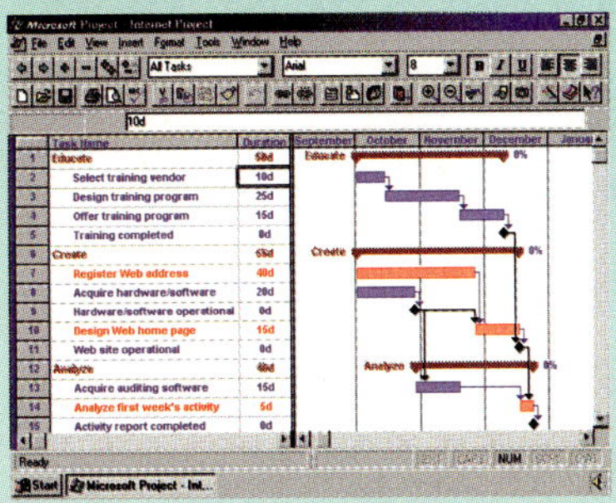

Project management software allows you to plan, schedule, and control the people, resources, and costs of a project.

Two important tools found in project management software are:

Gantt Charts

A **Gantt chart** uses bars and lines to indicate the time scale of a series of tasks so you can see whether the tasks are being completed on schedule.

PERT Charts

A **PERT chart** shows not only the timing of a project but also the relationships among its tasks.

Examples of Packages

Harvard Project Manager, Microsoft Project for Windows, Project Scheduler, SuperProject, Time Line

ARTIFICIAL INTELLIGENCE

Artificial intelligence is a research field to develop computer systems simulating human thought processes and actions. Three areas include:

Robotics

Robotics is a research field to develop machines that can be reprogrammed to do more than one task. Some types are industrial robots, perception systems, and mobile robots.

Knowledge-Based (Expert) Systems

These are computer programs that duplicate the knowledge humans have for performing specialized tasks. They are unlike conventional programs in that they provide advice, use a knowledge base, fire rules, and process according to user interaction. **Fuzzy logic** is used to allow humanlike input.

Virtual Reality

Also known as **artificial reality** or **virtual environments,** this consists of interactive sensory equipment to simulate alternative realities to the physical world.

System Software

Becoming a microcomputer end user is like becoming the driver of a car. You can learn just enough to start up the car, take it out on the street, and pass a driver's license test. Or you can learn more about how cars work. That way you can drive any number of vehicles, know their limitations, and compare performance. Indeed, you could go so far as to learn to be a mechanic. Similarly, by expanding your knowledge about microcomputers, you extend what you can do with them. You don't have to be the equivalent of a mechanic—a computer technician. But the more you know, the more you expand your computer competency and productivity.

COMPETENCIES

After you have read this chapter, you should be able to:

1. **Understand the importance of learning about system software.**
2. **Distinguish among five kinds of operating systems.**
3. **Explain the advantages and disadvantages of DOS.**
4. **Discuss the differences among the four Microsoft Windows programs.**
5. **Discuss the benefits and drawbacks of OS/2 Warp.**
6. **Describe what's good and bad about Macintosh system software.**
7. **Explain the advantages and disadvantages of Unix for microcomputers.**

4

All cars do the same thing—take you somewhere. But there was a time when you could choose between different automotive power systems: steam, electricity, diesel, or gasoline. Some systems were better for some purposes than others. You could have a car that was quiet or cheap to run, for instance. However, that same car perhaps took too long to start, wouldn't take you very far, or didn't have enough power on the hills.

Microcomputers are in a comparable phase of evolution. Some computers do some things better than others—are easier to learn, for instance, or run more kinds of application software. Why is this? One important reason is the *system software,* the "background" software that acts as an interface between the microcomputer and the user. System software also acts as an interface between the application program and the input, output, and processing devices. (See Figure 4-1.) The most important types of microcomputer system software are *DOS, Microsoft Windows, OS/2 Warp, Macintosh,* and *Unix.* Which of these you can use depends in part on what kind of computer you have.

FIGURE 4-1
End users interact with application software. System software interacts with the computer hardware.

Why Learn About System Software?

Because standards are changing, users need to know more about system software than was previously required.

Are you buying a pricey racing machine that you don't really need? Or are you buying an inexpensive, practical vehicle that may nonetheless soon become obsolete? These are the kinds of things many people think about when buying cars. Similar considerations apply in buying microcomputers and software. It's important to know what each type of operating system can and can't do. (See Figure 4-2.) Moreover, you hope the buying decision you make will be good for the next several years.

FIGURE 4-2
The IBM ValuePoint (left) and the Apple PowerPC (right) use different system software. Although similar in many ways, these systems have significant differences.

If the study of system software seems to be remote from your concerns, it shouldn't be. Here's why:

- **Competing system software:** In earlier editions of this book there might not have been a need for this chapter. The kind of microcomputer system software that predominated was the one for IBM and IBM-compatibles known as DOS. These IBM and IBM-compatibles are often referred to as *DOS-based* microcomputers. The other popular system software was the one designed for the Apple Macintosh. Without specialized hardware and software, Macintosh programs wouldn't run on DOS-based microcomputers, and DOS programs wouldn't run on Macintosh computers. Today's very powerful microcomputers are demanding more and more from last year's system software. Now there are several competing forms of system software.
- **One computer, many kinds of system software:** Now there are microcomputers that run more than one kind of system software. Employers may require that you know more than one kind. For instance, many office workers may need to know how to work with Microsoft Windows and OS/2 Warp. These systems can run on the same computer.
- **More networking:** More and more computers are being connected together to share information and resources. Not all operating systems can efficiently support network operations. And some of the ones that do can support only certain types of networks.
- **More sophisticated users:** Previously, microcomputer users were satisfied with the performance offered by DOS. However, users are becoming more sophisticated. Now they want to be able to fully exploit the power of these newer microcomputers. They are beginning to demand that microcomputers run programs that previously could run only on minicomputers and mainframes. To do this, more sophisticated system software is required.

Even if you use only *one* type of system software, such as Windows 95, it's important to realize that such software is frequently revised. Revisions are made in order to handle new technology such as newly developed input and output devices. As system software changes, you need to know what the effects are on your old application software.

Four Kinds of Programs

System software consists of the bootstrap loader, diagnostic routines, basic input-output system, and operating system.

System software deals with the physical complexities of how the hardware works. System software consists of four kinds of programs: bootstrap loader, diagnostic routines, basic input-output system, and operating system. The last one, the operating system, is the one we are most concerned with in this chapter. However, we will briefly mention the others, which operate automatically.

- The **bootstrap loader** is a program that is stored permanently in the computer's electronic circuitry. When you turn on your computer, the bootstrap loader obtains the operating system from your hard disk (or floppy disk) and loads it into memory. This is commonly called **booting** the system.
- The **diagnostic routines** are also programs stored in the computer's electronic circuitry. They start up when you turn on the machine. They test the primary storage, the central processing unit (CPU), and other parts of the system. Their purpose is to make sure the computer is running properly. On some computers, the screen may say "Testing RAM" (a form of computer memory) while these routines are running.
- The **basic input-output system** consists of service programs stored in primary storage. These programs enable the computer to interpret keyboard characters and transmit characters to the monitor or to a floppy disk.
- The **operating system,** the collection of programs of greatest interest to us, helps the computer manage its resources. The operating system takes care of a lot of internal matters so that you, the user, don't have to. For instance, it interprets the commands you give to run programs. It also enables you to interact with the programs while they are running. It manages memory, data, and files.

One set of programs within the operating system is called **utility programs.** These programs perform common repetitious tasks or "housekeeping tasks." One important utility program is used for **formatting** (or **initializing**) blank floppy disks. This program is very important. Although you can purchase disks already formatted, many are not and must be formatted before you can use them. Formatting prepares the disk so that it will accept data or programs. With a formatted disk, you can use a utility program to **copy** or duplicate files and programs from another disk. You can **erase** or remove old files from a disk. You can make a **backup** or duplicate copy of a disk. You can **rename** the files on a disk—that is, give them new filenames.

Every computer has an operating system. Larger computer systems like mainframes and minicomputers have very sophisticated ones. A popular operating system for IBM's mainframes, for example, is MVS. Digital Equipment Corporation (DEC) uses VAX/VMS as the operating system for its minicomputers. These operating systems have very powerful capabilities, including virtual memory, multiprogramming, and multiprocessing.

An operating system with **virtual memory** increases the amount of memory available to run programs. Without virtual memory, an entire program must be read into the computer system's memory before it can run. Therefore, the size of memory determines the largest program that can be run. With virtual memory, the operating system divides large programs into parts and stores these parts on a secondary storage device, usually a disk. Each part is then read into the computer system's memory only when needed. This allows a computer system to run very large programs.

Multiprogramming and multiprocessing allow more than one person to use a computer system. For **multiprogramming,** the operating system interrupts and

SYSTEM SOFTWARE PROGRAMS

PROGRAM	FUNCTION
Bootstrap loader	Reads operating system from disk and loads into memory.
Diagnostic routines	Tests parts of system to ensure computer is running properly.
Basic input-output	Transmits characters from the keyboard to a monitor or disk.
Operating system	Helps manage computer resources. Most important types are DOS, Microsoft Windows, OS/2 Warp, Macintosh, and Unix.

FIGURE 4-3
Types of system programs.

switches rapidly back and forth between several programs while they are running. This allows several different users to run different programs seemingly at the same time. For **multiprocessing,** the operating system controls two or more central-processing units. This allows several different users to independently run different programs at the same time.

There are several similarities between larger computer and microcomputer operating systems. One difference, however, is that the larger systems tend to focus on multiple users of a computer system. Microcomputer operating systems, on the other hand, tend to focus on single users.

For end users, the most important operating systems are those for microcomputers. To achieve computer competency, it is important for you to know something about the principal types of operating systems on the market for microcomputers today. These are *DOS, Microsoft Windows, OS/2 Warp, Macintosh,* and *Unix.*

For a summary of system software programs, see Figure 4-3.

DOS

DOS was the original standard. It is still used, runs thousands of applications, and requires inexpensive hardware.

DOS stands for *D*isk *O*perating *S*ystem. Its original developer, Microsoft Corporation, sells it under the name *MS-DOS.* (The "MS," of course, stands for Microsoft.) It was the original standard operating system for all microcomputers advertising themselves as "IBM-compatible" or "DOS-based," such as Compaq. Whatever machine it is used with, it is usually referred to simply as *DOS.*

There have been several upgrades since MS-DOS was introduced. The 1981 original was labeled version 1.0. Since then there have been numerous newer versions, including 6.0, 6.1, and 6.2. An important characteristic of the more recent or newer versions is that they are "backward compatible." That is, you can still run application programs with them that you could run on the older versions. The newer versions feature pull-down menus. (See Figure 4-4.) With pull-down menus, you use your mouse-directed insertion point or cursor to unfold ("pull down") a menu from the top of your display screen.

Advantages

There is no question that DOS has many advantages.

- **Widely used:** Even today DOS is still used on a significant percentage of all the microcomputers in the world.
- **Number of applications:** An enormous number of application programs have been written for DOS. Indeed, more specialized software is available for DOS than for any other operating system. This software includes not just the basic and advanced applications mentioned in Chapters 2 and 3 but many others as well.
- **Runs on inexpensive hardware:** DOS runs on many computers—old and new—that are reasonably priced. In addition, DOS is available for all kinds of domestic- and foreign-made IBM-compatible machines. The IBM Personal Computer set

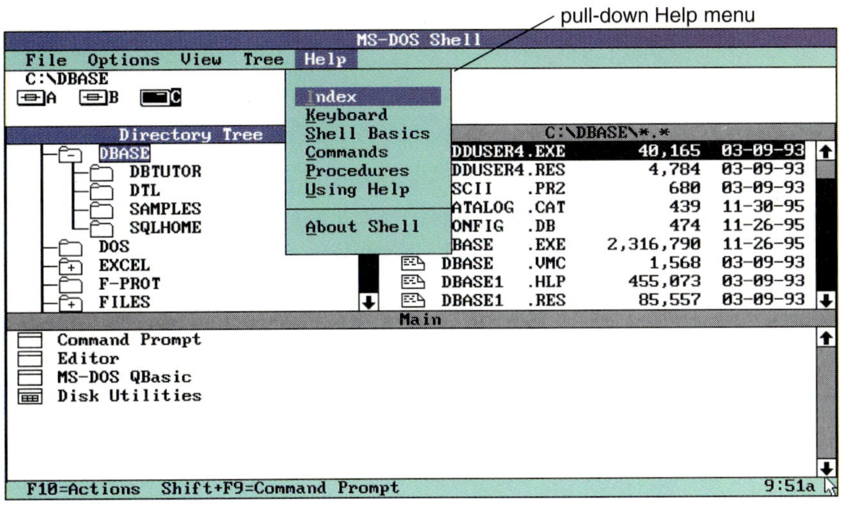

FIGURE 4-4
Pull-down menu (MS-DOS 6.0).

the standard for the business market. However, the appearance of similarly designed competitors has driven prices down, making microcomputers available to more people.

Disadvantages

DOS is software, and software can perform only as well as the hardware for which it was designed. The first version of DOS was introduced in 1981 for microcomputers with floppy-disk drives. This first version did not support hard-disk drives. Since that time, hardware has evolved significantly, and new versions have also evolved. Fortunately, these newer versions of DOS were written so that older application programs could still work with them. Unfortunately, DOS's ability to fully use all the power of today's microcomputers has been constrained. This is because DOS must support these older application packages.

- **Limited primary storage:** Before an application program can be used, it must be stored in the computer's primary storage. An application program running with DOS has direct access to only 640 kilobytes (about 640,000 characters) of primary storage. With the newer versions of DOS, several additional kilobytes can be accessed. However, almost all of the new spreadsheet, database management, and graphics programs require more primary storage. New microcomputers have much more primary storage. Still, DOS by itself as the operating system cannot access all of this available primary storage. This restriction is an inherent limitation of DOS.
- **"Single tasking" only: Multitasking** is the term given to operating systems that allow a single user to run several application programs at the same time. We discuss multitasking further in the next section. Unfortunately, MS-DOS by itself can do only *single tasking:* It can support only one user and one application program at the same time. The newer versions of MS-DOS, however, do support *task switching.* That is, they can switch or interrupt one application to do another application. But they cannot run both applications at the same time.

- **Character-based interface:** In DOS, users issue commands by typing or by selecting items from a menu. This approach is called a **character-based interface** or **command line interface.** Many users find another arrangement for issuing commands, the graphical user interface, much easier.

The widespread use and success of Microsoft's MS-DOS has encouraged other software companies to introduce similar competing products. The two best known are PC-DOS by IBM and Novell DOS by Novell Incorporated. Although the most recent versions of MS-DOS, PC-DOS, and Novell DOS are very similar, Microsoft's MS-DOS is by far the most widely used.

The long-term future of DOS is clear. It will likely continue to be updated, with newer versions designed to minimize its current disadvantages. However, DOS has been replaced by newer operating systems that take advantage of new technologies.

Microsoft Windows

Windows is an operating environment, while Windows 95, Windows 98, and Windows NT are operating systems.

There are four basic variations of Microsoft Corporation's windowing programs. The first is simply called Windows. The other three are Windows 95, Windows 98, and Windows NT.

Windows

Unlike Windows 95, Windows 98, and Windows NT, **Windows** is not an operating system. It is a program that runs with DOS. (See Figure 4-5.) Windows extends the capabilities of DOS by creating an easy-to-use **operating environment.** Other companies make similar programs: Desqview by Quarterdeck Office Systems and NewWave by Hewlett-Packard Company.

Windows is designed to run on IBM and compatible microcomputers with particular kinds of microprocessors. They are the Intel 80486 ("486") chip and Pentium chip.

ADVANTAGES Windows extends the capabilities of DOS to include:

- **Multitasking:** When DOS is combined with Windows, a number of applications ("multiple tasks") can share the same microprocessor. With multitasking you could be running a word processing program and a database management program at the same time. While you are printing a report using the word processing program, the other program could search a database for more information. Windows does this by switching back and forth between the two applications.
- **Graphical user interface:** Windows (and other windowing programs available for DOS) offers a graphical user interface (GUI). A graphical user interface allows you to use a mouse (or keyboard commands) to move a pointer or cursor on the screen. To make a selection, position the pointer on a graphic symbol called an **icon** or on a pull-down menu and then click (press a button on) the mouse.

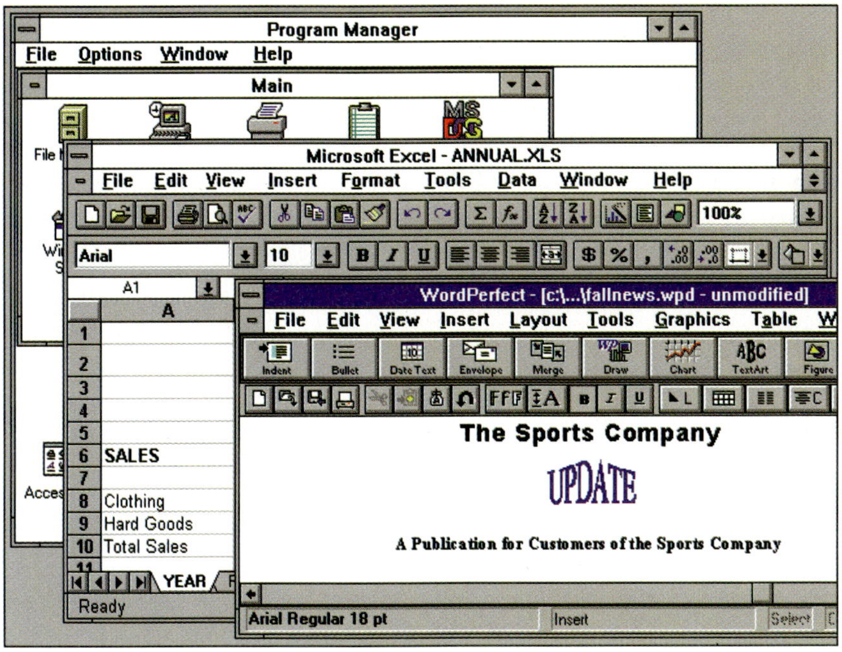

FIGURE 4-5
Windows 3.1 running with DOS.

For example, to specify printer commands using Windows, you can simply click on the printer icon.

- **Number of applications:** Although more programs have been written for DOS, there are nevertheless thousands of programs written for Windows.
- **More memory:** As mentioned before, DOS by itself has limited access to memory, thereby severely limiting software and hardware capabilities. Windows, however, has a **memory manager** that allows access well beyond 640 kilobytes. Windows can access billions of characters of memory.
- **Sharing data between applications:** Windows can share data from one application with data from other applications. For example, you may have created a cost report using a word processing program. The report contains a table based on a spreadsheet analysis of various items. If the two applications were linked, a change in the spreadsheet's values would automatically be reflected in the word processing document.

DISADVANTAGES Windows has dramatically improved upon DOS. Of course, Windows has some limitations.

- **Minimum system configuration:** Windows requires a more powerful microcomputer to run. To effectively use Windows, the system should have at least a 486 microcomputer. It also requires at least four times as much memory as DOS and a hard disk.
- **Unrecoverable errors:** When running the earlier versions of Windows, users sometimes encountered the message "Unrecoverable application error" on their screen. This means that the application program cannot proceed and you must restart the program to begin again. Fortunately, these unrecoverable errors are rare with the newer versions of Windows.

Windows 95

Unlike Windows, **Windows 95** does not require DOS to run. (See Figure 4-6.) Introduced by Microsoft in 1995, it is an operating system designed for powerful microcomputers.

ADVANTAGES Windows 95 has some major advantages compared to Windows. These include:

- **Multiprocessing:** Multiprocessing is similar to multitasking except that the applications are run independently and at the same time. For instance, you could be printing a word processing document and using a database management program at the same time. With multitasking, the speed at which the document is printed is affected by the demands of the database management program. With multiprocessing, the demands of the database management program do not affect the printing of the document.
- **Flexibility:** Windows 95 does not require DOS and is able to run with a much wider variety of powerful computers and microprocessors.
- **Internet access:** As we will discuss in the Guide to the Internet, to connect to the Internet through an online service, your microcomputer must have TCP/IP and Internet utilities. Both are built into Windows 95. To gain access using Windows 95, all you have to do is click the appropriate icon. (Refer to Figure 4-6.)
- **Easy upgrades:** Installation of new hardware such as a modem can be very complex and difficult. A new standard called Plug and Play (to be discussed in detail in Chapter 5) promises to greatly simplify the installation process. Windows 95 is the first operating system for DOS-based computers to fully support Plug and Play.

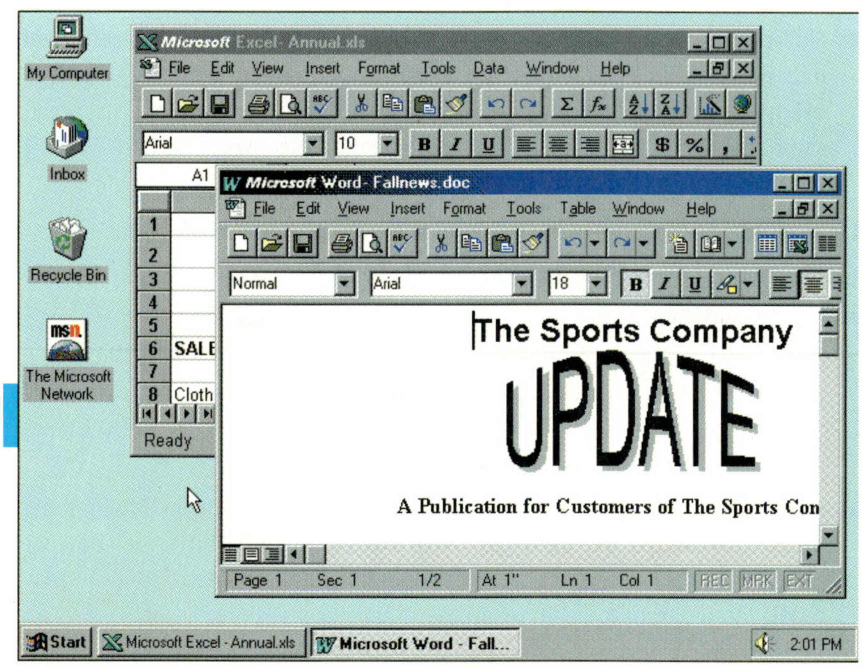

FIGURE 4-6
Windows 95.

DISADVANTAGES Compared to Windows, Windows 95 has two major disadvantages.

- **Minimum system configuration:** Like Windows, Windows 95 requires at least a 486 microprocessor and a hard-disk drive to operate effectively. However, Windows 95 requires more hard disk space—nearly five times as much. Additionally, Windows 95 requires much more memory—three to four times as much.
- **Fewer applications:** Compared to DOS and Windows, fewer applications have been written specifically for Windows 95. It can, however, run most DOS and Windows applications.

Windows 98

Windows 98 is one of the newest operating systems from Microsoft. It was previously known by the code name **Memphis** and at one time referred to as Windows 97. It is an advanced operating system designed for today's very powerful microcomputers. (See Figure 4-7.)

ADVANTAGES Windows 98 has some major advantages compared to Windows 95. These include:

- **Performance:** It is faster in many common tasks like starting up, loading applications, and shutting down. Windows 98 includes a Tune-up Wizard that automatically monitors system operations and suggests ways to improve performance.
- **Internet integration:** Windows 98 is fully integrated with Microsoft's browser, Internet Explorer, making Internet access easier and faster.
- **Ease of use:** Plug and play capability is extended to support the newest advances in technology. Multiple views of an application or multiple applications can be viewed on separate monitors simultaneously.

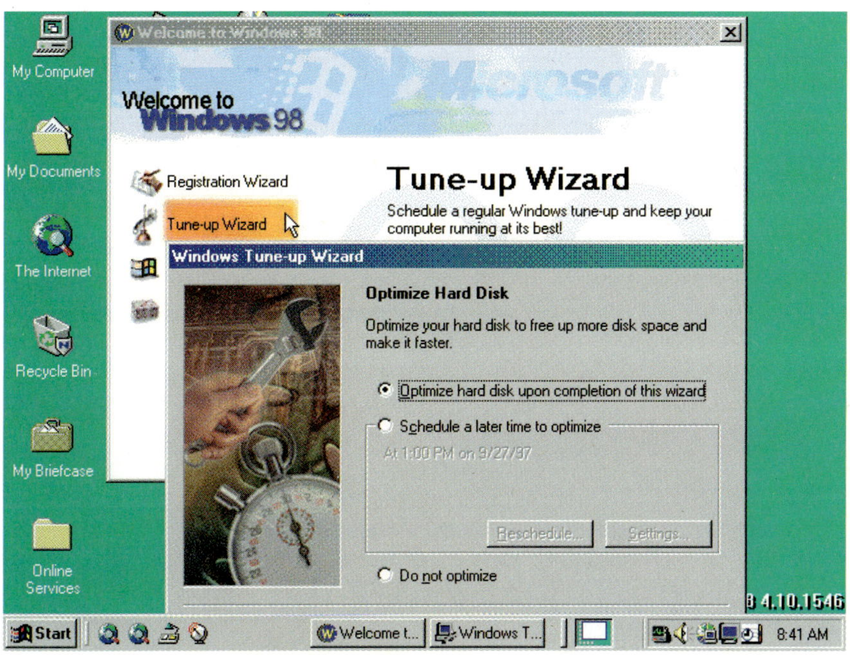

FIGURE 4-7
Windows 98.

- **Multimedia:** Windows 98 has advanced audio and video capability. With a tuner card, you can watch television on your microcomputer monitor.

DISADVANTAGES Compared to Windows 95, Windows 98 has some disadvantages.

- **Minimum system configuration:** Windows 98 requires at least a Pentium microprocessor to operate effectively. Additionally, more hard disk space and memory are necessary.
- **Fewer applications:** Of course since Windows 98 is a new operating system, fewer applications have been written specifically for it. It can, however, run most DOS, Windows, and Windows 95 applications.

Windows NT

Windows NT is a very sophisticated and powerful operating system. (See Figure 4-8.) It is not considered a replacement for Windows 95. Rather, it is an advanced alternative designed for very powerful microcomputers and networks.

ADVANTAGES Windows NT has some major advantages when compared to Windows 95. These advantages include:

- **Multiuser:** Windows NT allows more than one person, or **multiusers,** to use the same computer at the same time. At one time, multiuser systems were considered to have a very significant cost advantage. Now, as hardware costs have come down, this advantage for microcomputers is not nearly as significant.
- **Networking:** In many business environments, workers often use computers to communicate with one another and to share software using a network. This is made possible and controlled by special system software. Windows NT has network capabilities and security checks built into the operating system. This makes network installation and use relatively easy.

FIGURE 4-8
Windows NT.

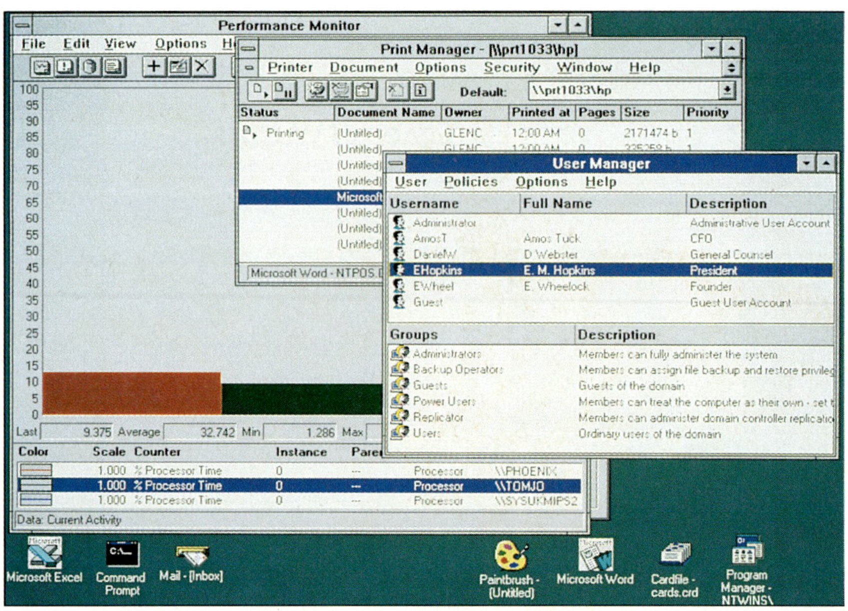

DISADVANTAGES Windows NT has some disadvantages when compared to Windows 95.

- **Minimum system configuration:** Windows NT requires more memory and more than twice the hard-disk space as Windows 95.
- **Upgrade support:** Windows NT does not provide the same level of support for Plug and Play. Therefore, upgrading or installation of new hardware under Windows NT can be much more difficult.

OS/2

OS/2 was originally developed jointly by IBM and Microsoft.

O**S/2** stands for Operating System/2. (See Figure 4-9.) It was originally developed jointly by IBM and Microsoft (who have since gone their separate ways). The most recent version is OS/2 Warp.

Advantages

Like Windows 98 and Windows NT, OS/2 Warp is designed for very powerful microcomputers and has several advanced features. Some of its advantages include:

- **Minimum system configuration:** OS/2 Warp requires nearly the same system configuration as Windows 98. Compared to Windows NT, however, OS/2 requires only one third the memory and less than half the hard-disk space.
- **Voice recognition:** OS/2 Warp has built-in voice recognition. Voice commands can be used to perform many basic operations such as opening, closing, and deleting files.

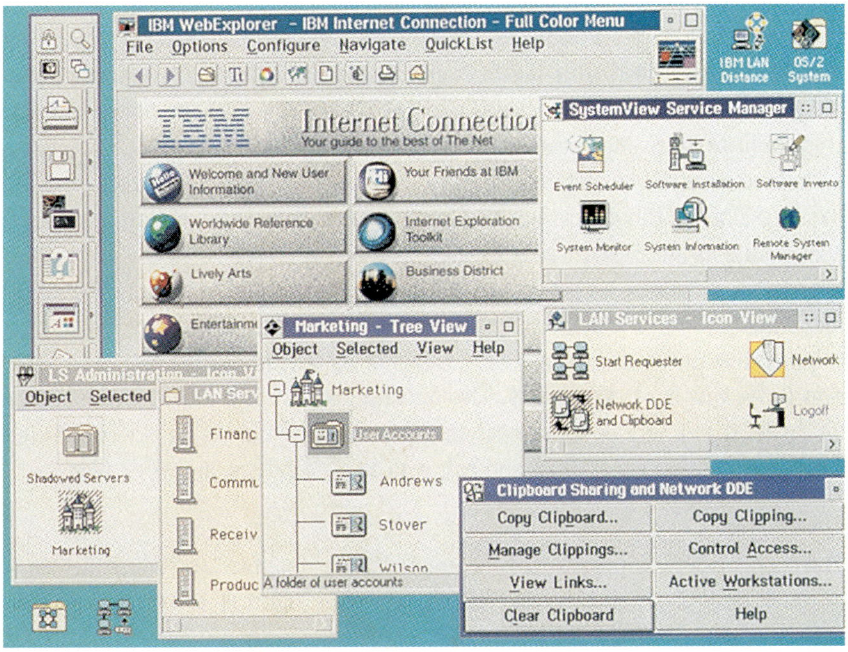

FIGURE 4-9
OS/2 Warp.

Disadvantages

OS/2 Warp has some disadvantages compared to Windows 98 and Windows NT:

- **Networking:** Compared to Windows NT, neither OS/2 Warp nor Windows 98 have the same level of network and security capabilities.
- **Upgrade support:** Like Windows NT, OS/2 Warp does not provide the same level of support for Plug and Play as does Windows 98. Therefore, upgrading or installation of new hardware can be more difficult.

Macintosh Operating System

The Macintosh operating system, which runs only on Macintosh computers, offers a high-quality graphical user interface and is very easy to use.

What can you do with OS/2 Warp or Microsoft Windows that you can't do with an Apple Macintosh computer? That's what many people are asking. If it's a graphical user interface or Plug and Play capabilities you want, that's been available for some time with the Mac. In the opinion of many industry observers, OS/2 Warp and Microsoft Windows look very similar to the Macintosh operating system. To appreciate the differences, let us look at how the Macintosh works.

The **Macintosh operating system** is contained in two primary files—the System file and the Finder. These two files work together to perform the standard operating system procedures. These procedures include tasks such as formatting disks, copying files, erasing files, and running application programs. These two files also manage the user interface, displaying menus and activating tasks that are chosen from the menus by the user.

Remember that the advantages and disadvantages of microcomputer operating systems are associated with the microprocessors for which they were originally designed. DOS, Microsoft Windows, and OS/2 were designed for microprocessor chips built by Intel. Macintoshes, on the other hand, are built around Motorola's microprocessors. These Motorola chips cannot run DOS application programs, and the Intel chips cannot run Macintosh application programs. In the beginning, Apple found its Macintoshes hard to sell to corporations because nearly all business application programs—such as Lotus 1-2-3—were written to run on DOS-based machines.

Apple has introduced numerous versions of its operating system. A recent version is the Macintosh **System 8.** This operating system is a significant milestone for Apple. It is a very powerful operating system like Windows NT and OS/2. System 8 has network capabilities and can read DOS, Windows, and OS/2 files.

Advantages

The Apple Macintosh popularized the graphical user interface, including the use of windows, pull-down menus, and the mouse. (See Figure 4-10.) The Macintosh operating system has several advantages:

FIGURE 4-10
The Macintosh graphical user interface.

- **Ease of use:** The graphical user interface has made the Macintosh popular with many newcomers to computing. This is because it is easy to learn. In fact, studies show that user training costs are *half* as much for Macintoshes as for DOS-based computers.
- **Multimedia:** Macintosh has established a high standard for graphics processing. This is a principal reason why the Macintosh is popular for desktop publishing. Additionally, System 8 includes special viewer programs that support powerful three-dimensional graphics.
- **Easy upgrades:** Like Windows 95 and Windows 98, the Macintosh System 8 supports Plug and Play. As mentioned earlier, Macintosh was the first operating system to support this concept.

Disadvantages

Many characteristics that were previously considered disadvantages may no longer prove to be so. Nevertheless, let us consider what these disadvantages are.

- **A "business" machine?** Apple has had to struggle against the corporate perception that its products are not for "serious business users." Corporate buyers have had a history of purchasing from IBM and other vendors of large computers. Many have viewed Apple from the beginning as a producer of microcomputers for students, game players, and hobbyists. This, however, has been changing.
- **Multiprocessing:** Unlike Windows NT and OS/2 Warp, Macintosh System 8 does not support multiprocessing.
- **Compatibility difficulties:** The incompatibility of DOS with Macintosh microprocessors made Macintoshes less attractive to corporate users interested in compatibility and connectivity. However, hardware and software are available for the Mac

to allow it to run DOS, Windows, and OS/2 applications. In addition, communications networks connect Macintoshes to other computers that use DOS. Apple has cooperated with Digital Equipment Corporation (DEC) and others to produce communications links between Macintoshes, IBM PCs, and mainframe computers.

Unix

Unix can run on many different computers (is "portable"), can perform multitasking, can be shared by several users at once, and can network reliably.

Unix has been around for some time. It was originally developed by AT&T for minicomputers and is very good for multitasking. It is also good for networking between computers. It has been, and continues to be, popular on very powerful microcomputers called workstations. (See Figure 4-11.)

Unix initially became popular in industry because for many years AT&T licensed the system to universities for a nominal fee. This led to Unix being carried by recent computer science and engineering graduates to their new places of employment.

One important consequence of its scientific and technical orientation is that Unix has remained popular with engineers and technical people. It is less well

FIGURE 4-11
UNIX workstation (SunIPX).

known among businesspeople. All that, however, is changing. The reason: With the arrival of very powerful microcomputers, Unix is becoming a larger player in the microcomputer world.

Let us consider the advantages and disadvantages of Unix.

Advantages

Unix has the advantage of being a portable operating system. That means that it is used with ("is portable to") different types of computer systems. It is used with microcomputers, minicomputers, mainframes, and supercomputers. The other operating systems are designed for microcomputers and are not nearly as portable. Having said this, however, we must hastily state that there are *different versions* of Unix, as we will describe. Let us first consider the advantages.

- **Multitasking:** Unix enables you to do multitasking. It allows you to run several programs at the same time, each one sharing the CPU.
- **Multiprocessing:** Unix, like Windows NT and OS/2 Warp, is able to run several programs independently and at the same time.
- **Networking:** Unix is able to share files over electronic networks with several different kinds of equipment. Although the other operating systems can also do this, Unix systems have been successfully and reliably sharing across networks for years.

Disadvantages

Unix was a minicomputer operating system used by programmers and computer science professionals some time before the rise of the microcomputer. This means it has certain qualities that make it useful to programmers—lots of supporting utility programs and documentation, for instance. But some of these features make Unix difficult for end users. Let us consider the disadvantages.

- **Limited business application software:** This is a great barrier at the moment. There are many engineering application programs. Unfortunately, there are fewer business application programs. Businesses that depend on off-the-shelf programs for microcomputers will find offerings very limited.
- **No Unix standard:** This may be *the* biggest stumbling block. There is no Unix standard. This means that an application written for one version of Unix may not run on other versions. The principal microcomputer versions are AT&T's Unix System V, IBM's AIX, Novell's UnixWare 2, and the University of California/Berkeley's 4.2 Unix. An organization called the X/Open Co. is trying to create a standard. This organization is a consortium of major computer suppliers led by DEC, Hewlett-Packard, Novell, and SunSoft.
- **More difficult to learn:** Unix is a very powerful and complex operating system. Its commands are frequently long and complex. Because of this, many microcomputer users find Unix difficult to learn and use.

Unix is a popular operating system for researchers and educators. Some observers think it could yet become a leader among microcomputer operating systems.

COMPARISONS OF OPERATING SYSTEMS

OPERATING SYSTEM	ADVANTAGES	DISADVANTAGES
DOS	Many existing users and applications; system requirements	Limited primary storage; single tasking only; character-based interface
Windows	Multitasking; graphical user interface; many applications; more memory; share data between applications	System requirements; occasional unrecoverable errors
Windows 95	Multitasking; graphical user interface; more memory; share data between applications; multiprocessing; flexibility; Internet access; easy upgrades	System requirements; few applications
Windows 98	Multitasking; graphical user interface; more memory; share data between applications; multiprocessing; flexibility; Internet access; easy upgrades, faster, multimedia support	System requirements; few applications
Windows NT	Multitasking; graphical user interface; more memory; share data between applications; multiprocessing; multiuser; flexibility; networking capabilities	System requirements; few applications; upgrade support
OS/2 Warp	Multitasking; graphical user interface; more memory; share data between applications; system requirements; multiprocessing; flexibility	Few applications; networking capabilities; upgrade support
Macintosh	Ease of use; quality graphics; graphical user interface; multitasking; upgrade support	Market perception; no multiprocessing compatibility
Unix	Multitasking; multiprocessing; multiuser; networking capabilities	Limited business applications; no standard version; difficult to learn

FIGURE 4-12
Advantages and disadvantages of different microcomputer operating systems.

The principal advantages and disadvantages of the present microcomputer operating systems are summarized in Figure 4-12.

A Look at the Future

Have you ever gotten really frustrated with a computer? Human surrogates like Bob and the Office Assistants might help.

Did you ever want to just yell at a computer? Have you ever threatened one? Sometimes they seem so stupid. Other times, hopefully more often than not, computers do just want we want. Perhaps you have even praised one or patted it on the monitor. If you have, don't feel alone. Research at Microsoft has found that many people see their computers as people!

Wouldn't it be nice to be able to communicate with a computer by talking to it and gesturing? How useful it would be to be able to ask questions or to receive advice on how to do things. Hold on because that's part of the future of operating systems and application programs.

Microsoft started along this path a few years ago with an operating system called Bob. Although greeted with limited success, Microsoft continued by providing Office Assistants in Office 97. IBM has experimented with more human and sophisticated assistants they call human surrogates. But this is just the beginning. Microsoft estimates that 90% of the programming for future operating systems will be devoted to these new input and interface technologies.

Will we be able to communicate directly with computers by talking and gesturing to them within the next decade? Microsoft CEO Bill Gates thinks we will. Who knows?

KEY TERMS

backup (75)
basic input-output system (75)
booting (75)
bootstrap loader (75)
character-based interface (78)
command line interface (78)
copy (75)
diagnostic routine (75)
DOS (76)
erase (75)
formatting (75)
icon (78)
initializing (75)
Macintosh operating system (84)
memory manager (79)
multiprocessing (76)
multiprogramming (75)
multitasking (77)
multiuser (82)
operating environment (78)
operating system (75)
OS/2 (83)
rename (75)
System 8 (84)
Unix (86)
utility program (75)
virtual memory (75)
Windows (78)
Windows 95 (80)
Windows 98 (81)
Windows NT (82)

REVIEW QUESTIONS

True/False

1. One computer can only run one kind of system software.
2. Virtual memory increases the amount of memory available to run application programs.
3. Mainframe and minicomputer systems tend to focus on multiple users of a single computer system.
4. Macintosh computers are designed to use the Pentium microprocessor.
5. One of Unix's primary strengths is the large number of applications written for it.

Multiple Choice

1. The collection of programs that helps the computer manage its resources:
   a. bootstrap loader
   b. applications
   c. operating system
   d. diagnostic routines
   e. backup

2. An operating environment:
   a. Windows
   b. Windows 98
   c. Windows NT
   d. OS/2
   e. Macintosh
3. The ability to have a number of applications running at the same time:
   a. GUI
   b. integrated
   c. windowing software
   d. multitasking
   e. networking
4. An operating system developed jointly by IBM and Microsoft Corporation:
   a. Unix
   b. OS/2
   c. Windows NT
   d. Windows 97
   e. Macintosh
5. Designed to run the System 8 operating system:
   a. Unix
   b. OS/2
   c. Windows
   d. Desqview
   e. Macintosh

Fill in the Blank

1. __________ the system means that the computer has been turned on and the operating system has been loaded into memory.
2. Of all the microcomputer operating systems, __________ is able to run on the least expensive hardware.
3. Windows 95 is an operating __________ .
4. The System file and the Finder are the two primary files in the __________ operating system.
5. The lack of a standard version for __________ is likely its most significant disadvantage.

Open Ended

1. What, in a phrase, is the difference between application software and system software?
2. What are utility programs?
3. What is meant by multitasking?
4. What is a graphical user interface?
5. What is meant by the term *multiuser*?

DISCUSSION QUESTIONS

1. *Apple or IBM?* Suppose you're working for a small company that needs 10 new microcomputers. The computers must all be the same and will be networked to share data and programs. It's your decision—you can buy either Apple Macintoshes or IBM-compatibles. Which microcomputer and what operating system would you choose, and why?
2. *Windows CE?* Windows CE is a specialized operating system not discussed in this chapter. Use the library or the Internet to learn about it. What is it? How is it used? How is it different from the other Microsoft Windows operating systems?

on the web

Exercises and Explorations

1 Apple's Macintosh Operating System

The Apple Corporation is widely recognized as the originator of user-friendly visual graphic interfaces. To learn more about the newest Macintosh operating system, visit our Web site at http://www.magpie.org/essentials/chapter-4.html to link to Apple's site. Once connected to their site, locate information about the latest Macintosh operating system. Print out the Web page describing this new operating system and write a paragraph summarizing its new features.

2 Microsoft's Windows

Microsoft created the famous Windows operating systems. To learn more about the most recent operating system from Microsoft, visit our Web site at http://www.magpie.org/essentials/chapter-4.html to connect to the Microsoft site. Once connected to that site, locate information about the newest operating system. Print out the most informative Web page and write a paragraph describing the most important features of this new operating system.

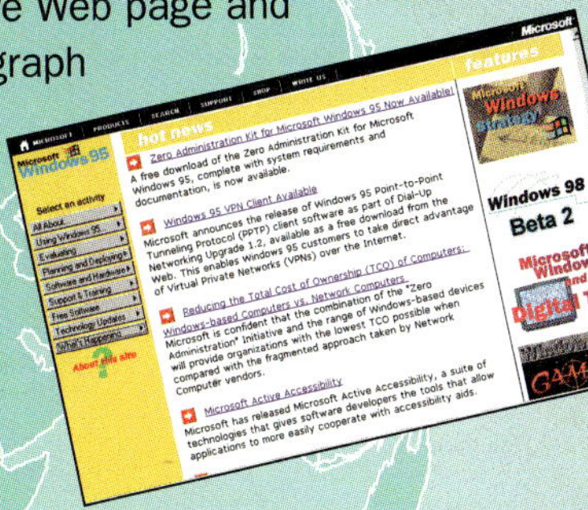

3 IBM's OS/2 Warp

Find the latest information on OS/2 Warp by visiting the site http://www.yahoo.com, where you can search with keywords such as "OS/2 Warp", "IBM", and "Operating System" or use categories to look in "Computers and Internet Channel: Operating Systems: OS/2." Print out the Web page you find most informative and write a paragraph describing how OS/2 differs from other operating systems

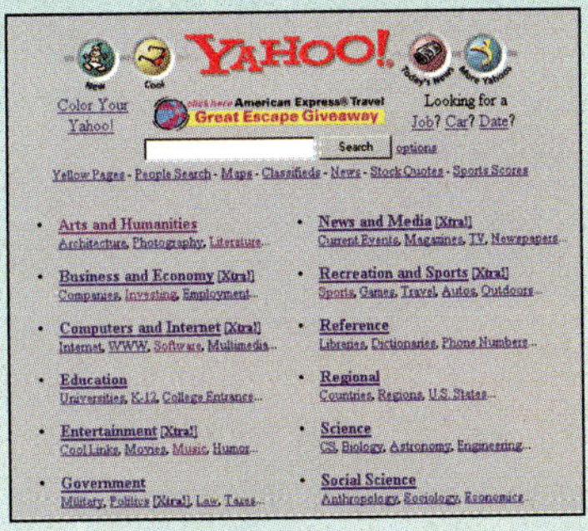

4 Comic Strips

Many of your favorite syndicated comic strips can be found on the World Wide Web. Visit our Web site at http://www.magpie.org/essentials/chapter-3.html to link to a syndicated site that contains several popular comic strips. Once connected, find one that you like and print it out. Why do you suppose the syndication is providing its comics on the Internet? Answer in a paragraph and include suggestions on how the syndication could improve its Web site.

VISUAL SUMMARY

4 Systems Software

Systems software does "background work" (like helping the computer do internal tasks). Five different kinds of operating systems are: DOS, Microsoft Windows, OS/2, Macintosh, and Unix.

WINDOWS 95

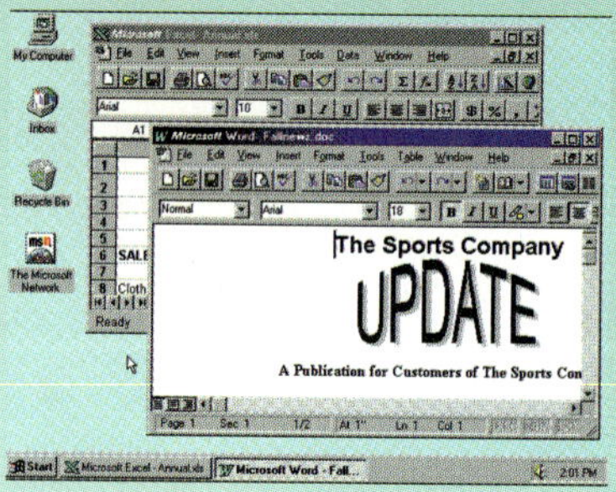

Windows 95 is an operating system. It does not require DOS. Windows 95 is an advanced operating system for powerful microcomputers. Compared to Windows:

Advantages

Like Windows, it supports multitasking, graphical user interface, more memory access, and data sharing. Additionally:

- **Multiprocessing** capability allows multiple applications to run independently and at the same time.
- Flexibility to run with wider variety of powerful computers and microprocessors.
- Internet utilities to connect to an online service.
- Plug and Play support to simplify new hardware installation.

Disadvantages

- System requirements are much greater than Windows.
- Few applications written specifically for Windows 95.

WINDOWS 98

Windows 98 is one of the newest operating systems from Microsoft. Previously known by the code name **Memphis** and at one time referred to as Windows 97. Compared to Windows 95:

Advantages

Like Windows 95, it supports multitasking, graphical user interface, more memory access, data sharing, multiprocessing, and flexibility. Additionally:

- Better performance of many common tasks and Tune-up Wizard to monitor and improve performance.
- Better Internet integration.
- Extended Plug and Play capability and multiple monitor support.
- Advanced multimedia and television support.

Disadvantages

- System requirements greater than for Windows 95.
- Fewer applications written specifically for Windows 98.

WINDOWS NT

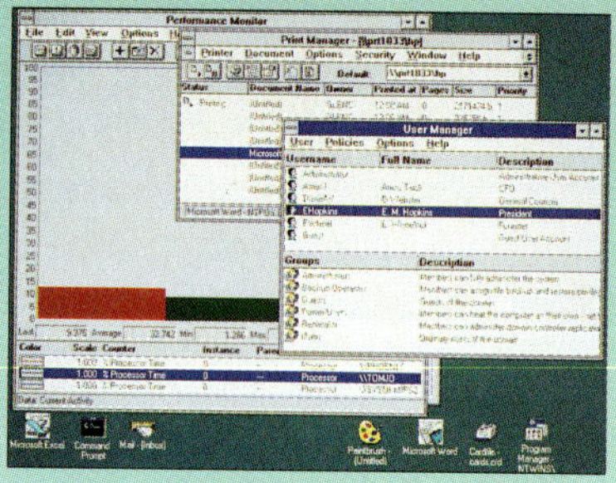

Windows NT is an operating system that offers an advanced alternative to Windows 95. It is designed for very powerful microcomputers and networks. Compared to Windows 95:

Advantages

Like Windows 95, it supports multitasking, graphical user interface, more memory access, data sharing, multiprocessing, and flexibility. Additionally:

- **Multiuser** capability allows more than one user to operate at the same time.
- Easy to install and use networking capabilities.

Disadvantages

- System requirements greater than for Windows 95.
- Plug and Play is not supported.

DOS was the first standard operating system for microcomputers. Windows, an **operating environment,** provided a graphical user interface, multitasking, more memory, and data sharing.

SYSTEM SOFTWARE PROGRAMS

PROGRAM	FUNCTION
Bootstrap loader	Reads operating system from disk and loads into memory.
Diagnostic routines	Tests parts of system to ensure computer is running properly.
Basic input-output	Transmits characters from the keyboard to a monitor or disk.
Operating system	Helps manage computer resources. Most important types are DOS, Microsoft Windows, OS/2, Macintosh, and Unix.

OS/2

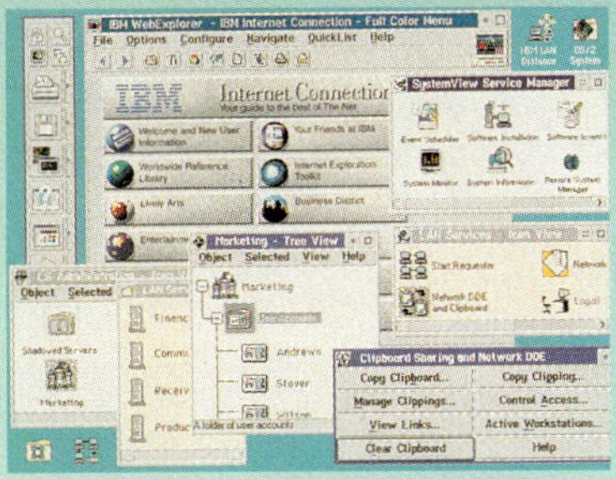

OS/2 is an operating system initially developed jointly by IBM and Microsoft. Compared to Windows NT:

Advantages

Like Windows NT, it supports multitasking, graphical user interface, more memory access, data sharing, flexibility, and multiprocessing.

- System requirements are slightly less.
- Built-in **voice recognition** to perform basic operations.

Disadvantages

Like Windows NT, it does not support Plug and Play and system requirements greater than Windows 95. Additionally:

- Networking capabilities are not as advanced.
- Multiuser capability not supported.

MACINTOSH OPERATING SYSTEMS

Several operating systems have been designed for Apple's **Macintosh.** One of the newest is **System 8.**

Advantages

- Easy to learn and to use.
- Multimedia support with high graphics standards and viewers for three-dimensional graphics.
- Plug and Play support.

Disadvantages

- Some corporate buyers do not view Macintosh as a serious business machine.
- Does not support multiprocessing.
- Programs written for DOS will not run on a Macintosh unless specialty hardware and software have been installed.

UNIX

Unix, originally developed for minicomputers, is able to run on more powerful models of microcomputers. Unix is available in a number of different versions, many of which are not compatible.

Advantages

- Allows multitasking—running of multiple programs.
- Allows multiprocessing—running multiple programs independently and at the same time.
- Allows multiple users to share computer simultaneously.
- History of sharing files over electronic networks with different equipment.

Disadvantages

- Few business applications programs are presently available.
- No one Unix standard exists; there are several versions (principal ones: Unix System V, Berkeley 4.2 Unix, SunOS).
- Commands are often long and complex, making it difficult for some users to learn and to use.

COMPETENCIES

After you have read this chapter, you should be able to:

1. **Explain the two main parts of the central processing unit—the control unit and the arithmetic-logic unit.**
2. **Understand the workings and the functions of memory.**
3. **Describe how a computer uses binary codes to represent data in electrical form.**
4. **Describe the components of the system unit in a microcomputer.**

5

The Processing Unit

How are application programs executed? That is the subject of this chapter. Why are some microcomputers more powerful than others? The answer lies in three words: *speed, capacity,* and *flexibility.* After reading this chapter, you will be able to judge how fast, powerful, and versatile a particular microcomputer is. As you might expect, this knowledge is valuable if you are planning to buy a new microcomputer system. (The Buyer's Guide at the end of this book provides additional buying information.) It will also help you to evaluate whether or not an existing microcomputer system is powerful enough for today's new and exciting applications.

Sometime you may get the chance to watch when a technician opens up a microcomputer to fix it. You will see that it is basically a collection of electronic circuitry. There is no need for you to understand how all these components work. However, it is important to understand the principles. Once you do, you will then be able to determine how powerful a particular microcomputer is. This will help you judge whether it can run particular kinds of programs and can meet your needs as a user.

The CPU

The central processing unit has two components—the control unit and the arithmetic-logic unit.

The part of the computer that runs the program (executes program instructions) is known as the **processor** or *central processing unit (CPU).* In a microcomputer, the CPU is on a single electronic component. The **micro-**

processor chip is within the *system unit* or *system cabinet.* The system unit also includes circuit boards, memory chips, ports, and other components. A microcomputer's system cabinet may also house disk drives, but these are considered separate from the CPU. (See Figure 5-1.)

In Chapter 1 we said the system unit consists of electronic circuitry with two main parts, the processor (the CPU) and memory. Let us refine this further by stating that the CPU itself has two parts: the control unit and the arithmetic-logic unit. In a microcomputer, these are both on the microprocessor chip.

Control Unit

The **control unit** tells the rest of the computer system how to carry out a program's instructions. It directs the movement of electronic signals between memory—which temporarily holds data, instructions, and processed information—and the arithmetic-logic unit. It also directs these control signals between the CPU and input and output devices.

Arithmetic-Logic Unit

The **arithmetic-logic unit,** usually called the **ALU,** performs two types of operations—arithmetic and logical. *Arithmetic* operations are, as you might expect, the fundamental math operations: addition, subtraction, multiplication, and division. *Logical* operations consist of comparisons. That is, two pieces of data are compared to see whether one is equal to (=), less than (<), or greater than (>) the other.

FIGURE 5-1
Inside a microcomputer system unit.

Memory

Memory temporarily holds data, program instructions, and information.

Memory—also known as **RAM, primary storage, internal storage,** or **main memory**—is the part of the microcomputer that holds

- Data for processing
- Instructions for processing the data—that is, the *program*
- Information—that is, processed data—waiting to be output or sent to secondary storage such as a floppy disk in a disk drive

One of the most important facts to know about memory is that part of its content is held only temporarily. In other words, it is stored only as long as the microcomputer is turned on. When you turn the machine off, the contents immediately vanish. We have said this before, but it bears repeating: The stored contents in memory are *volatile* and can vanish very quickly, as during a power failure, for example. It is therefore a good practice to repeatedly save your work in progress to a secondary storage medium such as a floppy disk or hard disk. For instance, if you are writing a report on a word processor, every 5 to 10 minutes you should stop and save your work. Many word processors and other application software have the ability to automatically save every few minutes.

The next important fact to know about memory is that its capacity varies in different computers. The original IBM Personal Computer, for example, could hold about half a million characters of data or instructions. By contrast, the IBM ValuePoint can hold 128 million characters, or over 250 times as much. If you are using an older computer with small memory, it may not be able to run such powerful programs as Excel. Thus, you need to look at the software package before you buy, and see how much memory it requires.

Registers

Computers also have several additional storage locations called **registers.** These appear in the control unit and ALU and make processing more efficient. Registers are special high-speed staging areas that hold data and instructions temporarily during processing. They are parts of the control unit and ALU rather than memory. Their contents can therefore be handled much faster than the contents of memory can.

Processing Cycle

To locate the characters of data or instructions in main memory, the computer stores them at locations known as **addresses.** Each address is designated by a unique number. Addresses may be compared to post office mailboxes. Their numbers stay the same, but the contents continually change.

Our illustration gives an example of how memory and the CPU work to process information. (See Figure 5-2.) In this example, the program will multiply two numbers—20 × 30, yielding 600. Let us assume the program to multiply these two numbers has been loaded into memory. The program asks the user to enter the

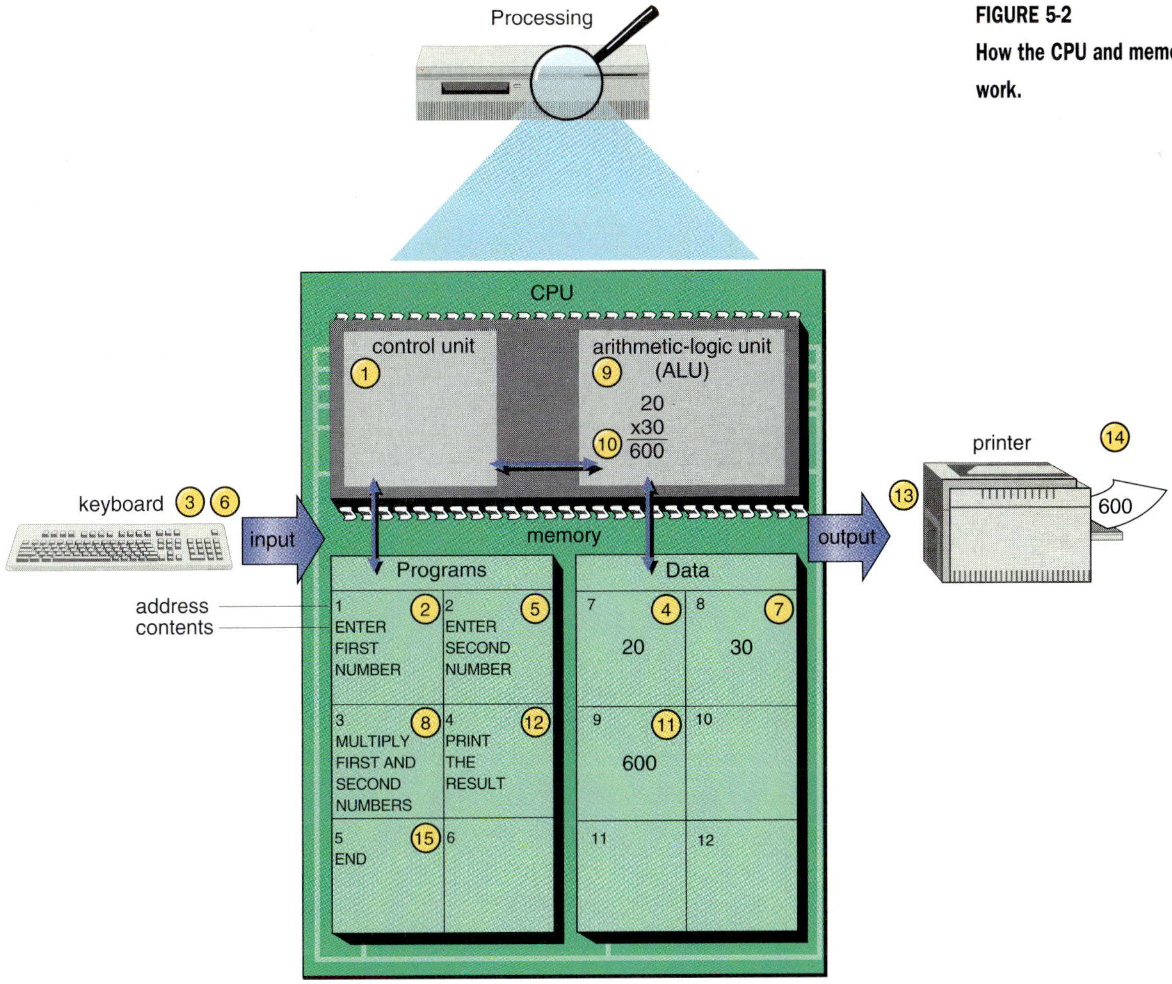

FIGURE 5-2
How the CPU and memory work.

1. The control unit recognizes that the entire program has been loaded into memory. It begins to execute the first step in the program.
2. The program tells the user, ENTER FIRST NUMBER.
3. The user types the number *20* on the keyboard. An electronic signal is sent to the CPU.
4. The control unit recognizes this signal and routes the signal to an address in memory—address 7.
5. After completing the above program instruction, the next program instruction tells the user, ENTER SECOND NUMBER.
6. The user types the number *30* on the keyboard. An electronic signal is sent to the CPU.
7. The control unit recognizes this signal and routes it to memory address 8.
8. The next program instruction is executed: MULTIPLY FIRST AND SECOND NUMBERS.
9. To execute this instruction, the control unit informs the arithmetic-logic unit (ALU) that two numbers are coming and that the ALU is to multiply them. The control unit next sends the ALU a copy of the contents of address 7 (*20*) and then sends a copy of the contents of address 8 (*30*).
10. The ALU performs the multiplication: *20* x *30* = *600*.
11. The control unit sends a copy of the multiplied results (*600*) back to memory, to address 9.
12. The next program instruction is executed: PRINT THE RESULT.
13. To execute this instruction, the control unit sends the contents of address 9 (*600*) to the printer.
14. The printer prints the value *600*.
15. The final instruction is executed: END. The program is complete.

two values (20 and 30). It then multiplies these two values together (20 × 30). Finally, it prints out the result (600) on a printer. Our illustration describes the process just after the program has been loaded into memory. Follow the steps in the figure to walk yourself through the diagram.

Note: This figure simplifies the actual processing activity in order to demonstrate the essential operations of the CPU. For instance, there are actually many more memory addresses—thousands or millions—than are shown here. Moreover, the addresses are in a form the computer can interpret—electronic signals rather than the numbers and letters shown here.

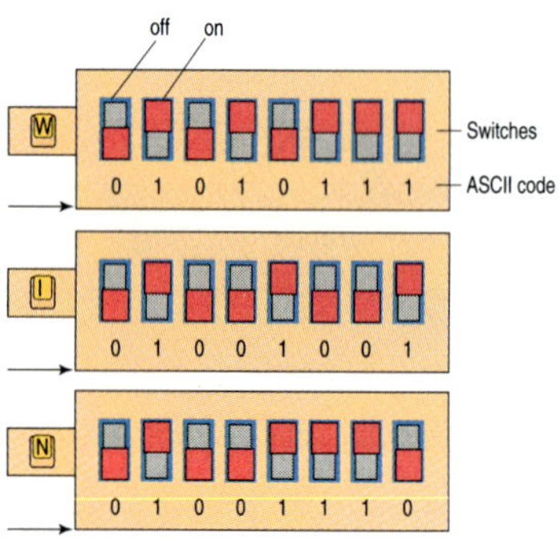

FIGURE 5-3
How the letters W-I-N are represented in on/off, 0/1 binary code (ASCII).

The Binary System

Data and instructions are represented electronically with a binary, or two-state, numbering system. The three principal binary coding schemes are ASCII, EBCDIC, and Unicode.

We have described the storage and processing of data in terms of *characters.* How, in fact, are these characters represented inside the computer?

We said that when you open up the system cabinet of a microcomputer, you see mainly electronic circuitry. And what is the most fundamental statement you can make about electricity? It is simply this: It can be either *on* or *off.*

Indeed, there are many forms of technology that can make use of this two-state on/off, yes/no, present/absent arrangement. For instance, a light switch may be on or off, or an electric circuit open or closed. A magnetized spot on a tape or disk may have a positive charge or a negative charge. This is the reason, then, that the binary system is used to represent data and instructions.

The decimal system that we are all familiar with has 10 digits (0, 1, 2, 3, 4, 5, 6, 7, 8, 9). The **binary system,** however, consists of only two digits—0 and 1. In the computer, the 0 can be represented by electricity being off, and the 1 by electricity being on. Everything that goes into a computer is converted into these binary numbers. (See Figure 5-3.) For example, the letter *W* corresponds to the electronic signal 0 1 0 1 0 1 1 1.

Units of Measure for Capacity

Each 0 or 1 in the binary system is called a **bit**—short for *b*inary dig*it*. In order to represent numbers, letters, and special characters, bits are combined into groups of eight bits called **bytes.** Each byte typically represents one character—in many computers, one addressable storage location. The capacity of main memory, then, is expressed in numbers of bytes. There are four commonly used units of measurement to describe memory capacity. (See Figure 5-4.)

MEMORY CAPACITY

UNIT	CAPACITY
Kilobyte (KB)	one thousand bytes
Megabyte (MB)	one million bytes
Gigabyte (GB)	one billion bytes
Terabyte (TB)	one trillion bytes

FIGURE 5-4
Memory capacity.

- One **kilobyte**—abbreviated **K** or **KB**—is equivalent to approximately 1000 bytes. (More precisely, 1 kilobyte is equal to 1024 bytes. However, the figure is commonly rounded to 1000 bytes.) This is a common unit of measure for the size of a file.
- One **megabyte**—**MB**—represents 1 million bytes. Thus, a microcomputer system listed with a "16MB main memory" has primary storage capacity of about 16 million bytes.
- One **gigabyte**—**GB**—represents about 1 billion bytes. This is a measure that until recently was used only with larger computers. Now it is also used to describe disk storage capacity.
- One **terabyte**—**TB**—represents about 1 trillion bytes. This is a measure used with large computers.

Binary Coding Schemes

Now let us consider an important question. How are characters represented as 0s and 1s ("off" and "on" electrical states) in the computer? The answer is in the use of *binary coding schemes.*

Two of the most popular binary coding schemes use eight bits to form each byte. These two codes are *ASCII* and *EBCDIC.* (See Figure 5-5.) A recently developed code, *Unicode,* uses sixteen bits.

- **ASCII,** pronounced "*as*-key," stands for *A*merican *S*tandard *C*ode for *I*nformation *I*nterchange. This is the most widely used binary code for microcomputers.
- **EBCDIC,** pronounced "*eb*-see-dick," stands for *E*xtended *B*inary *C*oded *D*ecimal *I*nterchange *C*ode. It was developed by IBM and is used primarily for large computers.
- **Unicode** is a sixteen-bit code designed to support international languages like Chinese and Japanese. These languages have too many characters to be represented by the eight-bit ASCII and EBCDIC codes. Unicode was developed by Unicode, Inc., with support from Apple, IBM, and Microsoft.

When you press a key on the keyboard, a character is automatically converted into a series of electronic pulses. The CPU can recognize these pulses. For example, pressing the letter *W* on a keyboard causes an electronic signal to be sent to the CPU. The CPU then converts it to the ASCII value of 01010111.

Why are coding schemes important? Whenever files are used or shared by different computers or applications, the same coding scheme must be used. Generally, this is not a problem if both computers are microcomputers since both would most likely use ASCII code. And most microcomputer applications store files using this code. However, problems occur when files are shared between microcomputers and larger computers that use EBCDIC code. The files must be translated from one coding scheme to the other before processing can begin. Fortunately, special conversion programs are available to help with this translation.

BINARY CODES

CHARACTER	ASCII	EBCDIC
A	0100 0001	1100 0001
B	0100 0010	1100 0010
C	0100 0011	1100 0011
D	0100 0100	1100 0100
E	0100 0101	1100 0101
F	0100 0110	1100 0110
G	0100 0111	1100 0111
H	0100 1000	1100 1000
I	0100 1001	1100 1001
J	0100 1010	1101 0001
K	0100 1011	1101 0010
L	0100 1100	1101 0011
M	0100 1101	1101 0100
N	0100 1110	1101 0101
O	0100 1111	1101 0110
P	0101 0000	1101 0111
Q	0101 0001	1101 1000
R	0101 0010	1101 1001
S	0101 0011	1110 0010
T	0101 0100	1110 0011
U	0101 0101	1110 0100
V	0101 0110	1110 0101
W	0101 0111	1110 0110
X	0101 1000	1110 0111
Y	0101 1001	1110 1000
Z	0101 1010	1110 1001
0	0011 0000	1111 0000
1	0011 0001	1111 0001
2	0011 0010	1111 0010
3	0011 0011	1111 0011
4	0011 0100	1111 0100
5	0011 0101	1111 0101
6	0011 0110	1111 0110
7	0011 0111	1111 0111
8	0011 1000	1111 1000
9	0011 1001	1111 1001

FIGURE 5-5
ASCII and EBCDIC binary coding schemes.

The Parity Bit

As you know, there is often static on the radio. Similarly, there can be "static," or electronic interference, in a circuit or communications line transmitting a byte. When you are typing the letter *W,* for example, the *W* should be represented in the CPU (in ASCII) as

0 1 0 1 0 1 1 1

However, if the last 1 is garbled and becomes a 0, the byte will be read as 01010110—*V* instead of *W.* Is there a way, then, for the CPU to detect whether it is receiving erroneous data?

Indeed there is. Detection is accomplished by using a **parity bit**—an extra bit automatically added to a byte for purposes of testing accuracy. There are even-parity systems and odd-parity systems. In a computer using an even-parity system, the parity bit is set to either 0 or 1 so that the number of 1s is even. (See Figure 5-6.) For instance, when the letter *W* is pressed on the keyboard, the signal 01010111 is emitted. Before the signal is sent to the CPU, the number of 1s is counted—in this case, 5. A parity bit is added to the front and set to 1, thereby making the number of 1s even. The signal 101010111 is sent. When the signal is received by the CPU, the number of 1s is checked again. If it is odd, it means an error has occurred. This is called a *parity error.* When a parity error occurs, the CPU requests that the signal be sent again. If the parity error occurs again, the message "parity error" might appear on your display. (Odd-parity systems act just the reverse of even-parity systems.)

Of course, the system does not guarantee accuracy. For example, if *two* erroneous 0s were introduced in the byte for *W,* the computer would accept the byte as correct. This is because the two erroneous 0s would add up to an even four bits.

We have explained the principles by which a computer stores and processes data. We can now open up the system unit and take a look at some of the parts.

FIGURE 5-6
How parity bits check for transmission errors.

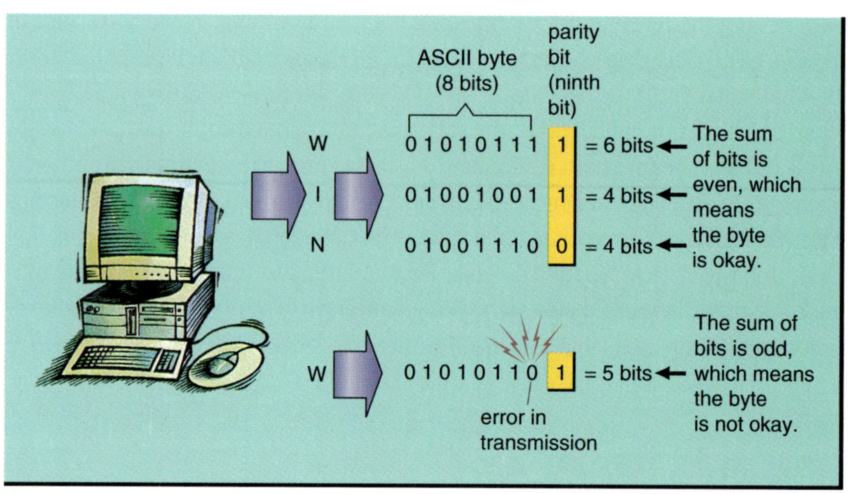

The System Unit

It's important to understand what's inside the system unit, so that you can talk intelligently to computer specialists.

As mentioned, the part of the microcomputer that contains the CPU is called the *system unit.* The system unit is housed within the system cabinet. If you take off the cabinet, you will find that many parts can be easily removed for replacement. Almost all computers are modular. That is, entire sections can be replaced, as one would the parts of a car. In addition, microcomputers are *expandable.* That is, more memory may be added, as well as certain other devices.

Let us consider the following components of the system unit:

- System board
- Microprocessor chips
- Memory chips
- System clock
- Expansion slots and boards
- Bus lines
- Ports

System Board

The **system board** is also called the **motherboard.** (See Figure 5-7.) It consists of a flat board that usually contains the CPU and some memory *chips.* A **chip** consists of a tiny circuit board etched on a small square of sandlike material called silicon. A chip is also called a **silicon chip, semiconductor,** or **integrated circuit.** Chips are mounted on carrier packages, which then plug into sockets on the system board. In addition, system boards usually contain expansion slots, as we describe in another few paragraphs.

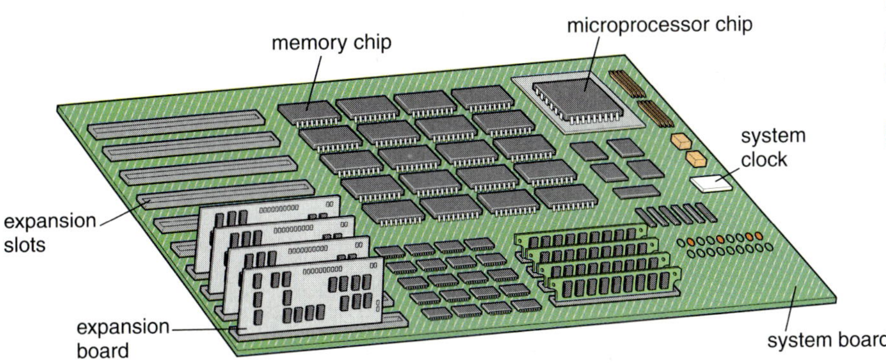

FIGURE 5-7
A microcomputer system board.

FIGURE 5-8
Typical microprocessor applications and users.

MICROPROCESSORS

MICROPROCESSOR	TYPICAL APPLICATIONS	USERS
Intel Pentium MMX	Windows 95, Windows 98, OS/2 Warp, groupware, desktop publishing, project management, multimedia	Single user, office staff, home user, home office user, networked users, workgroups
Pentium Pro	Windows NT, Unix, artificial intelligence, network communications, large database applications	All of the above, specialists
Pentium II	Windows 95, Windows 98, Windows NT, UNIX, multimedia	All of the above, multimedia specialists
Motorola 68040	Macintosh operating system, basic tools, personal information management, desktop publishing	Single user, home user, home office user
Power PC	Unix, groupware, project management, artificial intelligence, network communications, large database applications	All of the above, networked users, workgroups, specialists

Microprocessor Chips

In a microcomputer, the CPU is contained on a single silicon chip called the *microprocessor*—"microscopic processor." Different microprocessors have different capabilities. (See Figure 5-8.)

Typically, the microprocessor connects directly to the system board. Recently, however, Intel has introduced the Pentium II microprocessor, which connects to the system board through a plug-in cartridge.

Chip capacities are often expressed in word sizes. A **word** is the number of bits (such as 16, 32, or 64) that can be accessed at one time by the CPU. The more bits in a word, the more powerful—and the faster—the computer is. A 32-bit-word computer can access 4 bytes at a time. A 64-bit-word computer can access 8 bytes at a time. Therefore, the 64-bit computer is faster.

Microcomputers process data and instructions in millionths of a second, or **microseconds.** Supercomputers, by contrast, operate at speeds measured in nanoseconds and even picoseconds—1 thousand to 1 million times as fast as microcomputers. (See Figure 5-9.)

PROCESSING SPEEDS

UNIT	SPEED
Millisecond	thousandth of a second
Microsecond	millionth of a second
Nanosecond	billionth of a second
Picosecond	trillionth of a second

FIGURE 5-9
Processing speeds.

As we mentioned, the growing power of microprocessor chips is what is changing everything about microcomputers. Intel's Pentium Pro chip, for example, is twice as powerful as its predecessor. Intel's new microprocessor, code-named P55C, promises multimedia capabilities that far exceed the Pentium Pro. Motorola's Power PC chip used in Apple's Power PC Macintosh 7200 is four times faster than its predecessor.

There are two types of microprocessors.

- **CISC chips:** The most common type of microprocessor is **CISC** ("complex instruction set computer"). This design was popularized by Intel and is the basis for their line of microprocessors. It is the most widely used chip design with thousands of programs written specifically for it. Intel's Pentium is a recent CISC chip.

- **RISC chips: RISC** ("reduced instruction set computer") chips use fewer instructions. The design is becoming more widely used. This design is simpler, faster, and less costly than CISC chips. A recent Motorola chip developed with IBM and Apple is the Power PC chip. Two other recent RISC chips are Digital Equipment Corporation's (DEC) Alpha chip and MIPS's R4400 chip. These chips are used in many of today's most powerful microcomputers. (See Figure 5-10.)

The major advantage of the CISC chip is that it can run a large number of existing application programs. However, this advantage is offset somewhat by special programs called *emulation programs.* Emulation programs allow RISC chips to run CISC application programs. Unfortunately, the RISC advantage in speed is lost when the emulation programs are used. Another approach taken by two competitors to Intel's Pentium chip is to produce "RISC-like" or *hybrid* chips. These chips are based on the CISC design but incorporate some of the techniques used in RISC chips. They can run applications designed for CISC chips with speeds comparable to those of RISC chips. Two such chips are AMD's K6 and Cyrix's M2 chips.

Some specialized processor chips are available. One example is the tiny built-in microprocessor used in **smart cards.** Smart cards are about the size of a credit card. They can be used to hold health insurance information, frequent flier records, or driver license information, to name a few. While this technology has been around for some time, it has received more attention lately. President Clinton has suggested a National Health Security smart card for all individuals. This card would be used for a number of applications, including monitoring federal financial assistance programs.

FIGURE 5-10
This IBM RISC System/6000 is one of several IBM workstations using the fast RISC chip.

Memory Chips

There are two well-known types of memory chips. One type is called *RAM*. The other type is *ROM*. **RAM (random-access memory)** chips hold the program and data that the CPU is presently processing. That is, it is *temporary* or volatile storage. (Secondary storage, which we shall describe in Chapter 7, is *permanent* storage, such as the data stored on diskettes. Data from this kind of storage must be loaded into RAM before it can be used.)

RAM is called temporary because as soon as the microcomputer is turned off, everything in RAM is lost. It is also lost if there is a power failure that disrupts the electric current going to the microcomputer. For this reason, as we mentioned earlier, it is a good idea to save your work in progress. That is, if you are working on a document or a spreadsheet, every few minutes you should save, or store, the material.

In addition, when programs or data are written, or encoded, to RAM, the previous contents of RAM are lost. This is called the *destructive write process*. However, when programs and data are read, or retrieved, from RAM, their contents are not destroyed. Rather, the read process simply makes a copy of those contents. Consequently, this activity is called the *nondestructive read process*.

RAM storage is frequently expressed in megabytes. Thus, a microcomputer with 16MB RAM has memory that will hold about 16 million characters of data and programs.

Knowing the amount of RAM is important! Some software programs may require more memory capacity than a particular microcomputer offers. For instance, Excel 97 requires 8MB of RAM. Additional RAM is needed to hold any data. However, many microcomputers—particularly older ones—may not have enough memory to hold the program, much less work with it.

Microcomputer memory in RAM is of four types. (See Figure 5-11.) These types are mentioned in the instruction manuals you use to install system software like DOS or application software like Excel.

- **Conventional memory:** **Conventional memory** consists of the first 640K of RAM. It is the area used by DOS and application programs.
- **Upper memory:** **Upper memory** is located between 640K and 1MB of RAM. DOS uses this area to store information about the microcomputer's hardware. However, it is frequently underused and can be used by application programs.
- **Extended memory:** **Extended memory** is available on most microprocessors. It includes directly accessible memory above 1MB. Some programs can use extended memory (for example, Windows), and some cannot.
- **Expanded memory:** **Expanded memory** is intended to help older microprocessors that cannot directly access memory over 1MB. Expanded memory is a special "island" of memory of up to 32MB that exists outside of the DOS 640K limit. That is, it temporarily uses a portion of the reserved memory area between 640K and 1MB and switches it with information from the island.

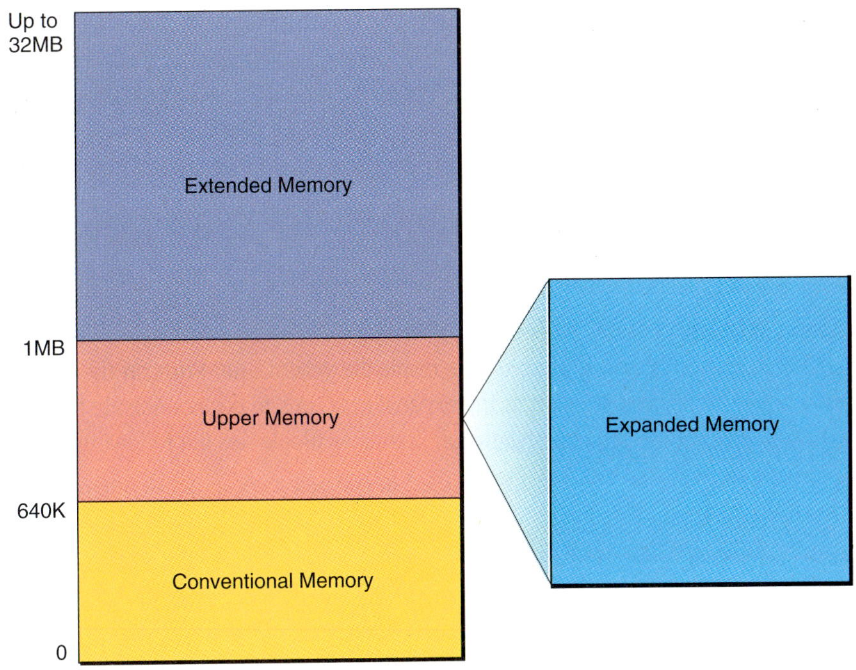

FIGURE 5-11
Types of RAM: conventional, upper, extended, expanded.

Another term you are apt to hear about in conjunction with RAM is **cache memory.** Cache (pronounced "cash") memory is an area of RAM set aside to store the most frequently accessed information stored in RAM. The cache acts as a temporary high-speed holding area between the memory and the CPU. In a computer with a cache (not all machines have one), the computer detects which information in RAM is most frequently used. It then copies that information into the cache, so that the CPU can access that information more quickly than usual.

ROM (read only memory) chips have programs built into them at the factory. Unlike RAM chips, the contents of ROM chips cannot be changed by the user. "Read only" means that the CPU can read, or retrieve, the programs written on the ROM chip. However, the computer cannot write—encode or change—the information or instructions in ROM.

ROM chips typically contain special instructions for detailed computer operations. For example, ROM instructions may start the computer, give keyboard keys their special control capabilities, and put characters on the screen. ROMs are also called **firmware.**

System Clock

The **system clock** controls the speed of operations within a computer. This speed is expressed in **megahertz** (abbreviated **MHz**). One megahertz equals 1 million cycles (beats) per second. The faster the clock speed, the faster the computer can process information. In computer ads, you may see that microcomputers built with Intel's Pentium chip typically have a 266 MHz or 300 MHz speed.

FIGURE 5-12
A network adapter card.

Expansion Slots and Boards

Computers are known for having different kinds of "architectures." Machines that have **closed architecture** are manufactured in such a way that users cannot easily add new devices. Most microcomputers have **open architecture.** They allow users to expand their systems by inserting optional devices known as **expansion boards.** Expansion boards are also called **plug-in boards, controller cards, adapter cards,** or **interface cards.**

The expansion boards plug into slots inside the system unit. Ports on the boards allow cables to be connected from the expansion boards to devices outside the system unit. Among the kinds of expansion boards available are the following:

- **Network adapter cards:** These cards are used to connect a computer to one or more other computers. This forms a communication network whereby users can share data, programs, and hardware. The network adapter card plugs into a slot inside the system unit. The network adapter card typically connects the system unit to a cable that connects to the other devices on the network. (See Figure 5-12.)
- **Small computer system interface (SCSI—pronounced "scuzzy") card:** Most computers have only a limited number of expansion slots. A **SCSI card** uses only one slot and can connect as many as seven devices to the system unit. These cards are used to connect such devices as printers, hard-disk drives, and CD-ROM drives to the system unit.
- **Television boards:** Now you can watch television and surf the Internet at the same time. **Television boards** contain a TV tuner and a video converter that changes the TV signal into one that can be displayed on your monitor. This **PC/TV** combination has become increasingly popular and has led to specialized large-screen systems with high-quality audio called **home PCs.**
- **PC cards:** To meet the size and constraints of portable computers, credit card–sized expansion boards have been developed. These cards can be easily inserted and replaced from the outside of a portable computer. They are called **PC cards** or **PCMCIA (Personal Computer Memory Card International Association) cards.** (See Figure 5-13.) These cards can be used for a variety of purposes, including increasing memory and connecting to other computers.

FIGURE 5-13
A PCMCIA card.

A wide variety of other expansion boards exist. Some of the most widely used are the following: Video adapter cards are used to adapt a variety of color video display monitors to a computer. CD-ROM cards connect optical disk drives (which we discuss in Chapter 7), and sound boards can record and play back digital sound.

To access the capabilities of an expansion board, the board must be inserted into a slot in the system unit and the system reconfigured to recognize the new board. Reconfiguration may require setting special switches on the expansion board and creating special configuration files. This can be a complex and difficult task. A recent development known as **Plug and Play** promises to eliminate this task.

Plug and Play is a set of hardware and software standards recently developed by Intel, Microsoft, and others. It is an effort by hardware and software vendors to create operating systems, processing units, and expansion boards, as well as other devices, that are able to configure themselves. Ideally, to install a new expansion board all you have to do is insert the board and turn on the computer. As the computer starts up, it will search for these Plug and Play devices and automatically configure the devices and the computer system.

Plug and Play is an evolving capability. Only a few completely Plug and Play–ready systems exist today. However, observers predict that within the next few years this will become a widely adopted standard, and adding expansion boards will be a simple task.

Bus Lines

A **bus line**—or simply **bus**—connects the parts of the CPU to each other. It also links the CPU with other important hardware. Examples are RAM and ROM chips and ports connecting with outside devices. A bus is a data roadway along which bits travel. Such data pathways resemble a multilane highway. The more lanes there are, the faster traffic can go through. Similarly, the greater the capacity of a bus, the more powerful and faster the operation. A 64-bit bus has greater capacity than a 32-bit bus, for example.

Why should you even have to care about what a bus line is? The answer is that, as microprocessor chips have changed, so have bus lines. Many devices, such as expansion boards, will work with only one type of bus line.

The four principal bus lines (or "architectures") are the following:

- **Industry Standard Architecture (ISA)** was developed for the IBM Personal Computer. First it was an 8-bit-wide data path, then it was 16 bits wide. The older microprocessors and add-on expansion boards were able to satisfactorily move data along this 16-bit roadway. But then along came the 386 chip—which requires data paths that are 32 bits wide. And suddenly there was a competition between two 32-bit standards.

FIGURE 5-14
Ports in the back of a system unit.

- **Micro Channel Architecture (MCA)** was developed by IBM to support the 386 chip. The first MCA was a 32-bit bus line that was entirely new. Recently, a 64-bit MCA bus was introduced. You cannot simply remove your expansion boards from an older computer and put them into a new IBM computer with Micro Channel. It simply won't work. If you are not concerned about transferring boards, IBM's new standard is not a problem. You can take full advantage of the faster processor.
- **Extended Industry Standard Architecture (EISA)** is a 32-bit bus standard that was proposed in September 1988 by nine manufacturers of IBM-compatibles, led by Compaq Computer Corporation. The purpose of EISA is to extend and amend the old ISA standard, so that all existing expansion boards can work with the new architecture. Like MCA, EISA has introduced a 64-bit bus.
- **Peripheral Component Interconnect (PCI)** is in the most recently developed category of buses called **local buses.** These buses were originally developed to meet the tremendous video demands of today's graphical user interfaces. PCI is the most widely used local bus. **VESA local bus (VL-bus)** is another widely used local bus. PCI is a high-speed 64-bit bus that is nearly ten times faster than either MCA or EISA buses. Now PCI buses are widely used to connect the CPU, memory, and expansion boards. Many observers predict that PCI will replace MCA and EISA buses in the future.

Ports

A **port** is a connecting socket on the outside of the system unit. It allows you to plug in a variety of devices, such as keyboards, mouse devices, video displays, modems, and printers. The four most widely used ports are (see Figure 5-14):

- **Serial ports** are used for a wide variety of purposes. They are used to connect a mouse, keyboard, modem, and many other devices to the system unit. Serial ports send data one bit at a time and are very good for sending information over a long distance.
- **Parallel ports** are used to connect external devices that need to send or receive a lot of data over a short distance. These ports typically send eight bits of data simultaneously across eight parallel wires. Parallel ports are mostly used to connect printers to the system unit.
- **USB (universal serial bus) ports** are expected to gradually replace serial and parallel ports. They are faster, and one USB port can be used to connect several devices to the system unit.
- **FireWire ports** are the newest type. They are even faster than USB ports and are used to connect high-speed printers and even video cameras to the system unit.

Ports are used to connect input and output devices to the system unit. We usually refer to all hardware outside the system unit—but not necessarily outside the system *cabinet*—as **peripheral devices.** In many microcomputers, disk drives are built into the system cabinet. In some laptop computers, the keyboard and monitor are also an integral part of the system cabinet.

For a summary of system unit components, see Figure 5-15.

SYSTEM UNIT

COMPONENT	FUNCTION
System board	Holds the various other system components
Microprocessor	Contains the CPU on a single chip
Memory	Holds programs and instructions
System clock	Controls the speed of computer operations
Expansion slots and boards	Connects to network and other system capabilities
Bus lines	Connects various internal system components
Ports	Connects outside devices to system unit

FIGURE 5-15
Components of a system unit.

A Look at the Future

Intel's Mobil Module and Xircom's PC cards could lead the way to desktop computing power in notebook computers.

Wouldn't it be nice if you could conveniently carry one of today's most powerful microcomputers? One that was light, compact, and would run on batteries? You could take it to class, to a group project meeting, or even to the beach.

Of course that's what notebook computers are all about. Unfortunately, the power of today's notebook microprocessors lags behind their desktop counterparts. Additionally, notebooks are priced higher than desktops with comparable performance. But all that may change in the next few years.

Intel, the leader in microprocessor technology, has recently taken steps to reduce the performance lag between notebooks and desktops. One step is the recent development of the Intel Mobil Module. This module combines multiple functions including the microprocessor onto a single circuit board. It will allow notebook manufacturers to readily switch to newer processors as they become available. Another step is Intel's purchase of 12.5% of Xircom, a maker of PC cards used to connect notebooks to corporate networks. Observers note that future Xircom products will likely encourage managers to replace their corporate desktop systems with notebooks.

Will your next computer be a notebook? There is a clear trend. Today 1 in 4 microcomputer buyers purchases a notebook computer and that number is expected to increase in the next few years.

KEY TERMS

adapter card (106)
address (96)
arithmetic-logic unit (ALU) (95)
ASCII (99)
binary system (98)
bit (98)
bus line, bus (107)
byte (98)
cache memory (105)
chip (101)
CISC (102)
closed architecture (106)
control unit (95)
controller card (106)
conventional memory (104)
EBCDIC (99)
expanded memory (104)
expansion board (106)
Extended Industry Standard Architecture (EISA) (108)
extended memory (104)
FireWire ports (108)
firmware (105)
gigabyte, GB (99)
home PC (106)
Industry Standard Architecture (ISA) (107)
integrated circuit (101)
interface card (106)
internal storage (96)
kilobyte, K or KB (99)
local bus (108)
main memory (96)
megabyte, MB (99)
megahertz, MHz (105)
memory (96)
Micro Channel Architecture (MCA) (108)
microprocessor chip (94)
microseconds (102)
motherboard (101)
open architecture (106)
parallel ports (108)
parity bit (100)
PC card (106)
PC/TV (106)
PCMCIA (Personal Computer Memory Card International Association) card (106)
Peripheral Component Interconnect (PCI) (108)
peripheral device (108)
Plug and Play (107)
plug-in board (106)
port (108)
primary storage (96)
processor (94)
RAM (random-access memory) (96, 104)
register (96)
RISC (103)
ROM (read-only memory) (105)
SCSI card (106)
semiconductor (101)
serial ports (108)
silicon chip (101)
smart card (103)
system board (101)
system clock (105)
television board (106)
terabyte, TB (99)
Unicode (99)
USB (universal serial bus) (108)
upper memory (104)
VESA local bus (VL-bus) (108)
word (102)

REVIEW QUESTIONS

True/False

1. In a microcomputer, the CPU is located on a single chip called the microprocessor.
2. A grouping of eight bytes is called a bit.
3. Another name for the system board is the processor board.
4. CISC chips use fewer instructions than RISC chips.
5. A SCSI card can be used to connect several different devices to the system unit.

Multiple Choice

1. The ALU performs arithmetic operations and:
   a. stores data
   b. logical operations
   c. binary calculations
   d. reduced instruction calculations
   e. parity checks
2. The binary code that is widely used with microcomputers is:
   a. ASCII
   b. EBCDIC
   c. BCD
   d. DEC/MVS
   e. Unicode
3. The number of bits that can be processed at one time is a:
   a. register
   b. cycle
   c. byte
   d. word
   e. PROM
4. Two types of memory chips are RAM and:
   a. RISC
   b. main
   c. MCA
   d. CD-ROM
   e. ROM
5. The local bus that is predicted to replace the other types in the future is called:
   a. EISA
   b. ISA
   c. PCI
   d. MCA
   e. PCMCIA

Fill in the Blank

1. Data and instructions are stored in memory at locations known as __________.
2. A __________ bit is an extra bit that is added to a byte to help detect errors.
3. __________ memory is directly accessible above 1MB.
4. The system clock controls the __________ of operations within a computer.
5. __________ and __________ is a set of standards designed to assist in the reconfiguration of computer systems.

Open Ended

1. Describe how the control unit, arithmetic-logic unit, and memory work together to execute a program.
2. What are the four commonly used units of measurement to describe memory capacity? Define each.
3. What is the difference between RISC and CISC chips?
4. Name four expansion boards.
5. Describe the four most widely used ports.

DISCUSSION QUESTIONS AND PROJECTS

1. *An inexpensive microcomputer system:* The prices of microcomputer systems have been decreasing for some time. You can buy them from computer stores, mail-order companies, and oftentimes from your college bookstore. Look through your local newspaper or through a computer magazine to locate three low-priced systems. Read each advertisement, make a list of all the computer terms used, and write down their definitions. Prepare a table comparing the three systems. Some factors to include in your table are: price, memory capacity, storage capacity, processor type, display type, expansion capability, and software included. If you were to purchase one of these systems, which one would you select, and why?
2. *The mobile office:* The mobile office does not have a fixed location, but like the traditional office has support facilities such as computers, printers, and fax and copy machines. The central piece of equipment is the notebook computer. Many jobs require being on the road away from home one week every month. For those road warriors, the mobile office is essential.

   Many hotels now offer specially equipped hotel rooms and business centers. For example, many Hyatt Hotels have the Hyatt Business Plan that provides guest rooms with microcomputers, modems, and fax machines. Additionally, a 24-hour business center provides printer, photocopy, and office-supply support.

   Suppose you have a job that requires a mobile office. Before making any hotel reservations, you should ensure that essential support facilities are available. Contact a major hotel chain to determine their support for mobile computing. Specifically, find out the following:

   a. Are in-room microcomputers and fax machines available? What are the charges?
   b. Is there a business center on site? What support is provided? What are the hours? What are the charges?
   c. If a business center is not available, will the front desk provide basic services such as faxing, copying, and printing? What are the charges?

on the web

Exercises and Explorations

1 Microprocessors

The Intel Corporation is one of the leaders in microprocessor design. To learn more about their most recent microprocessors, visit our Web site at http://www.magpie.org/essentials/chapter-5 to link to Intel's Web site. Once connected to that site, select one microprocessor and find a chart that compares this microprocessor to other Intel microprocessors. Print out the chart and describe the process you went through to find the chart.

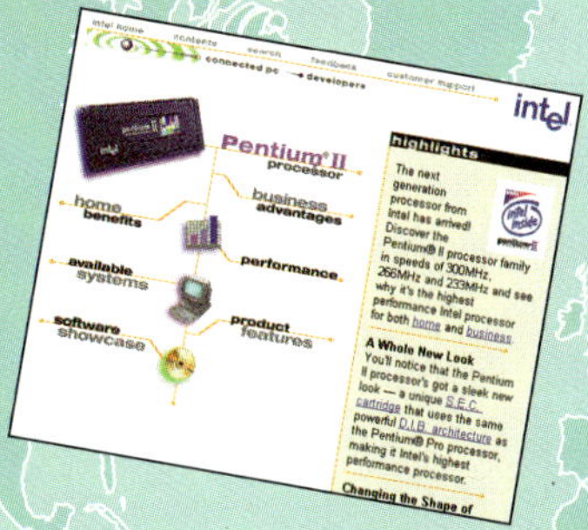

2 Desktops and Notebooks

There are several sites on the Web from which you can learn more about the newest desktops and notebooks on the market today. Visit our Web site at http://www.magpie.org/essentials/chapter-5 to link to one of these sites. Once connected to that site, check out the different models and select the one that best meets your needs. Print out the specifications for your chosen computer and write a paragraph on why this computer best suits your needs.

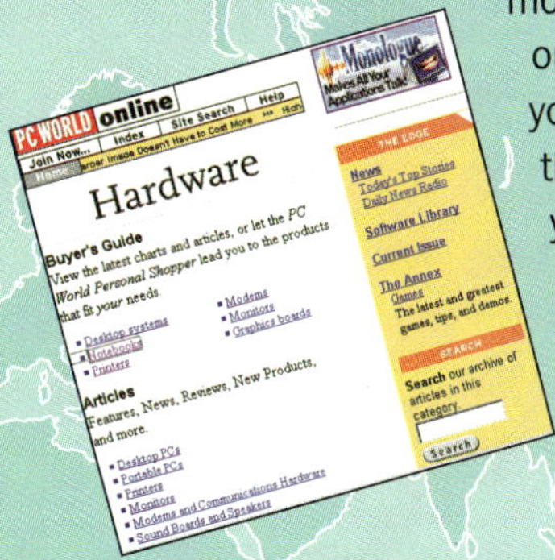

3 Universal Serial Bus

The Universal Serial Bus (USB) is the next evolution of computer ports. It was developed through the collaboration of seven leading-edge companies. To learn more about this technology, search with the keywords "USB" and "Universal Serial Bus" in yahoo, at http://www.yahoo.com. Pay special attention to FAQ (Frequently Asked Questions) pages. Print out the Web page you find the most informative. Write a paragraph listing the names of the seven companies that collaborated to develop the USB and a brief summary of what you learned about USB.

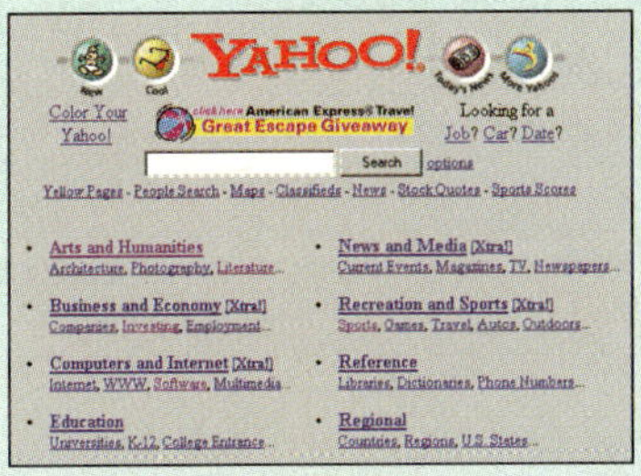

4 Wired

Several magazines now publish their works on the Internet. One of the leading ones is the techno-savy magazine, *Wired.* Visit our Web site at http://www.magpie.org/essentials/chapter-5 to link to the *Wired* site. Once connected, select an article of interest to you. Print out the article and write a paragraph summarizing the article and explaining why you selected it.

VISUAL SUMMARY

The Processing Unit

The central processing unit (CPU) and memory are two major parts of a microcomputer system unit.

PROCESSING SPEEDS

UNIT	SPEED
Millisecond	thousandth of a second
Microsecond	millionth of a second
Nanosecond	billionth of a second
Picosecond	trillionth of a second

THE CPU AND MEMORY

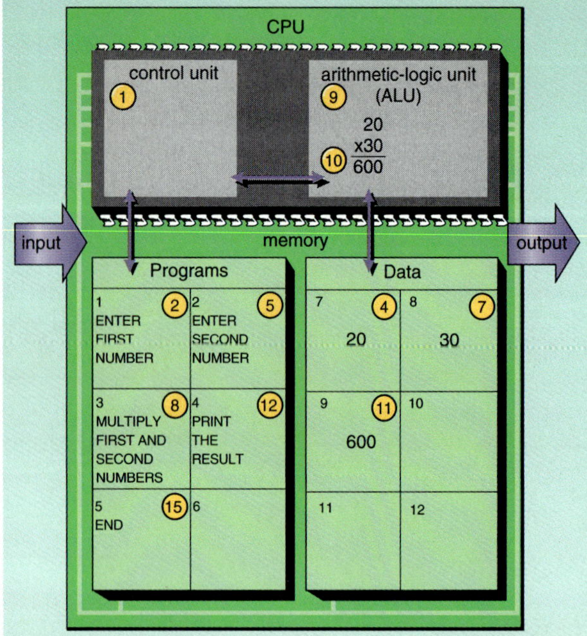

Central Processing Unit

The central processing unit (CPU) is the **processor,** the part of the computer that runs the program. The CPU has two parts:

- The **control unit** directs electronic signals between memory and the ALU, and between the CPU and input/output devices.
- The **arithmetic-logic unit (ALU)** performs *arithmetic* (math) operations and *logical* (comparison) operations.

Memory

Memory (**primary** or **internal storage**) holds data, instructions for processing data (the program), and information (processed data). The contents are held in memory only temporarily. Capacity varies with different computers.

- Additional storage units (in control unit and ALU) called **registers** help make processing more efficient.
- Characters of data or instructions are stored in memory locations called **addresses.**

THE BINARY SYSTEM

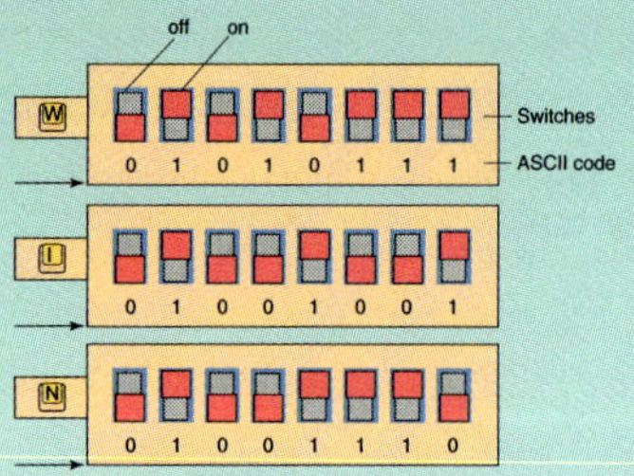

Data and instructions are represented electronically with a two-state **binary system** of numbers (0 and 1).

Measure of Capacity

- **Bit** (*bi*nary digi*t*)—0 or 1, corresponding to electricity being *on* or *off.*
- **Byte**—eight bits. Each byte represents one character. The primary storage capacity of a computer is measured in bytes.

MEMORY CAPACITY

UNIT	CAPACITY
Kilobyte (KB)	one thousand bytes
Megabyte (MB)	one million bytes
Gigabyte (GB)	one billion bytes
Terabyte (TB)	one trillion bytes

Binary Coding Schemes

Two popular schemes for representing bytes are:

- **ASCII**—used in microcomputers.
- **EBCDIC**—used in larger computers.

Parity Bit

A **parity bit** is an extra bit added to a byte for error detection purposes.

SYSTEM UNIT

COMPONENT	FUNCTION
System board	Holds the various other system components
Microprocessor	Contains the CPU on a single chip
Memory	Holds programs and instructions
System clock	Controls the speed of computer operations
Expansion slots and boards	Increases memory and other system capabilities
Bus lines	Connects various internal system components
Ports	Connects outside devices to system unit

THE SYSTEM UNIT

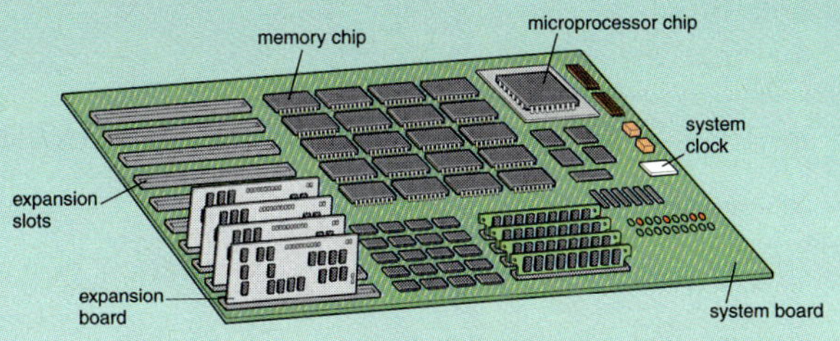

System Board

The **system board** contains the CPU and primary storage on **chips** (also called **silicon chips, semiconductors, integrated circuits**).

MICROPROCESSORS

MICROPROCESSOR		TYPICAL APPLICATIONS	USERS
Intel	Pentium	Windows 95, OS/2 Warp, groupware, desktop publishing, project management	Single user, office staff, home user, home office user, networked users, workgroups
	Pentium Pro	Windows NT, Unix, artificial intelligence, network communications, large database applications	All of the above, specialists
	P55C	Windows 95, Windows NT, UNIX, multimedia	All of the above, multimedia specialists
Motorola	68040	Macintosh operating system, basic tools, personal information management, desktop publishing	Single user, home user, home office user
	Power PC	Unix, groupware, project management, artificial intelligence, network communications, large database applications	All of the above, networked

Microprocessor Chips

The **microprocessor chip** contains the CPU. Capacities are expressed in word sizes. A **word** is the number of bits accessed at one time by the microprocessor. Two types are **CISC** and **RISC.**

Memory Chips

- **RAM chips** temporarily hold data and instructions. Four types of memory are: **conventional, upper, extended,** and **expanded.**
- **ROM chips (firmware)** have programs built into them for operating important system devices.

System Clock

System clock controls the speed of computer operations. It is measured in **megahertz (MHz).**

Expansion Slots and Boards

Expansion (or **plug-in**) **boards** can connect to networks, increase portable computers' expansion capabilities, contain TV tuner, and more.

Bus Lines

A **bus line** (or **bus**) is a data roadway. Four bus standards: **ISA, MCA, EISA,** and **PCI.** Local buses support video demands for graphical user interfaces. Two local bus standards: **PCI** and **VL-bus.**

Ports

Ports connect outside devices to the system unit. Four types: **serial, parallel, USB,** and **FireWire.**

Input and Output

How do you get data to the CPU? How do you get information out? Here we describe the two most important places where the computer interfaces with people. The first half of the chapter covers input devices; the second half covers output devices.

People understand language, which is constructed of letters, numbers, and punctuation marks. However, computers can understand only the binary machine language of 0s and 1s. Input and output devices are essentially translators. Input devices translate symbols that people understand into symbols that computers can process. Output devices do the reverse: They translate machine output to output people can comprehend. Let us, then, look at the devices that perform these translations.

COMPETENCIES

After you have read this chapter, you should be able to:

1. **Explain the difference between keyboard and direct-entry input devices and the POS terminal.**
2. **Describe the features of keyboards and the four types of terminals. These are dumb, intelligent, network terminal, and Internet terminal.**
3. **Describe direct-entry devices used with microcomputers. These include the mouse, touch screen, light pen, digitizer, digital camera, image scanner, fax, bar-code reader, MICR, OCR, OMR, and voice-input devices.**
4. **Describe monitors (cathode-ray tube and flat-panel) and monitor standards (CGA, EGA, VGA, Super VGA, and XGA).**
5. **Describe printers (ink-jet, laser, dot-matrix, thermal) and plotters (pen, ink-jet, electrostatic, and direct-image).**
6. **Describe voice-output devices.**

Input: Keyboard versus Direct Entry

Input devices convert people-readable data into machine-readable form. Input may be by keyboard or direct entry.

Input devices take data and programs people can read or understand and convert them to a form the computer can process. This form consists of the machine-readable electronic signals of 0s and 1s that we described in the last chapter. Input devices are of two kinds: keyboard entry and direct entry.

- **Keyboard entry:** Data is input to the computer through a *keyboard* that looks like a typewriter keyboard but has additional keys. In this method, the user typically reads from an original document called the **source document.** The user enters that document by typing on the keyboard.
- **Direct entry:** Data is made into machine-readable form as it is entered into the computer; no keyboard is used.

FIGURE 6-1
A point-of-sale terminal.

An example of an input device that uses both keyboard and direct entry is a **point-of-sale (POS) terminal.** This is the sort of "electronic cash register" you see in department stores. (See Figure 6-1.) When clerks sell a sweater, for example, they can record the sale by typing in the information (product code, purchase amount, tax) on the keyboard. Or they can use a hand-held **wand reader** or **platform scanner** to read special characters on price tags as direct entry. The wand reflects light on the characters. The reflection is then changed by photoelectric cells to machine-readable code. Whether by keyboard entry or direct entry, the results will appear on the POS terminal's digital display. (Refer to Figure 6-1.)

Keyboard Entry

In keyboard entry, people type input. There are four types of terminals: dumb, intelligent, network computer, and Internet terminal.

Probably the most common way in which you will input data, at least at the beginning, is by using a keyboard.

Keyboards

Keyboards have different kinds of keys. (See Figure 6-2.)

- **Typewriter keys:** The keys that resemble the regular letters, numbers, and punctuation marks on a typewriter keyboard are called **typewriter keys.** Note the position of the **Enter** key, which is used to enter commands into the computer.
- **Function keys:** The keys labeled *F1, F2,* and so on are the **function keys.** These keys are used for tasks that occur frequently (such as underlining in word processing). They save you keystrokes.

FIGURE 6-2
Traditional keyboard.

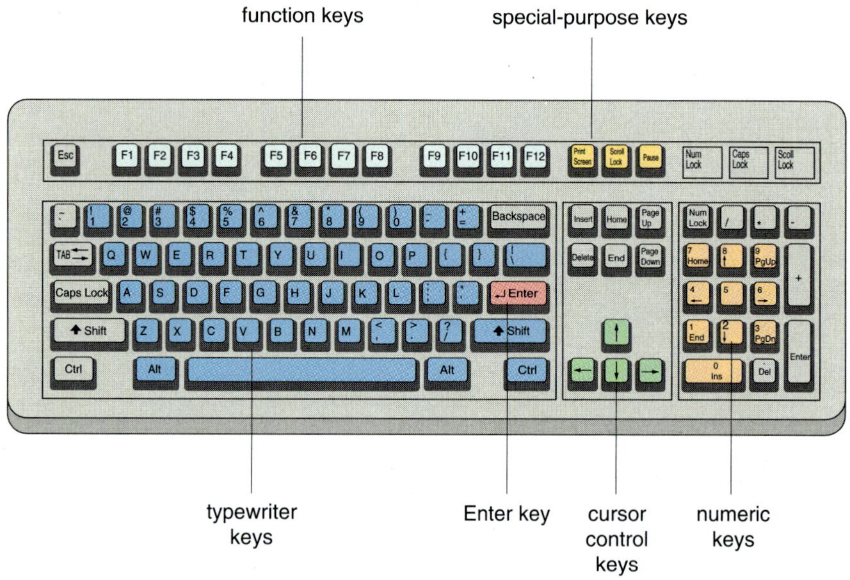

- **Numeric keys:** The keys 0 to 9, called the **numeric keys** or **numeric keypad,** are used for tasks principally involving numbers. These may be useful when you are working with spreadsheets.
- **Special-purpose and cursor control keys:** Examples of **special-purpose keys** are *Esc* (for "Escape"), *Ctrl* (for "Control"), *Del* (for "Delete"), and *Ins* (for "Insert"). These keys are used to help enter and edit data and execute commands. The **cursor control keys** or **directional arrow keys** are used to move the cursor.

As we mentioned in Chapter 5, these keys convert letters, numbers, and other characters into electrical signals that are machine readable. These signals are sent to the computer's CPU.

There are two basic keyboard designs. The traditional design or straight design is shown in Figure 6-2. The contour design splits and slopes the keyboard. (See Figure 6-3.) Many people prefer the contour design because it is more natural and comfortable.

FIGURE 6-3
Microsoft's Natural Keyboard.

Terminals

A **terminal** is a form of input (and output) device that connects you to a mainframe or other type of computer called a *host computer* or *server.* There are four types of terminals:

- A **dumb terminal** can be used to input and receive data, but it cannot process data independently. It is used only to gain access to information from a computer. Such a terminal may be used by an airline reservations clerk to access a mainframe computer for flight information.
- An **intelligent terminal** includes a processing unit, memory, and secondary storage such as a magnetic disk. Essentially, an intelligent terminal is a micro-

computer with communications software and a telephone hookup (modem) or other communications link. These connect the terminal to the larger computer or to the Internet. Microcomputers operating as intelligent terminals are widely used in organizations.

- A **network terminal,** also known as a **thin client** or **network computer,** is a low-cost alternative to an intelligent terminal. Most network terminals do not have a hard-disk drive and must rely on the host computer or server for application and system software. These devices are becoming increasingly popular in many organizations.
- An **Internet terminal,** also known as a **Web terminal,** provides access to the Internet and displays Web pages on a standard television set. These special-purpose terminals have just recently been introduced to offer Internet access to people without microcomputers. Unlike the other types of terminals, Internet terminals are used almost exclusively in the home.

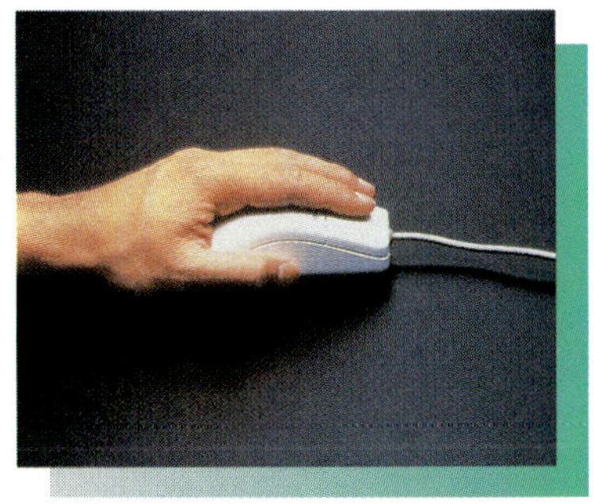

FIGURE 6-4
Microsoft mouse.

Direct Entry

Direct entry creates machine-readable data that can go directly to the CPU. Direct entry includes pointing, scanning, and voice-input devices.

Direct entry is a form of input that does not require data to be keyed by someone sitting at a keyboard. Direct-entry devices create machine-readable data on paper or magnetic media, or feed it directly into the computer's CPU. This reduces the possibility of human error being introduced (as often happens when data is being entered through a keyboard). It is also an economical means of data entry. Direct-entry devices may be categorized in three ways: pointing devices, scanning devices, and voice-input devices.

Pointing Devices

Pointing, of course, is one of the most natural of all human gestures. There are a number of devices that use this method as a form of direct-entry input, as follows.

- **Mouse:** There are three basic **mouse** types. One type of mouse has a ball on the bottom and is attached with a cord to the system unit. (See Figure 6-4.) When rolled on the tabletop, the mouse controls the cursor or pointer. The second type does not require a flat surface. The cursor is controlled by rotating a ball with your thumb. This type of mouse is often called a trackball or rollerball. The newest type is a touch-surface. The cursor is controlled by moving and tapping your finger on the surface of a pad. (See Figure 6-5.) The trackball and touch-surface are common on portable computers and are often built into keyboards.

FIGURE 6-5 Touch-surface (Epson ActionNote 880).

FIGURE 6-6
A touch screen: an industrial application.

- **Touch screen:** A **touch screen** is a particular kind of monitor screen covered with a plastic layer. (See Figure 6-6.) Behind this layer are crisscrossed invisible beams of infrared light. This arrangement enables someone to select actions or commands by touching the screen with a finger. Touch screens are easy to use, especially when people need information quickly. You may see touch screens at bank automatic teller machines (ATMs) and at visitor information centers in airports and hotels.
- **Light pen:** A **light pen** is a light-sensitive penlike device. (See Figure 6-7.) The light pen is placed against the monitor. This closes a photoelectric circuit and identifies the spot for entering or modifying data. Light pens are used by engineers, for example, in designing anything from microprocessor chips to airplane parts.
- **Digitizer:** A **digitizer** is a device that can be used to trace or copy a drawing or photograph. The shape is converted to digital data. A computer can then represent the data on the screen or print it out on paper. A **digitizing tablet** enables you to create your own images using a special stylus. (See Figure 6-8.) The images are then converted to digital data that can be processed by the computer. Digitizers are often used by designers and architects.
- **Digital camera:** **Digital cameras** are similar to traditional cameras except that images are recorded digitally in the camera's memory rather than on film. (See Figure 6-9.) Instant photography used to mean using a Polaroid camera and getting a photograph in two minutes. Now, you can take a picture, view it immediately, and even place it on your own Web page, all within minutes. Although faster than traditional photography, digital camera prices are typically higher, and image quality is not quite as good. Real estate agents use digital cameras to capture images of homes to be displayed on their Web pages.

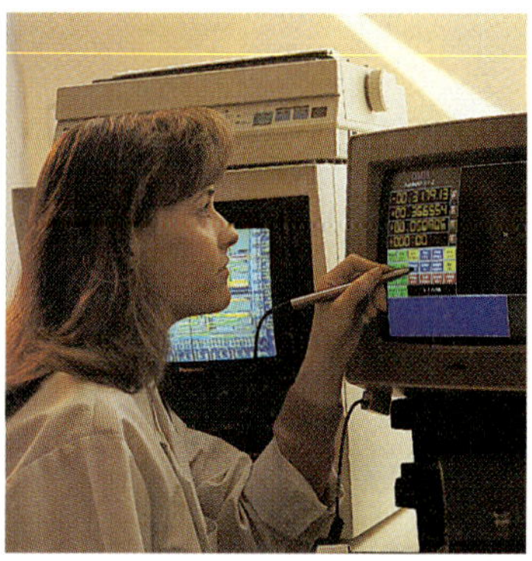

FIGURE 6-7
A light pen: a hospital application.

FIGURE 6-8
A digitizer: an industrial design application.

FIGURE 6-9
A digital camera: Apple QuickLake 200.

FIGURE 6-10
An image scanner: reproducing color images.

FIGURE 6-11
A fax machine: sending documents electronically.

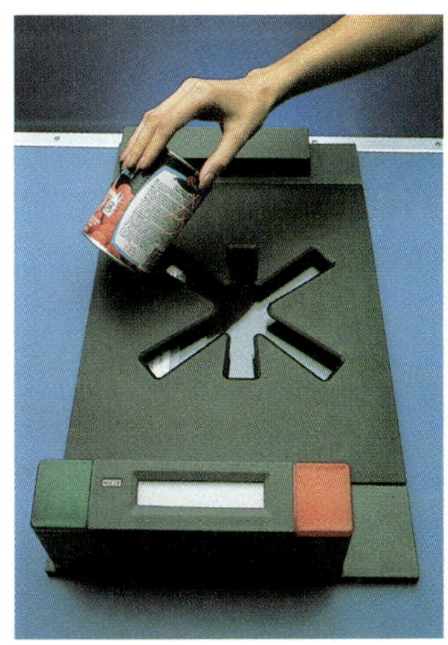

FIGURE 6-12
A bar-code reader: recording product codes.

Scanning Devices

Direct-entry scanning devices record images of text, drawings, or special symbols. The images are converted to digital data that can be processed by a computer or displayed on a monitor. Scanning devices include the following:

- **Image scanner:** An **image scanner** identifies images on a page. (See Figure 6-10.) It automatically converts them to electronic signals that can be stored in a computer. The process identifies pictures or different typefaces by scanning each image with light and breaking it into dots. The dots are then converted into digital code for storage. Image scanners are becoming widely used input devices. They are commonly used in desktop publishing to scan graphic images that can then be placed in a page of text.
- **Fax machines: Facsimile transmission machines,** commonly called **fax machines,** scan the image of a document to be sent. (See Figure 6-11.) The light and dark areas of the image are converted into a format that can be sent electronically over telephone lines. The receiving fax machine converts the signals back to an image and recreates it on paper.

  Although dedicated fax machines are popular, many people use their microcomputers with a **fax/modem board** that provides the independent capabilities of a fax and a modem.
- **Bar-code readers:** You are probably familiar with **bar-code readers** from grocery stores. (See Figure 6-12.) Bar-code readers are photoelectric scanners that read the **bar codes,** or vertical zebra-striped marks, printed on product containers. Supermarkets use a bar-code system called the Universal Product Code (UPC). The bar code identifies the product to the supermarket's computer, which has a description and the latest price for the product. The computer automatically tells the POS terminal what the price is. And it prints the price and the product name on the customer's receipt.

FIGURE 6-13

A wand reader: recording product codes.

- **Character and mark recognition devices:** There are three kinds of scanning devices—formerly used only with mainframes—now found in connection with the more powerful microcomputers.

  Magnetic-ink character recognition (MICR) is a direct-entry method used in banks. This technology is used to automatically read those futuristic-looking numbers on the bottom of checks. A special-purpose machine known as a **reader/sorter** reads characters made of ink containing magnetized particles.

  Optical-character recognition (OCR) uses special preprinted characters, such as those printed on utility and telephone bills. They can be read by a light source and changed into machine-readable code. A common OCR device is the hand-held *wand reader* discussed earlier in this chapter. (See Figure 6-13.) These are used in department stores to read retail price tags by reflecting light on the printed characters.

  Optical-mark recognition (OMR) is also called **mark sensing.** An OMR device senses the presence or absence of a mark, such as a pencil mark. OMR is often used to score multiple-choice tests such as the College Board's Scholastic Aptitude Test and the Graduate Record Examination.

Voice-Input Devices

Voice-input devices convert a person's speech into a digital code. (See Figure 6-14.) These input devices, when combined with the appropriate software, form **voice recognition systems.** These systems enable users to operate microcomputers and to create documents using voice commands.

Some of these systems must be "trained" to the particular user's voice. This is done by matching the user's spoken words to patterns previously stored in the computer. More advanced systems that can recognize the same word spoken by many different people have been developed. However, until recently the list of words has been limited. One voice recognition system, the Dragon Dictate, identifies over 30,000 words and adapts to individual voices. There are even systems that will translate from one language to another, such as from English to Japanese.

There are two types of voice recognition systems:

- **Continuous speech: Continuous speech recognition systems** are used to control a microcomputer's operations and to issue commands to special appli-

FIGURE 6-14
A voice-input device: dictating a letter.

cation programs. For example, rather than using the keyboard to save a spreadsheet file, the user could simply say "save the file." Two popular systems are Apple Computer's PlainTalk and IBM's Continuous Speech Series.

- **Discrete-word:** A common activity in business is preparing memos and other written documents. **Discrete-word recognition systems** allow users to dictate directly into a microcomputer using a microphone. The microcomputer stores the memo in a word processing file where it can be revised later or directly printed out. Two such systems are available from Kurzweil Applied Intelligence Inc. and IBM's Voice Type Dictation.

Output: Monitors, Printers, Plotters, Voice

Output devices convert machine-readable information into people-readable form.

Data that is input to and then processed by the computer remains in machine-readable form until output devices make it people-readable. The output devices we shall describe for microcomputers are monitors, printers, plotters, and voice-output.

Monitors

Monitor standards indicate screen quality. Some monitors are used on the desktop, others are portable.

The most frequently used output device is the monitor, also known as the **display screen, video display, video display terminal,** and **VDT.** Two important characteristics of monitors are the number of colors that can be displayed and the clarity of images produced. Images are represented on monitors by individual dots or "picture elements" called **pixels.** A pixel is the smallest unit on the screen that can be turned on and off or made different shades. The *density* of the dots—that is, the number of rows and columns of dots—determines the images' clarity, the resolution.

Standards

To indicate a monitor's color and resolution capabilities, several standards have been created. The three most common are VGA, Super VGA and XGA. (See Figure 6-15.)

- **VGA** stands for *V*ideo *G*raphics *A*rray. You can display 16 colors at a resolution of 640 by 480. Or, you can display 16 times as many colors—256 colors—with a resolution of 320 by 200. VGA has been a widely used monitor standard for general use.
- **Super VGA** or **SVGA** stands for *S*uper *V*ideo *G*raphics *A*rray. SVGA has a higher resolution capability. It has a minimum of 800 by 600 resolution. Some higher-priced models have a 1600 by 1200 resolution. SVGA is the most common standard today. It is widely used in many applications, including industrial design, which requires precise measurements taken directly from the screen.
- **XGA** stands for *E*xtended *G*raphic *A*rray and has a resolution of up to 1024 by 768 pixels. It can display more than 18 million colors. XGA may become the next widely accepted standard. It is used primarily by experts in engineering design and in graphic arts.

Cathode-Ray Tubes

The most common type of monitor for the office and the home is the **cathode-ray tube** or **CRT.** (See Figure 6-16.) These monitors are typically placed directly on the system unit or on the desktop. CRTs are similar in size and technology to televisions.

An important characteristic is how the cathode-ray tube creates images on the screen. **Interlaced monitors** create images by scanning down the screen, skipping every other line. This technology can cause flickering and may lead to eye strain. **Noninterlaced monitors** avoid these problems by scanning each line.

FIGURE 6-15
Monitor standards.

MONITORS

STANDARD	PIXELS	COLORS
CGA	320 × 200	4
EGA	640 × 350	16
VGA	640 × 480 320 × 200	16 256
Super VGA	800 × 600 1024 × 768	256 256
XGA	1024 × 768	65,536

FIGURE 6-16 A CRT monitor.

FIGURE 6-17 A flat-panel monitor.

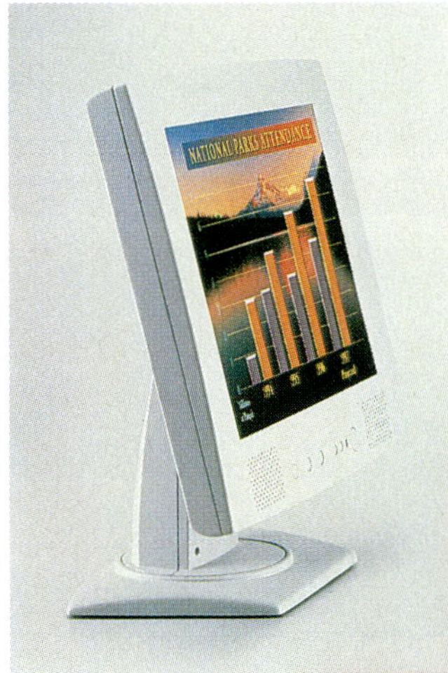

Flat-Panel Monitors

Because CRTs are too bulky to be transported, portable monitors (see Figure 6-17) known as **flat-panel monitors** or **liquid crystal display (LCD) monitors** were developed. Unlike the technology used in CRTs, the technology for portable monitors involves liquid crystals. Flat-panel monitors are much thinner than CRTs. Once used exclusively for portable computers, flat-panel monitors are now starting to be used for desktop systems as well.

There are two basic types of flat-panel monitors: *passive-matrix* and *active-matrix*. **Passive-matrix monitors** create images by scanning the entire screen. This type requires very little power, but the clarity of the images is not as sharp. **Active-matrix monitors** do not scan down the screen; instead, each pixel is independently activated. More colors with better clarity can be displayed. Active-matrix monitors are more expensive and require more power.

As we mentioned earlier, an exciting recent development is the merger of microcomputers and television called **PC/TV.** This is becoming possible through the establishment of all-digital **high-definition television (HDTV).** HDTV delivers a much clearer and more detailed wide-screen picture. Additionally, because the output is digital, it enables users to readily freeze video sequences to create still images. These images can then be digitized and output as artwork or stored on laser disks. This technology will likely be very useful to graphic artists, publishers, and educators.

Cable operators such as Time Warner Cable have recently introduced **ITV,** also known as **interactive TV,** to select markets. ITV provides viewers with videos on demand, video games, interactive shopping, and a dazzling array of entertainment and informational services. ITV uses normal telephone lines to transmit informa-

FIGURE 6-18
Microcomputer printers.

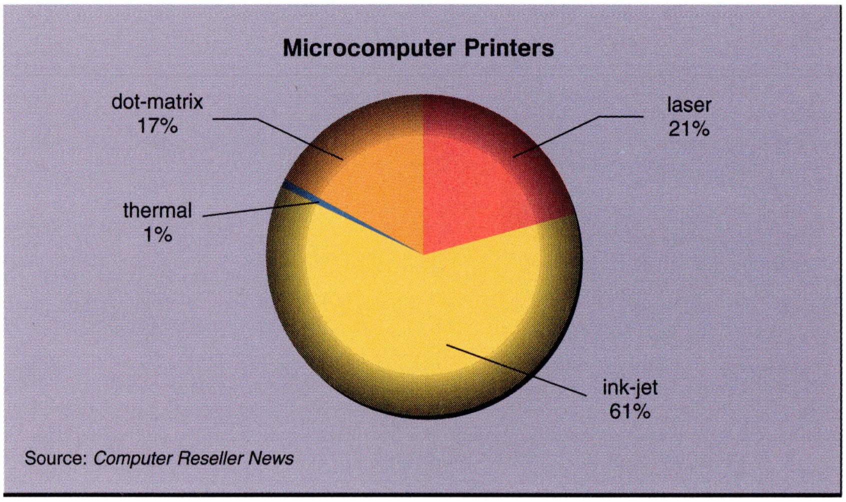

tion, a terminal or microcomputer connected to the television to interpret information, and a supercomputer at a centralized site to coordinate the entire system. ITV promises to revolutionize the TV world.

Printers

There are four types of printers: ink-jet, laser, dot-matrix, and thermal.

The images output on a monitor are often referred to as **soft copy.** Information output on paper—whether by a printer or by a plotter—is called **hard copy.** Four popular kinds of printers used with microcomputers are dot-matrix, ink-jet, laser, and thermal. (See Figure 6-18.)

FIGURE 6-19
An ink-jet printer: Hewlett-Packard PaintJet XL 300.

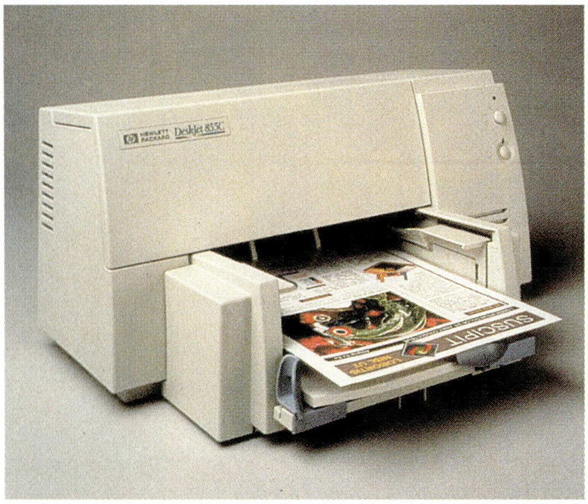

Ink-Jet Printer

An **ink-jet printer** sprays small droplets of ink at high speed onto the surface of the paper. This process not only produces a letter-quality image but also permits printing to be done in a variety of colors. (See Figure 6-19.) Ink-jet printers have recently become the most widely used printer. They are reliable, quiet, and inexpensive. Ink-jet printers are used wherever color and appearance are important, as in advertising and public relations.

Laser Printer

The **laser printer** uses a technology similar to that used in a photocopying machine. (See Figure 6-20.) It uses a laser beam to produce images with excellent letter and graphics quality. Laser printers are widely used in applications requiring high-quality output.

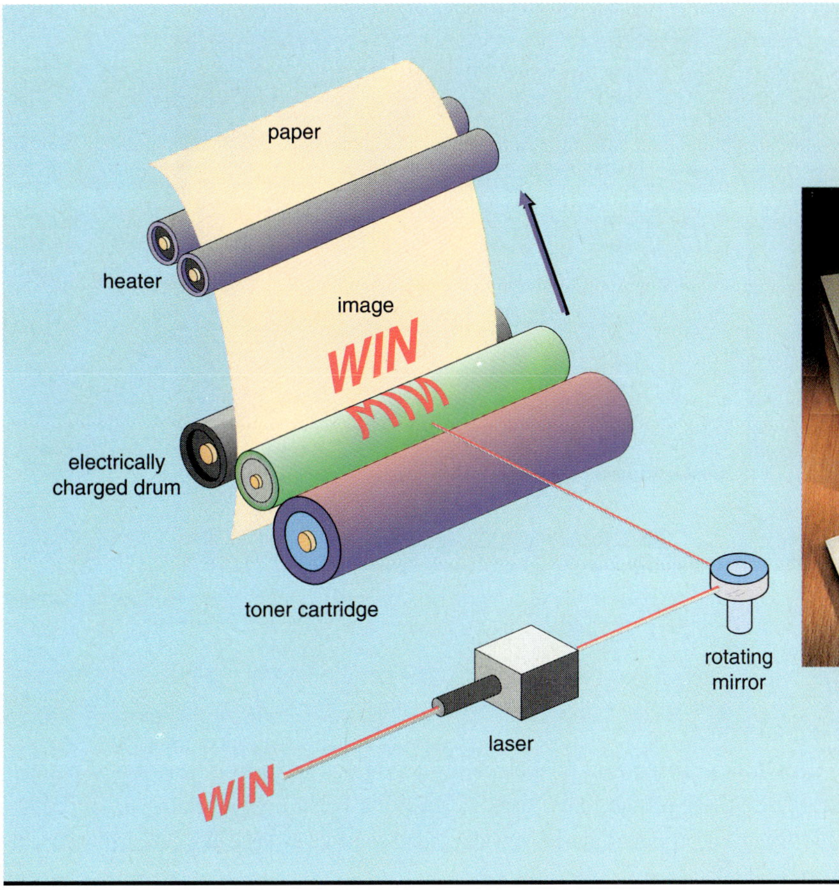

FIGURE 6-20
A laser printer: Hewlett-Packard LaserJet.

There are two categories of laser printers. **Personal laser printers** are inexpensive and used by many single users to produce black-and-white documents. They typically can print 4 to 6 pages a minute. **Shared laser printers** are more expensive and are used (shared) by a group of users to produce color as well as black-and-white documents. Shared laser printers typically print over 30 pages a minute.

Dot-Matrix Printer

Dot-matrix printers form characters or images using a series of small pins on a print head. (See Figure 6-21.) Once the most widely used microcomputer printers, dot-matrix printers are inexpensive and reliable but quite noisy. In general, they are used for tasks where a high-quality image is not essential. Thus, they are often used for documents that are circulated within an organization rather than shown to clients and the public.

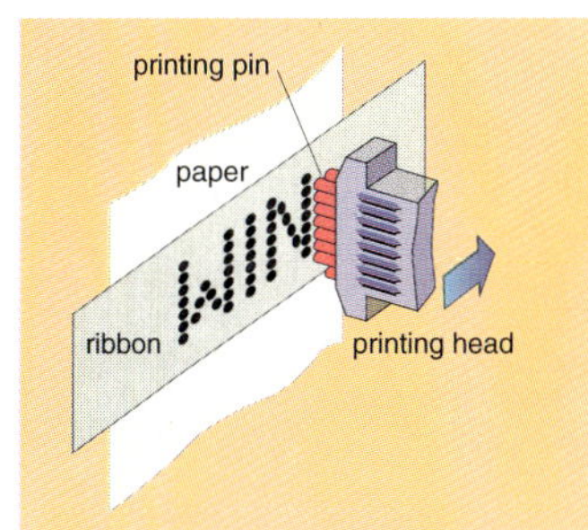

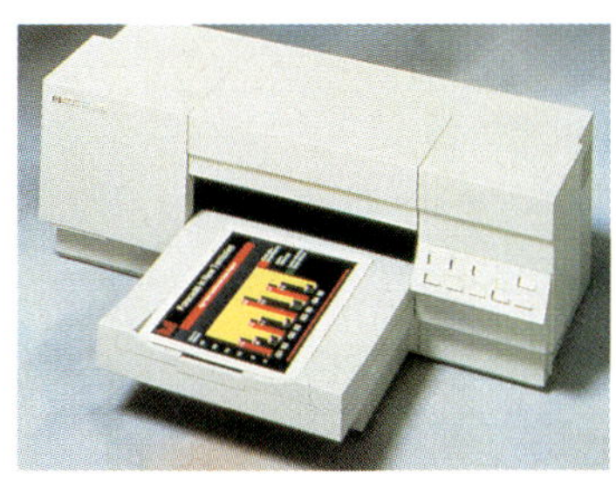

FIGURE 6-21
A dot-matrix printer: Epson ActionPrinter 5000+

FIGURE 6-22
A thermal printer: Tektronic's Phaser 200i.

Thermal Printer

A **thermal printer** uses heat elements to produce images on heat-sensitive paper. Originally these printers were used in scientific labs to record data. More recently, color thermal printers have been widely used to produce very high quality color artwork and text. (See Figure 6-22.)

Color thermal printers are not as popular because of their cost and the requirement of specially treated paper. They are a more special-use printer that produces near-photographic output. They are widely used in professional art and design work where very high quality color is essential.

Some of the important characteristics of the four most widely used microcomputer printers are summarized in Figure 6-23.

FIGURE 6-23
Four types of printers.

PRINTERS

PRINTER	CHARACTERISTICS	TYPICAL USE
Ink-jet	High color quality; inexpensive; sprays drops of ink on paper	Internal and external communications, advertising pieces
Laser	Very high quality; uses photocopying process	Desktop publishing, external documents
Dot-matrix	Reliable, inexpensive; noisy; forms text and graphics by dots	In-house communications
Thermal	Very high quality; uses heat elements on special paper	Art and design work

Other Printers

There are several other types of printers. Two are the daisy-wheel printer and the chain printer. Daisy-wheel printers produce very high quality, professional-looking correspondence. However, they are slower and less reliable than dot-matrix, ink-jet, and laser printers. Their sales have declined dramatically in the past few years.

You probably won't find a chain printer standing alone on a desk next to a microcomputer. This is because a chain printer is an expensive, high-speed machine originally designed to serve minicomputers and mainframes. However, you may see one in organizations that link several microcomputers together by a communications network.

Printer Features

Some general qualities to note about microcomputer printers are as follows:

- **Friction and tractor feed:** In a typewriter the paper is gripped by the roller (platen). Some printers use this method. It is called **friction feed.** In other microcomputer printers the paper is held in place by a **tractor feed** mechanism. This reduces the chance of the paper's getting out of alignment. The tractor feed has sprockets that advance the paper, using holes on the edges of continuous-form paper.
- **Shared use:** Laser and chain printers can be quite expensive. Thus, in organizations they are often found linked to several microcomputers through a communications network. Ink-jet printers are quite often used to serve individual microcomputers.
- **Portability:** Some people (travelers, for instance) require not only a portable computer but also a portable printer. Rugged ink-jet printers are available that are battery-powered and weigh less than 7 pounds. Such printers are recharged using a special connection that can be plugged into an AC outlet. Some can even be recharged through a car's cigarette lighter.

Plotters

Plotters are special-purpose drawing devices.

Plotters are special-purpose output devices for producing bar charts, maps, architectural drawings, and even three-dimensional illustrations. Plotters can produce high-quality multicolor documents and also documents that are larger in size than most printers can handle. There are four types of plotters: pen, ink-jet, electrostatic, and direct imaging.

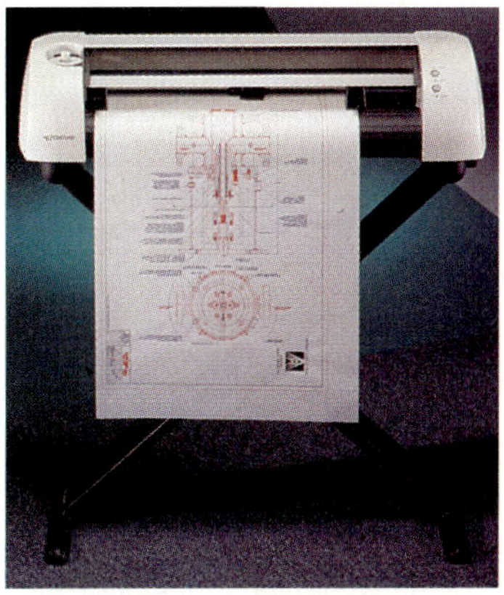

FIGURE 6-24
A pen plotter.

Pen Plotter

Pen plotters (see Figure 6-24) create plots by moving a pen or pencil over drafting paper. (With some pen plotters, the paper moves and the pen remains stationary.) Pen plotters are the least expensive plotters and the easiest to maintain. Their major limitations are slower speed and an inability to produce solid fills and shading. Nevertheless, they have been the most popular type of plotter.

FIGURE 6-25
An electrostatic plotter.

Ink-Jet Plotter

Ink-jet plotters create line drawings and solid-color output by spraying droplets of ink onto paper. Their best features are their speed, high-quality output, and quiet operation. The major disadvantage of ink-jet plotters is that the spray jets can become clogged and thus require more maintenance. Ink-jet plotters are used by a wide variety of workers, including engineers and automotive designers.

Electrostatic Plotter

Whereas pen plotters use pens, **electrostatic plotters** use electrostatic charges to create images made up of tiny dots on specially treated paper. (See Figure 6-25.) The image is produced when the paper is run through a developer. Electrostatic plotters produce high-resolution images and are much faster than either pen or ink-jet plotters. These plotters, unfortunately, use expensive chemicals that are considered hazardous. Electrostatic plotters are used for applications that require high-volume and high-quality outputs such as in advertising and graphic arts design.

Direct-Imaging Plotter

Direct-imaging plotters or thermal plotters create images using heat-sensitive paper and electrically heated pins. This type of plotter is comparably priced with electrostatic plotters, quite reliable, and good for high-volume work. However, direct-imaging plotters require expensive paper and typically create only two-color output. These plotters are typically used for very specific applications such as creating maps.

Voice-Output Devices

Voice-output devices vocalize prerecorded sounds.

Voice-output devices make sounds that resemble human speech but actually are prerecorded vocalized sounds. With one Macintosh program, the computer speaks the synthesized words "We'll be right back" if you type in certain letters and numbers. (The characters are *Wiyl biy ray5t bae5k*—the numbers elongate the sounds.) Voice output is not anywhere near as difficult to create as voice input. In fact, there are many occasions when you will hear synthesized speech being used. Examples are found in soft-drink machines, on the telephone, and in cars.

FIGURE 6-26
Stereo speakers: Boise MediaMate Computer Speakers.

For multimedia applications, the output device is typically a set of stereo speakers or headphones. (See Figure 6-26.) These devices are connected to a sound card in the system unit. The sound card is used to capture as well as play back recorded sounds.

Voice output is used as a reinforcement tool for learning, such as to help students study a foreign language. It is also used in many supermarkets at the checkout counter to confirm purchases. Of course, one of its most powerful capabilities is to assist the physically challenged.

A Look at the Future

Microsoft's Investment in WebTV and introduction of Broadcast Technology could lead the way to the merger of all digital television and microcomputers.

Have you been hearing a lot about digital TV? It promises to combine the power and flexibility of a microcomputer with the entertainment capabilities of a large screen TV. You and a whole group of friends could play computer games, interact with life-sized figures, surf the Web, capture video, edit it, and paste into electronic presentations.

Of course, that's what PC/TV is all about. These systems contain special devices that convert analog signals required for today's television sets to digital signals required for microcomputers. Unfortunately, this conversion greatly constrains the speed, flexibility, and quality of these systems. But, all that's going to change in the next few years.

All-digital television broadcasts are just around the corner and promise greater image and sound quality. The Federal Communications Commission is leading the way. Every major network is required to offer digital signals to their top 10 markets within the next year and to their top 30 markets within the following year.

Microsoft, a leader in software technology, has recently taken steps to position itself for this change. One step has been the recent investment of nearly a half billion dollars in WebTV, a company that manufactures Internet terminals for television sets. Another step is the introduction of Broadcast Technology in Microsoft Windows 98. This technology presents a cable TV interface that lets you choose content on screen from the Internet, local TV, cable TV, and other sources.

Will your current television set become useless? It will not be able to display the new digital signals; however, the transition to digital will be gradually phased over the next few years. By the year 2006, however, all analog broadcasts are expected to be eliminated.

KEY TERMS

active-matrix monitor (125)
bar codes (121)
bar-code reader (121)
cathode-ray tube (CRT) (124)
continuous speech recognition system (122)
cursor control keys (118)
digital camera (120)
digitizer (120)
digitizing tablet (120)
direct entry (119)
direct-imaging plotter (130)
directional arrow keys (118)
discrete-word recognition system (123)
display screen (123)
dot-matrix printer (127)
dumb terminal (118)
electrostatic plotter (130)
Enter (117)
facsimile transmission (fax) machine (121)
fax/modem board (121)
flat-panel monitor (125)
friction feed (129)
function keys (117)
hard copy (126)
high-definition television (HDTV) (125)
image scanner (121)
ink-jet plotter (129)
ink-jet printer (126)
intelligent terminal (118)
interactive TV (ITV) (125)
interlaced monitor (124)
Internet terminal (119)
laser printer (126)
light pen (120)
liquid crystal display (LCD) monitor (125)
magnetic-ink character recognition (MICR) (122)
mark sensing (122)
mouse (119)
network computer (119)
network terminal (119)
noninterlaced monitor (124)
numeric keypad (118)
numeric keys (118)
optical-character recognition (OCR) (122)
optical-mark recognition (OMR) (122)
passive-matrix monitor (125)
PC/TV (125)
pen plotter (129)
personal laser printer (126)
pixels (124)
platform scanner (117)
plotters (129)
point-of-sale (POS) terminal (117)
reader/sorter (122)
shared laser printer (126)
soft copy (126)
source document (116)
special-purpose keys (118)
Super VGA, SVGA (124)
terminal (118)
thermal printer (127)
thin client (119)
touch screen (120)
tractor feed (129)
typewriter keys (117)
VGA (124)
video display (123)

video display terminals (VDTs) (123)
voice recognition systems (122)
voice-input device (122)
voice-output device (130)
wand reader (117)
Web terminal (119)
XGA (124)

REVIEW QUESTIONS

True/False

1. Input devices translate symbols that people understand into symbols that computers can process.
2. A plotter is a device that can be used to trace or copy a drawing or photograph.
3. Banks use a method called magnetic-ink character recognition (MICR) to automatically read and sort checks.
4. Laser printers are highly reliable, but the quality of their output limits their use to rough drafts and in-house communications.
5. Plotters are special-purpose drawing devices.

Multiple Choice

1. Esc, Ctrl, Del, and Ins are __________ keys.
   a. function
   b. numeric
   c. directional arrow
   d. cursor control
   e. special-purpose
2. A device that converts images on a page to electronic signals that can be stored in a computer:
   a. monitor
   b. scanner
   c. plotter
   d. MICR
   e. POS
3. The type of flat-panel monitor that can display more colors, with better clarity:
   a. active-matrix
   b. passive-matrix
   c. monochrome
   d. CGA
   e. VGA
4. The printer that can produce very high quality images using heat elements on heat-sensitive paper:
   a. dot-matrix
   b. laser
   c. ink-jet
   d. plotter
   e. thermal
5. The plotter that creates images using heat-sensitive paper and electrically heated pins:
   a. pen
   b. ink-jet
   c. direct-imaging
   d. scanner
   e. electrostatic

Fill in the Blank

1. Another name for the mouse that has a ball controlled with the thumb is __________.
2. __________ machines are popular office machines that scan the image of a document to be sent.
3. The __________ printer is a reliable, inexpensive printer that forms letters by a series of small pins on a print head.
4. The __________ printer is the most widely used.
5. __________ devices make sounds that resemble human speech.

Open Ended

1. What are the differences between keyboard entry and direct entry as forms of input?
2. What is a POS terminal? What are two input devices on it that represent the two methods of inputting data?
3. Distinguish among the four kinds of terminals: dumb, intelligent, network, and Internet.
4. What are pixels? What do they have to do with screen resolution?
5. What are the differences between personal and shared lasers?

DISCUSSION QUESTION

1. *Evaluating laser printers:* When shopping for an inexpensive personal laser printer, you can't expect to get all of the fancy fonts. Nor can you expect the speedy, sophisticated paper handling more expensive printers offer. At the very least, you'd want crisp, professional-looking output and reasonably fast performance. Evaluate your printer needs in terms of the following criteria:
    a. Output quality
    b. Print speed
    c. Price
    d. Service and support
    e. Design and construction
    f. Font/graphics options
    g. Paper handling

on the web

Exercises and Exploration

1 SoundBlaster

Creative Lab is one of the pioneers in sound input and output technologies. Its SoundBlaster family of sound cards is an industry standard for affordability, quality, and reliability. Visit our Web site at http://www.magpie.org/essentials/chapter-6 to link to the SoundBlaster site. Once connected to that site, check out the newest sound card. Print out the Web page describing the specifications of this card and write a paragraph comparing the card to its predecessors.

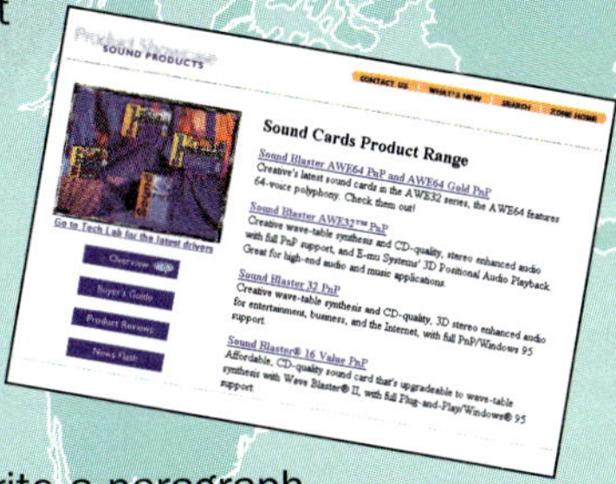

2 WebTV

In order to provide Internet access to a wider audience, the company WebTV Networks, Inc. has eliminated the need for a traditional computer when surfing the Web. Using a Web terminal connected to a TV set can offer anyone access to the Internet without the expense of a computer. To learn more about WebTV's Web terminal, visit our Web site at http://www.magpie.org/essentials/chapter-6 to link to WebTV's site. Once connected to that site, learn how to use your TV to access the Web. Print out the information page from this site. Write a paragraph identifying the names of two companies that use WebTV Networks' technology and discuss the relative advantages and disadvantages of TV versus computer access to the Internet.

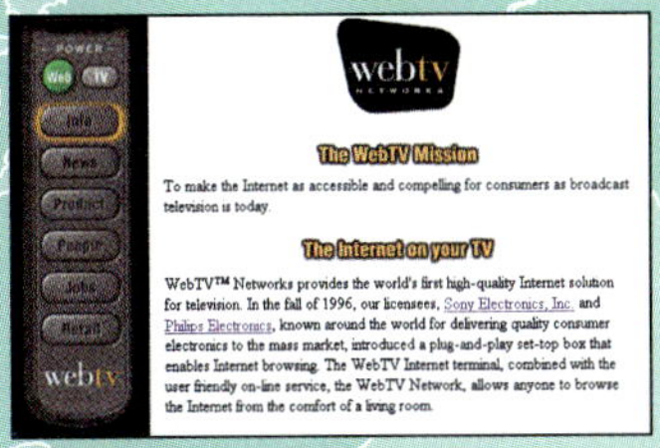

3 Speech Recognition

Apple Corporation is one of the leaders in speech recognition technology. Visit our Web site at http://www.magpie.org/essentials/chapter-6 to link to Apple's speech recognition and speech synthesis home page. Once connected to the Apple site, investigate the latest in speech recognition and speech synthesis software. Print out the Web page you find most informative. Write a paragraph describing why these new developments will or will not be useful in real-world business applications.

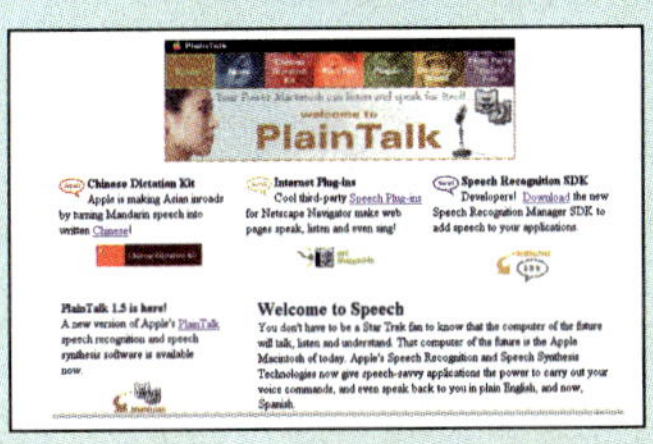

4 Movie Magic

3D Scanners and specialized input and output devices allowed director James Cameron to realize his vision that terrified and fascinated audiences in the ground-breaking film *Terminator 2*. To learn how such devices were used to create movie magic, visit our Web site at http://www.magpie.org/essentials/chapter-6 to link to a Web site on special effects. Once connected to that site, explore and learn how film magic is created. Print out the Web page that you find most interesting and write a brief paragraph on one movie magic technique that most interests you and how you found it on the web site.

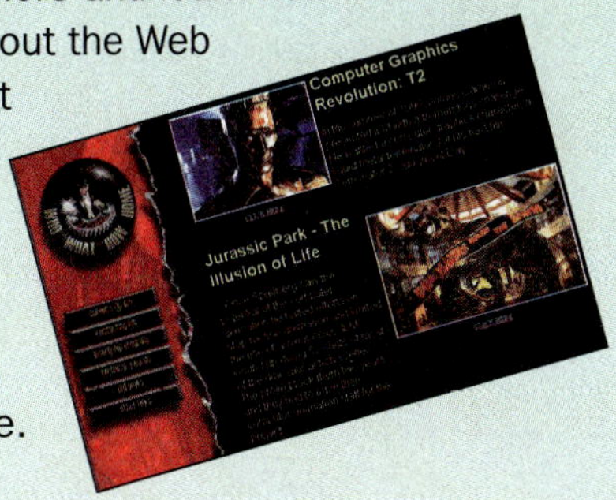

VISUAL SUMMARY

Input and Output

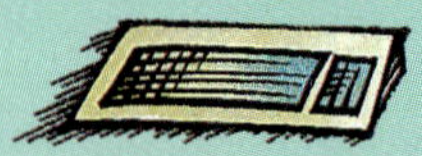

Input devices translate symbols that people understand into symbols the computer can process. Two kinds of input are keyboard and direct entry.

INPUT

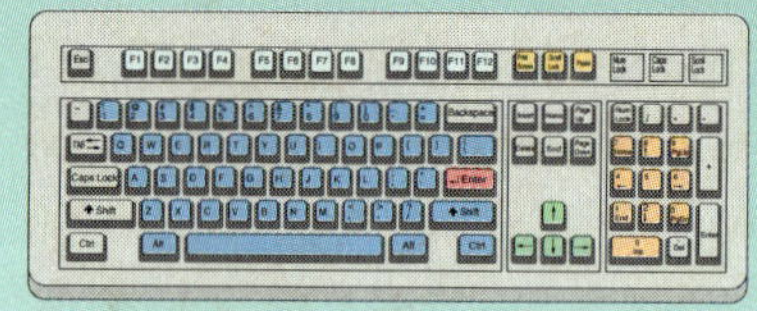

Keyboard entry may be categorized as keyboards and terminals.

Keyboards

In keyboard entry, data is typed. A keyboard consists of:

- **Typewriter keys,** for regular letters, numbers, etc., and **Enter** key to enter commands.
- **Function keys** (*F1, F2,* etc.), for special tasks.
- **Numeric keys,** for typing in numbers.
- **Special-purpose keys** (e.g., *Del* for Delete) and **cursor control (directional arrow) keys** (to move cursor).

Terminals

A **terminal** is an input/output device that connects to a host computer or server. Terminals are of four types:

- **Dumb**—sends and receives only; does no processing.
- **Intelligent**—has processing unit, memory, and secondary storage.
- **Network**—**network computers** (**thin clients**) are low cost alternatives to intelligent terminals
- **Internet**—(**Web terminals**) access Internet and display on television set.

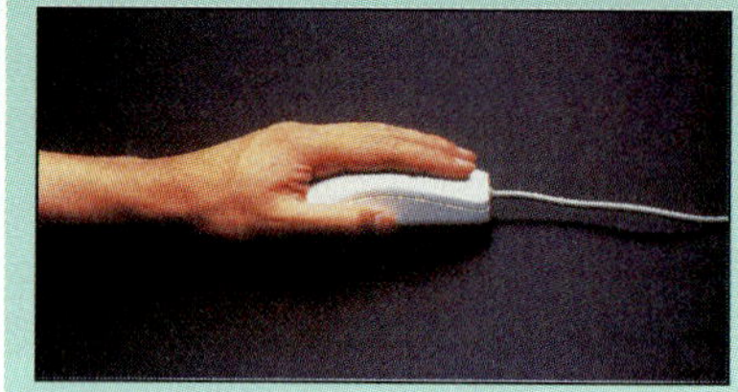

Direct-entry devices may be categorized as pointing, scanning, or voice-input devices.

Pointing Devices

- **Mouse**—directs cursor on screen.
- **Touch screen**—touching your finger to the screen selects actions.
- **Light pen**—recognizes a spot on the screen as input.
- **Digitizer**—converts image to digital data. A **digitizing tablet** converts images using a stylus.
- **Digital camera**—records images in memory.

Scanning Devices

- **Image scanner (bit-mapping device)**—converts an image to digital code.
- **Facsimile transmission (fax) machine**—converts images to electronic signals for sending over telephone lines. **Fax/modem boards** may be inserted in microcomputers to provide the independent capabilities of a fax and a modem.
- **Bar-code reader**—scans zebra-striped **bar codes** on products to reveal their prices.
- Character and mark recognition devices include **magnetic-ink character recognition (MICR),** used by banks to read magnetized-ink numbers on checks, which are sorted by a **reader/sorter** machine; **optical-character recognition (OCR),** used to read special preprinted characters (e.g., on utility bills); **optical-mark recognition (OMR),** which senses pencil marks (e.g., on College Board tests.).

Voice-Input Devices

Voice-input devices convert a person's spoken words to digital code. Combined with appropriate software, these devices are part of the **voice recognition system** that allows users to operate microcomputers using voice commands.

- **Continous speech recognition systems** control operations and issue commands for application packages.
- **Discrete-word recognition systems** convert and store dictation in a word processing file.

Output devices translate machine output to output that people can understand. Output devices include monitors, printers, plotters, and voice-output.

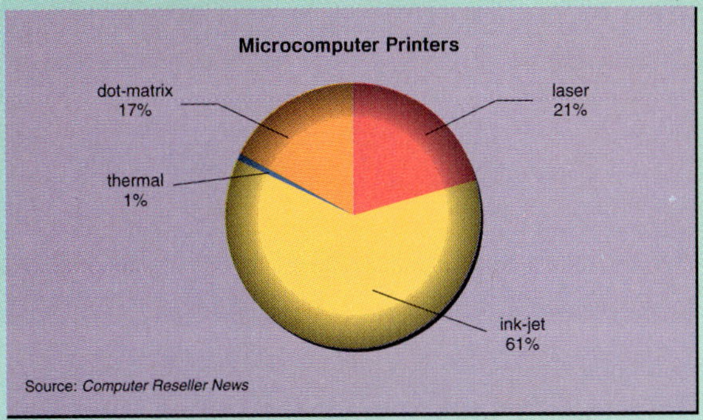

OUTPUT

MONITORS

STANDARD	PIXELS	COLORS
CGA	320 × 200	4
EGA	640 × 350	16
VGA	640 × 200 320 × 200	I16 256
Super VGA	800 × 600 1024 × 768	256 256
XGA	1024 × 768	65,536rts

Monitors

Monitors (**display screens**) create images by individual dots ("picture elements") called **pixels.** The three most common monitor standards are shown above.

- **Cathode-ray tube (CRT) monitors** typically are placed on the system unit or desk. **Interlaced monitors** create images by scanning down and skipping every other line. They can cause eye strain. **Noninterlaced monitors** avoid problems by scanning down each line.
- **Flat-panel monitors** are less bulky and flat. **Passive-matrix monitors** require little power but images not as sharp. **Active-matrix monitors** require more power, are more expensive, produce better images.

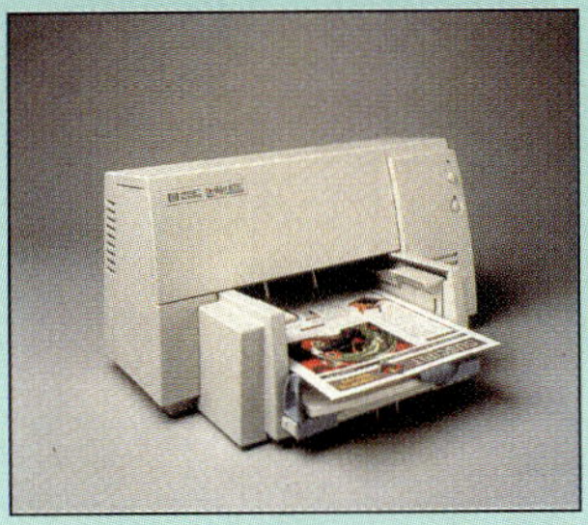

Printers

Output from display screens is called **soft copy.** Output from a printer is called **hard copy.** Four types of printers are:

- **Ink-jet**—sprays droplets of ink on paper; it is good for color and provides very good quality.
- **Laser**—uses a technology like photo copiers. Lasers print high-quality text and graphics; **personal lasers** used by the individual user; **shared lasers** used by many.
- **Dot-matrix**—forms text and graphic images with a matrix of pins.
- **Thermal**—heat elements produce images on special heat-sensitive paper; expensive; produces very high quality art and design output.

Plotters

Plotters produce multicolor bar charts, maps, architectural drawings. Four types are:

- **Pen**—has been most popular and least expensive.
- **Ink-jet**—fastest and very good at producing solid-color output.
- **Electrostatic**—electrostatic charges create high-quality and high-volume work on specially treated paper (shown).
- **Direct-imaging**—electrically charged pins create two-color output on special heat-sensitive paper.

Voice-Output Devices

- **Voice-output devices** make sounds resembling human speech.

Secondary Storage

Data may be input, processed, and output as information. But one of the best features about using a computer is the ability to save—that is, store—information. Computers can save information permanently, after you turn them off. This way, you can save your work for future use, share information with others, or modify information already available. Secondary storage holds information external from the CPU. Secondary storage allows you to store programs, such as Word and Excel. It also allows you to store the data processed by programs, such as text or the numbers in a spreadsheet.

7

COMPETENCIES

After you have read this chapter, you should be able to:

1. Contrast direct access and sequential access storage.
2. Describe how diskettes and disk drives work and how to take care of them.
3. Describe the following kinds of disks: internal hard disks, hard-disk cartridges, and hard-disk packs.
4. Describe ways to improve hard-disk operations: disk caching, data compression, and redundant arrays of inexpensive disks.
5. Describe the different types of optical disks: CD-ROM, CD-R, erasable, and DVD.
6. Describe magnetic tape streamers and magnetic tape reels.

What if you could buy a microcomputer and use your portable audiotape recorder to store programs and data? Actually, this was once advertised as a feature. In the early 1980s there were over 150 kinds of microcomputers being offered. Some inexpensive computers were advertised at that time that could store information on the tape in one's audiotape recorder.

To find a particular song on an audiotape, you may have to play several inches of tape. Finding a song on an audio compact disk, in contrast, can be much faster. You select the song, and the disk player moves directly to it. That, in brief, represents the two different approaches to external storage. The two approaches are called *sequential access* and *direct access*.

Magnetic tape is an example of **sequential access storage** media. Information is stored in sequence, such as alphabetically. You may have to search a tape past all the information from A to P, say, before you get to Q. This may involve searching several inches or feet, which takes time.

Generally speaking, disk storage falls in the category of **direct access storage.** That is, you select what you want and then move directly to it. Therefore, retrieving selected data and programs is much faster with disks than with tape.

Four Types of Secondary Storage

Microcomputer secondary storage may be on floppy disk, hard disk, optical disk, or magnetic tape.

We described random-access memory (RAM) in Chapter 5. This is the *internal* and *temporary* storage of data and programs in the computer's memory. Once the power is turned off or interrupted, everything in internal storage disappears. Such storage is therefore said to be **volatile.** Thus, we need *external, more permanent,* or **nonvolatile,** ways of storing data and programs. We also need external storage because users need much more capacity than is possessed by a computer's primary memory.

The most widely used external storage media are floppy disks, hard disks, optical disks, and magnetic tape. It is important for end users to understand the advantages, disadvantages, and typical uses for each.

Any particular microcomputer could use all of the different media. However, a typical system has a hard-disk drive and one or two other drives. The hard-disk drive is designated as the C drive and is typically used for storing system and application programs. Drives A and B are generally floppy-disk drives used for data files. The D drive is typically a CD-ROM drive for programs and reference materials. (See Figure 7-1.)

FIGURE 7-1
Apple's Macintosh Performa 6200 CD with both floppy-disk drive and optical drive.

FIGURE 7-2
A 3½-inch floppy disk.

Floppy Disks

Floppy disks are removable storage media that are inserted into disk drives.

Floppy disks, often called **diskettes** or simply **disks,** are flat, circular pieces of mylar plastic that rotate within a jacket. Data and programs are stored as electromagnetic charges on a metal oxide film coating the mylar plastic. Data and programs are represented by the presence or absence of these charges, using the ASCII or EBCDIC data representation codes. The two most popular sizes of floppy disks are 3½-inch diameter and 5¼-inch diameter. Larger and smaller sizes are also available, although they are not standard for most microcomputers.

Floppy disks are also called **flexible disks,** and **floppies.** This is because the plastic disk inside the diskette covers is flexible, not rigid. The 3½-inch standard is encased in a hard plastic jacket. (See Figure 7-2.)

The Disk Drive

The *disk drive* obtains stored data and programs from a floppy disk. It is also used to store data and programs on a floppy disk.

A disk drive consists of a box with a slot into which you insert the floppy disk. Often the slot is covered by a door, called the **drive gate.** A motor inside the drive rotates the floppy disk. As the floppy disk rotates, electronic heads can "read" data from and "write" data to it. As we stated earlier, *read* means that the disk drive *copies* data (stored as magnetic impulses) from the floppy disk. *Write* means that the disk drive *transfers* data, the electronic signals in the computer's memory, onto the floppy disk.

It's important to realize that reading makes a copy from the original data; it does not alter the original. Writing, in contrast, *writes over*—and replaces—any data that is already there. This is like recording a new song over an old one on a tape recorder. The same is true of programs on a floppy disk.

How a Disk Drive Works

A floppy disk is inserted into the slot in the front of the disk drive, and the drive gate is closed. (See Figure 7-3.) Closing the gate positions the floppy disk around a spindle and holds it so that it can revolve without slipping. When the drive is in motion, the floppy disk can turn at about 360 revolutions per minute, depending on the drive.

The magnetic data signals are transferred from floppy disk to computer (and computer to floppy disk) through **read-write heads.** (See Figure 7-3.) The read-write head is on an **access arm,** which moves back and forth over the floppy disk. To read or write on a particular part of the floppy disk, the access arm moves the read-write head on the floppy disk. This is called the **seek** operation. The drive then rotates the floppy disk to the proper position. This is called the **search** operation.

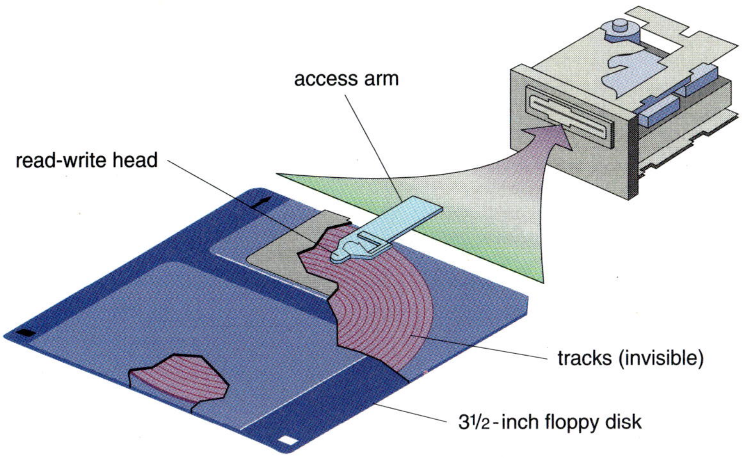

FIGURE 7-3
Reading from and writing to a floppy disk.

The Parts of a Floppy Disk

Both 3½-inch and 5¼-inch floppy disks work the same way in principle, although there are some differences.

Data is recorded on a floppy disk in rings called **tracks.** (See Figure 7-4.) These tracks are closed concentric circles, not a single spiral as on a phonograph record. Unlike a phonograph record, these tracks have no visible grooves. Looking at an exposed floppy disk, you would see just a smooth surface. Each track is divided into invisible wedge-shaped sections known as **sectors.**

Many disks are manufactured without tracks and sectors in place. They must be adapted to the particular brand of microcomputer and disk drive you are using. Thus, you must put the tracks and sectors on yourself, using a process called *formatting,* or *initializing.*

There are two standard types of floppy disks:

- The *3½-inch floppy disk* is the most widely used. (Refer to Figure 7-4.) It is sturdier than the 5¼-inch disk, having an exterior **jacket** made of hard plastic to protect the flexible disk inside. The **write-protect notch** is covered by

FIGURE 7-4
The parts of a 3½-inch floppy disk.

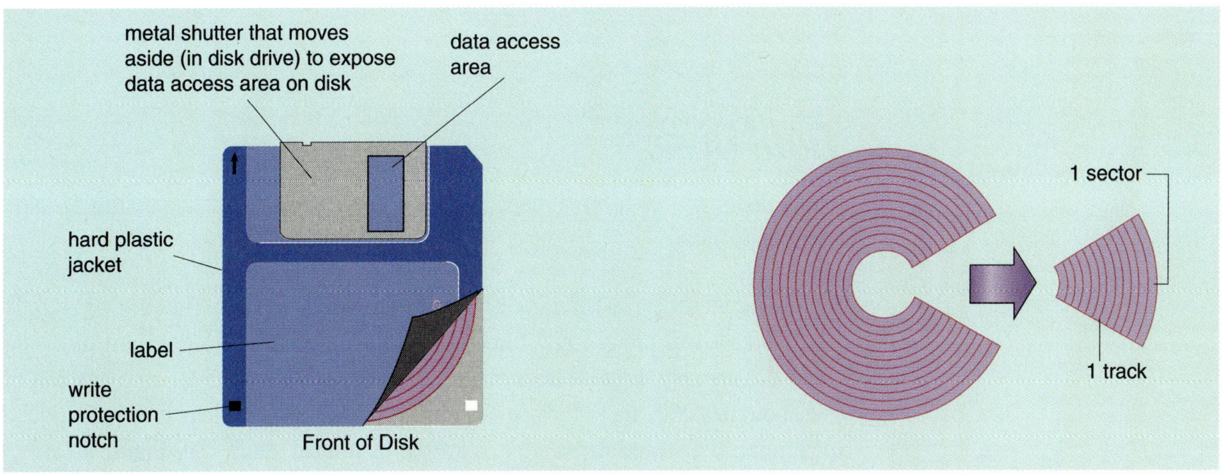

a sliding shutter. When you open the shutter, the write-protect notch prevents the computer from accidentally writing over information on the disk that you want to keep. The most widely used 3½-inch floppy disk is labeled "2HD," which means "two-sided, double-density." These disks can store 1,474,560 bytes or 1.44 megabytes—the equivalent of 400 typewritten pages.

- On the *5¼-inch floppy disk,* the exterior jacket is made of flexible plastic or cardboard. The disk is protected by a paper envelope, or sleeve, when it is not in the disk drive. The write-protect notch can be covered with a removable tab, which comes with the disk when you buy it. The most widely used 5¼-inch floppy disk is also labeled "2HD" but has a lower capacity of 1,228,800 bytes or 1.2 megabytes.

Taking Care of Floppy Disks

Taking care of floppy disks boils down to four rules:

1. *Don't bend the disks, put heavy weights on them, or use sharp objects on them.* For 5¼-inch disks, do not write on them with ballpoint pens. Use a felt-tip pen when writing on the index label.
2. *Don't touch anything visible through the protective jacket* (such as the data access area).
3. *Keep disks away from strong magnetic fields* (like motors or telephones). Also, *keep them away from extreme heat* (like a car trunk) *and chemicals* (such as alcohol and solvents). Keep 5¼-inch disks in their paper envelopes and store them in a file box when they are not in use.
4. *Store disks in a sturdy plastic storage box.* Even though the 3½-inch disks have a hard plastic jacket, they can be damaged.

Of course, the best protection is to make a *backup,* or duplicate, copy of your disk.

Despite these cautions, you will find floppy disks are actually quite durable. For instance, you can send them through the mail if you enclose them in cardboard or use special rigid mailing envelopes. They usually can also be put through the x-ray machines at airport security checkpoints without loss of data.

Hard Disks

Hard disks are of three types: internal hard disk, hard-disk cartridge, and hard-disk pack.

Hard disks consist of metallic rather than plastic platters. They are also tightly sealed to prevent any foreign matter from getting inside. Hard disks are extremely sensitive instruments. The read-write head rides on a cushion of air about 0.000001 inch thick. It is so thin that a smoke particle, fingerprint, dust, or human hair could cause what is known as a head crash. (See Figure 7-5.)

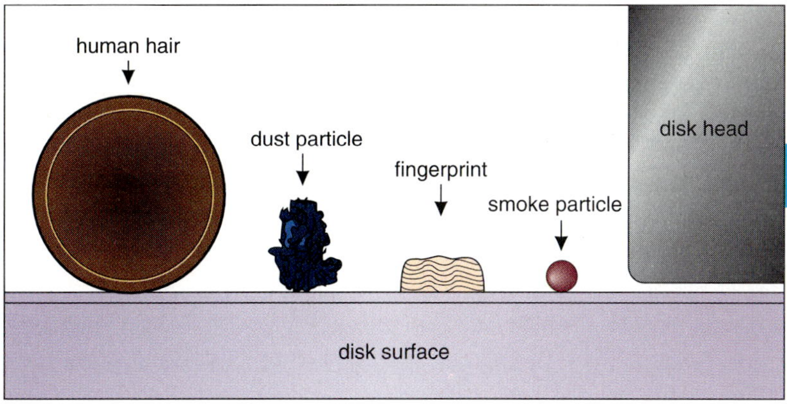

FIGURE 7-5
Materials that can cause a head crash.

A **head crash** happens when the surface of the read-write head or particles on its surface contact the magnetic disk surface. A head crash is a disaster for a hard disk. It means that some or all of the data on the disk is destroyed.

There are three types of hard disks: *internal hard disk, hard-disk cartridge,* and *hard disk pack.*

Internal Hard Disk

An **internal hard disk** consists of one or more metallic platters sealed inside a container. The container includes the motor for rotating the disks. It also contains an access arm and read-write heads for writing data to and reading data from the disks. Like a floppy-disk drive, an internal hard-disk drive has a seek operation and a search operation for reading and writing data in tracks and sectors. From the outside of a microcomputer, an internal hard disk looks like part of a front panel on the system cabinet. Typically, inside are three 3½-inch metallic platters with access arms that move back and forth. (See Figure 7-6.)

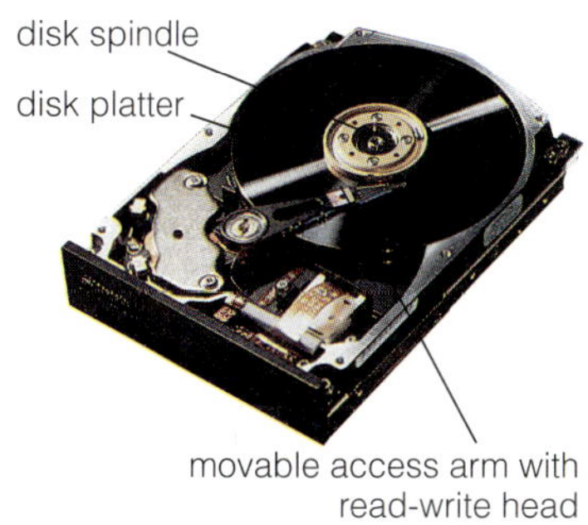

FIGURE 7-6
Inside of a hard-disk drive.

Internal hard disks have two advantages over floppy disks: capacity and speed. A hard disk can hold many times the information of a similar size floppy disk. A 2-gigabyte hard disk, for instance, can hold as much information as 1390 of the 3½-inch double-sided, high-density floppy disks. Moreover, access is faster: a hard disk spins 10 times faster than a floppy disk. For these reasons, almost all of today's powerful applications are designed to be stored and run from an internal hard disk. Adequate capacity or size of a microcomputer's internal hard disk is essential.

Hard-Disk Cartridges

The disadvantage of hard disks is that they have only a fixed amount of storage and cannot be easily removed. **Hard-disk cartridges** have the advantage of being as easy to remove as a cassette from a videocassette recorder. (See Figure 7-7.) They can give microcomputer systems fast access to very large quantities of data. The amount of storage available is limited only by the number of cartridges. For instance, the Omega Corporation has a removable hard-disk cartridge called the Jaz Drive that has a storage capacity of 1 gigabyte. They also have a widely used

FIGURE 7-7
Removable hard-disk cartridge.

floppy disk cartridge called the Zip Drive that has a 100-megabyte capacity. Thus, while a regular hard-disk system has a fixed storage capacity, a removable hard-disk cartridge system is unlimited—you can just buy more removable cartridges.

FIGURE 7-8
Hard-disk packs.

Hard-Disk Packs

Microcomputers that are connected to other microcomputers, minicomputers, or mainframes often have access to external hard-disk packs. (See Figure 7-8.) Microcomputer hard-disk drives typically have three disk platters. **Hard-disk packs** consist of several platters aligned one above the other. They resemble a stack of phonograph records. The difference is that there is space between the disks to allow the access arms to move in and out. (See Figure 7-9.) Each access arm has two read-write heads. One reads the disk surface above it; the other reads the disk surface below it. A disk pack with 11 disks provides 20 recording surfaces. This is because the top and bottom outside surfaces of the pack are not used.

All the access arms move in and out together. However, only one of the read-write heads is activated at a given moment. **Access time** is the time between the computer's request for data from secondary storage and the completion of the data transfer. Access time for most disk drives is under 25 milliseconds.

You may well use your microcomputer to gain access to information over a telephone or other communications line. (We show this in the next chapter.) Such information is apt to be stored on disk packs. One large information service (named Dialog), for example, has over 300 databases. These databases cover all areas of science, technology, business, medicine, social science, current affairs, and humanities. All of these are available through a telephone link with your desktop computer. There are more than 100 million items of information, including references to books, patents, directories, journals, and newspaper articles. Such an information resource may be of great value to you in your work.

FIGURE 7-9
How a disk pack works.

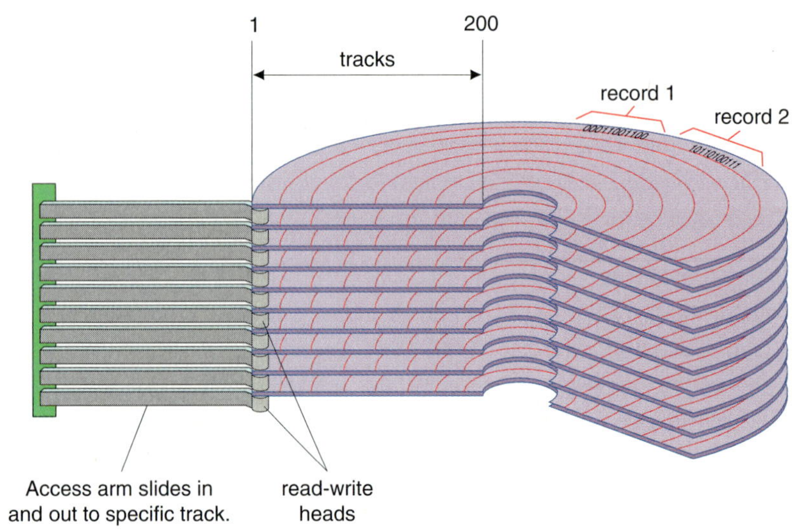

Performance Enhancements

Three ways to improve the performance of hard disks are disk caching, data compression, and redundant arrays of inexpensive disks.

Disk caching improves hard-disk performance by anticipating data needs. It requires a combination of hardware and software. During idle processing time, frequently used data is read from the hard disk into memory (cache). When needed, the data is then accessed directly from memory. The transfer rate from memory is much faster than from hard disk. As a result, overall system performance is often increased by as much as 30 percent.

Data compression and **decompression** increase storage capacity by reducing the amount of space required to store data and programs. In data compression, entering data is scanned for ways to reduce the amount of required storage. One way is to search for repeating patterns. The repeating patterns are replaced with a token, leaving enough so that the original can be rebuilt or decompressed. Data compression and decompression can be accomplished through the use of special software and/or hardware. An example is add-on boards inserted into the computer's expansion slots. Many times the software is included in the operating system. Also available are specialized programs. (See Figure 7-10.)

Data compression can regain or free as much as 80 percent of a microcomputer's hard disk. The major tradeoff is performance: A great deal of compression may slow down processing.

Redundant arrays of inexpensive disks (RAIDs) improve performance by expanding external storage. Groups of inexpensive hard-disk drives are related or grouped together using networks and special software. These grouped disks are treated as a single large-capacity hard disk. They can outperform single disks of comparable capacities.

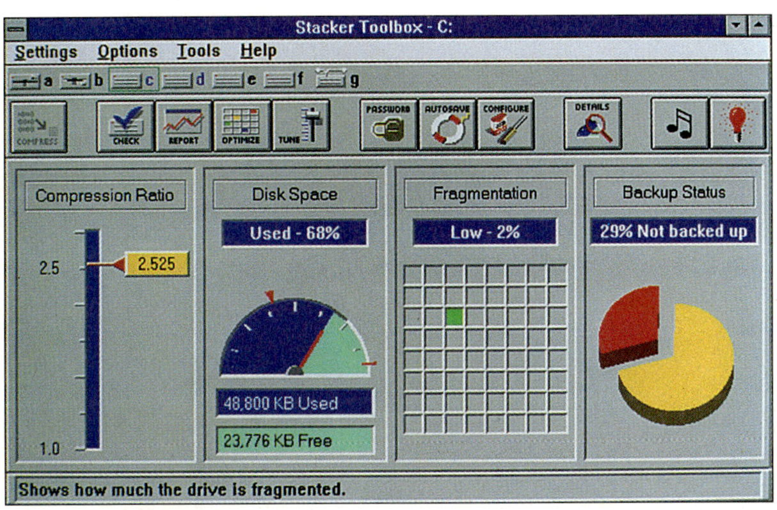

FIGURE 7-10
Data compression software (Stacker version 4.0).

Optical Disks

There are four kinds of optical disks: CD-ROM, CD-R, erasable, and DVD.

An **optical disk** can hold 4.7 gigabytes of data—the equivalent of hundreds of floppy disks. Moreover, an optical disk makes an immense amount of information available on a microcomputer. Optical disks are having a great impact on storage technology today, but we are probably only beginning to see their effects.

In optical-disk technology, a laser beam alters the surface of a plastic or metallic disk to represent data. To read the data, a laser scans these areas and sends the data to a computer chip for conversion. Optical disks are made in diameters of 3½, 4¾, 5¼, 8, 12, and 14 inches.

There are four kinds of optical disks available: *CD-ROM, CD-R, erasable optical disks,* and *DVD.*

CD-ROM

CD-ROM stands for *compact disk–read-only memory.* Unlike floppy and hard disks, which use magnetic charges to represent 1s and 0s, optical disks use reflected light. On a CD-ROM disk, 1s and 0s are represented by flat areas and bumpy areas (called "pits") on its bottom surface. The CD-ROM disk is read by a laser that pro-

FIGURE 7-11
How a CD-ROM works.

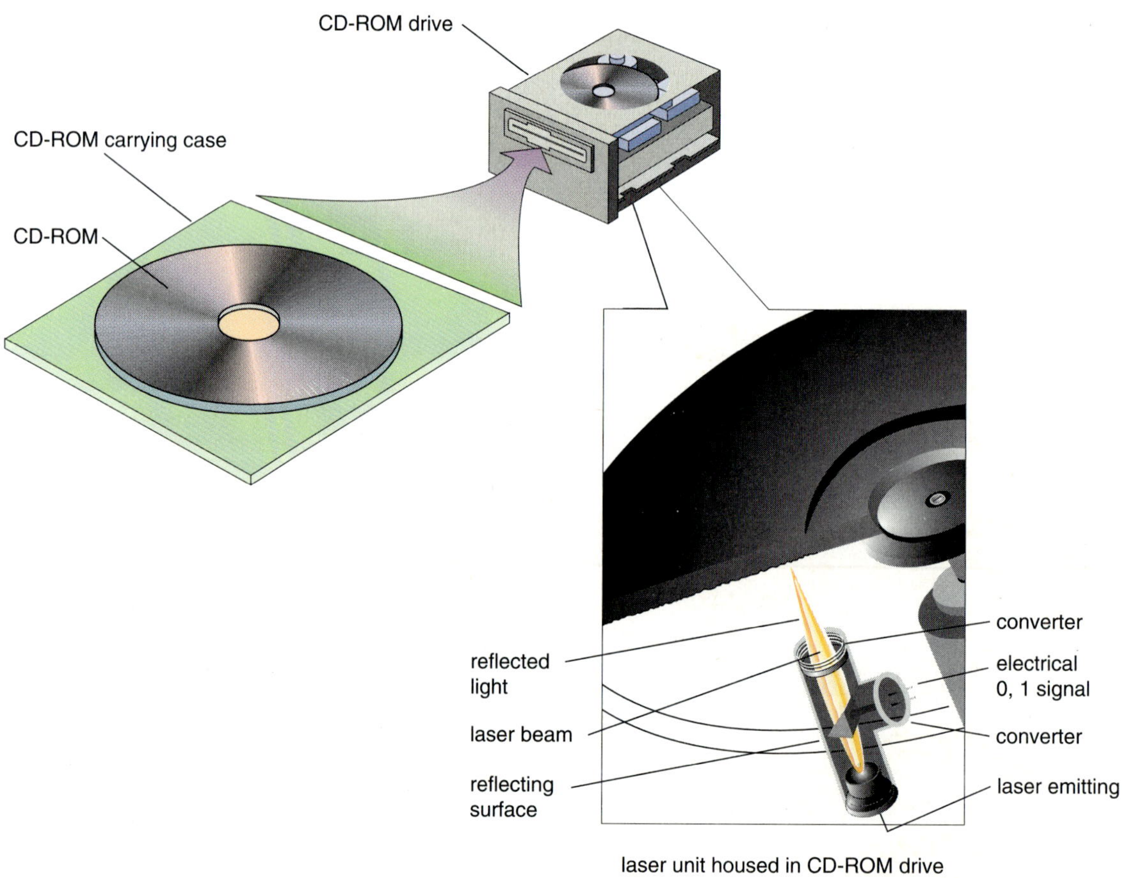

jects a tiny beam of light on these areas. The amount of reflected light determines whether the area represents a 1 or a 0. (See Figure 7-11.)

Like a commercial CD found in music stores, a CD-ROM is a "read-only" disk. **Read-only** means it cannot be written on or erased by the user. Thus, you as a user have access only to the data imprinted by the publisher. CD-ROM disks are used to distribute large databases and references. An example is the *Grolier Multimedia Encyclopedia,* a CD-ROM containing the *Academic American Encyclopedia,* with over 9 million words and 1500 pictures. (See Figure 7-12 for other CD-ROM titles.)

CD-ROMS are also used to distribute large software application packages. For example, Microsoft Office 97 is available on a single CD-ROM or on 38 floppy disks. One advantage of the CD-ROM version is that installation from one CD-ROM to the internal hard disk is much faster and easier.

A single CD-ROM disk can store 650 megabytes of data. That is equivalent to 451 floppy disks. With that much information on a single disk, the time to retrieve or access the information is very important. An important characteristic of CD-ROM drives is their access rate. (See Figure 7-13.)

CD-R

CD-R stands for *CD-Recordable*. Also known as **WORM** or *write once, read many,* CD-R disks can be written to once. After that they can be read many times

REFERENCE CD-ROMS

TITLE	DESCRIPTION
Grolier Multimedia Encyclopedia	presents information on a wide variety of topics, contains links to related Web sites, includes a powerful browsing tool called Knowledge Tree, and outlines topical coverage to efficiently locate specific information
Microsoft Encarta Encyclopedia	presents information on a wide variety of topics, provides links to related Web sites including its own site which provides monthly updates, incudes special tools called Find Wizard and Pinpointer to make searching for information easy
Microsoft Cinemania	provides detailed reviews of recent films, trivia questions, biographies of featured artists, and video celebrity tours all linked to its own Web site which provides additional related information and periodic updates
Complete Bible and Reference Guide	presents the Bible's text (displayed on scrolled parchment), sound, maps, tours, and biblical paintings to provide added depth and dimension, as well as Barron's Notes to the King James text and the capability for users to record their own notes and bookmarks

FIGURE 7-12
Leading CD-ROM reference materials.

FIGURE 7-13
Access speeds for CD-ROM drives.

CD-ROM DRIVES

TYPE	DESCRIPTION
Quad-speed	Introduced in 1994; transfer rate of 600 KB per second; marginally acceptable for full-motion video
Six-speed	Introduced in 1995; transfer rate of 900 KB per second; acceptable full-motion video
Eight-speed	Introduced in 1996; transfer rate of 1.2 MB per second; good full-motion video
Ten-speed	Also introduced in 1996; transfer rate of 1.5 MB per second; excellent full-motion video
Twelve-speed	Recently introduced along with sixteen-speed

without deterioration and cannot be written on or erased. A typical 5¼-inch CD-R disk can store between 600 and 650 megabytes of data.

Because the data cannot be erased, CD-R disks are ideal for use as archives to permanently store large amounts of important information. CD changers or CD Jukeboxes (see Figure 7-14) are used to give quick access to several CDs, allowing billions of bytes of data to be easily retrieved.

FIGURE 7-14
CD Jukebox.

Erasable Optical Disks

Erasable optical disks, also known as **rewriteable optical disks,** are like CD-Rs except that they can be written to many times. That is, a disk that has been written on can be erased and used over and over again. There are two basic types:

- **CD-RW** stands for *compact disk rewriteable.* Recently introduced, these disks are very similar to other CD-R disks except that the disk surface is not permanently altered when data is recorded. A typical 5¼-inch CD-RW disk can store between 600 and 650 megabytes of data.
- **MO** stands for *magnetic optical.* These disks use both magnetic and optical technologies to store data. A typical 5¼-inch MO disk can store between 600 megabytes and 1 gigabyte of data.

OPTICAL DISKS

DESCRIPTION	CAPACITY
CD-ROM	650 MB
CD-R	600–650 MB
Erasable	600–1000 MB
DVD	4.7 GB

FIGURE 7-15
Typical capacities for optical disks.

DVD

DVD stands for *digital versatile disk.* DVD disks and disk drives are very similar to CD-ROMs except that more data can be packed into the same amount of space. Recently introduced, DVD-ROM disks have a capacity of 4.7 gigabytes, or seven times more than CD-ROMs. They are being used for a variety of high-capacity needs such as recording and playing full-length motion pictures, advanced multimedia games, and interactive encyclopedias.

While CD-ROMs are the most widely used optical storage today, most observers are firmly convinced that DVD disks are the future. By the year 2000, DVD-R and DVD-RW (also known as DVD-RAM) disks will be available, and DVD storage capacity will increase to 17 gigabytes—enough storage for an 8-hour motion picture or an entire library of encyclopedias.

For a summary of optical disk storage capacities, see Figure 7-15.

Magnetic Tape

Magnetic tape streamers and magnetic tape reels are used primarily for backup purposes.

We mentioned the alarming consequences that can happen if a hard disk suffers a head crash. You will lose some or all of your data or programs. Of course, you can always make copies of your hard-disk files on floppy disks. However, this can be time-consuming and may require many floppy disks. Here is where magnetic tape storage becomes important. Magnetic tape falls into the category of sequential access storage and is therefore slower than direct access storage. However, it is an effective way of making a *backup,* or duplicate, copy of your programs and data.

There are two forms of tape storage. These are *magnetic tape streamers,* for use with microcomputers, and *magnetic tape reels,* for use with minicomputers and mainframes.

Magnetic Tape Streamers

Many microcomputer users with hard disks use a device called a **magnetic tape streamer** or a **backup tape cartridge unit.** (See Figure 7-16.) This enables you to duplicate or make a backup of the data on your hard disk onto a tape cartridge. Typical capacities of such tape cartridges are 120 megabytes to 5 gigabytes. Advanced forms of backup technology known as **digital audiotape (DAT) drives,** which use 2-inch by 3-inch cassettes, store 4 gigabytes or more. If your internal hard disk fails, you can have it repaired (or get another hard disk). You can restore all your lost data and programs in a matter of minutes from the backup tapes.

FIGURE 7-16
Backup software copying files to magnetic tape.

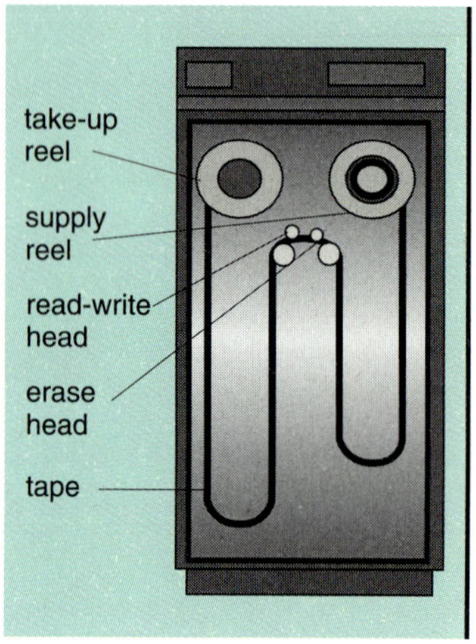

FIGURE 7-17
Data is recorded on magnetic tape on tape reels.

Magnetic Tape Reels

The cassette tapes you get for an audiotape recorder are only about 200 feet long. They record 200 characters to the inch. A reel of magnetic tape used with minicomputer and mainframe systems, by contrast, is ½-inch wide and ½-mile long. It stores 1600 to 6400 characters to the inch. Such tapes are run on **magnetic tape drives** or **magnetic tape units.** (See Figure 7-17.) You may never actually see these devices yourself. However, as a microcomputer user sharing storage devices with others, you may have access to them through a minicomputer or mainframe.

For the typical microcomputer user, the four storage options—floppy disk, hard disk, optical disk, and magnetic tape—are complementary, not competing. Almost all microcomputers today have at least one floppy-disk drive and one hard-disk drive. For those users who need access to vast amounts of data, an optical drive is added. Lastly, for those who need to back up lots of data and programs, magnetic tape drives are added.

For a summary comparison of the four types of secondary storage, see Figure 7-18.

FIGURE 7-18
Summary of storage options.

SECONDARY STORAGE

TYPE	ADVANTAGE	DISADVANTAGE	TYPICAL USE	COST/MEGABYTE
Floppy disk	Inexpensive, direct access, removable	Low capacity, slow access	Store files for word processors and spreadsheets	$1.00
Hard disk	Fast, direct access	Limited capacity	Store programs and data	$.40 to $.80
CD-ROM	High capacity, direct access	Slow access	Reference material	$.04 to $1.00
Magnetic tape	High capacity	Slow sequential data access	Backup programs and data	$.01 to $.40

A Look at the Future

Near-field recording devices use lasers and solid immersion lens. Holographic storage systems use three-dimensional holograms.

Have you ever wondered why we need such large capacity secondary storage devices? As we mentioned earlier, DVD-RW disks with a 17 gigabyte capacity are expected by the year 2000. When will this trend of increasing capacity end? Probably not in the near future.

As we use more graphical interfaces like Windows 98, store images from the Web, and work with more advanced applications like multimedia and virtual reality, the demand for larger and faster secondary storage devices will continue to grow. Fortunately, several new technologies promise to meet this demand.

One is called near-field recording. These devices use a revolutionary new drive head that utilizes lasers and a special focusing lens called a solid immersion lens. This lens precisely directs the laser's path, thereby allowing more information to be stored on a disk. Near-field recording devices are expected to cost the same as today's hard disk systems yet provide ten times more storage capacity.

A bit further on the horizon is holographic storage. Holograms, as you may know, are those shimmering, three-dimensional images often seen on credit cards. Holographic systems can store data equivalent to thousands of books inside a container the size of a sugar cube.

When will we be able to purchase systems using these new technologies? Prototypes have been created and we can expect to see near-field recording devices and holographic systems in the next few years.

KEY TERMS

access arm (140)
access time (144)
backup tape cartridge unit (148)
CD-R (147)
CD-ROM (146)
CD-RW (148)
data compression (145)
data decompression (145)
digital audiotape (DAT) drive (149)
direct access storage (139)
disk (140)
disk caching (145)
diskette (140)
drive gate (140)
DVD (148)
erasable optical disk (148)
flexible disk (140)
floppy (140)
floppy disk (140)
hard-disk cartridge (143)
hard-disk pack (144)
head crash (143)
internal hard disk (143)
jacket (141)
magnetic tape drive (150)
magnetic tape streamer (149)
magnetic tape unit (150)
MO (magnetic optical) disk (148)
nonvolatile storage (139)
optical disk (146)
read-only (147)
read-write head (140)
redundant arrays of inexpensive disks (RAIDs) (145)
rewriteable optical disk (148)
search (140)
sector (141)
seek (140)
sequential access storage (138)
track (141)
volatile storage (139)
WORM (147)
write-protect notch (141)

REVIEW QUESTIONS

True/False

1. Secondary storage holds information within the CPU.
2. Floppy disks are also known as flexible disks and as floppies.
3. Sectors are wedge-shaped sections on a disk.
4. CD-R disks can be erased and used over and over again.
5. Laser beams are used to record data on optical disks.

Multiple Choice

1. Which of the following is exclusively a sequential access storage media?
   a. floppy disk
   b. hard disk
   c. magnetic tape
   d. CD-ROM
   e. WORM
2. On a floppy-disk drive, data signals are transferred to the computer through:
   a. read-write heads
   b. access arms
   c. drive gate
   d. drive A
   e. sectors
3. The disk with the greatest capacity:
   a. 5¼-inch double-sided, high-density
   b. 3½-inch double-sided, double-density
   c. 3½-inch double-sided, high-density
   d. CD-ROM
   e. DVD-ROM
4. The hard-disk type that has several platters aligned one above the other:
   a. internal hard disk
   b. hard-disk pack
   c. floppy-disk array
   d. hard-disk cartridge
   e. disk cache
5. The method of improving hard-disk performance by anticipating data needs is:
   a. disk compression
   b. disk caching
   c. disk decompression
   d. RAIDs
   e. virtual processing

Fill in the Blank

1. A __________ disk is read by a laser projecting a beam of light.
2. Data is recorded on a disk in rings called __________.
3. Internal hard disks have two advantages over floppy disks: __________ and speed.
4. Data __________ time measures how long it takes to move data from the hard-disk track to memory.
5. The two forms of tape storage are magnetic tape streamers and magnetic tape __________.

Open Ended

1. Explain the difference between direct access storage and sequential access storage. Which is more apt to be identified with magnetic disk and which with magnetic tape?
2. What are the four kinds of secondary storage? What are their relative advantages and disadvantages?
3. State the four primary rules for taking care of floppy disks.
4. What is so disastrous about a head crash?
5. What are the four types of optical disk drives? Discuss their differences and similarities.

DISCUSSION QUESTIONS AND PROJECTS

1. *Looking for the right CD-ROM:* Perhaps you have had the difficulty of dealing with competing standards of media for something you want. Was a film you wanted to see available on Betamax but not on VHS videotape? Did a musical group have songs available on an LP or tape but not CD? Now you face a similar difficulty in evaluating the new storage medium of CD-ROM, for which competing versions exist. To help resolve the confusion, determine:
   a. How the CD-ROMs used for computer storage differ from those used as adjuncts to television sets, such as the CD-1 and CDTV.
   b. How the CD-ROMs normally associated with desktop computers differ from those used in the small electronic "book" players such as the Data Diskman put out by Sony.
   c. How the CD-ROMs available for Macintosh differ from those available for IBM and IBM-compatible microcomputers.
2. *Obtaining a CD-ROM drive:* Suppose you have a microcomputer system that does not have a CD-ROM drive, and you would like to have one. You have three options: (1) purchase an external CD-ROM drive that connects to one of the ports in the back of your system unit; (2) purchase and install an internal CD-ROM directly into your system unit; or (3) purchase a new microcomputer system that has a CD-ROM drive.

   Research each of the three options and prepare a set of written guidelines that could be used to make the best choice.

on the web

Exercises and Explorations

DVD Entertainment Systems

The DVD home entertainment system is more than just a new entertainment standard. It is also a new standard for CD-ROMs. To learn more about DVD home entertainment systems, visit our Web site at http://www.magpie.org/essentials/chapter-7 to link to a site that specializes in DVD. Once at the site, be sure to check out the FAQ (Frequently Asked Questions) page. Print out the Web page that you find most informative. Write a paragraph addressing the following questions: What is DVD? How does DVD-Video compare to Laserdisc?

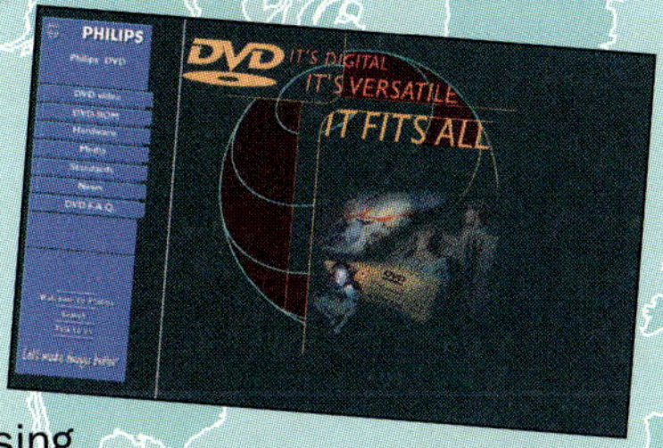

JAZ Drives

The ever-increasing demands on hard disk space has led to Iomega's innovations in high-capacity removable disk drives. For example, the Jaz drive can store 1 gigabyte on a single disk. To learn more about these drives, visit our Web site at http://www.magpie.org/essentials/chapter-7 to link to Iomega's Web site. Once connected to that site, check out the available drives. Choose a drive that would be helpful to you in your career and print out its specifications. Write a paragraph discussing how this drive would help you and how it is superior to the other drives available.

Advances in Storage Technology

Secondary storage technology is changing fast. One way to keep informed on the latest innovations is to search the many magazines that publish articles on the Web. Visit the Yahoo site at http://www.yahoo.com and look under the subcategory of "Computers and Internet: Magazines: Personal Computers: PC Compatibles." Find an article of interest, print it out, and write a brief paragraph summarizing the article.

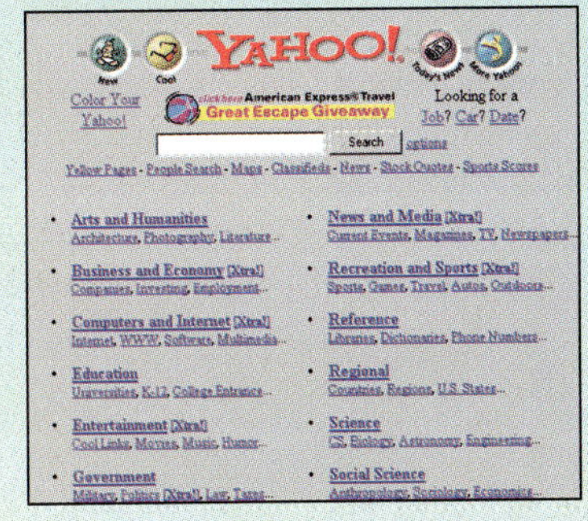

Buying a Car?

Looking for a new or used car? Interested in the Kelly blue book trade-in price on your current car? Visit our Web site at http://www.magpie.org/essentials/chapter-7 to link to a site that will answer many of your car-buying questions. Once at the site, find the best deal possible on a new or used car of your choice. Print out the information and write a brief paragraph on how you found it.

VISUAL SUMMARY

Secondary Storage

Primary storage in microcomputers is **volatile;** some things disappear when the power is turned off. Secondary storage is **nonvolatile;** it stores data and programs even after the power is turned off.

SECONDARY STORAGE

TYPE	ADVANTAGE	DISADVANTAGE	TYPICAL USE	COST/MEGABYTE
Floppy disk	Inexpensive, direct access, removable	Low capacity, slow access	Store files for word processors and spreadsheets	$1.00
Hard disk	Fast, direct access	Limited capacity	Store programs and data	$.40 to $.80
CD-ROM	High capacity, direct access	Slow access	Reference material	$.04 to $1.00
Magnetic tape	High capacity	Slow sequential data access	Backup programs and data	$.01 to $.40

FLOPPY DISK

Floppy disks (disks, diskettes) are circular plastic disks. Two principal types are 3½-inch and 5¼-inch.

- 3½-inch 2HD disks have 1.44 megabyte capacity.
- 5¼-inch 2HD disks have 1.2 megabyte capacity.

The Disk Drive

- A floppy disk is inserted through a **drive gate** into a *disk drive,* which has an **access arm** equipped with **read-write heads** that move on the disk (**seek** operation), which is rotated to the proper position (**search** operation).
- The read-write head *reads* (obtains) data or programs from the disk and sends it to the CPU or *writes* (transfers) data from the CPU to the disk.

Parts of Floppy Disk

- Data is recorded on a disk's **tracks** (rings) and **sectors** (sections). *Formatting (initializing)* is a process to insert tracks and sectors onto a disk.
- A disk is protected by the **jacket** (liner), paper envelope, and **write-protect notch** (covered by tab or shutter).

HARD DISK

Hard Disk

A **hard disk** is an enclosed disk drive that contains one or more metallic disks. Enclosing the disk in a sealed container prevents material entering that causes a **head crash.** Hard disks come in three forms:

- An **internal hard disk** has one or more metallic platters sealed inside a container. Hard disks have far more capacity than a floppy disks do.
- **Hard-disk cartridges** can be removed when they are filled or transported.
- Mini- and mainframe computers use **hard-disk packs,** which are hard disks consisting of several platters in a stack.

Performance Enhancements

- **Disk caching**—anticipates data needs by reading from hard disk to memory to reduce transfer rate of needed data.
- **Data compression (decompression)**—reduces amount of space required to store data and programs.
- **Redundant arrays of inexpensive disks (RAIDs)**—expands external storage by networking hard disks and grouping them so that they may be treated as a single large-capacity hard disk.

CD-ROM DRIVES

TYPE	FUNCTION
Quad-speed	Introduced in 1994; transfer rate of 600 KB per second; marginally acceptable for full-motion video
Six-speed	Introduced in 1995; transfer rate of 900 KB per second; acceptable full-motion video
Eight-speed	Introduced in 1996; transfer rate of 1.2 MB per second; good full-motion video
Ten-speed	Also introduced in 1996; transfer rate of 1.5 MB per second; excellent full-motion video
Twelve-speed	Recently introduced along with sixteen-speed

OPTICAL DISKS

OPTICAL DISKS

DESCRIPTION	CAPACITY
CD-ROM	650 MB
CD-R	600–650 MB
Erasable	600–1000 MB
DVD	4.7 GB

Optical Disks

An **optical disk** is a metallic disk that uses a laser beam for reading and writing. Four kinds are:

- **CD-ROM** (compact disc–read-only memory)—cannot be written on or erased by user **(read-only).** Used to distribute large databases, reference materials, and software.
- **CD-R** (CD-recordable) or **WORM** (write once, read many)—can be written to one time, after which it cannot be erased by users but can be read many times without deterioration.
- **Erasable optical disks**—can be written on and erased and reused. Two basic types: **CD-RW** (compact disk rewriteable) and **MO** (magnetic optical).
- **DVD** (digital versatile disk)—similar to CDs except greater capacity at 4.7 gigabytes for DVD-ROM. DVD-R and DVD-RW expected by the year 2000.

MAGNETIC TAPE

Magnetic Tape

Magnetic tape storage is mainly used to back up (duplicate) programs and data on disks. Two forms are:

- **Magnetic Tape Streamers (backup tape cartridge units)** consist of tape cartridges used to back up microcomputer hard disks.
- **Magnetic Tape Reels,** used to back up mini- and mainframe computer storage, run on **magnetic drives (magnetic tape units).**

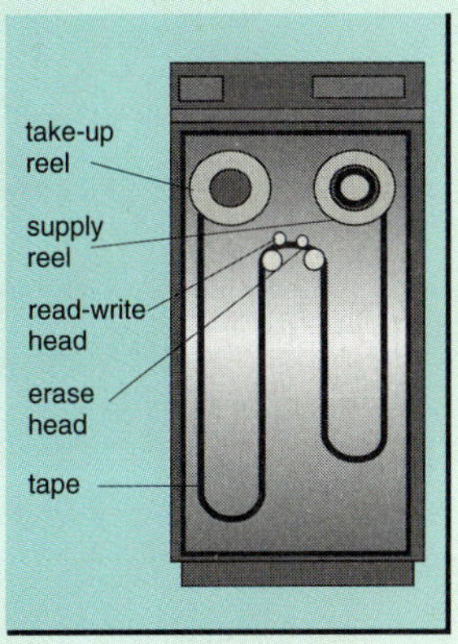

Communications and Connectivity

A familiar instrument—the telephone—has extended our uses for the microcomputer enormously. With the telephone or other kinds of communications equipment, you can connect your microcomputer to the microcomputers of other people, to the Internet, and to other, larger computers located throughout the world. As we've mentioned earlier, this *connectivity* puts incredible power on your desk. The result is increased productivity—for you as an individual and for the groups and organizations of which you are a member. Connectivity has become particularly important in business, where individuals now find themselves connected in networks to other individuals and departments.

COMPETENCIES

After you have read this chapter, you should be able to:

1. **Describe available communications resources and online services.**
2. **Describe the National Information Highway, the Internet, and the most common Internet applications.**
3. **Describe communications hardware, such as types of modems.**
4. **Describe the cable and air communications channels—telephone, coaxial, and fiber-optic cables; microwave relays; and satellites.**
5. **Discuss bandwidth, serial versus parallel transmission, direction of flow, modes of transmission, and protocols.**
6. **Explain network architecture—configurations and strategies.**
7. **Describe local area, metropolitan area, and wide area networks.**

8

Imagine: You are a real estate salesperson, and the telephone in your car rings. It is a client who is on the phone in his car across town. He asks you about a certain property, and you agree to meet him there. After you go back to look at the property, you connect your laptop computer to your car phone. You then dial the multiple listing service and get information on the property. This is an example of the use of communications to expand computer capabilities.

In Chapter 2, you learned about communications software. In this chapter, you will learn about communications systems. **Data communications systems** are the electronic systems that transmit data over communications lines from one location to another. You might use data communications through your microcomputer to send information to a friend using another computer. You might work for an organization whose computer system is spread throughout a building, or even throughout the country or world. That is, all the parts—input and output units, processor, and storage devices—are in different places and linked by communications. Or you might use *telecommunications* lines—telephone lines—to tap into information located in an outside data bank. You could then transmit it to your microcomputer for your own reworking and analysis.

Data communications is now considered essential in business. As we will see, an important part of communications is the *network,* a system connecting two or more computers. A popular form of network is the *local area network (LAN).* In a LAN, computers are connected together within a limited area, such as within the same building. In one survey, over 80 percent responded that there was a local area network within their company or organization. There are many occasions when you and coworkers need a network to gain access to one another's information. Such information may be on sales, customers, prices, schedules, or products. The list is nearly endless.

Communications and Connectivity

With communications capability, microcomputer users can transmit and receive data and gain access to electronic information resources.

You may have a desktop microcomputer next to a telephone. You may (or may someday) have a laptop microcomputer and a cellular phone in your car. Or you may have a microcomputer that is directly connected to other computers without telephone lines at all. Whatever the case, communications systems present many opportunities for transmitting and receiving information, giving you access to many resources. This brings up the important revolution represented by this chapter, that of connectivity.

Connectivity means you can connect your microcomputer by telephone or other telecommunications links to other computers and information sources almost anywhere. With this connection, you are linked to the world of larger computers. This includes minicomputers and mainframes and their large storage devices, such as disk packs, and their enormous volumes of information. Thus, computer competence becomes a matter of knowing not only about microcomputers. You should also know something about larger computer systems and their information resources.

Let us consider the options that connectivity makes available to you. These include *fax machines, electronic bulletin boards, electronic mail, voice-messaging systems, shared resources,* and *online services.* (See Figure 8-1.)

FIGURE 8-1
Connectivity options.

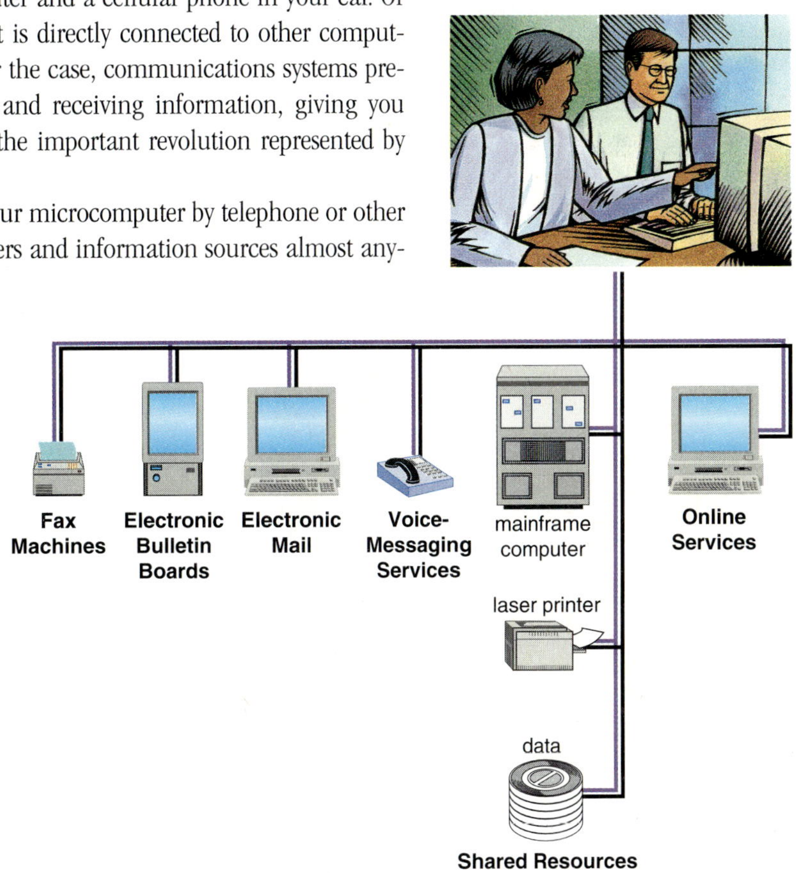

Fax Machines

Fax machines—facsimile transmission machines—have become essential machines in almost all offices. (See Figure 8-2.) As we mentioned earlier, these devices scan the image of a document. They convert the image to signals that can be sent over a telephone line to a receiving machine. This machine prints the image out on paper. Microcomputers, using fax/modem circuit boards, can be used to send and receive fax messages.

FIGURE 8-2
A fax machine.

Sending a document by fax is certainly faster—it arrives immediately—than any delivery service. It also is often cheaper than overnight delivery, unless you're sending more than 50 pages of a document. Almost every fax machine can exchange messages with every other fax machine. All you need is the receiving machine's phone number. The fax machine can transmit photographs and other artwork, as well as text in various typefaces.

If you are in the business of meeting deadlines—as most people are—a fax machine can be invaluable. Construction engineers can get cost estimates to major contractors. Lawyers can get contracts to other lawyers. Advertising people can get prospective ad layouts to their clients. Just as important, because people often respond better to pictures than to text, fax can get a picture to them quickly.

Electronic Bulletin Board Systems

Electronic bulletin board systems (BBS) are like public bulletin boards. You can post and read messages. These messages can be personal or intended for a group. The difference is that all the messages are electronic, and you need a microcomputer, telephone connection, and the electronic bulletin board's telephone number. The board's number connects you to a computer that receives messages, posts messages, and handles the details of administering the BBS. Such bulletin boards have been popular with microcomputer hobbyists and enthusiasts for many years. They are rapidly gaining favor with other people, too.

Bulletin boards exist for almost any subject. Many are concerned with new developments and problems related to particular brands of microcomputers. Others have to do with hobbies, such as rock music, science fiction, or genealogy. Still others serve special interests, such as political causes, or professional groups, such as lawyers. Finally, some companies offer bulletin boards as a means by which customers can get advice from other customers. They can also get advice from the company itself regarding a particular service or product. Finally, some companies use bulletin boards to communicate with employees working at home.

Electronic Mail

Also called **e-mail, electronic mail** resembles bulletin boards. (See Figure 8-3.) Often it uses a special communications line rather than a telephone line. In addition, electronic mail offers confidentiality. A **user name** and **password**—special number or letter sequences that limit access—are required to get into the "mailbox." The mailbox is simply a file stored on a computer system. Passwords

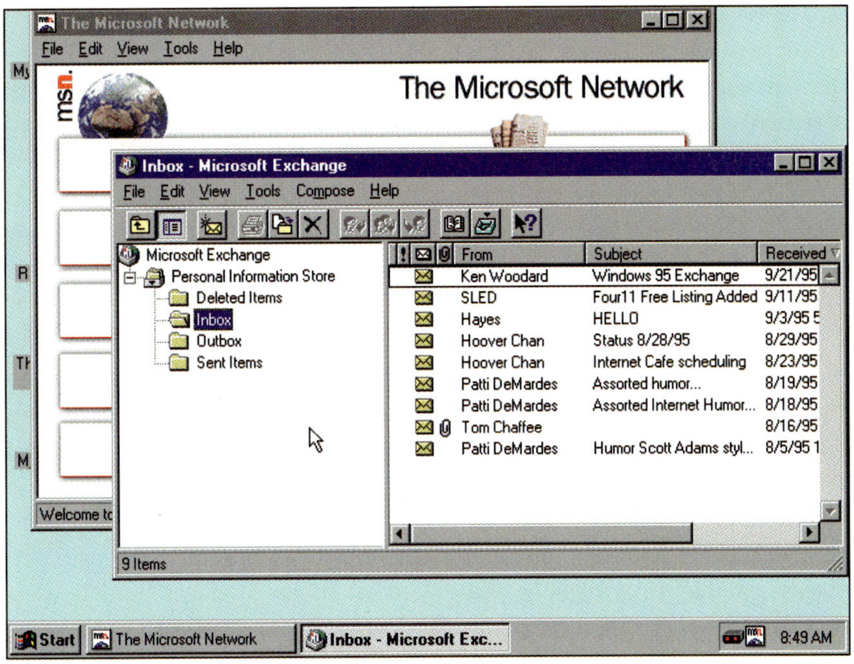

FIGURE 8-3

Microsoft Network's In-box.

are not limited to electronic mail. They are widely used to control access and use of restricted data and resources.

To send an electronic message, you dial the special number, specify the user name, password, and mailbox number, and type the message. You can also put the same message in several mailboxes at the same time. To access your own mailbox, dial the number of the e-mail system and type in your user name and password. You can look through the list of file names and transmission times of the messages. You then transfer to your own computer the messages you want to keep.

Electronic mail is used within companies to help employees exchange memos, set up meetings, and the like. It may also be used between companies. Sometimes outside electronic bulletin board services are used for these business purposes. We will further discuss electronic mail in the Guide to the Internet.

Voice-Messaging Systems

Voice-messaging systems are computer systems linked to telephones that convert the human voice into digital bits. They resemble conventional answering machines and also resemble electronic mail systems. However, they can receive large numbers of incoming calls and route them to the appropriate "voice mailboxes." They can deliver the same message to many people. These systems allow callers to leave "voice mail"—recorded voice messages. They can forward calls to your home or hotel, if you wish. When you check for your messages, you can speed through them or slow them down. You can dictate replies into the phone, and the system will send them out.

Shared Resources

An important aspect of connectivity is that it lets microcomputer users share expensive hardware. We have mentioned many of these: laser printers, chain printers, disk packs, and magnetic tape storage. Only in rare instances would a single microcomputer user need the use of, say, a disk pack. However, several microcomputers linked in a network make this option not only feasible but in many cases even essential. Communications networks also permit microcomputer users to share workstations, minicomputers, and mainframes. This is why we have stressed how important it is to know what these machines are.

Another important aspect of connectivity is the ability to share data. As we saw in Chapter 2, with a microcomputer you can have your own personal database. An example of such a database might be a collection of names and addresses. A *database,* as we mentioned, is a collection of integrated data. By "integrated," we mean the data consists of logically related files and records.

Your personal database might consist of data that only you use. However, it may also be data you share with others. The data might be stored on your microcomputer's hard disk. Or it might be located somewhere else. That is, you might use a shared database, like one a company might provide its employees so they can share information. This could be information stored on disk packs and accessible from the company's mainframe. You could gain access by using your microcomputer linked to your telephone and **downloading** selected data. That is, you could transfer the data from the larger computer to your microcomputer. Then you could process and manipulate the data as you chose. The reverse is **uploading**—transferring from your microcomputer to a mainframe or minicomputer. For example, a salesperson could record daily sales on a portable computer and upload monthly sales data to the company's mainframe.

Online Services

Several businesses offer services specifically for microcomputer users. Four well-known service providers are America Online, CSi, Microsoft Network, and AT&T Interchange. (See Figure 8-4.)

- **Teleshopping:** You dial into a database listing prices and descriptions of products such as appliances and clothes. You then order what you want and charge the purchase to a credit card number. The merchandise is delivered later by a package delivery service.
- **Home banking:** If you arrange it with your bank, you may be able to use your microcomputer to pay some bills. Such bills include those owed to big department stores and utility companies. You can also make loan payments and transfer money between accounts.
- **Investing:** You can get access to current prices of stocks and bonds and enter buy and sell orders.
- **Travel reservations:** Just like a travel agent, you can get information on airline schedules and fares. You can also order tickets, charging the purchase to your credit card.

See Figure 8-5 for a summary of the many connectivity options.

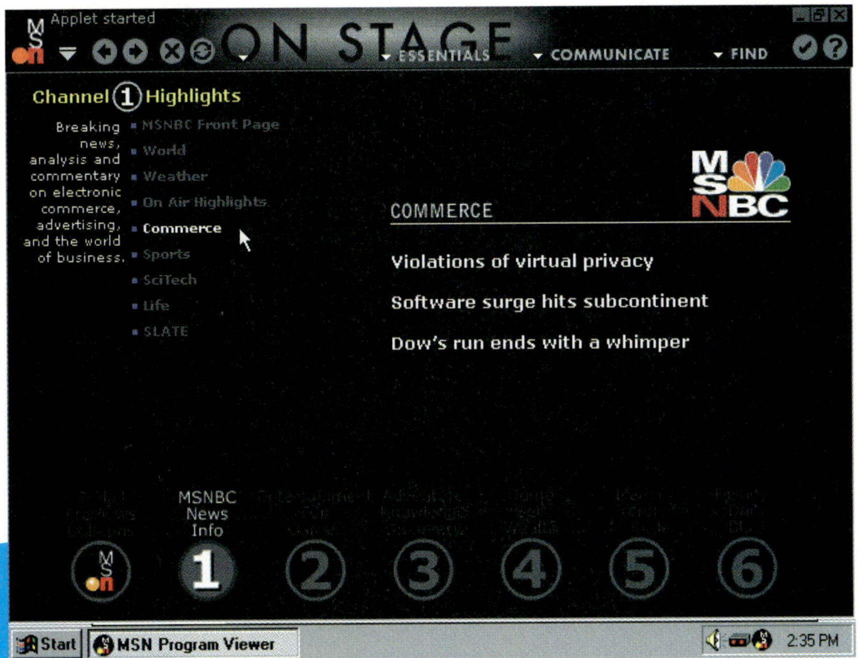

FIGURE 8-4
Microsoft Network's Program Viewer.

CONNECTIVITY OPTIONS

OPTION	FUNCTION
Fax machines	Convert images to signals and send them over telephone lines to receiving fax machines
Electronic bulletin boards	Provide forums on a variety of subjects available to telephone-linked microcomputer users
Electronic mail	Systems resembling bulletin boards but are restricted in access by passwords
Voice–mail systems	Convert a voice message to digital bits and distribute to many locations over telephone lines
Shared resources	Microcomputer users may share expensive hardware, data, and information
Online services	Provide wide range of activities including teleshopping, home banking, investments, and travel reservations services

FIGURE 8-5
Summary of connectivity options.

Information Superhighway and Internet

The Internet is the foundation for future communication networks. Four applications are to transfer electronic mail, participate in public discussions, copy files, and run programs. Two Internet utilities are Gopher and World Wide Web.

The **Information Superhighway** is also known as the **National Information Highway (NIH)** and as the **National Information Infrastructure (NII).** These popular phrases are used to describe the future of communication networks and computers. Legislation proposed and championed by Vice President Gore has laid the foundation for this billion-dollar project. Because of this legislation, Congress is now encouraging private investment, competition, and two-way universal access for the NIH. Such access would make computing resources available to everyone.

Internet

At the forefront of today's NIH is the **Internet.** It is a huge computer network available to nearly everyone who has a microcomputer and a means to connect to it. Once on the Internet it seems as if you are on a single giant computer that branches all over the world. It is an unprecedented resource for information about an infinite number of topics. Also, it connects people as close as the next office and as far as halfway around the world. (See Figure 8-6.)

FIGURE 8-6
Internet connections around the world.

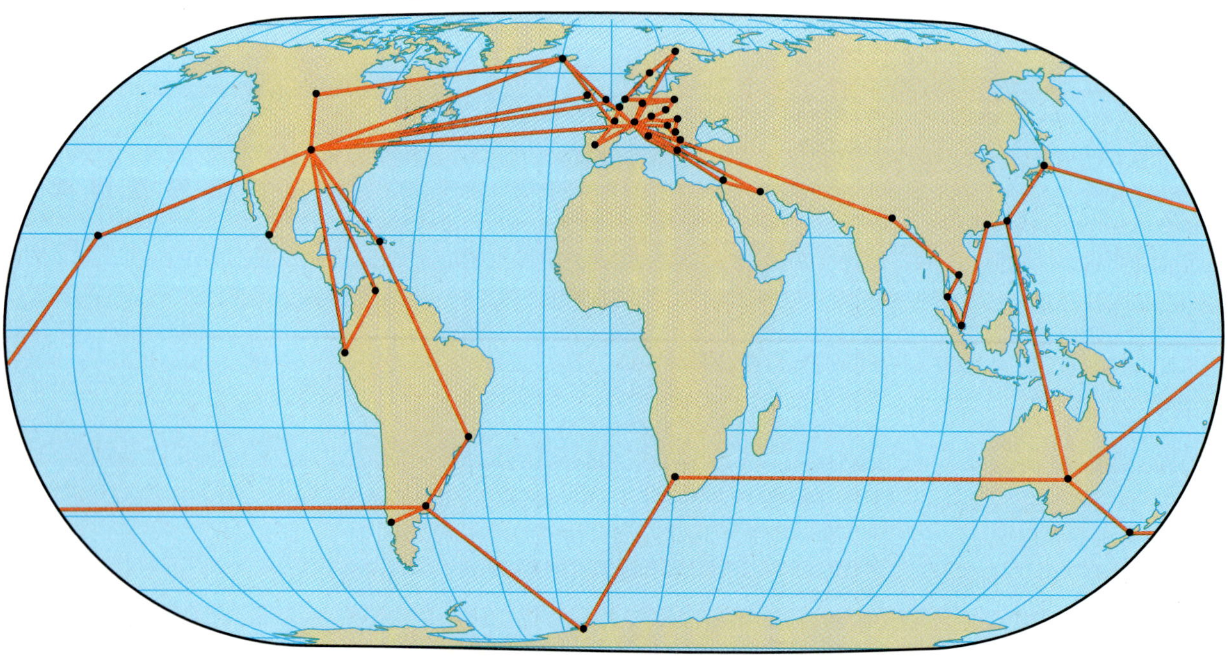

Technically, the Internet is a network connecting thousands of other networks and millions of computers; however, it represents much more. It is today's means to access and share knowledge. It is also tomorrow's foundation for a global community of users.

Applications

There are any number of uses for the Internet. The four most common applications are transferring electronic mail (e-mail), participating in public discussion groups, copying files, and running programs on a remote computer.

- **Electronic mail:** Sending and receiving e-mail is the most popular Internet service. You can send e-mail to anyone in the world if you know his or her e-mail address and have access to the Internet. You can even send and receive e-mail from other commercial service networks like America Online.
- **Public discussion groups:** You can join and listen to discussions and debates on a wide variety of topics on the Internet. This application is a variation of e-mail that uses a system called **UseNet.** UseNet creates an electronic forum of interested people in a particular subject. This forum of people is known as a *newsgroup.* There is an enormous number of newsgroups. They range from general-interest topics such as current events and movie reviews to specialized forums like computer trouble-shooting and Star Trek.
- **Files from remote databases:** The Internet service called **FTP** (file transfer protocol) lets you look at the names of files on other computers on the Internet and copy the ones you want. There are over 1500 FTP sites that have access to millions of publicly available files. These files can be downloaded to your microcomputer. FTP allows access to a large number of databases, from stock market quotations to personal income census data.
- **Programs on remote computers:** The Internet service called **Telnet** makes your computer a terminal for other computers on the Internet. It enables you to run selected programs from other computers. For example, you could access the NASA SPACElink computer. This Telnet link was originally designed for science teachers and is now available to the general public through the Internet. With it, you can learn about NASA's history, read about many exploration plans, view animated clips, and perform other space-related activities. Of course, not all Telnet connections are free. Medline, for example, is a fee-based application containing over 4000 medical journals and publications. You may have access to this application and others through a library or university near you.

See Figure 8-7 for a summary of Internet applications.

INTERNET APPLICATIONS

APPLICATION	DESCRIPTION
Electronic mail	Send and receive e-mail worldwide
Public discussion	Participate in discussions and debates using UseNet newsgroups
File transfer	Locate and copy selected files using FTP
Run programs	Allow terminal access to locate and run programs using Telnet

FIGURE 8-7
Summary of common Internet applications.

Utilities

Fortunately, there are several programs or utilities available to help you locate and use the Internet resources. Two of the most widely used Internet utility programs are Gopher and World Wide Web.

- **Gopher: Gophers** are programs that help individuals on the Internet access other computers on the Internet. There are two types of Gopher programs. One type, called the *Gopher client,* uses Telnet to request access. Once access is granted, the second type—the *Gopher server*—displays a menu system allowing access to the computer's available resources. There are hundreds of public computer systems on the Internet that can be accessed using Gopher software.

- **World Wide Web:** The **World Wide Web** is also known as **WWW** and the **Web.** Like Gopher, the Web helps users search for and retrieve information on the Internet. It uses clients and servers to provide menus to access a computer's resources. However, the Web goes one step further by providing a highly graphical interface to available resources and **hypertext links** that allow users to effortlessly jump from one computer's resources to another computer's resources. This is accomplished using special software called **browsers.** Four well-known browsers are Netscape Navigator, Microsoft Explorer, and NCSA Mosiac.

User Connection

Microcomputers require modems to send and receive messages over telephone lines.

FIGURE 8-8
Analog versus digital signals.

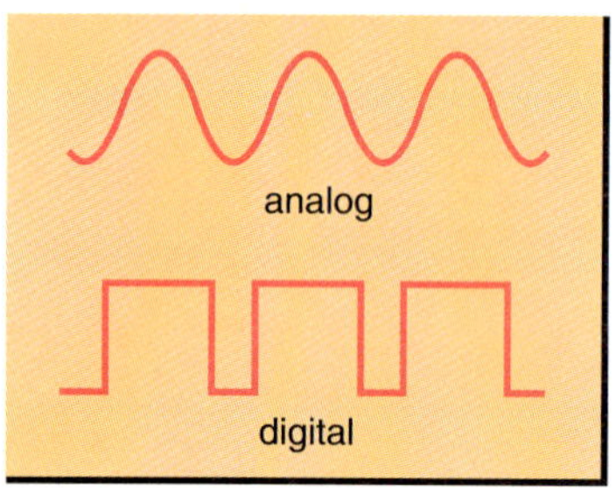

A great deal of computer communications is over telephone lines. However, because the telephone was originally designed for voice transmission, telephones typically send and receive **analog signals.** (See Figure 8-8.) Computers, in contrast, send and receive **digital signals.** These represent the presence or absence of an electronic pulse—the on/off binary signals we mentioned in Chapter 5. To convert the digital signals of your microcomputer to analog and vice versa, you need a modem.

Modems

The word *modem* is short for "*mo*dulator-*dem*odulator." **Modulation** is the name of the process of converting from digital to analog. **Demodulation** is the process of converting from analog to digital. The modem enables digital microcomputers to communicate across analog telephone lines. Both voice communications and data communications can be carried over the same telephone line.

The speed with which modems transmit data varies. Communications speed is often measured in **baud rate.** Baud rate represents the number of changes in the electrical state in the line per second. Unfortunately, this measure can be misleading. At low speeds, baud rate is equivalent to *bits per second (bps).* However, at higher speeds, baud rate is not equal to bits per second. For this reason, most communications professionals prefer to measure modem speed in bits per second.

The most popular microcomputer speeds are 28,800 bps, 36,600 bps, and 57,600 bps. The higher the speed, the faster you can send and receive information—and therefore the lower your line costs. For example, transmitting a 40-page single-spaced report could take nearly a minute at 28,800 bps and less than 30 seconds at 57,600 bps.

Types of Modems

The four types of traditional modems are external, internal, wireless, and fax.

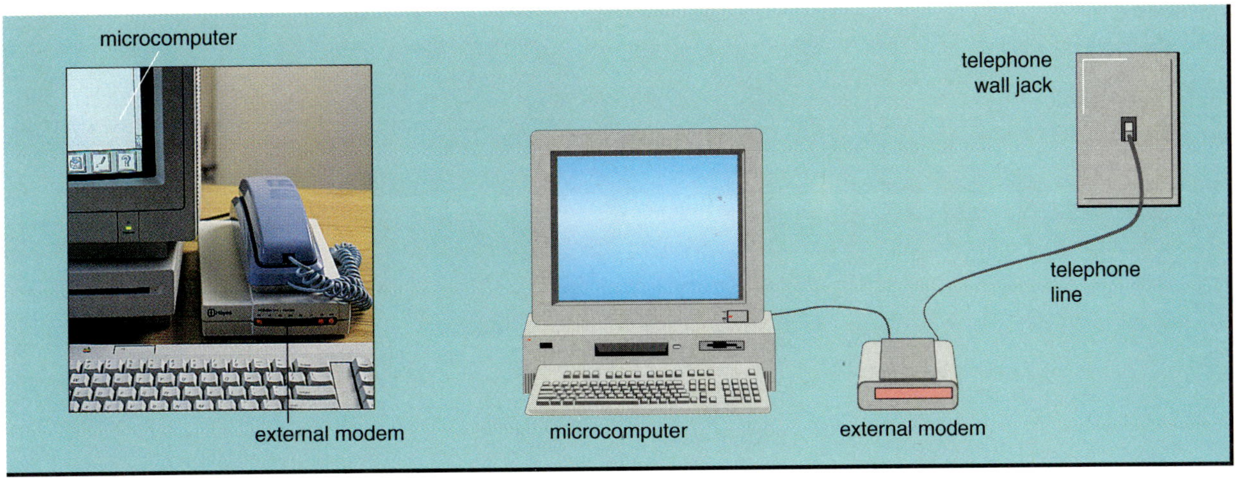

FIGURE 8-9
An external direct-connect modem.

- The **external modem** stands apart from the computer and is connected by a cable to the computer's serial port. Another cable connects the modem to the telephone wall jack. (See Figure 8-9.) Some modems weigh as little as 3 ounces, making them practical for use with portable computers.
- The **internal modem** consists of a plug-in circuit board inside the system unit. A cable directly connects the computer's serial port to the telephone wall jack.
- The **wireless modem** is very similar to the external modem. (See Figure 8-10.) It connects to the computer's serial port. Unlike an external modem, it does not connect to telephone lines. Rather, wireless modems receive through the air. This is a new type of modem using new technology. Although not as fast as the other modems, wireless modems are becoming popular with users of portable computers.
- A **fax modem** is a special modem that allows you to send and receive faxes. With the other modems, signals represent bits—0s and 1s combined to signify letters and numbers typically using an ASCII code. A fax modem uses the signals to represent a graphic image of a page. When a fax is received, the data is stored on the hard disk. The fax can be viewed on the screen or printed out.

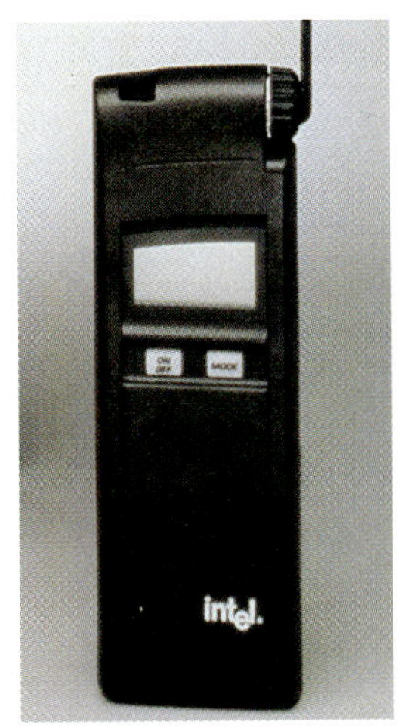

FIGURE 8-10
A wireless modem.

Not all computer communications require a traditional modem to convert from digital to analog and back. For example, **ISDN** adapters and telephone lines allow for all digital communication. ISDN service is available through many telephone companies and supports communication speeds of 128,000 bps. Some cable companies are now supporting all digital communication using coaxial television cables and special devices called **cable modems.** Although just in its infancy, the cable modem, with a communication speed of 27 million bps, is predicted to become widely used within the next five years.

FIGURE 8-11
Comparing cable size and capacity.

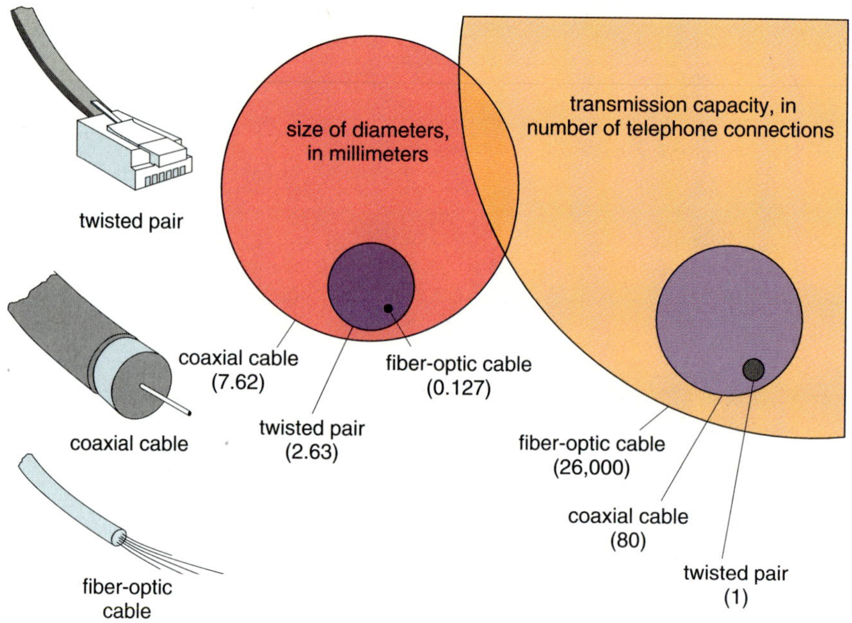

Communications Channels

Data may flow through five kinds of communications channels: telephone lines, coaxial cable, fiber-optic cable, microwave, and satellite.

The two ways of connecting microcomputers with each other and with other equipment are through the cable and through the air. Specifically, five kinds of technology are used to transmit data. These are telephone lines (twisted-pair), coaxial cable, fiber-optic cable, microwave, and satellite. The diameters and transmission capacities of the three kinds of cable are compared in Figure 8-11.

Telephone Lines

Most telephone lines you see strung on poles consist of cables made up of hundreds of copper wires, called **twisted pairs.** A single twisted pair culminates in a wall jack into which you can plug your phone. Telephone lines have been the standard transmission medium for years for both voice and data. However, they are now being phased out by more technically advanced and reliable media.

Coaxial Cable

Coaxial cable, a high-frequency transmission cable, replaces the multiple wires of telephone lines with a single solid-copper core. In terms of number of telephone connections, a coaxial cable has 80 times the transmission capacity of twisted pair. Coaxial cable is often used to link parts of a computer system in one building.

Fiber-Optic Cable

In **fiber-optic cable,** data is transmitted as pulses of light through tubes of glass. In terms of number of telephone connections, fiber-optic cable has 26,000 times the transmission capacity of twisted pair. (Refer to Figure 8-11.) However, it is significantly smaller. Indeed, a fiber-optic tube can be half the diameter of a human hair. Although limited in the distance they can carry information, fiber-optic cables have several advantages. Such cables are immune to electronic interference, which makes them more secure. They are also lighter and less expensive than coaxial cable and are more reliable at transmitting data. They transmit information using beams of light at light speeds instead of pulses of electricity, making them far faster than copper cable. Fiber-optic cable is rapidly replacing twisted-pair telephone lines.

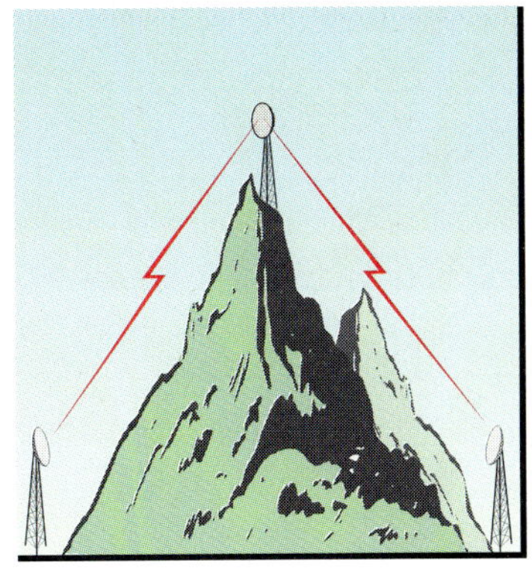

FIGURE 8-12
Microwave transmission.

Microwave

In the case of the microwave communications channel, the medium is not a solid substance but rather the air itself. **Microwaves** are high-frequency radio waves that travel in straight lines through the air. Because the waves cannot bend with the curvature of the earth, they can be transmitted only over short distances. Thus, microwave is a good medium for sending data between buildings in a city or on a large college campus. For longer distances, the waves must be relayed by means of "dishes," or antennas. These can be installed on towers, high buildings, and mountaintops, for example. (See Figure 8-12.)

Satellites

Orbiting about 22,000 miles above the earth, **satellites** are also used as microwave relay stations. Many of these are offered by Intelsat, the *In*ternational *Tel*ecommunications *Sat*ellite Consortium, which is owned by 114 governments and forms a worldwide communications system. Satellites rotate at a precise point and speed above the earth. This makes them appear stationary, so they can amplify and relay microwave signals from one transmitter on the ground to another. (See Figure 8-13.) Thus, satellites can be used to send large volumes of data. Their only drawback is that bad weather can sometimes interrupt the flow of data.

FIGURE 8-13
Satellite relaying microwave signals from earth.

Data Transmission

Several technical matters affect data communications. They are bandwidth, serial versus parallel transmission, direction of flow, modes of transmission, and protocols.

Several factors affect how data is transmitted. They include speed or bandwidth, serial or parallel transmission, direction of data flow, modes of transmitting data, and protocols.

Bandwidth

The different communications channels have different data transmission speeds. This bits-per-second transmission capability of a channel is called its **bandwidth.** Bandwidth may be of three types:

- **Voiceband:** **Voiceband** is the bandwidth of a standard telephone line and used often for microcomputer transmission; typical speeds are 9600 to 28,800, although with special equipment much higher speeds are possible.
- **Medium band:** The **medium band** is the bandwidth of special leased lines used mainly with minicomputers and mainframe computers; the bps is 56,000 to 264 million.
- **Broadband:** The **broadband** is the bandwidth that includes microwave, satellite, coaxial cable, and fiber-optic channels. It is used for very high speed computers whose processors communicate directly with each other. It is in the range of 56,000 to 30 billion bps.

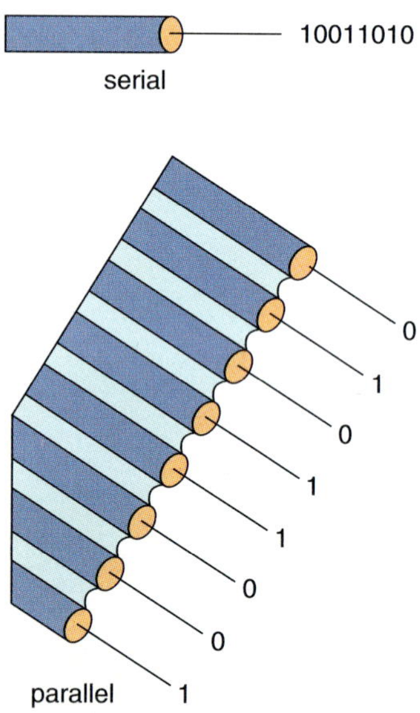

FIGURE 8-14
Serial versus parallel transmission.

Serial and Parallel Transmission

Data travels in two ways: serially and in parallel. (See Figure 8-14.)

- In **serial data transmission,** bits flow in a series or continuous stream, like cars crossing a one-lane bridge. Serial transmission is the way most data is sent over telephone lines. Thus, the plug-in board making up the serial connector in a microcomputer's modem is usually called a *serial port.* More technical names for the serial port are **RS-232C connector** and **asynchronous communications port.**
- With **parallel data transmission,** bits flow through separate lines simultaneously. In other words, they resemble cars moving together at the same speed on a multilane freeway. Parallel transmission is typically limited to communications over short distances and is not used over telephone lines. It is, however, a standard method of sending data from a computer's CPU to a printer.

Direction of Data Transmission

There are three directions or modes of data flow in a data communications system. (See Figure 8-15.)

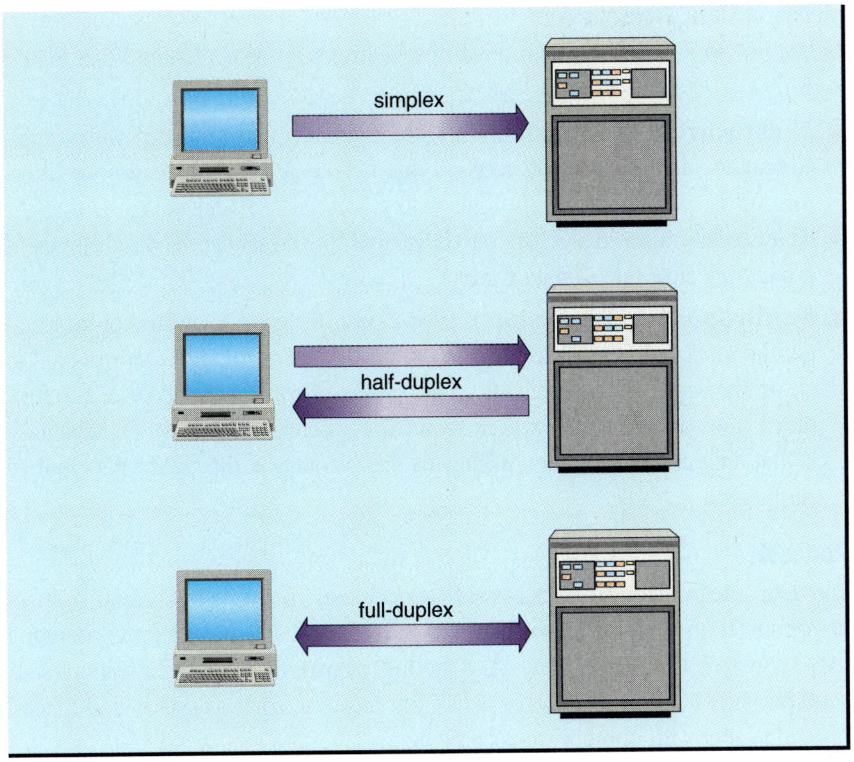

FIGURE 8-15
Simplex, half-duplex, and full-duplex communication.

- **Simplex communication** resembles the movement of cars on a one-way street. Data travels in one direction only. It is not frequently used in data communications systems today. One instance in which it is used may be in point-of-sale (POS) terminals in which data is being entered only.
- In **half-duplex communication,** data flows in both directions, but not simultaneously. That is, data flows in only one direction at any one time. This resembles traffic on a one-lane bridge. Half-duplex is very common and is frequently used for linking microcomputers by telephone lines to other microcomputers, minicomputers, and mainframes. Thus, when you dial into an electronic bulletin board through your microcomputer, you may well be using half-duplex communication.
- In **full-duplex communication,** data is transmitted back and forth at the same time, like traffic on a two-way street. It is clearly the fastest and most efficient form of two-way communication. However, it requires special equipment and is used primarily for mainframe communications. An example is the weekly sales figures and delivery schedules that a supermarket or regional office sends and receives from its corporate headquarters in another state.

Modes of Data Transmission

Data may be sent by asynchronous or synchronous transmission. (See Figure 8-16.)

- In **asynchronous transmission,** the method frequently used with microcomputers, data is sent and received one byte at a time. Asynchronous transmission is often used for terminals with slow speeds. Its advantage is that the data can be transmitted whenever convenient for the sender. Its disadvantage is a relatively slow rate of data transfer.
- **Synchronous transmission** is used to transfer great quantities of information by sending several bytes or a block at a time. For the data transmission to occur, the sending and receiving of the blocks of bytes must occur at carefully timed intervals. Thus, the system requires a synchronized clock. Its advantage is that data can be sent very quickly. Its disadvantage is the cost of the required equipment.

Protocols

For data transmission to be successful, sender and receiver must follow a set of communication rules for the exchange of information. These rules for exchanging data between computers are known as the line **protocol.** A communications software package like Crosstalk helps define the protocol, such as speeds and modes, for connecting with another microcomputer.

When different types of microcomputers are connected in a network, the protocols can become very complex. Obviously, for the connections to work, these network protocols must adhere to certain standards. The first commercially available set of standards was IBM's Systems Network Architecture (SNA). This works for IBM's own equipment, but other machines won't necessarily communicate with them.

The International Standards Organization has defined a set of communications protocols called the Open Systems Interconnection (OSI). The purpose of the OSI model is to identify functions provided by any network. It separates each network's

FIGURE 8-16
Asynchronous and synchronous communication.

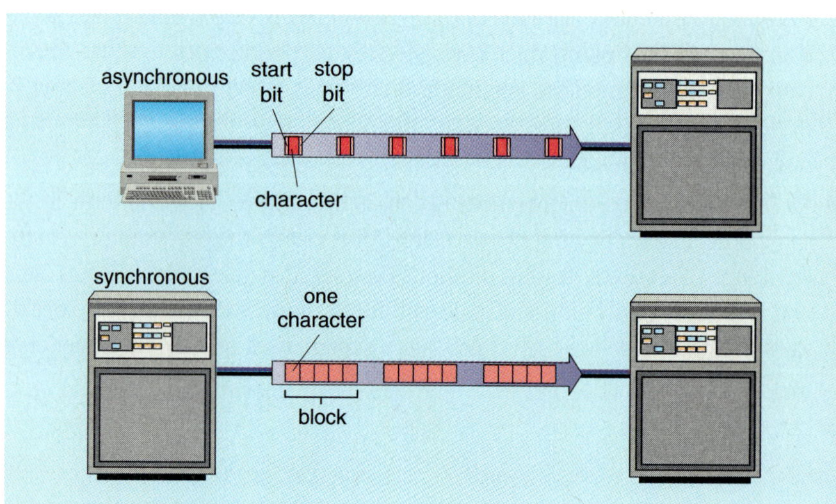

functions into seven "layers" of protocols, or communication rules. When two network systems communicate, their corresponding layers may exchange data. This assumes that the microcomputers and other equipment on each network have implemented the same functions and interfaces.

Network Architecture

Network architecture describes how a computer network is configured and what strategies are used.

Communications channels can be connected in different arrangements, or *networks,* to suit different users' needs. A *computer network* is a communications system connecting two or more computers that work together to exchange information and share resources. **Network architecture** describes how the network is arranged and how the resources are coordinated and shared.

Terms

There are a number of specialized terms that describe computer networks. Some terms often used with networks are:

- **Node:** A node is any device that is connected to a network. It could be a computer, printer, or data storage device.
- **Client:** A client is a node that requests and uses resources available from other nodes. Typically, a client is a user's microcomputer.
- **Server:** A server is a node that shares resources with other nodes. Depending on the resources shared, it may be called a file server, printer server, communication server, Web server, or database server.
- **Network Operating System (NOS):** Microcomputer operating systems like DOS and Windows interact with an application and a computer. On the other hand, network operating systems control and coordinate the activities between computers on a network. These activities include electronic communication and the sharing of information and resources.
- **Distributed processing:** In a distributed processing system, computing power is located and shared at different locations. This type of system is common in decentralized organizations where divisional offices have their own computer systems. The computer systems in the divisional offices are networked to the organization's main or centralized computer.
- **Host computer:** A host computer is a large centralized computer, usually a minicomputer or a mainframe.

A network may consist only of microcomputers, or it may integrate microcomputers or other devices with larger computers. Networks can be controlled by all nodes working together equally or by specialized nodes coordinating and supplying all resources. Networks may be simple or complex, self-contained or dispersed over a large geographical area.

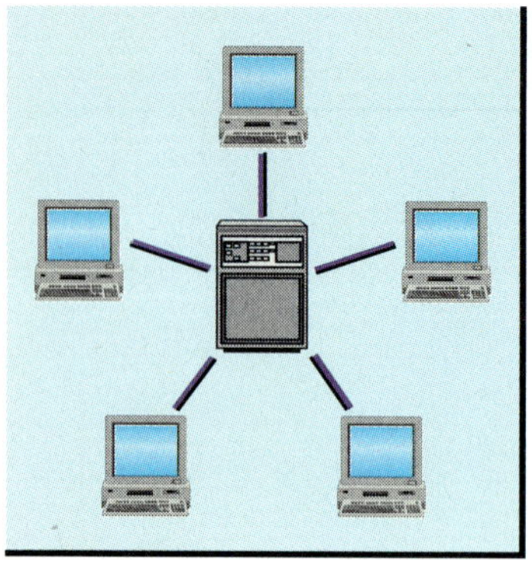

FIGURE 8-17
Star network.

Configurations

A network can be arranged or configured in several different ways. This arrangement is called the network's **topology.** The four principal network topologies are star, bus, ring, and hierarchical.

In a **star network,** a number of small computers or peripheral devices are linked to a central unit. (See Figure 8-17.) This central unit may be a *host computer* or a *file server.*

All communications pass through this central unit. Control is maintained by **polling.** That is, each connecting device is asked ("polled") whether it has a message to send. Each device is then in turn allowed to send its message.

One particular advantage of the star form of network is that it can be used to provide a **time-sharing system.** That is, several users can share resources ("time") on a central computer. The star is a common arrangement for linking several microcomputers to a mainframe that allows access to an organization's database.

In a **bus network,** each device in the network handles its own communications control. There is no host computer. All communications travel along a common connecting cable called a **bus.** (See Figure 8-18.) As the information passes along the bus, it is examined by each device to see if the information is intended for it.

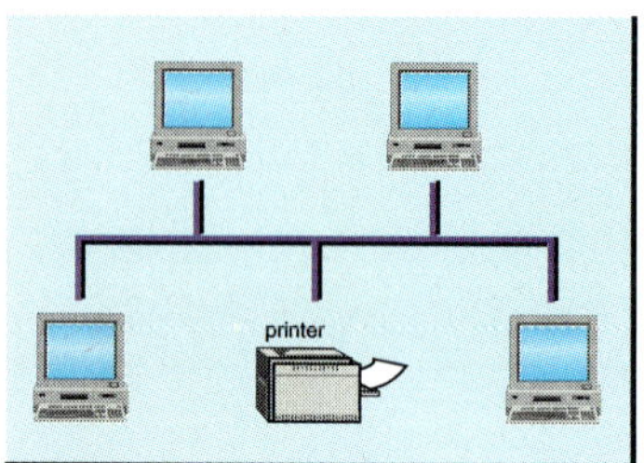

FIGURE 8-18
Bus network.

The bus network is typically used when only a few microcomputers are to be linked together. This arrangement is common in systems for electronic mail or for sharing data stored on different microcomputers. The bus network is not as efficient as the star network for sharing common resources. (This is because the bus network is not a direct link to the resource.) However, a bus network is less expensive and is in very common use.

In a **ring network,** each device is connected to two other devices, forming a ring. (See Figure 8-19.) There is no central file server or computer. Messages are passed around the ring until they reach the correct destination. With microcomputers, the ring arrangement is the least frequently used of the four networks. However, it often is used to link mainframes, especially over wide geographical areas. These mainframes tend to operate fairly autonomously. They perform most or all of their own processing and only occasionally share data and programs with other mainframes.

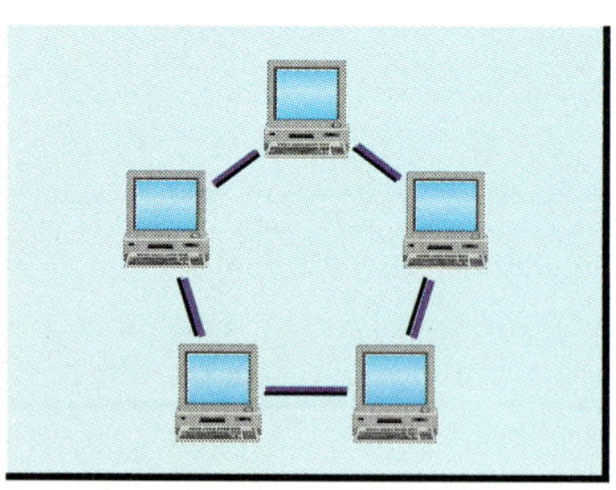

FIGURE 8-19
Ring network.

A ring network is useful in a decentralized organization because it makes possible a *distributed data processing system.* That is, computers can perform processing tasks at their own dispersed locations. However, they can also share programs, data, and other resources with each other.

The **hierarchical network**—also called a **hybrid network**—consists of several computers linked to a central host computer, just like a star network. However, these other computers are also hosts to other, smaller computers or to peripheral devices. (See Figure 8-20.)

Thus, the host at the top of the hierarchy could be a mainframe. The computers below the mainframe could be minicomputers, and those below, microcomputers. The hierarchical network allows various computers to share databases, processing power, and different output devices.

A hierarchical network is useful in centralized organizations. For example, different departments within an organization may have individual microcomputers connected to departmental minicomputers. The minicomputers in turn may be connected to the corporation's mainframe, which contains data and programs accessible to all.

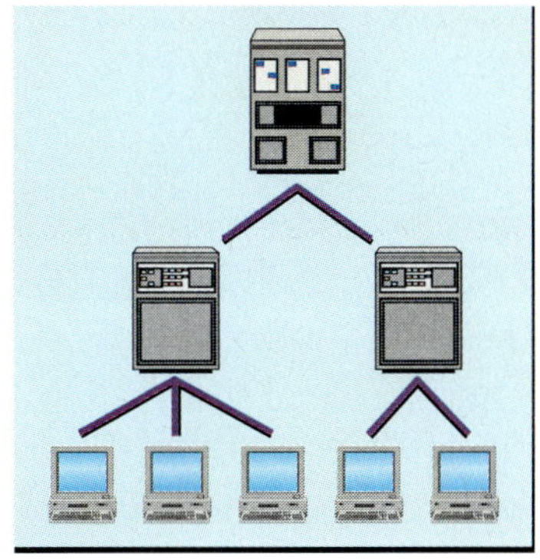

FIGURE 8-20
Hierarchical network.

Strategies

Every network has a *strategy,* or way of coordinating the sharing of information and resources. The most common network strategies are terminal, peer-to-peer, and client/server systems.

In a **terminal network system,** processing power is centralized in one large computer, usually a mainframe. The nodes connected to this host computer are terminals with little or no processing capabilities. The star and hierarchical networks are typical configurations with UNIX as the operating system.

Most airline reservation systems are terminal systems. A large central computer maintains all the airline schedules, rates, seat availability, and so on. Travel agents use terminals to connect to the central computer and use it to schedule reservations. Although the tickets may be printed along with travel itineraries at the agent's desk, nearly all processing is done at the central computer.

One advantage of terminal network systems is the centralized location and control of technical personnel, software, and data. One disadvantage is the lack of control and flexibility for the end user. Another disadvantage is that terminal systems do not use the processing power available with microcomputers. Once very popular, most new systems do not use the terminal strategy.

In a **peer-to-peer network system,** nodes can act as both servers and clients. For example, one microcomputer can *obtain* files located on another microcomputer and can also *provide* files to other microcomputers. A typical configuration for a peer-to-peer system is the bus network. Commonly used network operating systems are Artisoft LANtastic, Apple's Macintosh Peer-to-Peer LANs, Novell's NetWare Lite, and Microsoft's Windows for Workgroups.

There are several advantages to using this type of strategy. The networks are inexpensive and easy to install, and they usually work well for smaller systems with less than ten nodes. As the number of nodes increases, however, the performance of the network declines. Another disadvantage is the lack of powerful management software to effectively monitor a large network's activities. For these reasons, peer-to-peer networks are typically used by small networks.

Client/server network systems use one powerful computer to coordinate and supply services to all other nodes on the network. The server provides access to centralized resources such as databases, application software, and hardware. This strategy is based on specialization. Server nodes coordinate and supply specialized services, and client nodes request the services. Commonly used network operating systems are Novell's NetWare, IBM's LAN Server, Banyan Vines, and Microsoft's LAN Manager and Windows NT.

One advantage of client/server network systems is their ability to handle very large networks efficiently. Another advantage is the powerful network management software that monitors and controls the network's activities. The major disadvantages are the cost of installation and maintenance.

Computer networks in organizations have evolved over time. Most large organizations have a wide range of different network configurations, operating systems, and strategies. These organizations are moving toward integrating or connecting all of these networks together. That way, a user on one network can access resources available throughout the company. This is called **enterprise computing.**

Network Types

Communications networks differ in geographical size. Three important types are LANs, MANs, and WANs.

Clearly, different types of channels—cable or air—allow different kinds of networks to be formed. Telephone lines, for instance, may connect communications equipment within the same building. In fact, many new buildings—called *smart buildings*—have coaxial or fiber-optic cable installed inside the walls. This makes it easy to form communications networks.

Networks may also be citywide and even international, using both cable and air connections. Here let us distinguish among three types: *local area networks, metropolitan area networks,* and *wide area networks.*

Local Area Networks

Networks with computers and peripheral devices in close physical proximity—within the same building, for instance—are called **local area networks (LANs).** Linked by cable—telephone, coaxial, or fiber-optic—LANs often use a bus form of organization.

Our illustration shows an example of a LAN. (See Figure 8-21.) This typical arrangement has two benefits. People can share different equipment, which lowers

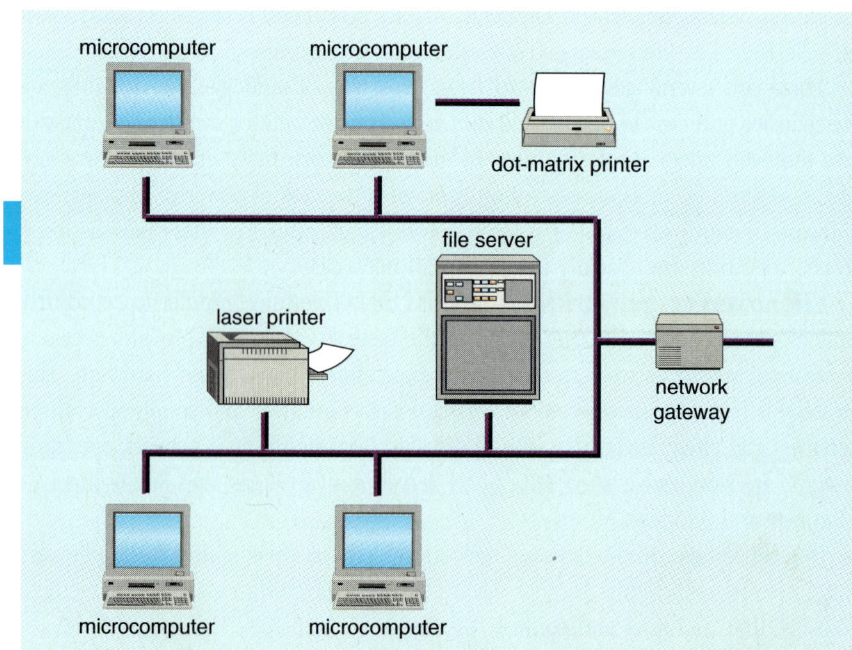

FIGURE 8-21
A local area network that includes a file server and network gateway.

the cost of equipment. For instance, here the four microcomputers share the laser printer and the file server, which are expensive pieces of hardware. (Individual microcomputers many times also have their own less expensive printers, such as the dot-matrix printer shown in our illustration.) Other equipment may also be added to the LAN—for instance, mini- or mainframe computers or optical-disk storage devices.

Note that the LAN shown in our illustration also features a **network gateway.** A LAN may be linked to other LANs or to larger networks in this manner. For example, the LAN of one office group may be connected to the LAN of another office group. It may also be connected to others in the wider world, even if their configurations are different. Alternatively, a **network bridge** would be used to connect networks with the same configurations.

Metropolitan Area Networks

The next step up from the LAN might be the **MAN**—the **metropolitan area network.** These networks are used as links between office buildings in a city. *Cellular phone systems* expand the flexibility of MANs by allowing links to car phones and portable phones.

Wide Area Networks

Wide area networks (WANs) are countrywide and worldwide networks. Among other kinds of channels, they use microwave relays and satellites to reach users over long distances—for example, from Los Angeles to Paris. (See Figure 8-22.) One of the most widely used WANs is the Internet, which allows users to connect to other users and facilities worldwide.

FIGURE 8-22
Wide area network.

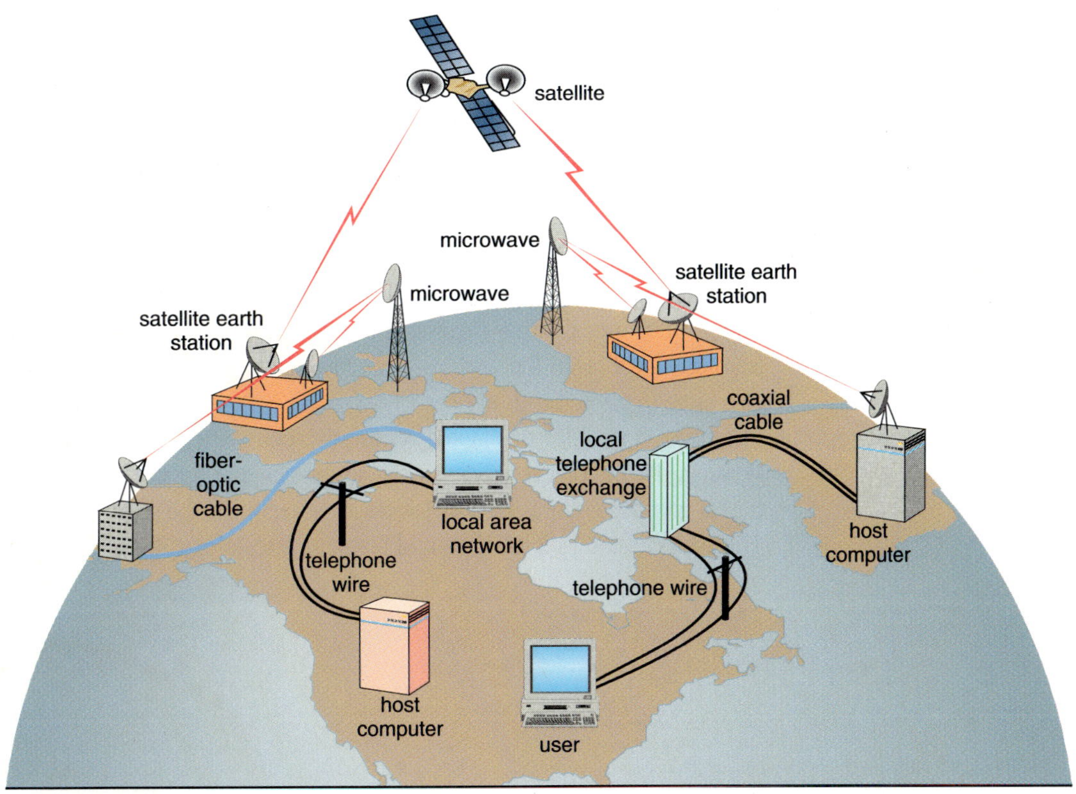

The primary difference between a LAN, MAN, and WAN is the geographical range. Each may have various combinations of hardware, such as microcomputers, minicomputers, mainframes, and various peripheral devices.

A Look at the Future

Teledesic Corporation hopes to create an airborne Internet that will connect the world community.

Can you imagine what it would be like if all of the world's people could directly communicate with one another? If you wanted to know more about life in a remote African village, you could directly connect to members of that village to share experiences and explore the future. Medical researchers from every corner of the world could meet daily to coordinate and share their work. The world community could quickly react to and unite to face global crises.

Of course, that's what the Internet is all about. All the major cities in North America and Europe are wired for fast, efficient Internet access. Most of the rest of the world, however, is not. While satellites can be used to connect these other areas, most satellites orbit at such high altitudes that Internet connections are not effective. But, that may be changing in the very near future.

Bill Gates from Microsoft and Craig McCaw from Cellular Communications have formed a corporation called Teledisc. This corporation plans to invest over 9 billion dollars in the next two years to launch over 800 low-orbit satellites. These satellites will hover just 435 miles above the earth and provide direct effective Internet access. Once this airborne Internet is in place, all a user will need to link up to it from any location in the world is a microcomputer with a sender/receiver the size of a large pizza and a signal decoder.

Is there a need for this global communication system? Probably not right now. However, the Internet is growing fast and the demand for world wide communication is growing even faster. Will Teledisc be a reality in the year 2000? Who knows? This project requires a lot of ground-breaking technology. We will have to wait and see.

KEY TERMS

analog signal (166)
asynchronous communications port (170)
asynchronous transmission (172)
bandwidth (170)
baud rate (166)
broadband (170)
browser (166)
bus (174)
bus network (174)
cable modem (167)
client/server network system (175)
coaxial cable (168)
data communications system (158)
demodulation (166)
digital signal (166)
downloading (162)
electronic bulletin board system (BBS) (160)
electronic mail (160)
e-mail (160)
enterprise computing (176)
external modem (167)
fax machine (160)
fax modem (167)
fiber-optic cable (168)
FTP (file transfer protocol) (165)
full-duplex communication (171)
Gopher (165)
half-duplex communication (171)
hierarchical network (174)
hybrid network (174)
hypertext link (166)
information superhighway (164)
internal modem (167)
Internet (164)
ISDN (167)
local area network (LAN) (176)
medium band (170)
metropolitan area network (MAN) (177)
microwave (169)
modulation (166)
National Information Highway (NIH) (164)
National Information Infrastructure (NII) (164)
network architecture (172)
network bridge (177)
network gateway (177)
parallel data transmission (170)
password (160)
peer-to-peer network system (175)
polling (174)
protocol (172)
ring network (174)
RS-232C connector (170)
satellite (169)
serial data transmission (170)
simplex communication (171)
star network (174)
synchronous transmission (172)
Telnet (165)
terminal network system (175)
time-sharing system (174)

topology (174)
twisted pair (168)
uploading (162)
UseNet (165)
user name (160)
voiceband (170)
voice-messaging system (161)
wide area network (WAN) (177)
wireless modem (167)
World Wide Web, WWW, W3, the Web (166)

REVIEW QUESTIONS

True/False

1. A local area network connects two or more computers within a limited area, such as within the same building.
2. Modems are used to convert data on a CD-ROM to an internal hard disk.
3. Frequently, computer communications over telephone lines require a modem.
4. In half-duplex communication, data flows in both directions at the same time.
5. In a client/server system, each node on the network has equal responsibility for coordinating the network's activities.

Multiple Choice

1. A special sequence of numbers or letters that limits access to electronic mailboxes is a:
   a. combination
   b. code
   c. fax
   d. password
   e. modem
2. Transferring data from a larger computer to your microcomputer is called:
   a. a LAN
   b. time-sharing
   c. downloading
   d. networking
   e. uploading
3. What communications channel transfers data as pulses of light?
   a. telephone lines
   b. coaxial cable
   c. fiber-optic cable

   d. microwave
   e. satellite
4. Rules for exchanging data on a network:
   a. protocol
   b. asynchronous transmission
   c. configuration
   d. channel
   e. serial transmission
5. A system frequently used in decentralized organizations in which computing power is located and shared at different sites:
   a. client/server
   b. ring
   c. centralized
   d. mainframe
   e. distributed

Fill in the Blank

1. __________ systems are computer systems linked to telephones that convert the human voice into digital bits.
2. Transferring data from your microcomputer to a minicomputer or mainframe is called __________.
3. Because __________ travel in straight lines through the air and cannot bend with the curvature of the earth, they can transmit data only over short distances.
4. A __________ __________ system controls and coordinates the activities on a network.
5. __________ are countrywide and worldwide networks that connect users over long distances.

Open Ended

1. What are electronic bulletin boards? How do they differ from electronic mail systems?
2. List and describe the five kinds of communications channels.
3. What are the differences between a terminal, a peer-to-peer, and a client/server system?
4. Describe the difference between simplex, half-duplex, and full-duplex communication.
5. Discuss the four basic network configurations.

DISCUSSION QUESTION AND PROJECTS

1. *Electronic bulletin boards:* Unquestionably there is an area of personal interest to you that is available on an electronic bulletin board. A glance at one local microcomputer publication shows bulletin boards available on such subjects as sports, restaurants, politics, religion, business opportunities, music, mental health, drug recovery, alternative lifestyles, and many other topics.

   What kind of electronic bulletin board would be of interest to you? See if you can find a printed list of bulletin boards in a local microcomputer publication. Or try contacting a users' group for help. Users' groups are clubs or volunteer organizations. Their members meet to help each other solve problems or share interests regarding particular personal computers.

on the web

Exercises and Explorations

1 ISDN

Are you tired of waiting for images and text to download from the World Wide Web? If you want to decrease the wait time, consider getting an Internet connection with a higher bandwidth, such as an ISDN connection. To learn more about ISDN, visit our Web site at http://www.magpie.org/essentials/chapter-8 to link to a site specializing in ISDN. Once connected to that site, print out the Web page you find most informative. Write a paragraph on who should and who shouldn't get an ISDN line and why. Consider individuals in different geographic locations, with different usage needs, and in large and small companies. Suggest alternatives to ISDN that might be more economical for some people.

2 Satellite Link

One way to speed up Internet access and delivery is by using a satellite link. All you need is a satellite service provider and satellite dish, and you can download information from the Web or upload information to the Web via a phone line. To learn more about satallite links, visit our Web site at http://www.magpie.org/essentials/chapter-8 to link to a site specializing in satellite links. Once connected to that site, print out the Web page you find most informative. Write a paragraph listing the pros and cons of using a satellite link for your Internet connection.

3 Cable Modems

Many observers look to cable modems to greatly increase Internet access and connection capabilities. Search the Internet to learn more about cable modems and cable modem service. Visit the Excite search service at http: //www.excite.com and use keywords such as "cable internet connection" and "high bandwidth," Also use Excite's topic areas to limit your search, and take advantage of Excite's [More Like This] buttons next to each site. Find out whether your local cable company provides Internet access and how much it costs. Print out the most informative Web page, and write a paragraph describing the site, and explaining how it is useful and how you found it.

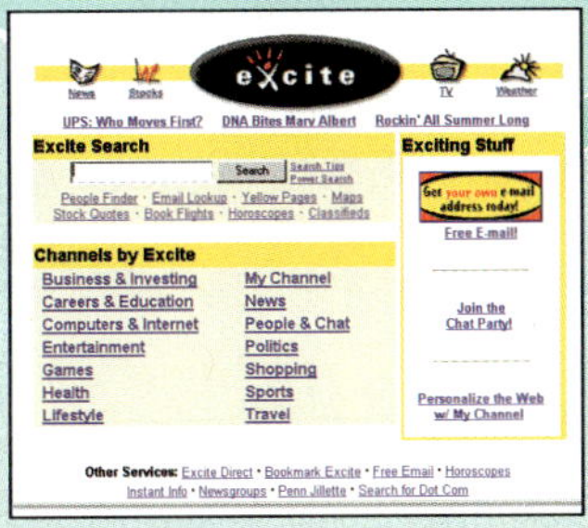

4 Travel

You can find all sorts of travel information and advice on the Internet. Visit our Web site at http://www.magpie.org/essentials/chapter-8 to link to one of the best travel sites on the Web. Once connected to that site, you'll find a wide range of travel information from tickets to theatrical and sporting events to plane, hotel, and cruise schedules. Plan the vacation of your dreams. Print out the most interesting Web page, and write a paragraph describing your vacation plans, including estimated budget, destinations, airline (or cruise) departure times, and accommodations.

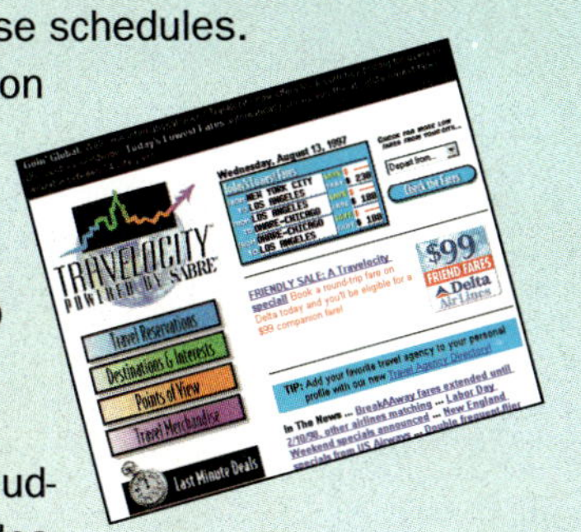

VISUAL SUMMARY

8 Communications and Connectivity

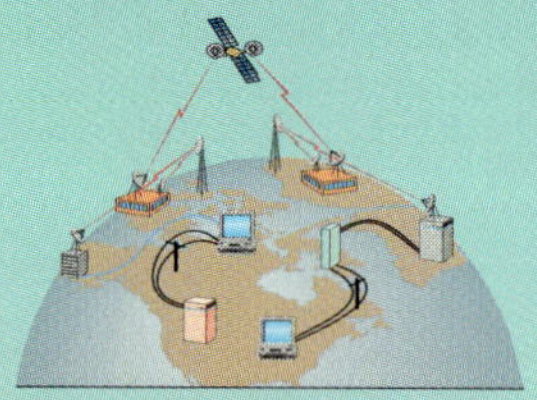

Data communications systems are the electronic systems that transmit data over communications lines from one location to another.

INFORMATION SUPERHIGHWAY AND INTERNET

Internet

At the **Internet** is a worldwide computer network that is at the forefront of the **Information Superhighway.**

Internet Applications

INTERNET APPLICATIONS

APPLICATION	DESCRIPTION
Electronic mail	Send and receive e-mail worldwide
Public discussion	Participate in discussions and debates using UseNet newsgroups
File transfer	Locate and copy selected files using FTP
Run programs	Allow terminal access to locate and run programs using Telnet

Utilities

Two widely known and used Internet utility programs:

- **Gophers** are programs to access computers on the Internet. **Gopher clients** request access. **Gopher servers** provide access by displaying menus.
- **World Wide Web** (**WWW** or **Web**) provides a graphical interface and **hypertext links. Browsers** are special software to jump from one computer to another.

USER CONNECTION

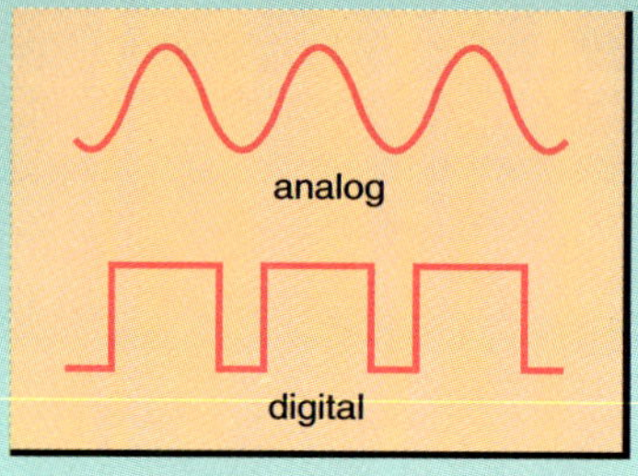

Telephones typically send and receive **analog signals.** Computers send and receive **digital signals.**

Modems and Communications Speeds

- A *modem* ("*mo*dulator *dem*odulator") converts digital to analog and vice versa. **Modulation**—digital to analog. **Demodulation**—analog to digital.
- Popular speeds are 28,000; 36,600; and 57,600 bits per second..

Types of Modems

- **External modem**—outside system cabinet and connected by cable.
- **Internal modem**—plug-in circuit board inside system unit.
- **Wireless modem**—does not connect to telephone line, receives data through the air.
- **Fax modem**—unlike other modems, fax modems send and receive signals that represent graphic images.
- **Cable modem**—supports all digital communication.

COMMUNICATIONS CHANNELS

Data may be transmitted by:

Telephone Lines

Most phone lines have consisted of copper wires called **twisted pairs.**

Coaxial Cable

Coaxial cable is high-frequency, solid-core cable.

Fiber-Optic Cable

Fiber-optic cable transmits data as pulses of light through tubes of glass.

Microwave

Microwaves are high-frequency radio waves that travel in a straight line.

Satellites

Satellites act as microwave relay stations rotating above the earth.

CONNECTIVITY OPTIONS

OPTION	FUNCTION
Fax machines	Convert images to signals and send them over telephone lines to receiving fax machines
Electronic bulletin boards	Provide forums on a variety of subjects available to telephone-linked microcomputer users
Electronic mail	Systems resembling bulletin boards but are restricted in access by passwords
Voice–mail systems	Convert a voice message to digital bits and distribute to many locations over telephone lines
Shared resources	Microcomputer users may share expensive hardware, data, and information
Online services	Provide wide range of activities including teleshopping, home banking, investments, and travel reservations services

DATA TRANSMISSION

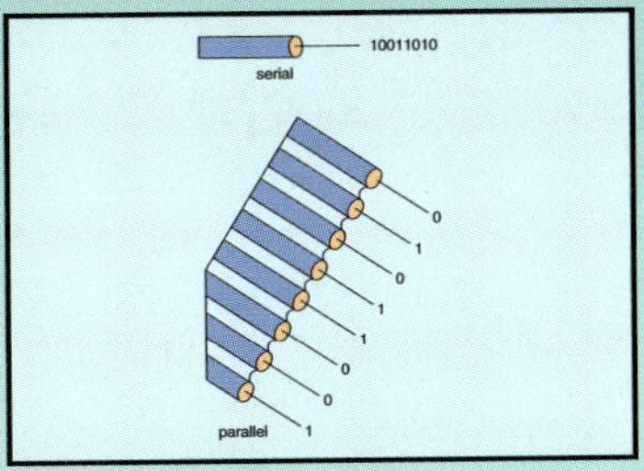

Data transmission factors:

Bandwidth

Bandwidth may be **voiceband, medium band,** or **broadband.**

Serial and Parallel Transmission

With **serial data transmission,** bits flow in a continuous stream. With **parallel data transmission,** bits flow through separate lines simultaneously.

Direction of Data Transmission

Three directions of data flow are **simplex communication, half-duplex communication,** and **full-duplex communication.**

Modes of Transmitting Data

Two modes are **asynchronous**—data is sent and received one byte at a time—and **synchronous**—several bytes (a block) are sent at one time.

Protocols

A **protocol** defines rules by which senders and receivers may exchange information.

NETWORK ARCHITECTURE

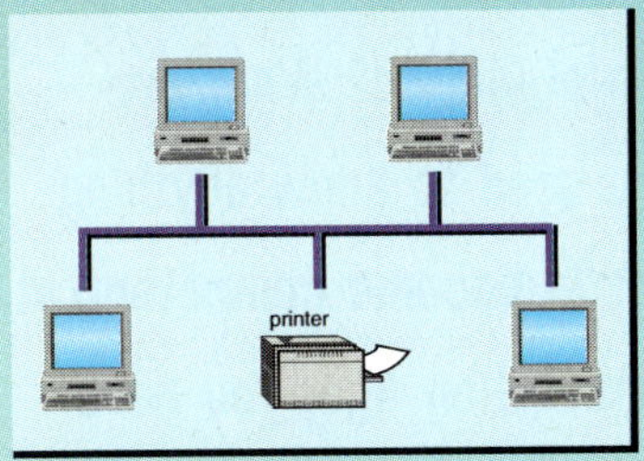

Network architecture describes how a computer network is configured and what strategies are used.

Configurations

Networks can be arranged or configured in several different ways. Four principal ways:

- **Star network**—small computers or peripheral devices are linked to a central unit.
- **Bus network**—each device handles its own communications.
- **Ring network**—each device is connected to two other devices, forming a ring.
- **Hierarchical network**—several computers are linked to a central host.

Strategy

Every network has a strategy for coordinating and sharing. The three most common are:

- With **terminal networks,** power is centralized in one large computer.
- With **peer-to-peer networks,** each node acts as both a server and a client.
- With **client/server networks,** one node coordinates and supplies services to all other nodes.

NETWORK TYPES

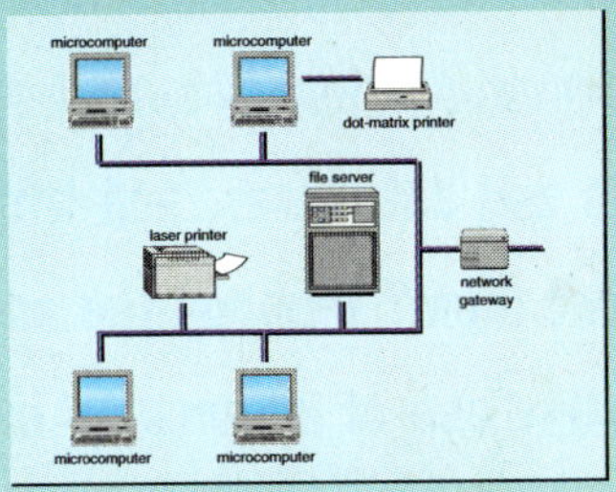

Three types of geographical networks are:

Local Area Networks

Local Area Networks (LANs) are computers and peripheral devices close together (for example, in same building). Linked by telephone, coaxial, or fiber-optic cable, LANs often take bus form. LANs may be linked to other LANs or networks by a **network gateway.**

Metropolitan Area Networks

A **metropolitan area network (MAN)** consists of citywide networks, often using cellular phones.

Wide Area Networks

Wide area networks (WANs) are countrywide and worldwide networks, often using microwave relays and satellites.

Data Files and Databases

Like a library, the purpose of secondary storage is to store information. How is such information organized? What are files and databases, and why do you need to know anything about them? Perhaps the answer is: To become competent at making use of information in the Information Age, you have to know how to *find* that information.

9

COMPETENCIES

After you have read this chapter, you should be able to:

1. **Describe how data is organized: characters, fields, records, and files.**
2. **Understand the difference between batch processing and real-time processing.**
3. **Describe the difference between master files and transaction files.**
4. **Define and describe the three types of file organization: sequential, direct, and index sequential.**
5. **Describe the advantages of a database.**
6. **Describe the two essential parts of a database management system (DBMS).**
7. **Describe three ways of organizing a DBMS: hierarchical, network, and relational.**
8. **Distinguish among individual, company, distributed, and proprietary databases.**
9. **Discuss some issues of productivity and security.**

At one time, it was not important for microcomputer users to know much about data files and databases. However, the recent arrival of very powerful microcomputers and their availability to communications networks and the Internet has changed that. To attain true computer competency, you need to know how to gain access to data files and databases. Communications lines and the Internet extend the reach of your microcomputer well beyond the desktop.

Data Files

Understanding how data files work means understanding data organization, key fields, batch versus real-time processing, master versus transaction files, and file organization.

You want to know your final grades for the semester. You call your school's registrar after your last semester exams to find out your grade point average. Perhaps you are told, "Sorry, that's not in the computer yet." Why can't they tell you? How is the school's computer system different from, say, your bank's, where deposits and withdrawals seem to be recorded right away?

Data Organization

To be processed by the computer or stored in secondary storage, data is typically organized into groups or categories. Each group is more complex than the one before:

- **Character:** A character is a single letter, number, or special character such as a punctuation mark or $.
- **Field:** A field contains a set of related characters. On a college registration form or a driver's license, a person's first name is a field. Last name is another field, street address another field, city yet another field, and so on.
- **Record:** A record is a collection of related fields. Everything on a person's college registration form or driver's license, including identification number, is a record.
- **File:** A data file is a collection of related records. All the driver's licenses issued in one county could be a file.
- **Database:** A database is a collection of related files. All the driver's license files for the state could be a database.

An example of how data is organized is shown in the illustration. (See Figure 9-1.) Note that a student's name is not one field, but three: first name, middle initial, and last name.

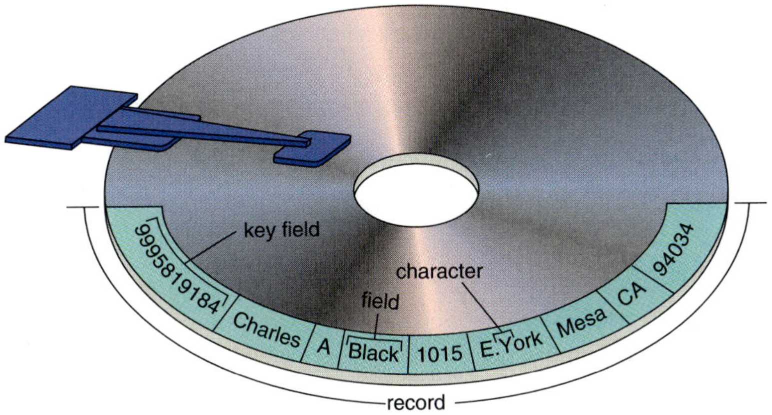

FIGURE 9-1
How data is organized.

The Key Field

Our illustration also shows the student's identification number. Is such a number really necessary? Certainly most people's names are different enough that at a small college, say, you might think identification numbers wouldn't be necessary. However, as anyone named John Smith or Linda Williams knows, there are plenty of other people around with the same name. Sometimes they even have the same middle initial. This is the reason for the student identification number: The number is unique, whereas the name may not be.

This distinctive number is called a *key field.* A **key field** is the particular field of a record that is chosen to uniquely identify each record. Some common key fields are social security numbers, employee identification numbers, and part numbers.

Batch versus Real-Time Processing

Traditionally data is processed in two ways. These are *batch processing,* what we might call "later," and *real-time processing,* what we might call "now." These two methods have been used to handle common record-keeping activities such as payroll and sales orders.

- **Batch processing:** In **batch processing,** data is collected over several hours, days, or even weeks. It is then processed all at once—as a "batch." If you have a bank credit card, your bill probably reflects batch processing. That is, during the month, you buy things and charge them to your credit card. Each time you charge something, a copy of the transaction is sent to the credit card company. At some point in the month, the company's data processing department puts all those transactions (and those of many other customers) together. It then processes them at one time. The company then sends you a single bill totaling the amount you owe.
- **Real-time processing:** Totaling up the sales charged to your bank credit card is an example of batch processing. You might use another kind of card—your bank's automatic teller machine (ATM) card—for the second kind of processing. **Real-time processing** occurs when data is processed at the same time the transaction occurs. As you use your ATM card to withdraw cash, the system automatically computes the balance remaining in your account.

At one time, only tape storage, and therefore only sequential access storage (as we discussed in Chapter 7), was available. All processing then was batch processing and was done on mainframe computers. Even today, a great deal of mainframe time is dedicated to this kind of processing. Many smaller organizations, however, use microcomputers for this purpose.

Real-time processing is made possible by the availability of disk packs and direct access storage (as we described in Chapter 7). Direct access storage enables the user to quickly go directly to a particular record. (In sequential access storage, by contrast, the user must wait for the computer to scan several records one at a time. It continues scanning until it comes to the one that's needed.) Not long ago, specialized terminals were used to enter data and perform real-time processing. Today, however, more and more microcomputers are being used for this purpose. As we have stated, microcomputers have become increasingly more powerful. Thus, smaller companies and departments of large companies use these machines by themselves for many real-time processing needs. That is, they use them without connecting to a mainframe.

Master versus Transaction Files

Two types of files are commonly used to update data—a *master file* and a *transaction file.*

- The **master file** is a complete file containing all records current up to the last update. An example is the data file used to prepare your last month's telephone bill or credit card bill.
- The **transaction file** contains *recent* changes to records that will be used to update the master file. An example could be a temporary "holding" file that accumulates telephone charges or credit card charges through the present month.

File Organization

File organization may be of three types: *sequential, direct,* and *index sequential.*

- **Sequential file organization:** The simplest organization is **sequential file organization,** in which records are stored physically one after another in predetermined order. This order is determined by the key field on each record, such as a student identification number. (See Figure 9-2.)

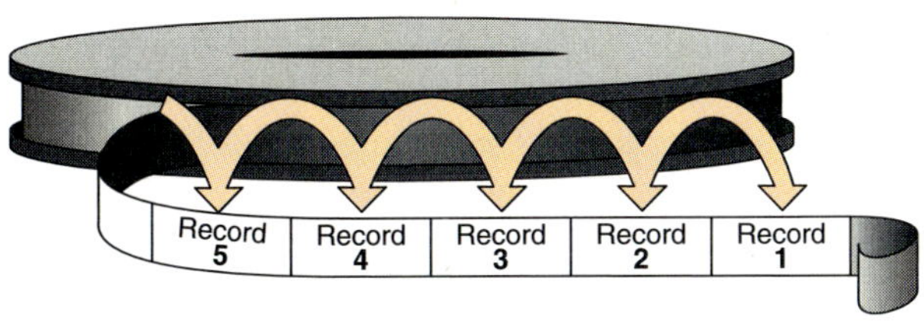

FIGURE 9-2
Sequential file organization.

This organization is very efficient whenever all or a large portion of the records need to be accessed—for example, when final grades are to be mailed out. There is also an equipment cost advantage because magnetic tapes and tape drives can be used. Both are less expensive than disks and disk drives. One disadvantage is that the records must be ordered in a specific way, and that can be time-consuming.

The major disadvantage, however, is that access to a particular record can be very slow. For example, to find the record about a particular student, the registrar's office would sequentially search through the records. It would search them one at a time until the student's number was found. If the number is 4315, the computer will start with record number 0000. It will go through 0001, 0002, and so on until it reaches the student's number.

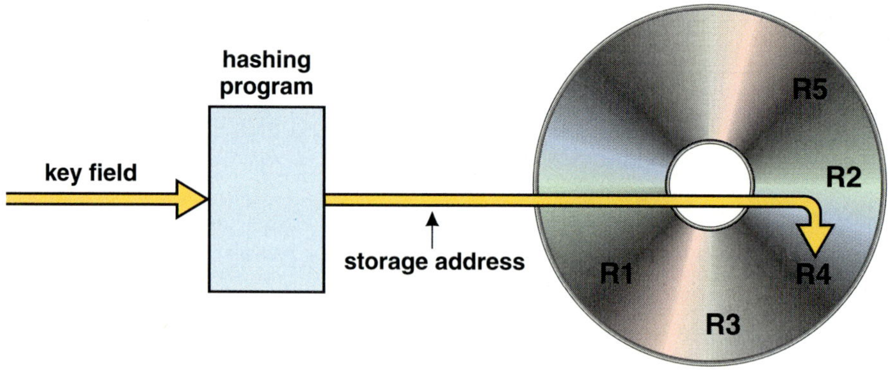

FIGURE 9-3
Direct file organization.

- **Direct file organization:** To obtain particular records, **direct file organization** is much better. Records are not stored physically one after another. Rather, they are stored on a disk in a particular address or location that can be determined by their key field. This address is calculated by a technique known as **hashing.** Hashing programs use mathematical operations to convert the key field's numeric value to a particular storage address. These programs are used to initially store records and later to relocate them. (See Figure 9-3).

  Unlike sequential access files, which are stored on either magnetic tape or disk, direct files can only be stored on disk. The primary advantage is that direct file organization can locate specific records very quickly. If your grades were stored in a direct file, the registrar could access them quickly using only your student identification number.

  The disadvantage of direct file organization is cost. It needs more storage space on disk. It also is not as good as sequential file organization for large numbers of updates or for listing large numbers of records.

- **Index sequential file organization: Index sequential file organization** is a compromise between sequential and direct file organizations. It stores records in a file in sequential order. However, an index sequential file also contains an index. The index lists the key to each group of records stored and the corresponding disk address for that group. When the user seeks a particular record, the computer starts searching sequentially by looking at the beginning of the record group. (See Figure 9-4.) Note: The disk addresses listed in Figure 9-4 represent the actual locations, which are identified by specific track and sector locations.

  For example, the college registrar could index certain ranges of student identification numbers—0000 to 1999, 2000 to 3999, and so on. For the computer to find your number (for example, 4315), it would first go to the index. The index would give the location of the range in which your number appears on the disk (for example, 4000 to 4999). The computer would then search that range (A4) sequentially to find your number.

  Index sequential file organization requires disks or other direct access storage devices. It is faster than sequential but not as fast as direct access. It's best used when large batches of transactions must occasionally be updated, yet users also

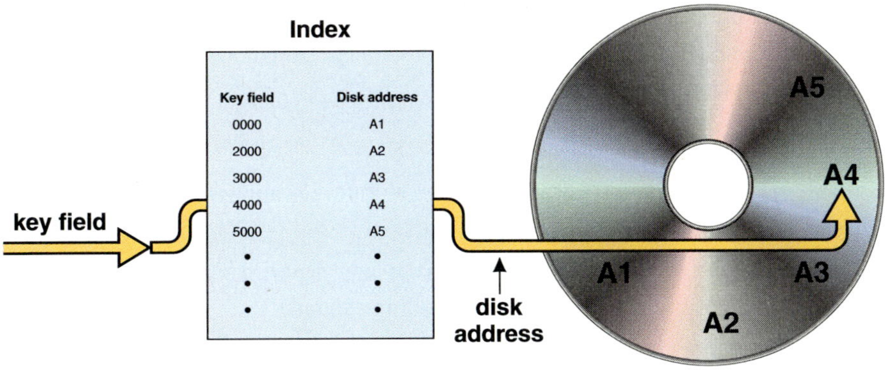

FIGURE 9-4
Index sequential file organization.

want frequent, quick access to data. For example, every month a bank will update bank statements to send to its customers. However, customers and bank tellers need to be able to have up-to-the-minute information about checking accounts.

See Figure 9-5 for a summary of the advantages and disadvantages of each type of file organization.

Database

Databases integrate data. DBMSs create, modify, and access databases using data dictionaries and query languages.

Many organizations have multiple files on the same subject or person. For example, records for the same customer may appear in different files in the sales department, billing department, and credit department. If the customer moves, then the address in each file must be updated. If one file is overlooked, it can cause embarrassments. For example, a product ordered might be sent to the new address, but the bill might be sent to the old address.

Moreover, data spread around in different files is not as useful. The marketing department, for instance, might want to offer special promotions to customers who

FILE ORGANIZATION

TYPE	ADVANTAGES	DISADVANTAGES
Sequential	Efficient access to all or large part of records, cost	Slow access to specific records
Direct	Fast access to specific records	Inefficient access to all or large part of records, cost
Index sequential	Faster than sequential, more efficient than direct	Not quite as efficient as sequential, not quite as fast as direct, cost

FIGURE 9-5
Summary of the three types of file organization.

order large quantities of merchandise. However, they may be unable to do so because that information is in the billing department. A database can make the needed information available.

The Need for Databases

For both individuals and organizations, there are many advantages to having databases:

- **Sharing:** In organizations, information from one department can be readily shared with others, as we saw in the preceding example.
- **Security:** Users are given passwords or access only to the kind of information they need to know. Thus, the payroll department may have access to employees' pay rates, but other departments would not.
- **Fewer files:** With several departments having access to one file, there are fewer files. Excess storage, or what is called "data redundancy," is reduced. Microcomputers linked by a network to a file server, for example, could replace the hard disks located in several individual microcomputers.
- **Data integrity:** Older filing systems many times did not have "integrity." That is, a change made in the file in one department might not be made in the file in another department. As you might expect, this can cause serious problems and conflicts when data is used for important decisions affecting both departments.

Software for a Database Management System

In order to create, modify, and gain access to the database, special software is required. This software is called a *database management system,* which is commonly abbreviated DBMS.

Some DBMSs, such as dBASE, are designed specifically for microcomputers. Other DBMSs are designed for minicomputers and mainframes. Once again, increased processing power and the wide use of communications networks linked to file servers are changing everything. Now microcomputer DBMSs have become more like the ones used for mainframes—and vice versa.

DBMS software is made up of a data dictionary and a query language.

Data Dictionary

A **data dictionary** contains a description of the structure of the data used in the database. For a particular item of data, it defines the names used for a particular field. It defines what type of data that field is (alphabetic, numeric, alphanumeric, date, time, or logic). It also specifies the number of characters in each field and whether that field is a key field. An example of a data dictionary appears in the illustration. (See Figure 9-6.)

Query Language

Access to most databases is accomplished with a **query language.** This is an easy-to-use language understandable to most users. The most widely used query language is **SQL** or **Structured Query Language.**

Query languages have commands such as DISPLAY, ADD, COMPARE, LIST, SELECT, and UPDATE. For example, imagine you wanted the names of all sales-

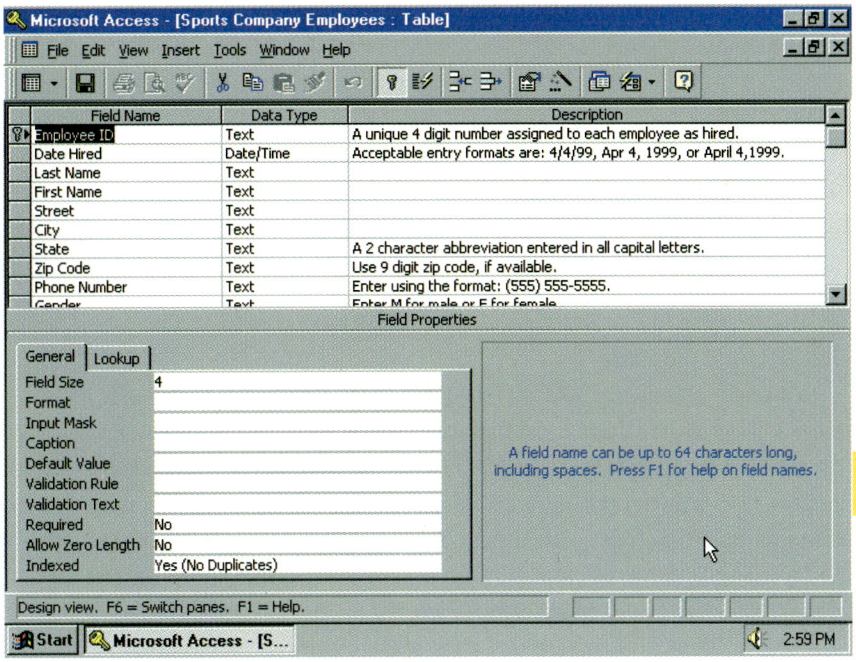

FIGURE 9-6

Data dictionary Access 97.

people in an organization whose sales were greater than their sales quotas. You might type the statement "DISPLAY ALL FOR SALES > QUOTA."

DBMS Organization

The three principal DBMS organizations are hierarchical, network, and relational.

The purpose of a database is to integrate individual items of data—that is, to transform isolated facts into useful information. We saw that files can be organized in various ways (sequentially, for example) to best suit their use. Similarly, databases can also be organized in different ways to best fit their use. Although other arrangements have been tried, the three most common formats are *hierarchical, network,* and *relational.*

The Hierarchical Database

In a **hierarchical database,** fields or records are structured in **nodes.** Nodes are points connected like the branches of an upside-down tree. Each entry has one **parent node,** although a parent may have several **child nodes.** This is sometimes described as a *one-to-many relationship.* To find a particular field you have to start at the top with a parent and trace down the tree to a child.

The nodes farther down the system are subordinate to the ones above, like the hierarchy of managers in a corporation. An example of a hierarchical database for part of a nationwide airline reservations system is shown in our illustration. (See

Figure 9-7.) The parent node is the "departure" city, Los Angeles. This parent has four children, labeled "arrival." New York, one of the children, has three children of its own. They are labeled "flight number." Flight 110 has three children, labeled "passenger."

The problem with a hierarchical database is that if one parent node is deleted, so are all the subordinate child nodes. Moreover, a child node cannot be added unless a parent node is added first. The most significant limitation is the rigid structure: one parent only per child, and no relationships or connections between the child nodes themselves.

The Network Database

A **network database** also has a hierarchical arrangement of nodes. However, each child node may have more than one parent node. This is sometimes described as a *many-to-many relationship*. There are additional connections—called **pointers**—between parent nodes and child nodes. Thus, a node may be reached through more than one path. It may be traced down through different branches.

An example of the use of a network organization is that shown in our illustration for students taking courses. (See Figure 9-8.) If you trace through the logic of this organization, you can see that each student can have more than one teacher. Each teacher can also teach more than one course. Students may take more than a single course. This demonstrates how the network arrangement is more flexible and in many cases more efficient than the hierarchical arrangement.

The Relational Database

The most flexible type of organization is the **relational database.** In this structure, there are no access paths down a hierarchy to an item of data. Rather, the data elements are stored in different tables, each of which consists of rows and columns. A table is called a **relation.**

FIGURE 9-7
Example of a hierarchical database.

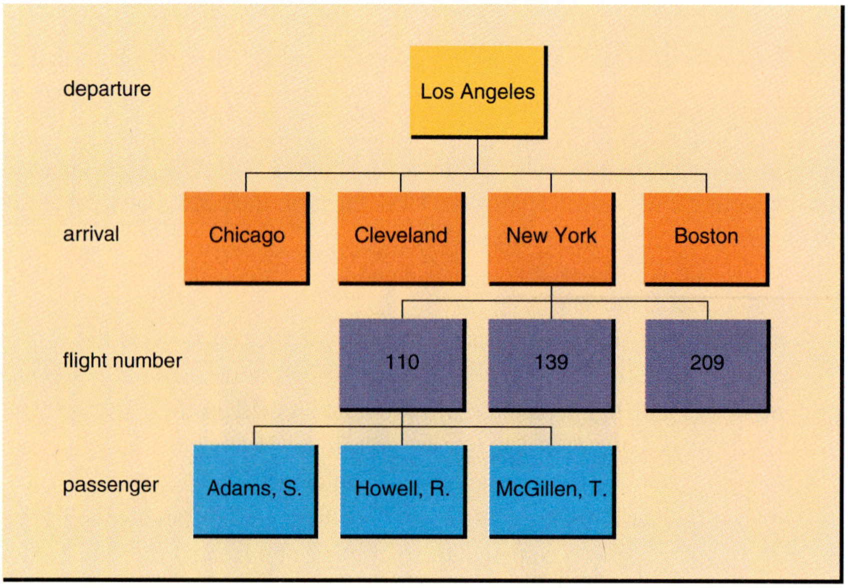

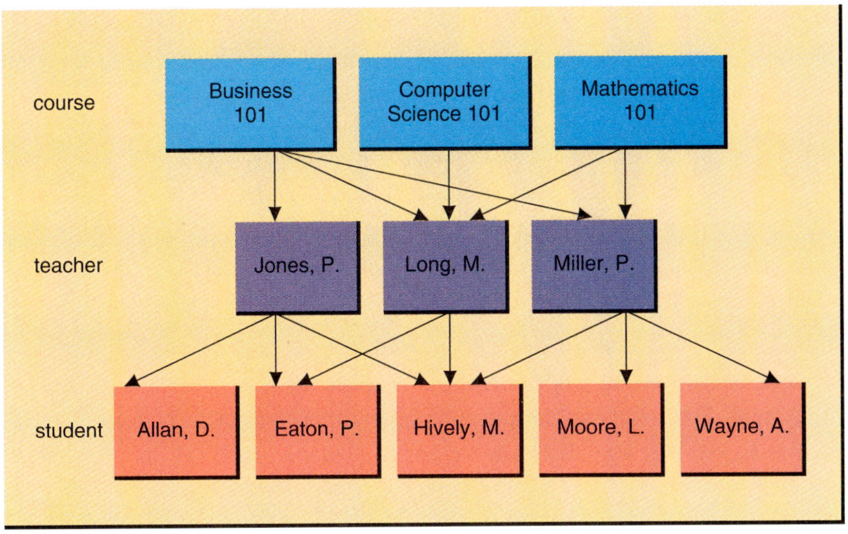

FIGURE 9-8
Example of a network database.

An example of a relational database is shown in our illustration. (See Figure 9-9.) The address table contains the names, drivers' license numbers, and addresses for all registered drivers in a particular state. Within the table, a row resembles a record—for example, information about one driver. A column entry resembles a field. The driver's name is one field; the driver's license number is another field. All related tables must have a *common data item* (a key field). Thus, information

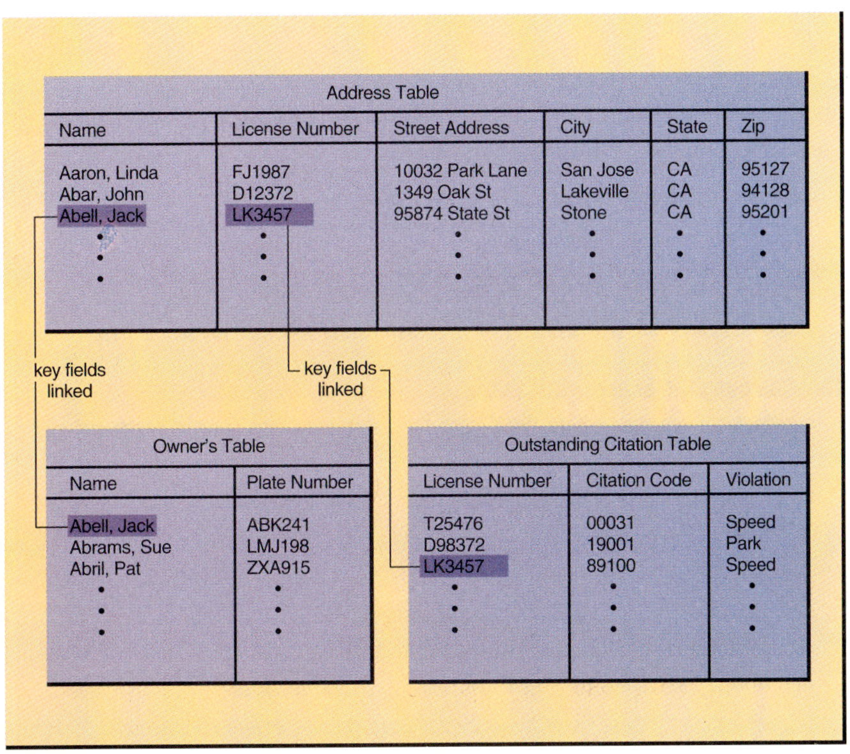

Address Table

Name	License Number	Street Address	City	State	Zip
Aaron, Linda	FJ1987	10032 Park Lane	San Jose	CA	95127
Abar, John	D12372	1349 Oak St	Lakeville	CA	94128
Abell, Jack	LK3457	95874 State St	Stone	CA	95201
• • •	• • •	• • •	• • •	• • •	• • •

Owner's Table

Name	Plate Number
Abell, Jack	ABK241
Abrams, Sue	LMJ198
Abril, Pat	ZXA915
• • •	• • •

Outstanding Citation Table

License Number	Citation Code	Violation
T25476	00031	Speed
D98372	19001	Park
LK3457	89100	Speed
• • •	• • •	• • •

FIGURE 9-9
Example of a relational database.

stored on one table can be linked with information stored on another. One common field might be a person's name. Another might be a driver's license number.

Thus, police officers who stop a speeding car can radio the driver's license number and the car's license plate number to the department of motor vehicles. They can use the driver's license number as the key field. With it they can find out about any unpaid traffic violations (such as parking tickets). Also using the license plate number they can obtain the car owner's name and address. If the owner's name and address do not match the driver who has been stopped, the police officer may check further for a stolen vehicle.

The most valuable feature of relational databases is their simplicity. Entries can be easily added, deleted, and modified. The hierarchy and network databases are more rigid. The relational organization is common for microcomputer DBMSs, such as Access, Paradox, dBASE, and R:Base. Relational databases are also becoming very popular for mainframe- and minicomputer-based systems.

Types of Databases

There are four kinds of databases: individual, company, distributed, and proprietary.

Databases may be small or large, limited in accessibility or widely accessible. Databases may be classified into four types: *individual, company* (or shared), *distributed,* and *proprietary.*

The Individual Database

The **individual database** is also called a **microcomputer database.** It is a collection of integrated files primarily used by just one person. Typically, the data and the DBMS are under the direct control of the user. They are stored either on the user's hard-disk drive or on a LAN file server.

There may be many times in your life when you will find this kind of database valuable. If you are in sales, for instance, a microcomputer database can be used to keep track of customers. If you are a sales manager, you can keep track of your salespeople and their performance. If you are an advertising account executive, you can keep track of what work and how many hours to charge each client.

The Company, or Shared, Database

Companies, of course, create databases for their own use. The **company database** may be stored on a mainframe and managed by a computer professional (known as a *database administrator*). Users throughout the company have access to the database through their microcomputers linked to local area networks or wide area networks. Company databases are of two types:

- The **common operational database** contains details about the operations of the company, such as inventory, production, and sales. It contains data describing the day-to-day operations of the organization.

- The **common user database** contains selected information both from the common operational database and from outside private (proprietary) databases. Managers can tap into this information on their microcomputers or terminals and use it for decision making.

As we will see in the next chapter, company databases are the foundation for management information systems. For instance, a department store can record all sales transactions in the database. A sales manager can use this information to see which salespeople are selling the most products. The manager can then determine year-end sales bonuses. Or the store's buyer can learn which products are selling well or not selling and make adjustments when reordering. A top executive might combine overall store sales trends with information from outside databases about consumer and population trends. This information could be used to change the whole merchandising strategy of the store.

The Distributed Database

Many times the data in a company is stored not in just one location but in several locations. It is made accessible through a variety of communications networks. The database, then, is a **distributed database.** That is, it is located in a place or places other than where users are located. Typically, database servers on a client/server network provide the link between users and the distant data.

For instance, some database information can be at regional offices. Some can be at company headquarters, some down the hall from you, and some even overseas. Sales figures for a chain of department stores, then, could be located at the various stores. But executives at district offices or at the chain's headquarters could have access to these figures.

The Proprietary Database

A **proprietary database** is generally an enormous database that an organization develops to cover particular subjects. It offers access to this database to the public or selected outside individuals for a fee. Sometimes proprietary databases are also called *information utilities* or *data banks.* An example is CompuServe, which sells a variety of consumer and business services to microcomputer users. (See Figure 9-10.)

Some important proprietary databases are the following:

- **CSi:** Offers consumer and business services, including electronic mail.
- **Dialog Information Services:** Offers business information, as well as technical and scientific information.
- **Dow Jones Interactive Publishing:** Provides world news and information on business, investments, and stocks.
- **Prodigy:** Offers news and information on business and economics, as well as leisure services.

There are also specialized proprietary databases for investors and financial analysts, such as Chase Econometric Associates.

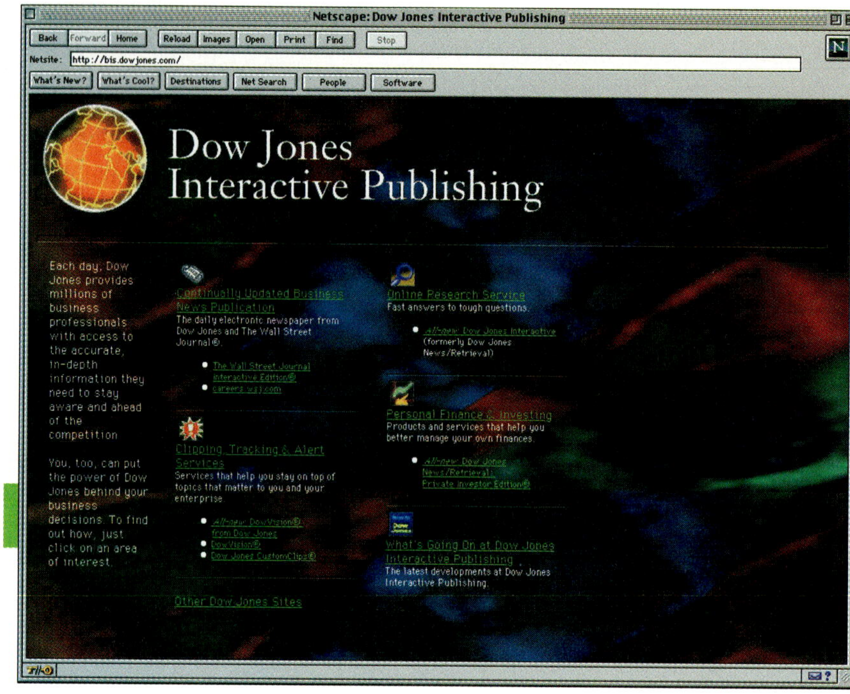

FIGURE 9-10
Proprietary Database (Dow Jones Interactive Publishing).

Costs

If you have a microcomputer, modem, and phone at home, many of these proprietary databases are available to you. Usually you pay a start-up fee, an hourly charge for searching the database, and the phone company or telecommunications line charges.

As you might expect, fees and charges are high during the normal nine-to-five business hours. However, proprietary databases often offer cheaper after-hours rates. Dialog Information Services, for example, offers The Knowledge Index nights and weekends for (as of this writing) a start-up fee of $9.95 through CSi. An online search charge (which includes telecommunications line costs) is $21.00 an hour. This service offers comprehensive coverage of journals, abstracts, research reports, reviews, news, tax information, and bibliographies. Topics covered range from agriculture to social science.

See Figure 9-11 for a summary of the four types of databases.

FIGURE 9-11
Summary of the four types of databases.

TYPES OF DATABASES

TYPE	DESCRIPTION
Individual	Integrated files used by just one person
Company	Common operational or commonly used files shared in an organization
Distributed	Database spread geographically and accessed using database server
Proprietary	Information utilities or data banks available to users on wide range of topics for a subscription fee

Database Uses and Issues

Databases help users keep current and plan for the future, but keeping them secure is important. Databases may be supervised by a database administrator.

Databases offer great opportunities for productivity. In fact, in corporate libraries, electronic databases are now considered more valuable than books and journals. However, maintaining databases means users must make constant efforts to keep them from being tampered with or misused.

Data for Strategic Uses

Databases help users keep up to date and plan for the future. Among the hundreds of databases available to help users with both general and specific business purposes are the following:

- *Business directories* providing addresses, financial and marketing information, products, and trade and brand names.
- *Demographic data,* such as county and city statistics, current estimates on population and income, employment statistics, census data, and so on.
- *Business statistical information,* such as financial information on publicly traded companies, market potential of certain retail stores, and other business data and information.
- *Text databases* providing articles from business publications, press releases, reviews on companies and products, and so on.

Importance of Security

Precisely because databases are so valuable, their security has become a vital issue. One concern is that personal and private information about people stored in databases will be used for the wrong purposes. For instance, a person's credit history or medical records might be used to make hiring or promotion decisions.

Another concern is with preventing unauthorized users from gaining access to a database. For example, there have been numerous instances in which a **computer virus** has been launched into a database or network. Computer viruses are hidden instructions that are often passed through networks and operating systems and become embedded in different programs and databases. Some are relatively harmless, but others may destroy data. Computer viruses and other security issues are discussed in detail in the Workplace Issues chapter.

Security may require putting guards on company computer rooms and checking the identification of everyone admitted. Some security systems electronically check fingerprints. (See Figure 9-12.) Security concerns are particularly important to organizations using WANs. Violations can occur without actually entering secured areas.

FIGURE 9-12
Security: Electronic fingerprint pads.

The Database Administrator

Librarians have had to be trained in the use of electronic databases so that they can help their corporate users. However, corporate databases of all sorts—not just those in the library—have become extremely important. Hence, many large organizations employ a **database administrator (DBA).** He or she helps determine the structure of the large databases and evaluates the performance of the DBMS. For shared databases, the DBA also determines which people have access to what kind of data; these are called **processing rights.** In addition, the DBA is concerned with such significant issues as security, privacy, and ethics.

A Look at the Future

The Internet on Wheels from Mercedes Benz is a leader in smart cars.

Did you see Bruce Willis' futuristic airborne taxi in *The Fifth Element*? Imagine a car that operates on its own, flies, has rocket boosters, monitors traffic conditions and weather, and entertains us as we travel. In the 23rd century, smart cars may well look and act a lot like Bruce Willis' taxi . . . hopefully more sleek and efficient but just as smart.

Of course, none of today's cars can do all those things. But you can expect more cars that navigate themselves and surf the Internet in the near future. Several car makers offer global positioning systems (GPS) that combine large databases of streets, highways, and interchanges with satellite communications. These GPS precisely track a vehicle as it travels to its destination. You can obtain specific directions and navigational advice without ever leaving your car.

Daimmler-Benz, maker of the Mercedes Benz cars, recently unveiled a concept car dubbed The Internet Multimedia on Wheels. This smart car allows occupants to access the Internet from most locations in Europe and North America. They foresee a day when you will be able to access Internet-based roadside services that will diagnose car problems remotely as well as deliver traffic advisories and headline news.

When will these smart cars be available? Don't expect to see any Internet applications in your sedan anytime soon. Most observers predict that it will be ten years away. However, many of the other applications are already here and more are on their way.

KEY TERMS

batch processing (188)
child node (193)
common operational database (196)
common user database (197)
company database (196)
computer virus (199)

data dictionary (192)
database administrator (DBA) (200)
direct file organization (190)
distributed database (197)
hashing (190)
hierarchical database (193)
index sequential file organization (190)
individual database (196)
key field (188)
master file (189)
microcomputer database (196)
network database (194)
nodes (193)
parent node (193)
pointer (194)
processing rights (200)
proprietary database (197)
query language (192)
real-time processing (188)
relation (194)
relational database (194)
sequential file organization (189)
Structured Query Language (SQL) (192)
transaction file (189)

REVIEW QUESTIONS

True/False

1. A record is a collection of related files.
2. In batch processing, data is processed at the same time the transaction occurs.
3. A data dictionary describes the structure of the data in a database.
4. A distributed database has data located in more than one location.
5. Processing rights are typically determined by the database administrator to specify which people have access to what kind of data.

Multiple Choice

1. A collection of related fields:
   a. byte
   b. word
   c. character
   d. record
   e. file
2. A temporary file containing recent changes to records:
   a. master
   b. data
   c. transaction
   d. indexed
   e. batch
3. The database organization in which fields and records are structured in nodes with each child node having only one parent.
   a. hierarchical
   b. network
   c. proprietary
   d. relational
   e. individual
4. The type of database that is sometimes called an information utility or a data bank:
   a. individual
   b. common operational
   c. common user
   d. distributed
   e. proprietary

5. Hidden instructions that "migrate" through networks and operating systems:
   a. file servers
   b. viruses
   c. nodes
   d. relation
   e. pointer

Fill in the Blank

1. The __________ field uniquely identifies each record.
2. __________ file organization is best for locating specific records.
3. A database is a collection of __________ data.
4. __________ databases are more flexible and easier to use than hierarchical and network databases.
5. Large organizations employ database __________ to help determine database structures and evaluate database performance.

Open Ended

1. Describe how data is organized and give an example.
2. What are the differences between sequential, direct, and index sequential file organizations?
3. What are databases, and why are they needed?
4. Discuss the three principal ways of organizing a database.
5. Describe each of the four types of database.

DISCUSSION QUESTIONS

1. *Useful information utilities:* What is your major or prospective major? What kinds of information are you apt to be required to obtain for research papers, projects, and assignments? If you're in the health field, you may be required to learn about diet, exercise, drug recovery, and the like. If you're in marketing, you may need to know about sales forecasting and product marketing.

   Take a few minutes to list the areas of information required in your field. Then go to the library and look up which information utilities or data banks would be most valuable to you. Examples are CompuServe, Dialog or The Knowledge Index, Dow Jones News Retrieval, and Prodigy.
2. *Your school's database:* Almost all organizations keep information about their employees and customers in databases. Surely your college or university does also. Without conducting extensive research, respond to each of the following:
   a. What information about you do you think is stored in your school's database?
   b. How do you suppose the data is organized? Specifically, give an example of a database, file, record, field, and character.
   c. Which type of file organization do you think is used, and why?
   d. Which type of DBMS organization is likely used, and why?

on the web

Exercises and Explorations

1 Financial Markets

There are several sites on the Web for financial information. These sites typically maintain a large, ever-expanding database that receives and organizes stock information. Visit our Web site at http://www.magpie.org/essentials/chapter-9 to link to one of the best data bases. Once connected to that site, look up the performance of Nike, Disney, and Coca-Cola. Print out the graph of each stock's price fluctuations, and write a paragraph on how businesses might use this information.

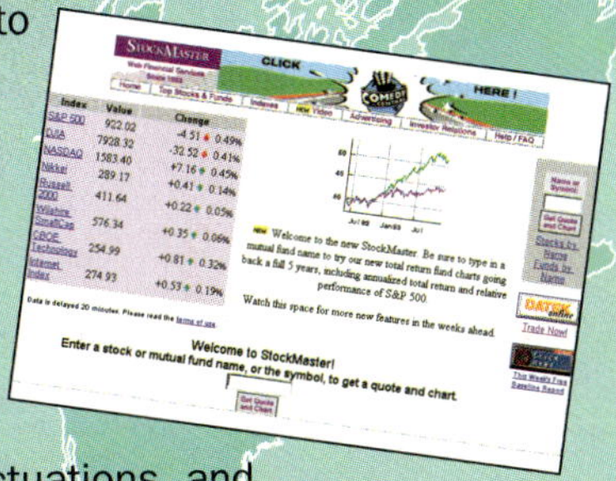

2 Information Please

If you forget a telephone number, you can always consult the telephone directory or call for directory assistance. Or, you can use the Web, and get even more information. To see how this works, connect to our site at http://www.magpie.org/essentials/chapter-9 to link to a site containing this type of information. Once connected to that site, use the white pages, and enter your family name, city, and state or province as indicated. Then use the map function to print out a map to your home. Use the directions option to print out directions for getting from your home to school. Write a brief paragraph describing who might use such a service and why.

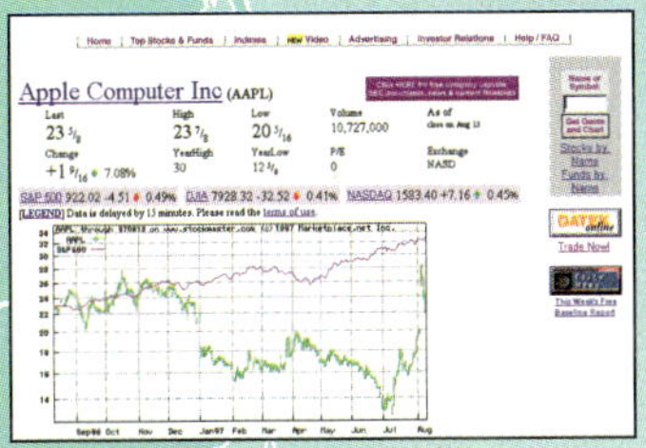

3 Search Tool

Numerous search tools are available on the Web. Typically, they create, maintain, and use an enormous database of Web sites. When users specify a search topic, a search tool investigates its database and returns a ranked list of all related Web sites.

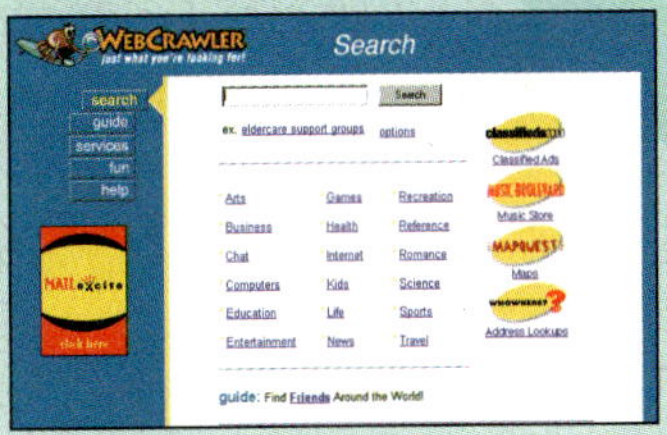

Choose a topic of interest to you and determine a few keywords that can be used to search for this topic. Then visit each of the following search tools using the same keywords each time: http://www.webcrawler.com; http://guide.infoseek.com; and http://www.lycos.com. Print out the first page of results for each search tool. Write a paragraph addressing the following questions: Are the lists identical? If not, why? Which search engine produced the best sites?

4 Music

The Web is full of sites that maintain large databases. For example, most large retail chains have sites containing databases listing all of their products. Visit our site at http://www.magpie.org/essentials/chapter-9 to link to a popular retail music chain. Once connected to that site, choose one of your favorite albums or artists. Print the information provided on the album or artist. Write a paragraph addressing the following questions: What type of file organization do you think is most likely used for this database? why?

VISUAL SUMMARY

Data Files and Databases

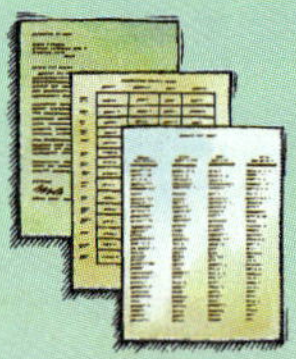

Through communication lines, users can gain access to files and databases.

FILE ORGANIZATION

TYPE	ADVANTAGES	DISADVANTAGES
Sequential	Efficient access to all or large part of records, cost	Slow access to specific records
Direct	Fast access to specific records	Inefficient access to all or large part of records, cost
Index sequential	Faster than sequential, more efficient than direct	Not quite as efficient as sequential, not quite as fast as direct, cost

FILES

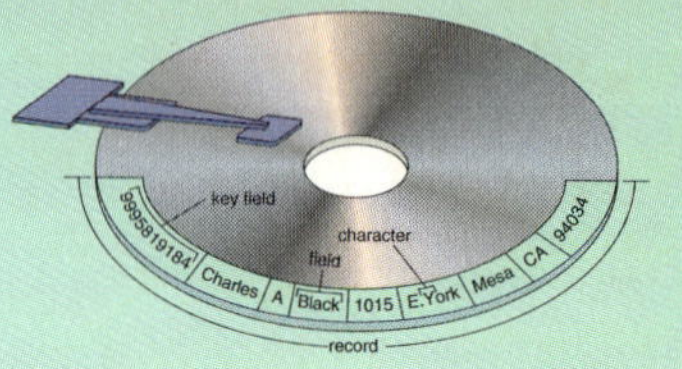

Understanding how data files work means understanding:

Data Organization

- **Character**—letter, number, special character.
- **Field**—set of related characters.
- **Record**—collection of related fields.
- **Data file**—collection of related records.
- **Database**—collection of related files.
- **Key field**—unique identifier for each record in a file.

Batch versus Real-Time Processing

Two methods of processing:

- **Batch processing**—transactions are collected over time, then processed all at once.
- **Real-time processing**—data is processed at the same time transactions occur.

Master versus Transaction Files

- **Master file**—complete file, current to the last update.
- **Transaction file**—temporary "holding file" used to update the master file.

Three types of file organization:

Sequential

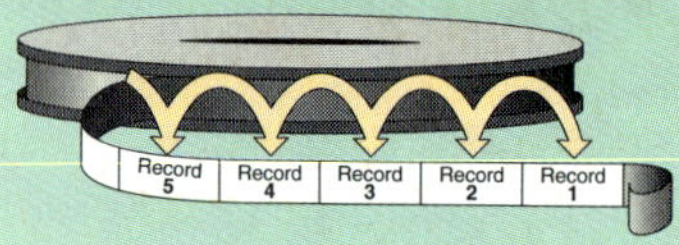

- **Sequential**—records are stored one after the other in ascending or descending order. This method is often used with magnetic tape.

Direct

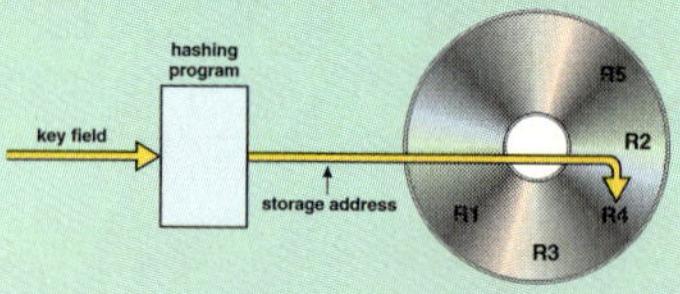

- **Direct**—records are stored in order by a key field such as a special number. This method is often used with magnetic disk.

Index Sequential

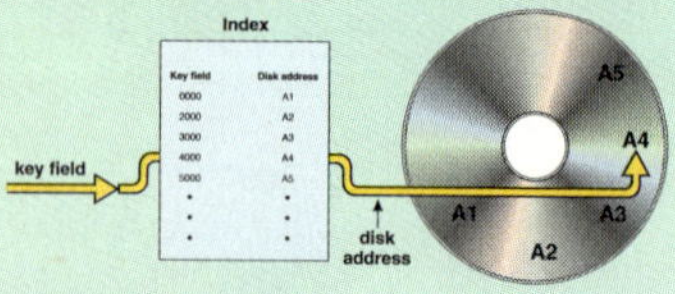

- **Index sequential**—a compromise organization with records stored sequentially and an index for near-direct access. Used with magnetic disk storage.

DATABASE

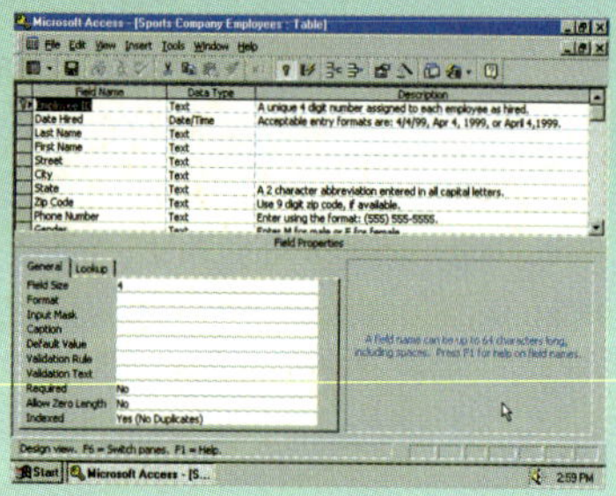

A *database* is a collection of integrated data—logically related files and records.

The Need for Databases

Advantages of databases:

- Sharing—users may share with others.
- Security—access is restricted to authorized people.
- Fewer files—a company avoids multiple files on the same subject.
- Database integrity—changes in one file are made in other files as well.

Software for a DBMS

A **database management system (DBMS)** is the software for creating, modifying, and gaining access to the database. A DBMS consists of:

- **Data dictionary**—describes the structure of the database.
- **Query language**—language to get access to the database.

Relational databases use **tables** where rows resemble records. Related tables have a **common data element** (key field). Table entries can be easily added, deleted, and modified.

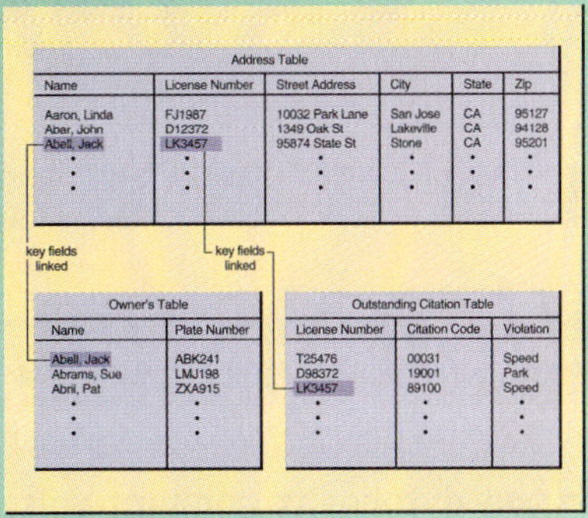

DBMS ORGANIZATION

Three principal DBMS organizations are:

Hierarchical Database

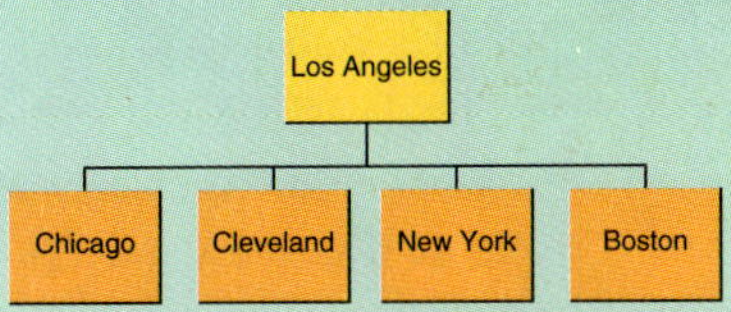

In a **hierarchical database**, fields and records are structured in **nodes**, points connected like tree branches. An entry may have a **parent** node with several **child** nodes. A node may be reached by only one path.

Network Database

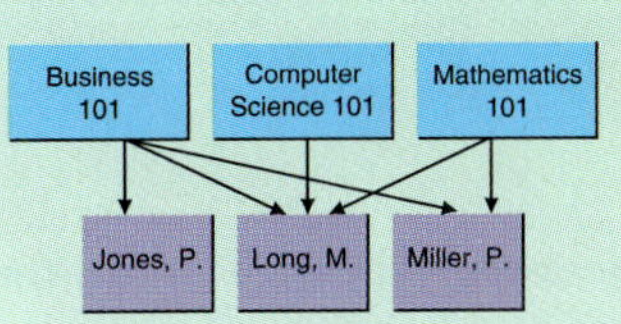

In a **network database**, nodes are arranged hierarchically, but a child node may have more than one parent. There are additional connections called **pointers**. A node may be reached by several paths.

Relational Database

In a **relational database,** data is stored in tables consisting of rows and columns; data items are found by means of an index.

TYPES OF DATABASE

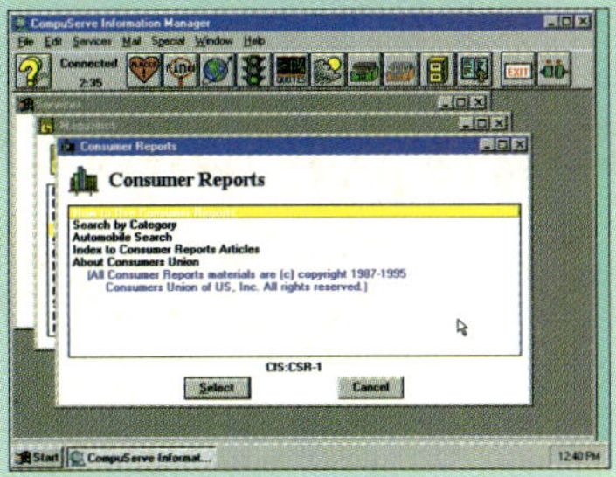

Four types of databases are:

Individual Database

The **individual database** is a collection of integrated files useful mainly to just one person.

Company, or Shared, Database

Two types of **company (shared) database** are:

- **Common operational database**—contains data on company operations.
- **Common user database**—contains data from common operational database and from outside private databases.

Distributed Database

The **distributed database** is spread out geographically and is accessible by communications links.

Proprietary Database

A **proprietary database** is available by subscription to customers.

DATABASE USES AND ISSUES

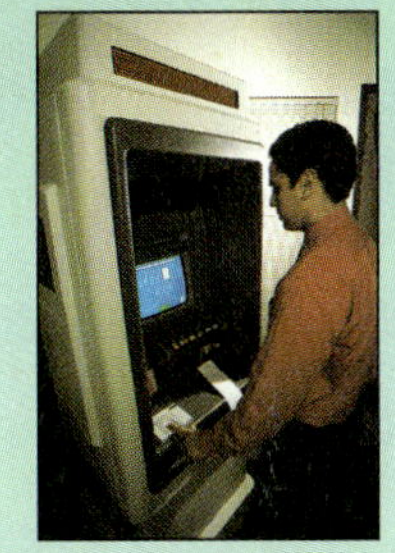

Databases offer increased productivity but also risks to security.

Data for Strategic Uses

Databases help users keep current and plan for the future.

Importance of Security

Two security concerns are illegal use of data and unauthorized access. **Computer viruses** are hidden instructions that "migrate" into programs and databases.

The Database Administrator

The **database administrator (DBA)** is a specialist who sets up and manages the database and determines **processing rights**—which people have access to what kind of data.

Information Systems

Communications links and databases connect you with information resources far beyond the surface of your desk. The microcomputer offers you access to a greater *quantity* of information than was possible a few years ago. In addition, you also have access to a better *quality* of information. As we show in this chapter, when you tap into a computer-based information system, you not only get information—you also get help in *making decisions.*

COMPETENCIES

After you have read this chapter, you should be able to:

1. Explain how organizations can be structured according to five functions and three management levels.
2. Describe how information flows in an organization.
3. Distinguish among a transaction processing system, a management information system, a decision support system, and an executive support system.
4. Distinguish between office automation systems and knowledge work systems.
5. Explain the difference between data workers and knowledge workers.
6. Describe how an intranet works.

10

Why are computers used in organizations? No doubt you can easily state one reason: to keep records of events. However, another reason might be less obvious: to help make decisions. For example, point-of-sale terminals record sales as well as recording which salesperson made each sale. This information can be used for decision making. For instance, it can help the sales manager decide which salespeople will get year-end bonuses for doing exceptional work.

Keeping accurate records and making good decisions are extremely important in running any successful organization, small or large. Let us see how some organizations are structured and how information flows within them.

How Information Flows in an Organization

Information flows up and down among managers and sideways among departments.

An **information system** (as we discussed in Chapter 1) is a collection of *people, procedures, software, hardware,* and *data.* They all work together to provide information essential to running an organization. This is information that will successfully produce a product or service and, for profit-oriented enterprises, derive a profit.

In large and medium-sized organizations, computerized information systems don't just keep track of transactions and day-to-day business operations. They also support the flow of information within the organization. This information flows both vertically and horizontally. In order to understand this, we need to understand how an organization is structured. One way to examine an organization's structure is to view it from a functional perspective. That is, you can study the different basic functional areas in organizations and the different types of people within these functional areas.

As we describe these, you might consider how they apply to any organization you are familiar with. Or consider how they apply to a hypothetical manufacturer of sporting goods, the HealthWise Group. Think of this as a large company that manufactures equipment for sports and physical activities, including those that interest you. These goods range from every type of ball imaginable (from golf to tennis to soccer) to hockey pads, leotards, and exercise bicycles.

Functions

Depending on the services or products they provide, most organizations have departments that specialize in one of five basic functions. These are *accounting, marketing, production, human resources,* and *research.* Even in very small organizations these functions must be performed—often by one person, the owner. (See Figure 10-1.) Their purposes are as follows:

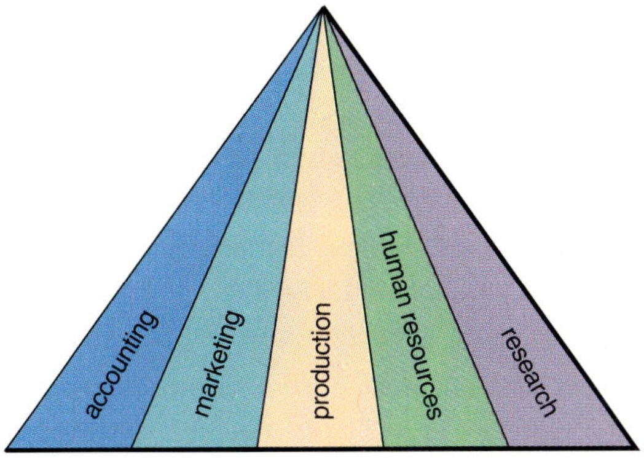

FIGURE 10-1
The five functions of an organization.

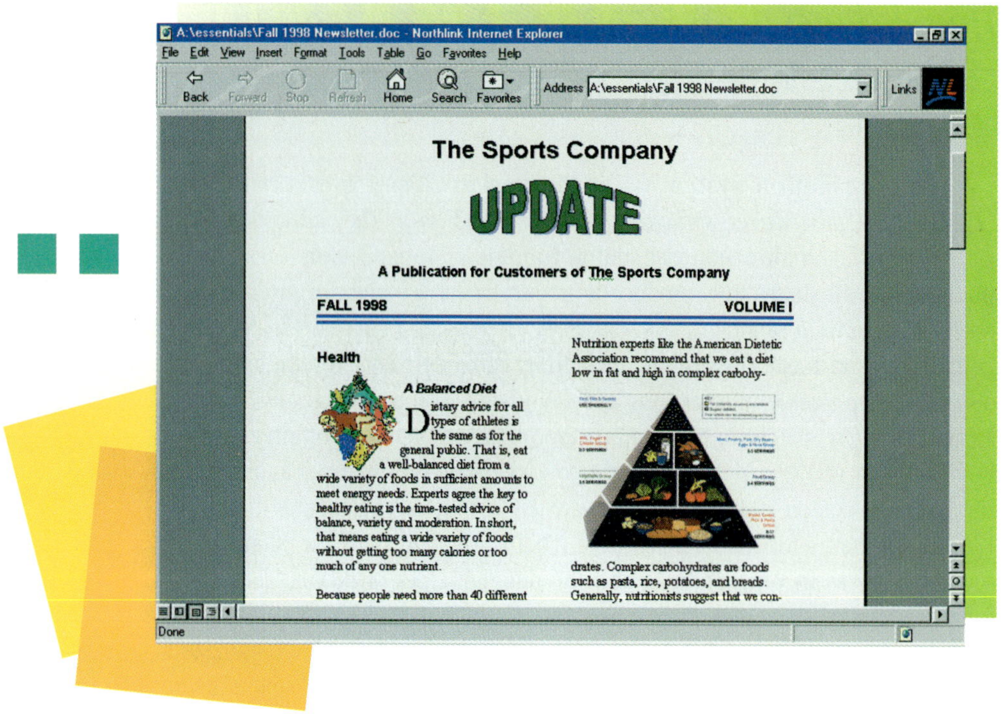

FIGURE 10-2
Newsletter on the Web.

- **Accounting:** This department keeps track of all financial activities. It pays bills, records payments, issues paychecks, and compiles periodic financial statements. At HealthWise, for example, this department performs two major activities. First, it records bills and other financial transactions with sporting goods stores and produces financial statements. Second, it produces financial budgets and forecasts of projected financial performance to help managers run the business.
- **Marketing:** Advertising, promotion, and sales are handled by this department. The people in this department plan, price, promote, sell, and distribute goods and services to customers. At HealthWise they even get involved with creating a customer newsletter that is distributed via the corporate Web page. (See Figure 10-2.)
- **Production:** This department makes the product. (See Figure 10-3.) It takes in raw materials and puts people to work to turn out finished goods (or services). The department may be a manufacturing activity or—in the case of a retail store, for example—an operations activity. It manages purchases, inventories, and flows of goods and services. At HealthWise, this department is a big purchaser of steel and aluminum, materials used in weight-lifting and exercise machines.
- **Human resources:** This department finds and hires people and handles matters such as sick leave and retirement benefits. In addition, it is concerned with evaluation, compensation, and professional development. As you might imagine, HealthWise has rather good health benefits.

FIGURE 10-3
Production is responsible for making products.

- **Research:** The research (or research and development) department has two tasks. First, it does product research. That is, it does basic research and relates new discoveries to the firm's current or new products. For instance, research people at HealthWise might look into new ideas from exercise physiologists about muscle development. They might use this knowledge in designing new physical fitness machines. Second, it does product development. That is, it develops and tests new products created by research people. It also monitors and troubleshoots new products as they are being produced.

Whatever your job in an organization, it is likely to be in one of these departments. Within the department, you may also be at one of the management levels.

Management Levels

Most people who work in an organization are not managers, of course. At the base of the organizational pyramid are the assemblers, painters, welders, drivers, and so on. These people produce goods and services. Above them, however, are various levels of managers—people with titles such as supervisor, director, regional manager, and vice president. These are the people who do the planning, leading, organizing, and controlling necessary to see that the work gets done. At HealthWise, for example, the northwest district sales manager directs and coordinates all the salespeople in her area. Other job titles might be vice president of marketing, director of human resources, or production manager. In smaller organizations, these titles are often combined.

Management in many organizations is divided into three levels: supervisors, middle-level, and top-level. (See Figure 10-4.) They may be described as follows:

- **Supervisors: Supervisors** manage and monitor the employees or workers, those who actually produce the goods and services. Thus, these managers have the responsibility relating to *operational matters.* They monitor day-to-day events and immediately take corrective action, if necessary. For example, at HealthWise, a production supervisor monitors the materials needed to build exercise bicycles. If parts begin to run low, the supervisor must take action immediately.

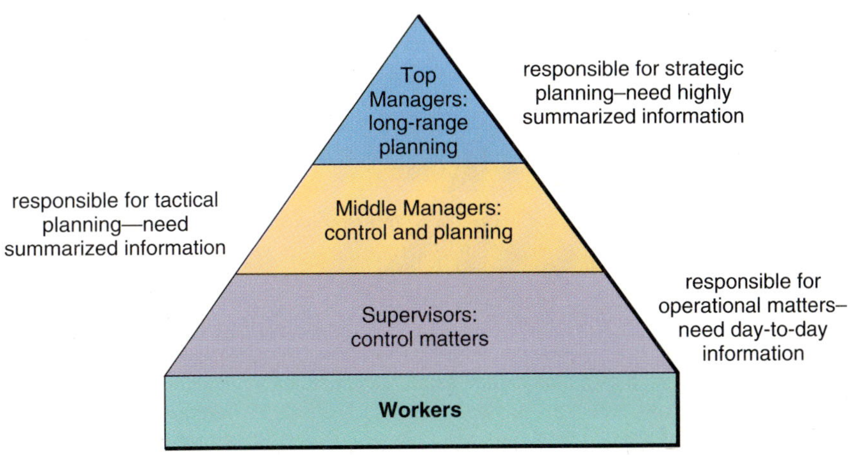

FIGURE 10-4

Three levels of management.

- **Middle management: Middle-level managers** deal with *control, planning* (also called *tactical planning*), and *decision-making.* They implement the long-term goals of the organization. For example, the HealthWise regional sales manager for the Northwest sets sales goals for district sales managers in Washington, Oregon, and Idaho. She or he also monitors their sales performance and takes corrective action if necessary.
- **Top management: Top-level managers** are concerned with *long-range planning* (also called *strategic planning*). They need information that will help them to plan the future growth and direction of the organization. For example, the HealthWise vice president of marketing might need to determine the demand and the sales strategy for a new product. Such a product might be a stationary exercise bicycle with a biometric feedback mechanism.

Information Flow

Each level of management has different information needs. Top-level managers need information that is summarized in capsule form to reveal the overall condition of the business. They also need information from outside the organization, because top-level managers need to forecast and plan for long-range events. Middle-level managers need summarized information—weekly or monthly reports. They need to develop budget projections as well as to evaluate the performance of supervisors. Supervisors need detailed, very current day-to-day information on their units so that they can keep operations running smoothly.

To support these different needs, information *flows* in different directions. (See Figure 10-5.) The top-level managers, such as the chief executive officer (CEO), need information from below and from all departments. They also need information from outside the organization. For example, at HealthWise, they are deciding whether to introduce a line of hockey equipment in the southwestern United States. The vice president of marketing must look at relevant data. Such data might include availability of ice rinks and census data about the number of young people. It might also include sales histories on related cold-weather sports equipment.

For middle-level managers, the information flow is both horizontal and vertical across functional lines within the organization. For example, the regional sales managers at HealthWise set their sales goals by coordinating with middle managers

FIGURE 10-5
Information flow within an organization.

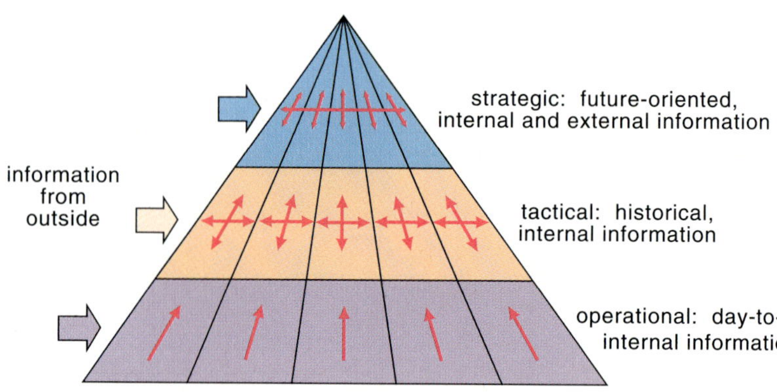

in the production department. They are able to tell sales managers what products will be produced, how many, and when. An example of a product might be an exercise bicycle. The regional sales managers also must coordinate with the strategic goals set by the top managers. They must set and monitor the sales goals for the supervisors beneath them.

For supervisory managers, information flow is primarily vertical. That is, supervisors communicate mainly with their middle managers and with the workers beneath them. For instance, at HealthWise, production supervisors rarely communicate with people in the accounting department. However, they are constantly communicating with production-line workers and with their own managers.

Now we know how a large organization is usually structured and how information flows within the organization. But how is a computer-based information system likely to be set up to support its needs? And what do you, as a microcomputer user, need to know to use it?

Computer-Based Information Systems

There are four kinds of computer-based information systems: transaction processing system, management information system, decision support system, and executive support system.

All large organizations have computer-based information systems. Some systems record routine activities: employees hired, materials purchased, products produced, and the like. Such recorded events are called **transactions.** Other systems use these recorded events to help managerial planning and control. The systems form a pyramid, each primarily (but not exclusively) supporting one level of management. (See Figure 10-6.)

FIGURE 10-6
The three levels of information systems.

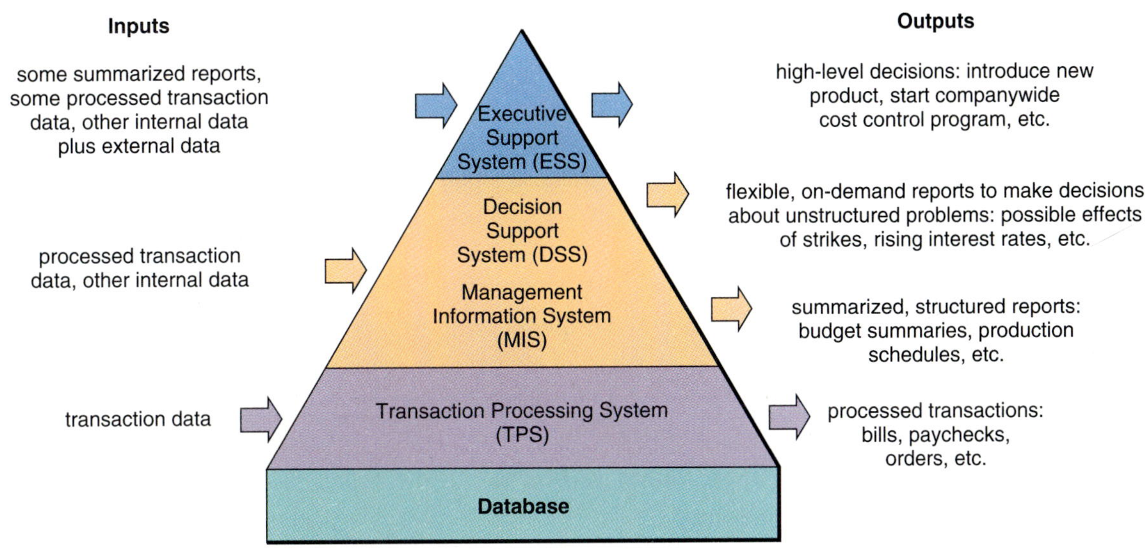

- **Transaction processing system:** The **transaction processing system (TPS)** records day-to-day transactions such as customer orders, bills, inventory levels, and production output. The TPS helps supervisors by generating databases that act as the foundation for the other information systems.
- **Management information system:** The **management information system (MIS)** summarizes the detailed data of the transaction processing system in standard reports for middle-level managers. Such reports might include production schedules and budget summaries.
- **Decision support system:** The **decision support system (DSS)** provides a flexible tool for analysis. The DSS helps middle-level managers and others in the organization analyze a wide range of problems, such as the effect of events and trends outside the organization. Like the MIS, the DSS draws on the detailed data of the transaction processing system.
- **Executive support system:** The **executive support system (ESS),** also known as the **executive information system (EIS),** is an easy-to-use system that presents information in a very highly summarized form. It helps top-level managers oversee the company's operations and develop strategic plans. The ESS combines the internal data from TPS and MIS with external data.

Let us describe these four kinds of information systems in more detail.

Transaction Processing Systems

A transaction processing system records routine operations.

A *transaction processing system (TPS)* helps an organization keep track of routine operations and records these events in a database. For this reason, some firms call this the **data processing system (DPS).** The data from operations—for example, customer orders for HealthWise's products—makes up a database that records the transactions of the company. This database of transactions is used to support an MIS, DSS, and ESS.

One of the most essential transaction processing systems for any organization is in the accounting area. (See Figure 10-7.) Every accounting department handles six basic activities. Five of these are sales order processing, accounts receivable, inventory and purchasing, accounts payable, and payroll. All of these are recorded in the general ledger, the sixth activity.

Let us take a look at these six activities. They will make up the basis of the accounting system for almost any office you might work in.

- The **sales order processing** activity records the customer requests for the company's product or service. (See Figure 10-8.) When an order comes in—a request for a set of barbells, for example—the warehouse is alerted to ship a product.
- The **accounts receivable** activity records money received from or owed by customers. HealthWise keeps track of bills paid by sporting goods stores and by gyms and health clubs to which it sells directly.

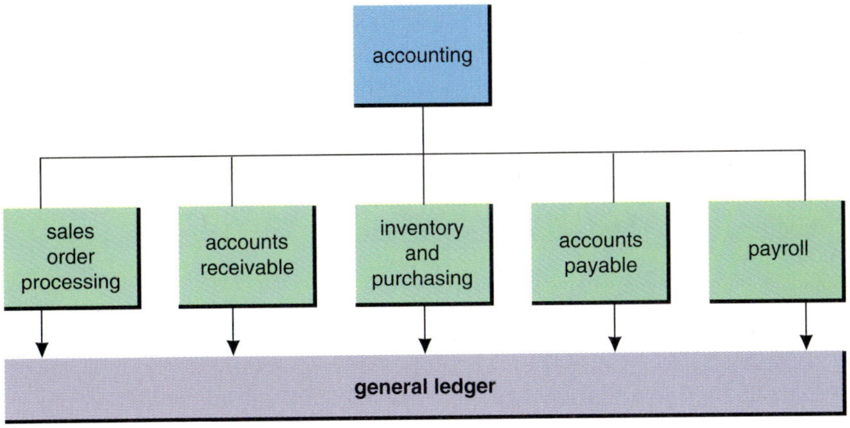

FIGURE 10-7
Transaction processing system for accounting.

- The parts and finished goods that the company has in stock are called **inventory**—all exercise machines in the warehouse, for example. An *inventory control system* keeps records of the number of each kind of part or finished good in the warehouse. **Purchasing** is buying of materials and services. Often a *purchase order* is used. This is a form that shows the name of the company supplying the material or service and what is being purchased.
- **Accounts payable** refers to money the company owes its suppliers for materials and services it has received—steel and aluminum, for example.
- The **payroll** activity is concerned with calculating employee paychecks. Amounts are generally determined by the kind of job, hours worked, and kinds of deductions (such as taxes, social security, medical insurance). Paychecks may be calculated from employee time cards or, in some cases, supervisors' time sheets.

FIGURE 10-8
Sales order processing for Canadian Airlines International.

- The **general ledger** keeps track of all summaries of all the foregoing transactions. A typical general ledger system can produce income statements and balance sheets. *Income statements* show a company's financial performance—income, expenses, and the difference between them for a specific time period. *Balance sheets* list the overall financial condition of an organization. They include assets (for example, buildings and property owned), liabilities (debts), and how much of the organization (the equity) is owned by the owners.

Management Information Systems

A management information system produces summarized, structured reports.

A *management information system (MIS)* is a computer-based information system that produces standardized reports in summarized, structured form. It is used to support middle managers. An MIS differs from a transaction processing system in a significant way. Whereas a transaction processing system *creates* databases, an MIS *uses* databases. Indeed, an MIS can draw from the databases of *several* departments. (See Figure 10-9.) Thus, an MIS requires a *database management system* that integrates the databases of the different departments. Middle managers need summary data often drawn from across different functional areas.

An MIS produces reports that are *predetermined.* That is, they follow a predetermined format and always show the same kinds of content. Although reports may differ from one industry to another, there are three common categories of reports:

- **Periodic reports** are produced at regular intervals—weekly, monthly, or quarterly, for instance. (See Figure 10-10.) Examples are HealthWise's monthly sales or production reports. The sales reports from district sales managers are

FIGURE 10-9
MIS uses databases created by various departments.

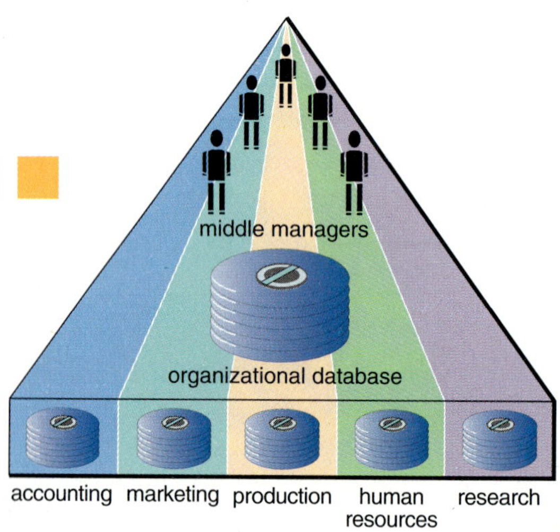

FIGURE 10-10
Periodic reports may be produced weekly, monthly, or quarterly.

combined into a monthly report for the regional sales managers. For comparison purposes, a regional manager is also able to see the sales reports of other regional managers.

- **Exception reports** call attention to unusual events. An example is a sales report that shows that certain items are selling significantly above or below marketing department forecasts. For instance, if fewer exercise bicycles are selling than were predicted for the northwest sales region, the regional manager will receive an exception report. That report may be used to alert the district managers and salespeople to give this product more attention.
- The opposite of a periodic report, a **demand report** is produced on request. An example is a report on the numbers and types of jobs held by women and minorities. Such a report is not needed periodically, but it may be required when requested by the U.S. government. At HealthWise, many government contracts require this information. It's used to certify that HealthWise is achieving certain government equal-opportunity guidelines.

Decision Support Systems

A DSS helps decision makers analyze unanticipated situations.

Managers often must deal with unanticipated questions. For example, the HealthWise manager in charge of manufacturing might ask how a strike would affect production schedules. A *decision support system (DSS)* enables managers to get answers to such unexpected and generally nonrecurring kinds of problems. Frequently, a team is formed to address large problems. A **group decision support system (GDSS)** is then used to support this collective work. The GDSS uses interactive terminals (or microcomputers) and software. **Interactive** means that there is immediate communication between the user and the computer system. That is, when input data is entered into the computer, it is processed immediately. The output results are promptly displayed on the screen.

A DSS, then, is quite different from a transaction processing system, which simply records data. It is also different from a management information system, which summarizes data in predetermined reports. A DSS is used to *analyze* data. Moreover, it produces reports that do not have a fixed format. This makes the DSS a flexible tool for analysis.

Many DSSs are designed for large computer systems. However, microcomputers, with their increased power and sophisticated software, such as spreadsheet and database programs, are being used for DSS. Users of a DSS are managers, not computer programmers. Thus, a DSS must be easy to use—or most likely it will not be used at all. Commands need to be in English-like language: "SEARCH" or "FIND," for instance. A HealthWise marketing manager might want to know which territories are not meeting their sales quotas and need additional advertising support. To find out, the executive might type "FIND ALL FOR SALES < QUOTA."

How does a decision support system work? Essentially, it consists of four parts: the user, system software, data, and decision models.

The User

The user could be you. In general, the user is someone who has to make decisions—a manager, often a middle-level manager.

System Software

The system software is essentially the operating system—programs designed to work behind the scenes to handle detailed operating procedures. In order to give the user a good, comfortable interface, the software typically is menu- or icon-driven. That is, the screen presents easily understood lists of commands or icons, giving the user several options.

The Data

The data in a DSS is stored in a database and consists of two kinds. *Internal data*—data from within the organization—consists principally of transactions from the transaction processing system. *External data* is data gathered from outside the organization. Examples are data provided by marketing research firms, trade associations, and the U.S. government (such as customer profiles, census data, and economic forecasts).

The Decision Models

The **decision models** give the DSS its analytical capabilities. There are three basic types of models: strategic, tactical, and operational. *Strategic models* assist top-level managers in long-range planning, such as stating company objectives or planning plant locations. *Tactical models* help middle-level managers control the work of the organization, such as financial planning and sales promotion planning. Such models help middle-level managers implement top managers' long-range plans. *Operational models* help lower-level managers accomplish the organization's day-to-day activities, such as evaluating and maintaining quality control.

Executive Support Systems

Executive support systems are specially designed, simplified systems for top executives.

Using a DSS requires some training. Many top managers have other people in their offices running DSSs and reporting their findings. Top-level executives also want something more concise than an MIS—something that produces very focused reports.

Executive support systems (ESSs) consist of sophisticated software that, like an MIS or a DSS, can draw together data from an organization's databases in meaningful patterns. However, an ESS is specifically designed to be easy to use. This is so that a top executive with little spare time can obtain essential information without extensive training. Thus, information is often displayed in very condensed form and in bold graphics.

Consider an executive support system used by the president of HealthWise. It is available on his microcomputer. The first thing each morning, the president calls up the ESS on his display screen, as shown in the left-hand illustration. (See Figure 10-11.) Note that the screen gives a condensed account of activities in the five different areas of the company. (These are Accounting, Marketing, Production, Human Resources, and Research.) On this particular morning, the ESS shows business in four areas proceeding smoothly. However, in the first area, Accounting, the percentage of late-paying customers—past due accounts—has increased 3 percent. Three percent may not seem like much. But HealthWise has had a history of problems with late payers, which has left the company at times strapped for cash. The president decides to find out the details. To do so, he presses *1* (corresponding to Accounting) on his keyboard.

The right-hand screen shows information about past due accounts expressed in graphic form. (Refer to Figure 10-11.) The status of today's late payers is shown in

FIGURE 10-11
An executive information system. Left: information in condensed text form. Right: details in graphic form.

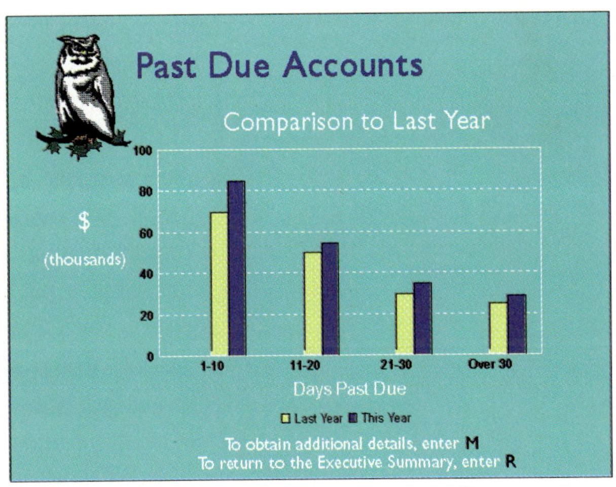

blue. The status of late payers at this time a year ago is shown in yellow. The differences between today and a year ago are very clearly presented. The differences are significant. For example, approximately $70,000 was late 1 to 10 days last year. This year, over $80,000 was late. The president knows that he must take some action to speed up customer payments. (For example, he or she might call this to the attention of the vice president of accounting. The vice president might decide to offer discounts to early payers or charge more interest to late payers.)

ESSs permit a firm's top executives to gain direct access to information about the company's performance. Some also have electronic mail setups that allow managers to communicate directly with other executives. Some systems even have structured forms to help managers streamline their thoughts before sending electronic memos. In addition, an ESS may be organized to retrieve information from databases outside the company, such as business-news services. This enables a firm to watch for stories on competitors and stay current on relevant news events that could affect its business. For example, news of increased sports injuries caused by running and aerobic dancing, and the consequent lessened interest by people in these activities, might cause HealthWise to alter its sales and production goals for its line of fitness-related shoes.

Other Information Systems

Information workers use office automation systems and knowledge work systems.

We have discussed only four information systems: TPS to support lower-level managers, MIS and DSS to support middle-level managers, and ESS to support top-level managers. There are many other information systems to support different individuals and functions. The fastest-growing are information systems designed to support information workers.

Information workers create, distribute, and communicate information. They are the secretaries, clerks, engineers, and scientists, to name a few, in the organization. Some are involved with distribution and communication of information (like the secretaries and clerks). They are called *data workers.* Others are involved with the creation of information (like the engineers and scientists). They are called *knowledge workers.*

Three systems to support information workers are:

- **Office automation systems:** **Office automation systems (OASs)** are designed primarily to support data workers. These systems focus on managing documents, communicating, and scheduling. Documents are managed using word processing, desktop publishing, and other image technologies. Communications use e-mail, voice-messaging, and videoconferencing. (See Figure 10-12.)
- **Knowledge work systems:** Knowledge workers use OAS systems. Additionally, they use specialized information systems called **knowledge work systems (KWSs)** to create information in their areas of expertise. For example, engineers involved in product design and manufacturing use **CAD/CAM (computer-aided**

FIGURE 10-12
Videoconferencing: individuals and groups can see and share information.

design/computer-aided manufacturing) systems. (See Figure 10-13.) These KWSs consist of powerful microcomputers running special programs that integrate the design and manufacture activities. CAD/CAM is widely used in the manufacture of automobiles and other products.

- **Intranets: Intranets** are privately owned organizationwide networks that look and act like the Internet. They use TCP/IP and linked Web pages. Users access internal information using browsers and locate information using search tools. Unlike the Internet, intranets are privately owned and access is carefully controlled.

FIGURE 10-13
CAD/CAM: Knowledge work systems used by design and manufacturing engineers.

A Look at the Future

Technology can cause information overload. E-mail is the major source of information overload.

Have you ever questioned the value of technology? Has it really helped us and made us more productive? Is it possible that the various devices intended to increase our productivity have actually had the opposite effect?

E-mail, cell phones, notebook computers, and the Web are great. They allow us to communicate, work almost anywhere, and provide access to vast amounts of data. However, unless we are careful, they can create information overload and have a negative effect on our ability to get work done.

Several studies have found that e-mail is the major source of information overload. It was recently reported that a typical knowledge worker in a large corporation sends and receives over 100 e-mail messages a day. Furthermore, the study concluded that the majority of these messages are not necessary. Here are some tips to control e-mail overload.

- *Be selective* look first at the subject line in an e-mail—read only those of direct and immediate interest to you; look next at the sender line—read only those from people important to you; postpone or ignore the others
- *Remove* after reading an e-mail, respond if necessary, then either file it in the appropriate folder or delete it
- *Protect* limit your e-mail by giving your address only to those who need it
- *Be brief* when responding, be concise and direct
- *Stop spam* spam is unwanted e-mail advertisements—avoid mailing lists, complain to those who send spam, and ask to have your name removed from their mailing list
- *Don't respond* you do not have to respond to an e-mail; be selective, respond only to those worthy of your time

Is information overload part of your future? If you are like today's busy executives, it probably will be.

KEY TERMS

accounts payable (213)
accounts receivable (212)
CAD/CAM (computer-aided design/ computer-aided manufacturing) (218)
data processing system (DPS) (212)
decision model (216)
decision support system (DSS) (212)
demand report (215)
exception report (215)
executive information system (EIS) (212)
executive support system (ESS) (212)
general ledger (214)
group decision support system (GDSS) (215)
information system (207)
information worker (218)
interactive (215)
intranet (219)
inventory (213)
knowledge work system (KWS) (218)
management information system (MIS) (212)
middle-level manager (210)
office automation system (OAS) (218)
payroll (213)
periodic report (214)
purchasing (213)
sales order processing (212)
supervisor (209)
top-level manager (210)
transaction (211)
transaction processing system (TPS) (212)

REVIEW QUESTIONS

True/False

1. For small companies, keeping accurate records and making good decisions are extremely important.
2. The production department takes in raw materials and puts people to work to turn out finished goods (or services).
3. In smaller organizations such titles as vice president of marketing and director of human resources are often combined.
4. CEO stands for chief executive officer.
5. Decision support systems summarize the detailed data of the transaction processing system in standard reports.

Multiple Choice

1. An information system is a collection of hardware, software, procedures, data, databases, and:
   a. people
   b. functions
   c. managers
   d. accounting systems
   e. information
2. This department finds and hires people and handles such matters as sick leave and retirement benefits:
   a. accounting
   b. production
   c. marketing
   d. human resources
   e. research
3. The level of manager who deals with control and planning:
   a. executive
   b. top manager
   c. middle manager
   d. supervisor
   e. vice president
4. The level of manager whose information is primarily vertical:
   a. supervisor
   b. top manager
   c. middle manager
   d. executive
   e. vice president
5. The information system that provides a flexible tool for analysis:
   a. database information system
   b. transaction processing system
   c. management information system
   d. executive information system
   e. decision support system

Fill in the Blank

1. The __________ department relates new discoveries and is responsible for product development.
2. __________ managers are concerned with long-range planning.
3. __________ __________ systems record day-to-day activities such as customer orders and inventory levels.
4. __________ information systems are specially designed, simplified systems for top-level executives.
5. __________ workers use office automation and knowledge work systems.

Open Ended

1. What are the five departments found in medium-sized and large organizations? Discuss the function of each department.
2. What are the three levels of management? What are the responsibilities of managers at each level?
3. Explain the differences between the three types of reports produced by a management information system.
4. Discuss the three types of decision models used in a DSS.
5. Explain what an executive support system is. Give an example.

DISCUSSION QUESTIONS AND PROJECTS

1. *The functions and transactions of an organization:* What is the equivalent of "production" in a hotel or "marketing" in a college? The five functions or departments of an organization—accounting, marketing, production, human resources, and research—clearly exist in a for-profit organization such as an apparel manufacturer. However, they would not be found—at least not in the same form—in an employment agency, a department store, or a hospital. Nevertheless, these organizations do offer products or services, and they probably (if large enough) have three management levels.

   Choose an organization, such as your college, and interview someone to find out what might constitute departments and management layers. Summarize your findings in a drawing identifying the departments and the levels of management. See if you can discover the transactions that go into the database of one of the departments—for example, registrar, housing, fund raising, financial aid, or alumni affairs.
2. Almost all organizations collect and use data. Large organizations typically have formal names for the systems designed to collect and use the data. Although different organizations may use different names, the most common names are transaction processing, management information, decision support, and executive information systems.

   Choose an organization, such as your college, and consider the data and information needs. Describe:

a. the transaction processing system—identify the data collected and briefly describe the six basic activities of the accounting department.
b. the management information system—describe a typical periodic report, exception report, and demand report.
c. the decision support system—discuss a problem that might be addressed.
d. the executive support system—present a typical display the president would see first thing each morning.

3. *Do computers really make us more productive?* The basic reason for installing and learning computers is that they help us increase our productivity. But do they really? Research has shown some of the following problems. (a) People in organizations spend time fine-tuning their word-processing documents when such polishing is not necessary. (b) They devote time to unnecessarily putting spreadsheet information into graphic form. (c) They fill up ordinary memos with unnecessary facts gleaned from expensive computer searches. (d) They create unnecessary pressure by transmitting messages via modem or fax when regular mail would do. (e) They spend unproductive hours surfing the Internet and browsing the Web. These are serious problems that you will run across in the workplace. Discuss the following:

a. Who or what creates these problems?
b. What would you do to prevent these problems if you were a supervisor in an office?
c. What can you do to avoid contributing to these problems yourself?

on the web

Exercises and Explorations

1 CAD

CAD (computer-aided drawing) programs are often used to build precise models of buildings or products on the computer. Visit our site at http://www.magpie.org/essentials/chapter-10 to link to a CAD site. Once connected to that site, locate the gallery, and print out images presented there. Write a brief paragraph describing how and why many businesses use CAD programs.

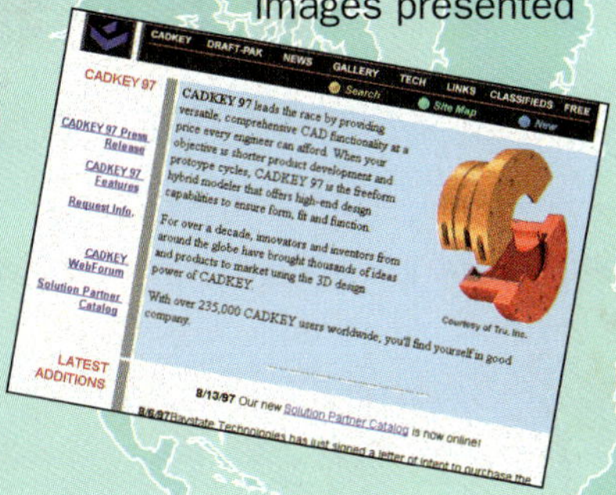

2 Global Positioning Systems

The global positioning systems (GPS) use a series of satellites that ring the world. Using these satellites, a special receiver can locate your exact location anywhere in the world. To learn more, visit our Web site at http://www.magpie.org/essentials/chapter-10 to link to a GPS service provider. Once connected to that site, print the opening Web page. Write a paragraph describing the GPS product and discussing its accuracy.

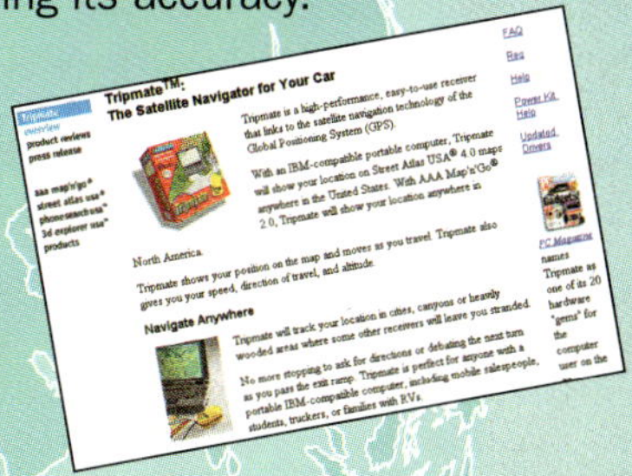

3 Intranets

Within corporate computing, intranets are rapidly growing in popularity. To learn more about this important topic, visit the Yahoo site at http://www.yahoo.com. Once connected to that site try using the keyword "intranet" or the subject heading "Computers and Internet: Communications and Networking: Intranets." Print the Web page you find the most informative. Write a paragraph on what kinds of companies use intranets, how intranets are helpful, and what the downsides are in using intranets in the workplace.

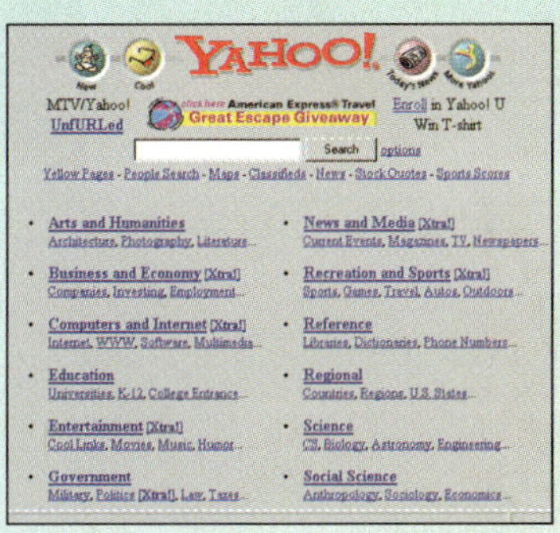

4 News

Current and late-breaking news often hits the Web before it is printed and sometimes before it makes the television news. Visit our Web site at http://www.magpie.org/essentials/chapter-10 to link to a site specializing in news. Once connected, locate an article of interest to you. Print the article and write a brief paragraph summarizing it.

VISUAL SUMMARY

10 Information Systems

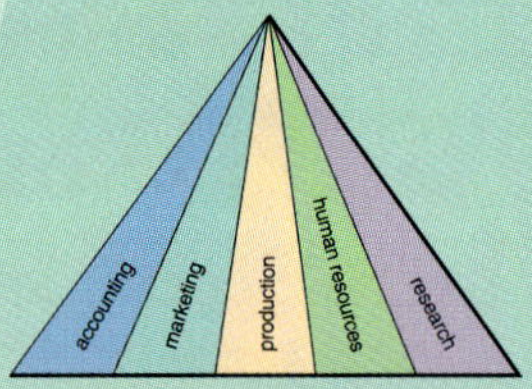

Technological advances in communications and database applications make available a greater *quantity* of information than was possible a few years ago. In addition, you have access to a better *quality* of information. Organizations use specialized information systems to provide accurate and timely information.

HOW INFORMATION FLOWS

Information flows up and down among managers and sideways among departments.

Functions

Most organizations have separate departments to perform five functions:

- *Accounting*—manages finances, including orders, bills, paychecks.
- *Marketing*—promotes and sells the product (or service).
- *Production*—makes the product (or service).
- *Human resources*—hires people, manages employee benefits.
- *Research*—develops new products (or services).

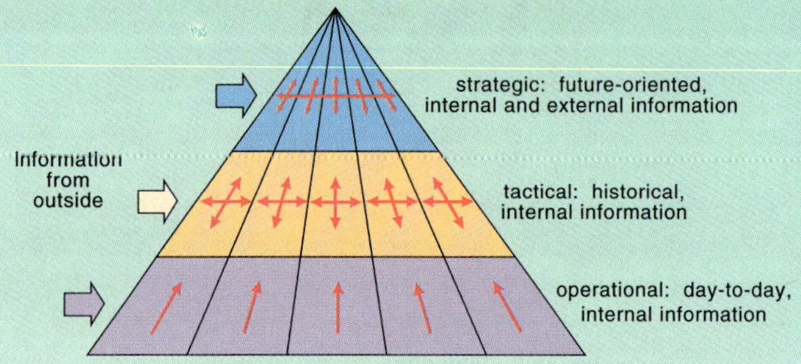

Management Levels

Management in many organizations has three levels:

- **Top-level managers** are concerned with long-range planning, forecasting future events.
- **Middle-level managers** are concerned with control and planning, implementing long-term goals.
- **Supervisors** are concerned with control of operational matters, monitoring day-to-day events, and supervising workers.

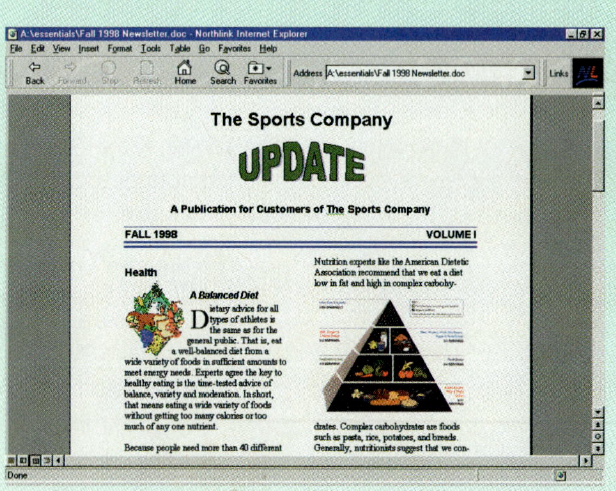

Information Flow

Information flows in different directions:

- For top-level managers—flow is up within the organization and into the organization from outside.
- For middle-level managers—flow is horizontally across and vertically within departments.
- For supervisors—flow is primarily vertical.

Executive Support System

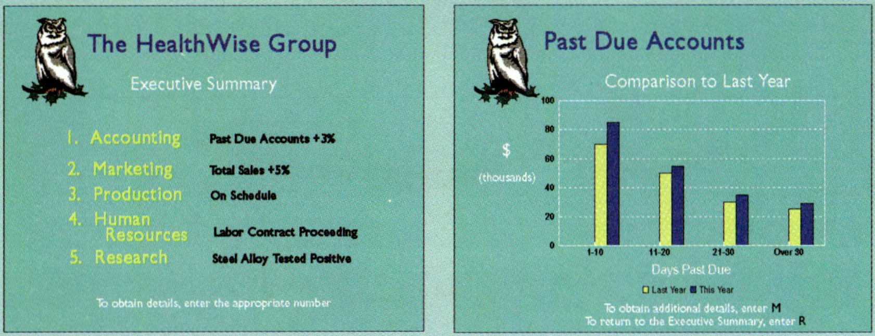

An **executive support system (ESS)** or **executive information system (EIS)** draws data together from an organization's databases but is designed to be easier to use than MISs or DSSs. Information is displayed in condensed form and in bold graphics.

TYPES OF INFORMATION SYSTEMS

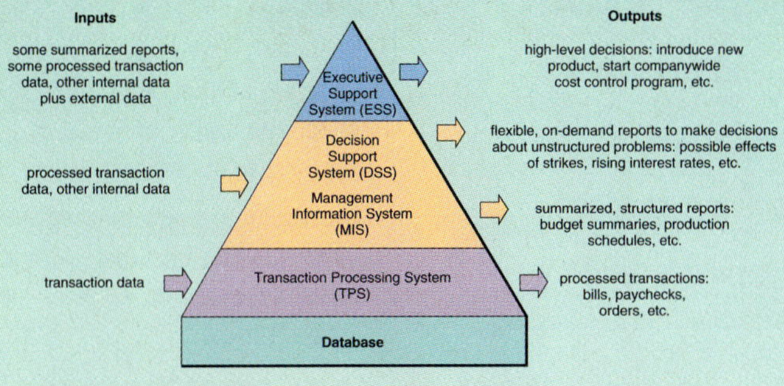

Transaction Processing System (TPS)

Records day-to-day transactions. An example is in accounting, which handles six activities: **sales order processing, accounts receivable, inventory and purchasing, accounts payable, payroll,** and **general ledger.**

Management Information System (MIS)

Produces predetermined **periodic, exception,** and **demand reports.** Management information systems use database management systems to integrate the databases of different departments.

Decision Support System (DSS)

Enables managers to get answers for unanticipated questions. A decision support system consists of the user, software system, data, and **decision models.** Teams formed to address large problems use **group decision support systems.**

Executive Support System (ESS)

Assists top-level executives. An executive support system is similar to an MIS and a DSS but easier to use. ESSs are designed specifically for top-level decision makers.

Other Information Systems

- **Office automation systems (OAS)** support data workers who are involved with distribution and communication of information.
- **Knowledge work systems (KWS)** support knowledge workers who create information.
- **Intranets** are private networks that look and act like the Internet. Browsers and search tools access internal information.

Systems Analysis and Design

Most people in an organization are involved with an information system of some kind, as we saw in the previous chapter. Assuredly, most microcomputer users in the future will have access to such a system, and they will also be part of it. For an organization to *establish* a system and for users to make it truly useful require considerable thought and effort. Fortunately, there is a six-step problem-solving process for accomplishing this. It is known as *systems analysis and design*.

11

COMPETENCIES

After you have read this chapter, you should be able to:

1. **Describe the six phases of the systems life cycle.**
2. **Discuss how problems or needs are identified during Phase 1, preliminary investigation.**
3. **Explain how the current system is studied and new requirements are specified in Phase 2, systems analysis.**
4. **Describe how a new or alternative information system is designed in Phase 3, systems design.**
5. **Explain how new hardware and software are acquired, developed, and tested in Phase 4, systems development.**
6. **Discuss how a new information system is installed and users are trained in Phase 5, systems implementation.**
7. **Describe Phase 6, systems maintenance, the systems audit and ongoing evaluation, to see if a new system is doing what it's supposed to.**
8. **Understand prototyping.**

Big organizations can make big mistakes. For example, General Motors spent $40 billion putting in factory robots and other high technology in its automaking plants. It then removed much of this equipment and reinstalled that basic part of the assembly line—the conveyor belt. Why did the high-tech production systems fail? The probable reason was that GM didn't devote enough energy to training its work force in using the new systems.

The government also can make big mistakes. In one year, the Internal Revenue Service computer system was so overwhelmed it could not deliver tax refunds on time. The reason? Despite extensive testing of much of the system, not all testing was completed. Thus, when the new system was phased in, the IRS found it could not process tax returns as quickly as it had hoped. Many tax refunds were delayed.

Both of these examples show the necessity for thorough planning—especially when an organization is trying to implement a new kind of system. Despite the spectacular failures just mentioned, there is a way to reduce the chances for such mistakes. It is called *systems analysis and design*.

Why should you, as a computer end user rather than a computer professional, know anything about this procedure? There are four reasons:

- If you work for a large organization, a systems analysis and design study will sometime undoubtedly focus on your job. Knowing how the procedure works will enable you to deal with it better.
- You can use the steps in systems analysis and design to improve your own productivity within the organization. That is, you can use the procedure to solve problems within your own corner of the organization. Or you can use it to assist professionals in solving larger problems within the organization.
- You can use this procedure to reduce the risk of a new project's failing. Many new information systems fail or do not work well for a variety of reasons. Using systems analysis and design can minimize the chances of these flaws occurring.
- You can use this procedure to choose an entire microcomputer system for any small business or for yourself.

Systems Analysis and Design

Systems analysis and design is a six-phase problem-solving procedure for examining and improving an information system.

We described different types of information systems in the last chapter. Now let us consider: What, exactly, is a **system?** We can define it as a collection of activities and elements organized to accomplish a goal. As we saw in the last chapter, an *information system* is a collection of hardware, software, people, procedures, and data. These work together to provide information essential to running an organization. This information helps to produce a product or service and, for profit-oriented businesses, derive a profit.

Information—about orders received, products shipped, money owed, and so on—flows into an organization from the outside. Information—about what supplies have been received, which customers have paid their bills, and so on—also flows inside the organization. In order to avoid confusion, these flows of information must follow some system. However, from time to time, organizations need to change their information systems. Reasons include organizational growth, mergers and acquisitions, new marketing opportunities, revisions in governmental regulations, availability of new technology, or other changes.

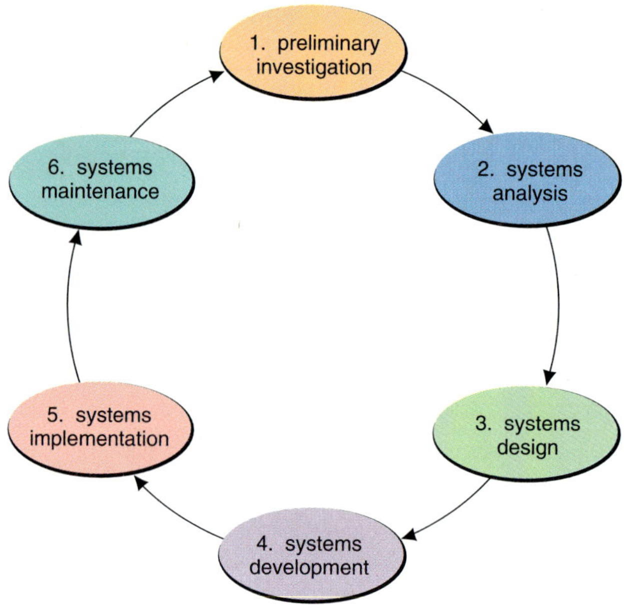

FIGURE 11-1
The six-phase systems life cycle.

Systems analysis and design is a six-phase problem-solving procedure for examining and improving an information system.

The six phases make up the **systems life cycle.** (See Figure 11-1.) The phases are as follows:

1. *Preliminary investigation:* The information problems or needs are identified.
2. *Systems analysis:* The present system is studied in depth. New requirements are specified.
3. *Systems design:* A new or alternative information system is designed.
4. *Systems development:* New hardware and software are acquired, developed, and tested.
5. *Systems implementation:* The new information system is installed and adapted to the new system, and people are trained to use it.
6. *Systems maintenance:* In this ongoing phase, the system is periodically evaluated and updated as needed.

In organizations, the six-phase systems life cycle is used by computer professionals known as **systems analysts.** These people study an organization's systems to determine what actions to take and how to use computer technology to assist them. A recent survey by *Money* magazine compared salary, prestige, and security of 100 widely held jobs. The top job classification was computer engineer, followed by computer systems analyst.

You may well find yourself working with a systems analyst. Or you may even become one yourself. It's important that you understand how the six phases work. After all, you better than anyone should understand what is needed in your part of the organization. And you should be the one best able to express that need. Developing a large computer-based information system requires the close collaboration of end users and systems analysts.

The procedure is also one that *you* as an end user can perform, working alone or with a systems analyst. In fact, you may *have* to use the procedure. More and more end users are developing their own information systems. This is because in many organizations there is a three-year backlog of work for systems analysts. For instance, suppose you recognize that there is a need for certain information within your organization. Obtaining this information will require the introduction of new hardware and software. You go to seek expert help from systems analysts in studying these information needs. At that point you discover they are so overworked it will take them three years to get to your request! You can see, then, why many managers are learning to do these activities themselves. In any case, learning these six steps will raise your computer competency. It will also give you skills to solve a wide range of problems. These steps can make you more valuable to an organization.

Let us now describe each phase in the systems life cycle.

Phase 1: Preliminary Investigation

In the preliminary investigation phase, the problems are briefly identified and a few solutions are suggested.

The first phase is a **preliminary investigation** of a proposed project to determine the need for a new information system. This usually is requested by an end user or a manager who wants something done that is not presently being done. For example, suppose you work for Advantage Advertising, a fast-growing advertising agency. (See Figure 11-2.) Advantage Advertising produces a variety of different ads for a wide range of different clients. The agency employs

FIGURE 11-2
Phase 1: preliminary investigation.

both regular staff people and on-call freelancers. One of your responsibilities is keeping track of the work performed for each client and the employees who performed the work. In addition, you are responsible for tabulating the final bill for each project.

How do you figure out how to charge which clients for which work done by which employees? This kind of problem is common to many service organizations (such as lawyers' and contractors' offices). Indeed, it is a problem in any organization where people charge for their "time" and clients need proof of hours worked.

In Phase 1, the systems analyst—or the end user—is concerned with three tasks. These are (1) briefly defining the problem, (2) suggesting alternative solutions, and (3) preparing a short report. This report will help management decide whether to pursue the project further. (If you are an end user employing this procedure for yourself, you may not produce a written report. Rather, you would report your findings directly to your supervisor.)

Defining the Problem

Defining the problem means examining whatever current information system is in use. Determining what information is needed, by whom, when, and why, is accomplished by interviewing and making observations. If the information system is large, this survey is done by a systems analyst. If the system is small, the survey can be done by the end user.

For example, suppose Advantage Advertising account executives, copywriters, and graphic artists currently just record the time spent on different jobs on their desk calendars. (Examples might be "Client A, telephone conference, 15 minutes"; "Client B, design layout, 2 hours.") This approach is somewhat helter-skelter. Written calendar entries look somewhat unprofessional to be shown to clients. Moreover, a large job often has many people working on it. It is difficult to pull together all their notations to make up a bill for the client. Some freelancers work at home, and their time slips are not readily available. These matters constitute a statement of the problem: The company has a manual time-and-billing system that is slow and difficult to implement.

As an end user, you might experience difficulties with this system yourself. You're in someone else's office, and a telephone call comes in for you from a client. Your desk calendar is back in your own office. You have two choices. You can always carry your calendar with you. As an alternative, you can remember to note the time you spent on various tasks when you return to your office. The secretary to the account executive is continually after you (and everyone else at Advantage) to provide photocopies of your calendar. This is so that various clients can be billed for the work done on various jobs. Surely, you think, there must be a better way to handle time and billing.

Suggesting Alternative Systems

This step is simply to suggest some possible plans as alternatives to the present arrangement. For instance, Advantage could hire more secretaries to collect the information from everyone's calendars (including telephoning those working at home). Or it could use the existing system of network-linked microcomputers that staffers and freelancers presently use. Perhaps, you think, there is already some off-the-shelf packaged software available that could be used for a time-and-billing system. At least there might be one that would make your own job easier.

Preparing a Short Report

For large projects, the systems analyst writes a short report summarizing the results of the preliminary investigation and suggesting alternative systems. The report may also include schedules for further development of the project. This document is presented to higher management, along with a recommendation to continue or discontinue the project. Management then decides whether to finance the second phase, the systems analysis.

For Advantage Advertising, your report might point out that billing is frequently delayed. It could say that some tasks may even "slip through the cracks" and not get charged at all. Thus, as the analyst has noted, you suggest the project might pay for itself merely by eliminating lost or forgotten charges.

Phase 2: Analysis

In the systems analysis phase, the present system is studied in depth, and new requirements are specified.

In Phase 2, **systems analysis,** data is collected about the present system. This data is then analyzed, and new requirements are determined. We are not concerned with a new design here, only with determining the *requirements* for a new system. Systems analysis is concerned with gathering and analyzing the data. It usually is completed by documenting the analysis in a report.

Gathering Data

In the step of gathering data, the systems analyst—or the end user doing systems analysis—expands on the data gathered during Phase 1. He or she adds details about how the current system works. Data is obtained from observation and interviews. It is also obtained from studying documents that describe the formal lines of authority and standard operating procedures. One document is the **organization chart,** which shows levels of management and formal lines of authority. (See Figure 11-3, top.) You might note that an organization chart resembles the hierarchy of three levels of management we described in Chapter 10. The levels are top managers, middle managers, and supervisors. (See Figure 11-3, bottom.) In addition, data may be obtained from questionnaires given to people using the system.

Note in our illustration that we have preserved the department labeled "Production." (Refer to Figure 11-3, top.) (However, the name in an advertising agency might be something like "Creative Services.") Obviously, the products an advertising agency produces are ads: radio and television commercials, magazine and newspaper ads, billboard ads, and so on. In any case, if the agency is working on a major advertising campaign, people from several departments might be involved. There might also be people from different management levels within the departments. Their time charges will vary, depending on how much they are paid.

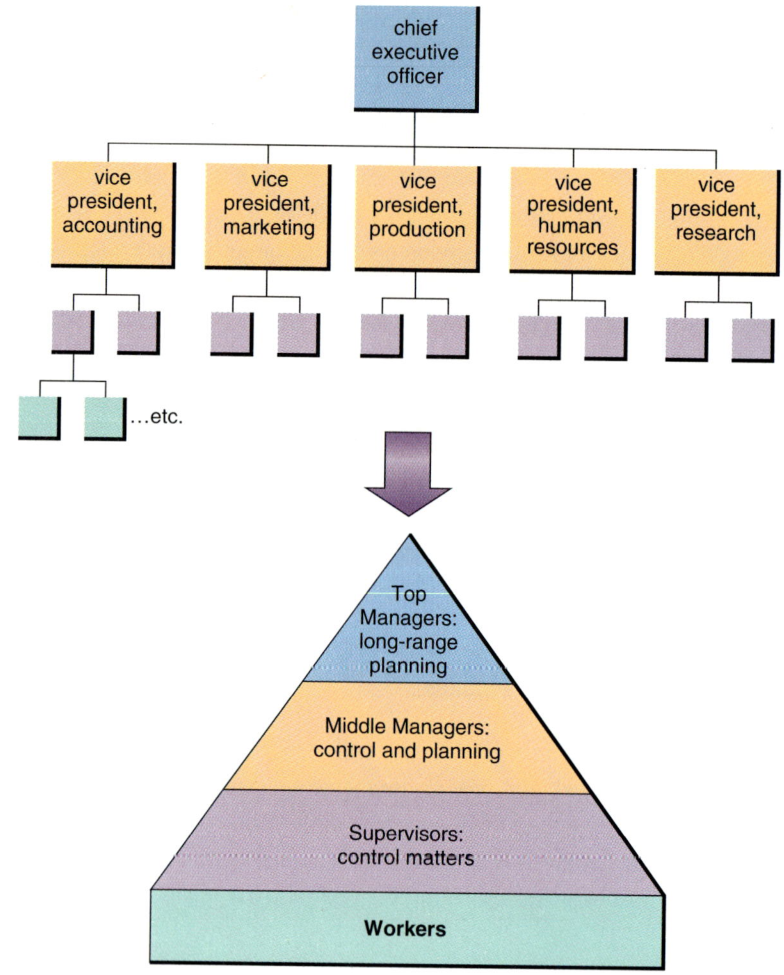

FIGURE 11-3
Example of an organization chart—and how it corresponds to the management pyramid.

Analyzing the Data

In the step of analyzing the data, the idea is to learn how information currently flows and to pinpoint why it isn't flowing appropriately. The whole point of this step is to apply *logic* to the existing arrangement to see how workable it is. Many times the current system is not operating correctly because prescribed procedures are not being followed. That is, the system may not really need to be redesigned. Rather, the people in it may need to be shown how to follow correct procedures.

Many different tools are available to assist systems analysts and end users in the analysis phase. Some of the principal ones are as follows:

- **Checklists:** Numerous checklists are available to assist in this stage. A **checklist** is a list of questions. It is helpful in guiding the systems analyst and end user through key issues for the present system.

  For example, one question might be "Can reports be easily prepared from the files and documents currently in use?" Another might be "How easily can the present time-and-billing system adapt to change and growth?"

- **Top-down analysis methodology:** The **top-down analysis methodology** is used to identify the top-level components of a complex system. Each component is then broken down into smaller and smaller components. This approach makes each component easier to analyze and deal with.

  For instance, the systems analyst might look at the present kind of bill submitted to a client for a complex advertising campaign. The analyst might note the categories of costs—employee salaries, telephone and mailing charges, travel, supplies, and so on.

- **Grid charts:** A **grid chart** shows the relationship between input and output documents. An example is shown in Figure 11-4 that indicates the relationship between the data input and the outputs.

  For instance, a time sheet is one of many inputs that produces a particular report, such as a client's bill. (Other inputs might be forms having to do with supplies, travel, and other costs of an advertising campaign.) Horizontal rows represent inputs, such as time card forms. Vertical rows represent output documents, such as different clients' bills. A checkmark at the intersection of a row and column means that the input document is used to create the output document.

- **Decision tables:** A **decision table** shows the decision rules that apply when certain conditions occur. Figure 11-5 shows a decision table to evaluate whether to accept a client's proposed advertising project. The first decision rule applies if both conditions are met. If the project is less than $10,000 and if the client has a good credit history, the firm will accept the project without requiring a deposit.

	Reports (output)		
Forms (input)	Client Billing	Personnel expense	Support cost
Time sheet	✓	✓	
Telephone log	✓		✓
Travel log	✓		✓

FIGURE 11-4
Example of a grid chart.

	Decision rules			
	1	2	3	4
Conditions:				
1. Project less than $10,000	Y	Y	N	N
2. Good credit history	Y	N	Y	N
Actions:				
1. Accept project	✓	✓	✓	
2. Require deposit		✓	✓	
3. Reject project				✓

FIGURE 11-5
Example of a decision table.

- **System flowcharts: System flowcharts** show the flow of input data to processing and finally to output, or distribution of information. An example of a system flowchart keeping track of time for advertising "creative people" is shown in Figure 11-6. The explanation of the symbols used (and others not used) appears in Figure 11-7. Note that this describes the present manual, or noncomputerized, system. (A *system* flowchart is not the same as a *program* flowchart, which is very detailed. Program flowcharts are discussed in the next chapter.)
- **Data flow diagrams: Data flow diagrams** show the data or information flow within an information system. The data is traced from its origination through processing, storage, and output. An example of a data flow diagram is shown in Figure 11-8.
- **Automated design tools: Automated design tools** are software packages that evaluate hardware and software alternatives according to requirements given by the systems analyst. They are also called **computer-aided software engineering tools,** or **CASE tools.** These tools are not limited to system analysis. They are used in system design and development as well. CASE tools relieve the system analysts of many repetitive tasks, develop clear documentation, and, for larger projects, coordinate team-member activities.

For a summary of the analysis tools, see Figure 11-9.

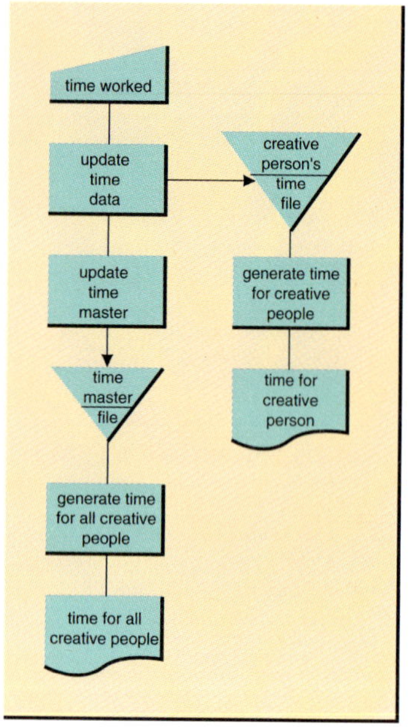

FIGURE 11-6
Example of a system flowchart.

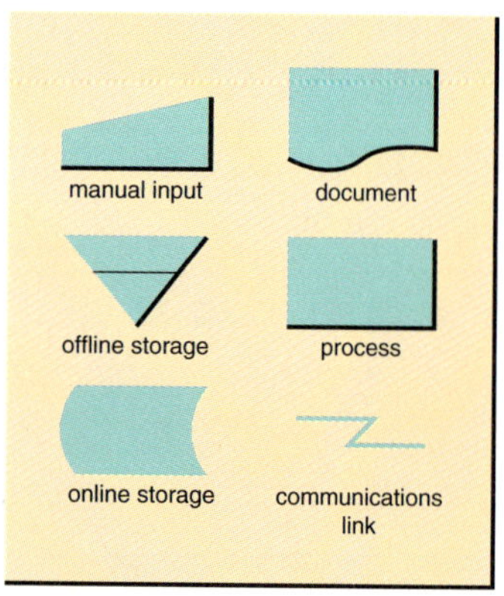

FIGURE 11-7
System flowchart symbols.

Documenting the Systems Analysis Stage

In larger organizations, the systems analysis stage is typically documented in a report for higher management. The systems analysis report describes the current information system, the requirements for a new system, and a possible development schedule. For example, at Advantage Advertising, the system flowcharts show the present flow of information in a manual time-and-billing system. Some boxes in the system flowchart might be replaced with symbols showing where a computer-

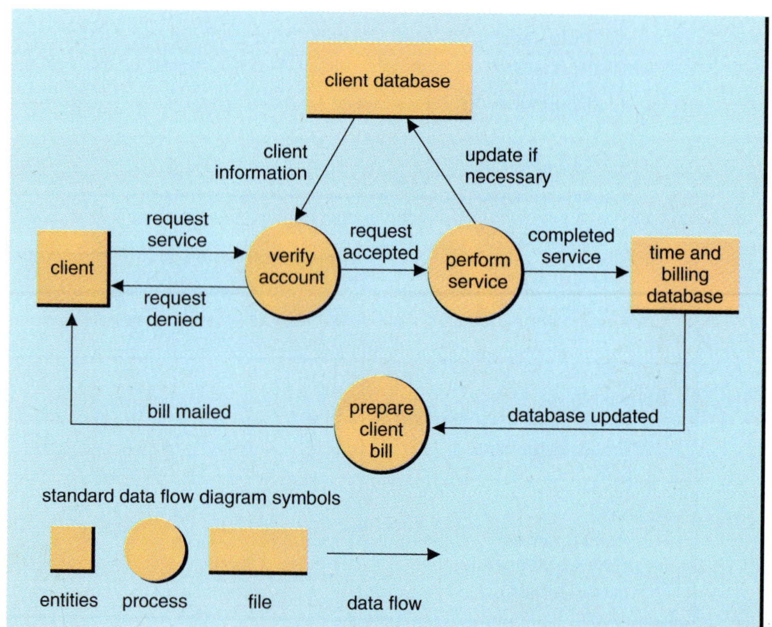

FIGURE 11-8
Example of a data flow diagram.

ANALYSIS TOOLS

TOOL	DESCRIPTION
Checklist	Provides a list of questions about key issues
Top-down analysis	Divides a complex system into components, beginning at the top
Grid chart	Shows relationships between inputs and outputs
Decision table	Specifies decision rules and circumstances when specific rules are to be applied
System flowchart	Shows movement of input data, processing, and output or distribution of information
Data flow diagram	Shows data flow within an organization or application
CASE	Automates the analysis, design, and development of information systems

FIGURE 11-9
Summary of analysis tools.

ized information system could work better. For example, in our flowchart, the offline storage symbol ("time master file") might be replaced by an online storage symbol. (Refer back to Figure 11-6.) That is, the information in the file would be instantly accessible.

Management studies the report and decides whether to continue with the project. Let us assume your boss and higher management have decided to continue. You now move on to Phase 3, systems design.

Phase 3: Design

In the systems design phase, a new or alternative information system is designed.

Phase 3 is **systems design.** (See Figure 11-10.) It consists of three tasks: (1) designing alternative systems, (2) selecting the best system, and (3) writing a systems design report.

FIGURE 11-10
Phase 3: design.

Designing Alternative Systems

In almost all instances, more than one design can be developed to meet the information needs. Systems designers evaluate each alternative system for feasibility. By "feasibility" we mean three things:

- **Economic feasibility:** Will the costs of the new system be justified by the benefits it promises?
- **Technical feasibility:** Are reliable hardware, software, and training available to make the system work?
- **Operational feasibility:** Can the system actually be made to operate in the organization, or will people—employees, managers, clients—resist it?

Selecting the Best System

When choosing the best design, managers must consider these four questions. (1) Will the system fit in with the organization's overall information system? (2) Will the system be flexible enough so it can be modified in the future? (3) Can it be made secure against unauthorized use? (4) Are the benefits worth the costs?

For example, one aspect you have to consider at Advantage Advertising is security. Should freelancers and outside vendors enter data directly into a computerized time-and-billing system, or should they keep submitting time slips manually? In allowing these outside people to directly input information, are you also allowing them access to files they should not see? Do these files contain confidential information, perhaps information of value to rival advertising agencies?

Writing the Systems Design Report

The systems design report is prepared for higher management and describes the alternative designs. It presents the costs versus the benefits and outlines the effect of alternative designs on the organization. It usually concludes by recommending one of the alternatives.

Phase 4: Development

In the systems development phase, new hardware and software are developed, acquired, and tested.

Phase 4 is **systems development.** (See Figure 11-11.) It has three steps: (1) developing software, (2) acquiring hardware, and (3) testing the new system.

Developing Software

Application software for the new information system can be obtained in two ways. It can be purchased as off-the-shelf packaged software and possibly modified, or it can be custom designed. If any of the software is being specially created, the steps we will outline on programming (in Chapter 12) should be followed.

With the systems analyst's help, you have looked at time-and-billing packaged software designed for service organizations. Such organizations might include advertising agencies, law firms, and building contractors. The systems analyst points out the importance of time-and-billing data's being collected in an appro-

FIGURE 11-11
Phase 4: development.

priate manner so that it can be used for a variety of purposes. Such a system will not only help supervisory and middle managers do their jobs but also help top managers make decisions.

Unfortunately, you find that none of the packaged software will do. Most of the packages seem to work well for one person (you). However, none seem to be designed for many people working together. It appears, then, that software will have to be custom designed. (We discuss the process of developing software in Chapter 12 on programming.)

Acquiring Hardware

Some new systems may not require new computer equipment, but others will. The kinds needed and the places they are to be installed must be determined. This is a very critical area. Switching or upgrading equipment can be a tremendously expensive proposition. Will a microcomputer system be sufficient as a company grows? Are networks expandable? Will people have to undergo costly training?

The systems analyst tells you that there are several different makes and models of microcomputers currently in use at Advantage Advertising. Fortunately, all are connected by a local area network to a file server that can hold the time-and-billing data. To maintain security, the systems analyst suggests that an electronic mailbox can be installed for freelancers and others outside the company. They can use this electronic mailbox to post their time charges. Thus, it appears that existing hardware will work just fine.

Testing the New System

After the software and equipment have been installed, the system should be tested. Sample data is fed into the system. The processed information is then evaluated to see whether results are correct. Testing may take several months if the new system is complex.

For this step, you take some time and expense charges from an ad campaign that Advantage ran the previous year. You then ask some people in Creative Services to test it on the system. You observe that time is often charged in fractions of minutes and that the software ignores these fractions of time. You also see that some of the people in Creative Services have problems knowing where to enter their

FIGURE 11-12
Phase 5: implementation.

times. To solve the first problem, you must see that the software is corrected to allow for fractional minutes. To solve the second problem, you must see that the software is modified so that it displays an improved user entry screen. After the system has been thoroughly tested and revised as necessary, you are ready to put it into use.

Phase 5: Implementation

In the systems implementation phase, the new information system is installed, and people are trained to use it.

Another name for Phase 5, **systems implementation,** is **conversion.** (See Figure 11-12.) It is the process of changing—converting—from the old system to the new.

Types of Conversion

There are four approaches to conversion: *direct, parallel, pilot,* and *phased.*

- In the **direct approach,** the conversion is done simply by abandoning the old and starting up the new. This can be risky. If anything is still wrong with the new system, the old system is no longer available to fall back on.

  The direct approach is not recommended precisely because it is so risky. Problems, big or small, invariably crop up in a new system. In a large system, a problem might just mean catastrophe.

- In the **parallel approach,** old and new systems are operated side by side until the new one has shown it is reliable.

  This approach is low-risk. If the new system fails, the organization can just switch to the old system to keep going. However, keeping enough equipment and people active to manage two systems at the same time can be very expensive. Thus, the parallel approach is used only in cases in which the cost of failure or of interrupted operation is great.

- In the **pilot approach,** the new system is tried out in only one part of the organization. Once the system is working smoothly in that part, it is implemented throughout the rest of the organization.

  The pilot approach is certainly less expensive than the parallel approach. It also is somewhat riskier. However, the risks can be controlled because problems will be confined to only certain areas of the organization. Difficulties will not affect the entire organization.
- In the **phased approach,** the new system is implemented gradually over a period of time.

  The entire implementation process is broken down into parts or phases. Implementation begins with the first phase and once it is successfully implemented, the second phase begins. This process continues until all phases are operating smoothly. This is an expensive proposition, because the implementation is done slowly. However, it is certainly one of the least risky approaches.

In general, the pilot and phased approaches are the most favored methods. Pilot is preferred when there are many people in an organization performing similar operations—for instance, all sales clerks in a department store. Phased is more appropriate for organizations in which people are performing different operations.

You and the systems analyst succeed in convincing the top managers of Advantage Advertising to take a pilot approach. The reason is that it is easy to select one trial group—the group of which you are a member. Moreover, this group is eager to try the new system. Thus, the new time-and-billing system is tried first with a handful of people in your particular department.

FIGURE 11-13
Phase 6: maintenance.

Training

Training people is important, of course. Unfortunately, it is one of the most commonly overlooked activities. Some people may begin training early, even before the equipment is delivered, so that they can adjust more easily. In some cases, a professional software trainer may be brought in to show people how to operate the system. However, at Advantage Advertising the time-and-billing software is simple enough that the systems analyst can act as the trainer.

Phase. 6: Maintenance

Systems maintenance is first a systems audit and then an ongoing evaluation to see whether a system is performing productively.

After implementation comes **systems maintenance,** the last step in the systems life cycle. (See Figure 11-13.) This phase is a very important and an ongoing activity. Most organizations spend more time and money on this phase than any of the others. Maintenance has two parts—a *systems audit* and a *periodic evaluation*.

In the **systems audit,** the system's performance is compared to the original design specifications. This is to determine if the new procedures are actually furthering productivity. If they are not, some further redesign may be necessary.

SYSTEMS DEVELOPMENT LIFE CYCLE

PHASE	ACTIVITY
1. Preliminary investigation	Define problem, suggest alternatives, prepare short report
2. Systems analysis	Gather data, analyze data, document
3. Systems design	Design alternatives, select best alternative, write report
4. Systems development	Develop software, acquire hardware, test system
5. Systems implementation	Convert, train
6. Systems maintenance	Perform system audit, evaluate periodically

FIGURE 11-14
Summary of systems life cycle.

After the systems audit, the new information system is periodically evaluated and further modified, if necessary. All systems should be evaluated from time to time to see if they are meeting the goals and providing the service they are supposed to.

For example, over time the transaction database at Advantage Advertising is expanded. After a year or two, the systems analyst might suggest that the time-and-billing part of it be reevaluated. For instance, the analyst might discover that telephone and mailing charges need to be separated. This might be because, with more people using the electronic mailbox and more people sharing data, telephone charges are now higher. The six-step systems life cycle is summarized in Figure 11-14.

Prototyping

Prototyping consists of devising a model of a new system for users to try out.

Is it necessary to follow every phase of the six phases of systems analysis and design? It may be desirable, but often there is no time to do so. For instance, hardware may change so fast that there is no opportunity for the evaluation, design, and testing just described.

A faster alternative is prototyping. **Prototyping** means to build a model, or prototype that can be modified before the actual system is installed. For instance, the systems analyst for Advantage Advertising might develop a menu as a possible screen display for the time-and-billing system. Users could try it before the system is put into place.

Prototyping is considered a "quickie" way of building a system. It allows users to find out right away how a change in the system can help their work. However, relying on prototyping alone can be risky. It might lead to a system's being changed or installed without all costs and other matters being considered.

A Look at the Future

The systems life cycle will be shortened using a method called rapid applications development.

The traditional systems life cycle can take a long time—sometimes years, in the case of large projects for large organizations. Because the pace of business is increasing, to stay competitive, corporations must shorten development life cycles so that products can be produced more quickly.

In the future, we will probably see increasing use of a new method called *rapid applications development (RAD),* which is intended to reduce development to months instead of years. RAD uses powerful development software (such as CASE), small teams, and highly trained people to produce applications much faster and with higher-quality results than traditional methods do.

KEY TERMS

automated design tool (236)
checklist (234)
computer-aided software engineering (CASE) tool (236)
conversion (240)
data flow diagram (236)
decision table (235)
direct approach (240)
grid chart (235)
organization chart (233)
parallel approach (240)
phased approach (241)
pilot approach (240)
preliminary investigation (231)
prototyping (242)
system (229)
system flowchart (236)
systems analysis (236)
systems analysis and design (230)
systems analyst (230)
systems audit (241)
systems design (237)
systems development (238)
systems implementation (240)
systems life cycle (230)
systems maintenance (241)
top-down analysis methodology (235)

REVIEW QUESTIONS

True/False

1. Systems analysis and design is a way to reduce the chance of creating an ineffective information system.
2. In large organizations, the person who uses the systems life cycle the most is called a database administrator.
3. Defining the problem is a task in Phase 2, design.
4. Software is either purchased or developed in the implementation phase.
5. In pilot conversion, one part of an organization initially tries out the new system.

Multiple Choice

1. A collection of hardware, software, people, procedures, and data:
   a. analysis and design
   b. system
   c. network
   d. microcomputer
   e. design
2. This phase in the systems life cycle focuses on evaluating and determining the need for a new information system:
   a. preliminary investigation
   b. systems design
   c. systems development
   d. systems implementation
   e. systems maintenance
3. Phase 2, analysis, involves gathering data, analyzing the data, and:
   a. designing the new system
   b. creating programs
   c. auditing the existing system
   d. documenting the systems analysis stage
   e. training

4. The evaluation of economic, technical, and operational feasibility is made during this phase:
   a. preliminary investigation
   b. systems design
   c. systems development
   d. systems implementation
   e. systems maintenance
5. The final step in Phase 4, development, is:
   a. designing alternative systems
   b. selecting the best system
   c. developing software
   d. acquiring hardware
   e. testing the new system

Fill in the Blank

1. The six-phase problem-solving procedure for systems analysis and design is the ________ ________ ________.
2. Defining the problem, suggesting alternative systems, and preparing a short report are all parts of ________ ________.
3. ________ ________ diagrams trace data from its origination through processing, storage, and output.
4. Once the new system is operational, a ________ ________ is performed to compare the original design specifications with the actual system.
5. A ________ is a model of a system.

Open Ended

1. What is the purpose of systems analysis and design? Who is involved with this process?
2. What are the six phases in the systems life cycle? Briefly describe each phase.
3. Describe top-down analysis methodology.
4. Explain the three steps in Phase 4, systems development.
5. Describe the four possible ways of implementing a system. Which one would you recommend?

DISCUSSION QUESTIONS

1. *Using systems analysis in your life:* Will the systems life cycle approach work in the real world? Will it work for you? To find out, try one of the following activities:
   a. Interview a systems analyst, perhaps one working at the computer center or in the information systems department of your college. Ask the analyst's opinion of the systems approach as applied to ordinary, non-computer-related problems.
   b. Apply the systems life cycle to activities at school or work that you find inefficient or irritating: parking problems, preregistration system, financial aid deadlines, and so on. Try to apply Phase 1, preliminary investigation, briefly identifying the problem and suggesting possible solutions. Write a short report to higher management or the college administration to help them decide whether to go ahead with Phase 2. See whether you can pose a few solutions, and find out who is in a position of authority to make possible changes.

on the web

Exercises and Explorations

1 Health and Fitness

One of the best resources for the latest information about health and fitness is the Web. Visit our Web site at http://www.magpie.org/essentials/chapter-11 to link to one of these sites. Once connected to that site, print out the page you find most informative. Write a paragraph on the ways that you can improve your nutrition.

2 Job Search

You can find almost anything on the Web – even a job. Visit our Web site at http://www.magpie.org/essentials/chapter-11 to link to one of these job-search sites. Once connected to that site, find one job opportunitiy that interests you. Print out the job description, and write a paragraph describing the value of the job-search service and who would most likely use it.

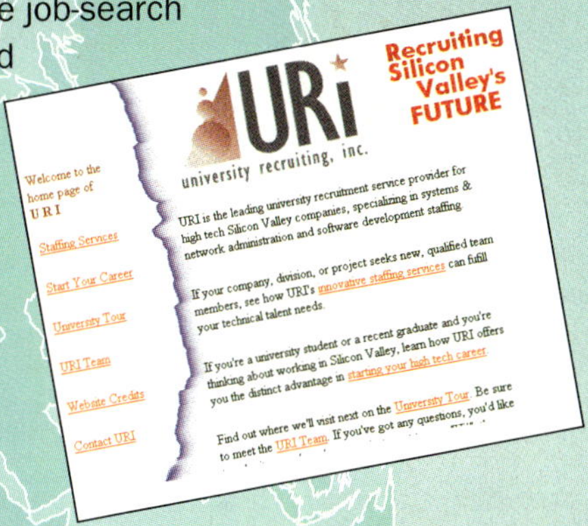

3 Management Information Sytems

Search the Internet for recent information on management information systems (MIS). Visit the Yahoo site at http://www.yahoo.com and investigate the category of "Business and Economy: Management Information Systems." Select the most interesting Web site. Print out the first page of the site, and write a paragraph summarizing its content.

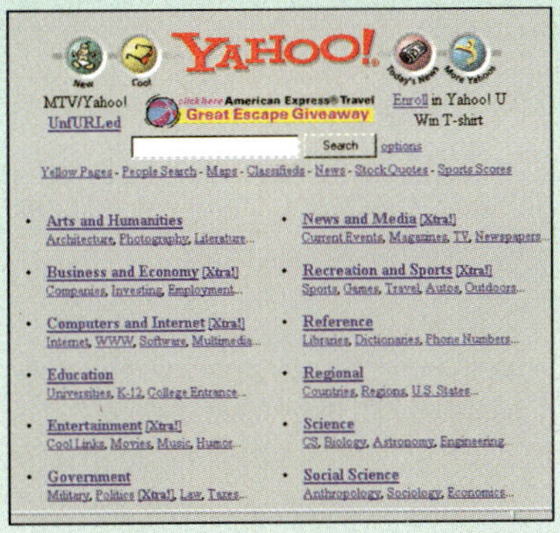

4 Astrology

There are numerous Web sites that provide horoscopes, including romance predictions and explanations of astrological terms. Visit our Web site at http://www.magpie.org/essentials/chapter-11 to link to one of these sites. Once connected to that site, print out your horoscope. Write a paragraph describing how the horoscope's prediction could relate to you.

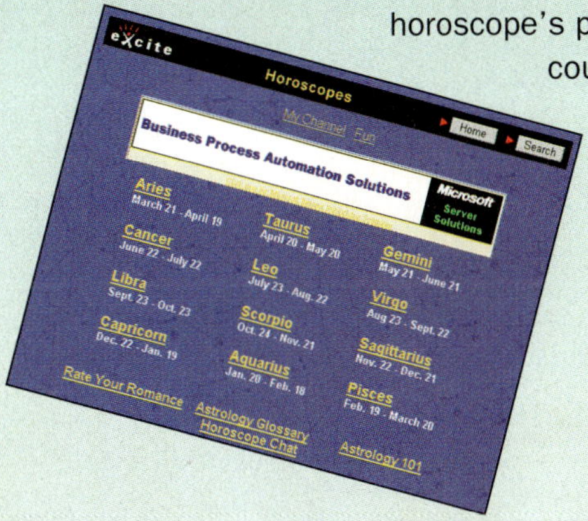

VISUAL SUMMARY

11 Systems Analysis and Design

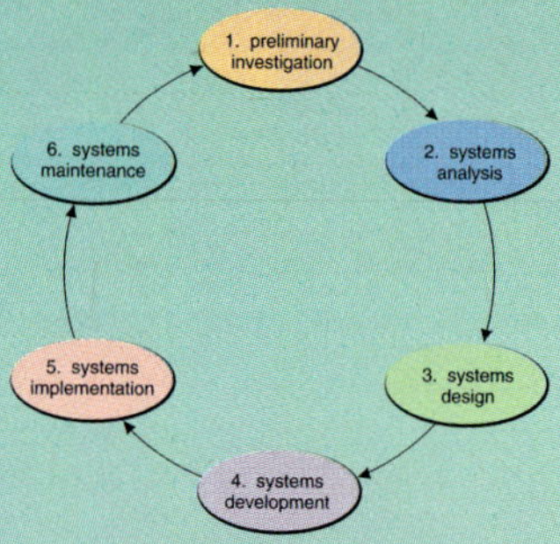

Systems analysis and design is a six-phase problem-solving procedure for examining an information system and improving it. The six phases are called the **systems life cycle.**

PHASE 1: PRELIMINARY INVESTIGATION

The **preliminary investigation** determines the need for a new information system. The tasks of this phase are:

Defining the problem

The current information system is examined to determine what information is needed by whom, when, and why.

Suggesting alternative systems

Based on interviews and observations made in defining the problem, alternative information systems are identified.

Preparing a short report

To document and to communicate the findings of Phase 1, preliminary investigation, a short report is prepared and presented to management.

PHASE 2: ANALYSIS

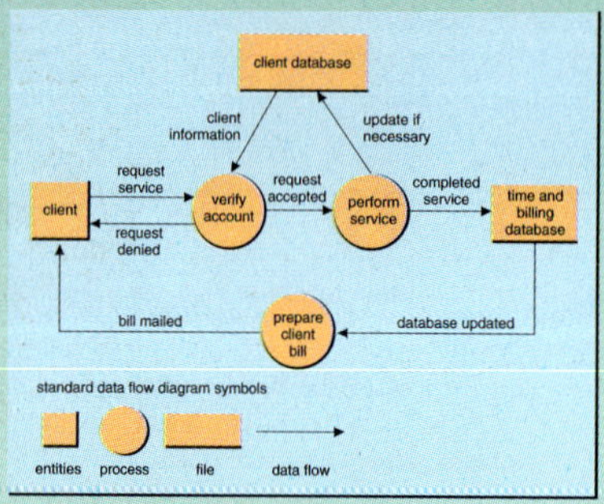

In **systems analysis** data is collected about the present system. The tasks of this phase are:

Gathering data

Data gathered by observation, interviews, questionnaire, and looking at documents. One helpful document is the organization chart, which shows a company's functions and levels of management.

Analyzing the data

There are several tools for the analysis of data, including checklists, top-down analysis, grid charts, decision tables. See the table on the next page for a more complete list and details.

Documenting systems analysis

To document and to communicate the findings of Phase 2, analysis, a report is prepared for higher management.

PHASE 3: DESIGN

Systems design consists of the following three tasks:

Designing alternative systems

Alternative information systems are designed. Each alternative is evaluated for economic, technical, and operational feasibility.

Selecting the best system

Four questions considered when selecting the best system:

- Will the system fit into an overall information system?
- Is the system flexible enough to be modified as needed in the future?
- Will it be secure against unauthorized use?
- Will the system's benefits exceed its costs?

Documenting system design

To document and to communicate the findings of Phase 3, design, a report is prepared for higher management.

ANALYSIS TOOLS

TOOL	DESCRIPTION
Checklist	Provides a list of questions about key issues
Top-down analysis	Divides a complex system into components, beginning at the top
Grid chart	Shows relationships between inputs and outputs
Decision table	Specifies decision rules and circumstances when specific rules are to be applied
System flowchart	Shows movement of input data, processing, and output or distribution of information
Data flow diagram	Shows data flow within an organization or application
CASE	Automates the analysis, design, and development of information systems

PHASE 4: DEVELOPMENT

The **systems development** phase has three steps:

Developing software

Two ways to acquire software are:

- **Purchase**—buying off-the-shelf software to be modified if necessary.
- **Custom designed**—create programs following programming steps presented in Chapter 11.

Acquiring hardware

Acquiring hardware is very critical and involves consideration for future company growth, existing networks, communication capabilities, and training.

Testing the system

Using sample data, the new system is tested. Can take several months.

PHASE 5: IMPLEMENTATION

Systems implementation (conversion) is the process of changing from the old system to the new.

Types of Conversion

Four ways to convert are:

- **Direct approach**—abandoning the old and starting up the new.
- **Parallel approach**—operating the old and new side by side until the new one proves its worth.
- **Pilot approach**—trying out the new system in only one part of an organization.
- **Phased approach**—implementing the new system gradually.

Training

A software trainer may be used to train end users on the new system.

PHASE 6: MAINTENANCE

Systems maintenance has two parts:

System audit

Once the new system is operational, the systems analyst compares it to the original design specifications. If the system does not meet these specifications, some further redesign of the system may be required.

Periodic evaluation

The new system is periodically evaluated to ensure that it is operating efficiently. If it is not, some redesign may be required.

Programming and Languages

How do you go about getting a job? You look through newspaper classified ads, check with employment services, write to prospective employers, and so on. In other words, you do some *general problem solving* to come up with a broad plan. This is similar to what you do in systems analysis and design. Once you have determined a *particular* job you would like to have, you then do some *specific problem solving.* That is what you do in programming. In this chapter, we describe programming in two parts. They are (1) the steps in the programming process and (2) some of the programming languages available.

COMPETENCIES

After you have read this chapter, you should be able to:

1. **Understand the six steps of programming.**
2. **Describe Step 1, program specification.**
3. **Describe Step 2, program design, and the program-design tools of top-down program design, pseudocode, flowcharts, and logic structures.**
4. **Explain Step 3, coding the program.**
5. **Describe Step 4, testing the program, and the tools for correcting programs.**
6. **Discuss Step 5, documenting the program.**
7. **Discuss Step 6, maintaining the program.**
8. **Describe CASE tools and object-oriented software development.**
9. **Explain the five generations of programming languages.**

Why should you need to know anything about programming? The answer is simple. You might need to deal with programmers in the course of your work. You may also be required to do some programming yourself in the future. A new field has emerged known as *end-user application development.* In this field, users like you create their own business application programs, without the assistance of a programmer. Thus, organizations avoid paying high software development costs. You and other end users avoid waiting months for programmers to get around to projects important to you.

In the last chapter, we described the six phases of the systems life cycle. They are preliminary investigation, systems analysis, systems design, systems development, systems implementation, and systems maintenance. Programming is part of Phase 4, systems development, as illustrated in Figure 12-1. Note that the bottom part of that illustration constitutes an outline of the six steps in programming. We follow that outline in this chapter.

Programs and Programming

Programming is a six-step procedure for producing a program—a list of instructions—for the computer.

What exactly *is* programming? Many people think of it as simply typing words into a computer. That may be part of it—but certainly not all of it. Programming, as we've hinted before, is actually a *problem-solving procedure.*

What Is a Program?

To see how programming works, think about what a program is. A **program** is a list of instructions for the computer to follow to accomplish the task of processing data into information. The instructions are made up of statements used in a programming language, such as BASIC, C, or Java.

Application software or *application programs,* as we said in Chapter 1, are the kind of programs that do "end-user work." These are things such as word processing and accounting tasks. *System software,* we said, is concerned with "background" tasks such as housekeeping chores involving computer operations. In this chapter we are concerned with application programs.

You are probably most familiar with one kind of application program—the *prewritten* or *packaged* programs. These are so-called off-the-shelf programs such as word processors, spreadsheets, and database managers. However, application programs may also be *created* or *custom-made*—either by a professional programmer or by you, the end user. In Chapter 11, we saw that the systems analyst looked into the availability of time-and-billing software for Advantage Advertising. Will off-the-shelf software do the job, or should it be custom written? This is one of the first things that needs to be decided in programming.

What Is Programming?

A program is a list of instructions for the computer to follow to process data. **Programming,** also known as **software development,** is a six-step procedure for creating that list of instructions. Only *one* of those steps consists of typing (keying) statements into a computer.

The six steps are as follows. (Refer to Figure 12-1.)

1. Program specification
2. Program design
3. Program code
4. Program test
5. Program documentation
6. Program maintenance

Step 1: Program Specification

In the program specification step, the objectives, outputs, inputs, and processing requirements are determined.

Program specification is also called **program definition** or **program analysis.** It requires that the programmer—or you, the end user, if you are following this procedure—specify five tasks. They are (1) the program's objectives, (2) the desired output, (3) the input data required, (4) the processing requirements, and (5) the documentation. Let us consider these.

FIGURE 12-1
Where programming fits in the systems life cycle.

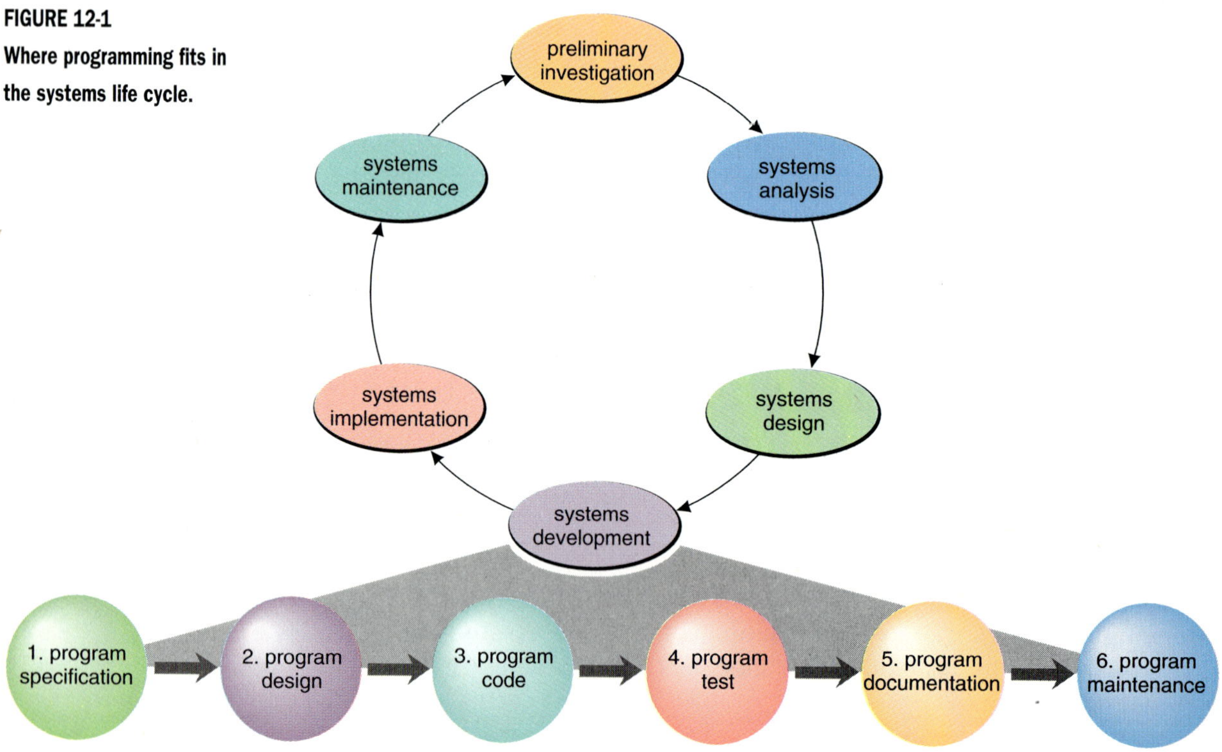

FIGURE 12-2
Problem definition: make a clear statement of the problem.

Determining Program Objectives

You solve all kinds of problems every day. A problem might be deciding how to commute to school or work or which homework or report to do first. Thus, every day you determine your *objectives*—the problems you are trying to solve. Programming is the same. You need to make a clear statement of the problem you are trying to solve. (See Figure 12-2.) An example would be "I want a time-and-billing system to record the time I spend on different jobs for different clients of Advantage Advertising."

Determining the Desired Output

It is best always to specify outputs before inputs. That is, you need to list what you want to *get out* of the computer system. Then you should determine what will *go into* it. The best way to do this is to draw a picture. You—the end user, not the programmer—should sketch or write how you want the output to look when it's done. It might be printed out or displayed on the monitor.

For example, if you want a time-and-billing report, you might write or draw something like Figure 12-3. Another form of output from the program might be bills to clients.

Determining the Input Data

Once you know the output you want, you can determine the input data and the source of this data. For example, for a time-and-billing report, you can specify that one source of data to be processed should be time cards. These are usually logs or statements of hours worked submitted on paper forms. The log shown in Figure

FIGURE 12-3
End user's sketch of desired output.

Client name: Allan Realty   Month and year: Jan '93

Date	Worker	Regular Hours & Rate	Overtime Hours & Rate	Bill
1/2	M. Jones	5 @ $10	1 @ $15	$65.00
	K. Williams	4 @ $30	2 @ $45	$210.00

12-4 is an example of the kind of input data used in Advantage Advertising's manual system. Note that military time is used. For example, instead of writing "5:45 P.M.," people would write "1745."

Determining the Processing Requirements

Here you define the processing tasks that must happen for input data to be processed into output. For Advantage, one of the tasks for the program will be to add the hours worked for different jobs for different clients.

Documenting the Program's Specifications

As in the systems life cycle, ongoing documentation is essential. You should record program objectives, desired outputs, needed inputs, and required processing. This leads to the next step, program design.

FIGURE 12-4
Example of statement of hours worked—manual system. Hours are expressed in military time.

Daily Log

Worker:
Date:

Client	Job	Time in	Time out
A	TV commercial	800	915
B	Billboard ad	935	1200
C	Brochure	1315	1545
A	Magazine ad	1600	1745

Step 2: Program Design

In the program-design step, a solution is created using programming techniques such as top-down program design, pseudocode, flowcharts, and logic structures.

After program specification, you begin **program design.** Here you plan a solution, preferably using **structured programming techniques.** These techniques consist of the following: (1) top-down program design, (2) pseudocode, (3) flowcharts, and (4) logic structures.

Top-Down Program Design

First you determine the outputs and inputs of the computer program you will create. Then you can use **top-down program design** to identify the program's processing steps. Such steps are called **program modules** (or just **modules**). Each module is made up of logically related program statements.

An example of a top-down program design for a time-and-billing report is shown in Figure 12-5. Each of the boxes shown is a module. Under the rules of top-down design, each module should have a single function. The program must pass in sequence from one module to the next until all modules have been processed by the computer. Three of the boxes—"obtain input," "compute hours for billing," and "produce output"—correspond to the three principal computer system operations. These operations are *input, process,* and *output.*

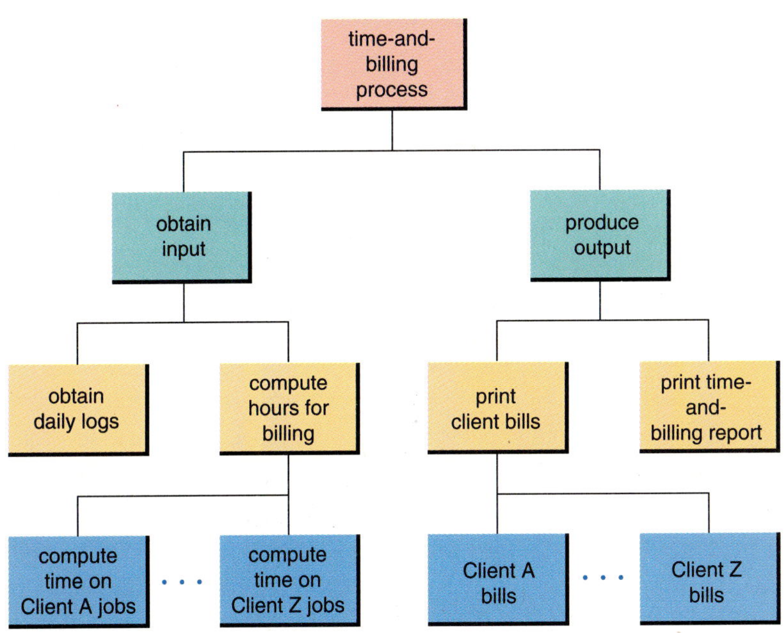

FIGURE 12-5
Example of top-down program design.

Pseudocode

Pseudocode (pronounced "*soo*-doh-code") is an outline of the logic of the program you will write. It is like doing a summary of the program before it is written. Figure 12-6 shows the pseudocode you might write for one module in the time-and-billing program. This shows the reasoning behind determining hours—including overtime hours—worked for different jobs for one client, Client A. Again, note this expresses the *logic* of what you want the program to do.

FIGURE 12-6
Example of pseudocode.

Compute time for Client A

Set total regular hours and total overtime hours to zero.
Get time in and time out for a job.
If worked past 1700 hours, then compute overtime hours.
Compute regular hours.
Add regular hours to total regular hours.
Add overtime hours to total overtime hours.
If there are more jobs for that client, go back and compute for that job as well.

Flowcharts

We mentioned system flowcharts in the previous chapter. Here we are concerned with **program flowcharts.** These graphically present the detailed sequence of steps needed to solve a programming problem. Figure 12-7 presents the standard flowcharting symbols and gives an example of a program flowchart. This flowchart expresses all the logic for just *one* module—"Compute time on Client A jobs"—in the top-down program design.

Perhaps you can see from this flowchart why a computer is a computer, and not just a fancy adding machine. A computer does more than arithmetic. It also *makes comparisons*—whether something is greater than or less than, equal to or not equal to.

But have we skipped something? How do we *know* which kind of twists and turns to put in a flowchart so that it will logically work? The answer is based on the use of logic structures, as we will explain.

Logic Structures

How do you link the various parts of the flowchart? The best way is a combination of three **logic structures** called *sequence, selection,* and *loop.* Using these arrangements enables you to write so-called *structured programs,* which take much of the guesswork out of programming. Let us look at the logic structures.

- In the **sequence structure,** one program statement follows another. (See Figure 12-8.)

  Consider, for example, the "compute time" flowchart. (Refer back to Figure 12-7.) The two "add" boxes are "Add regular hours to total regular hours" and

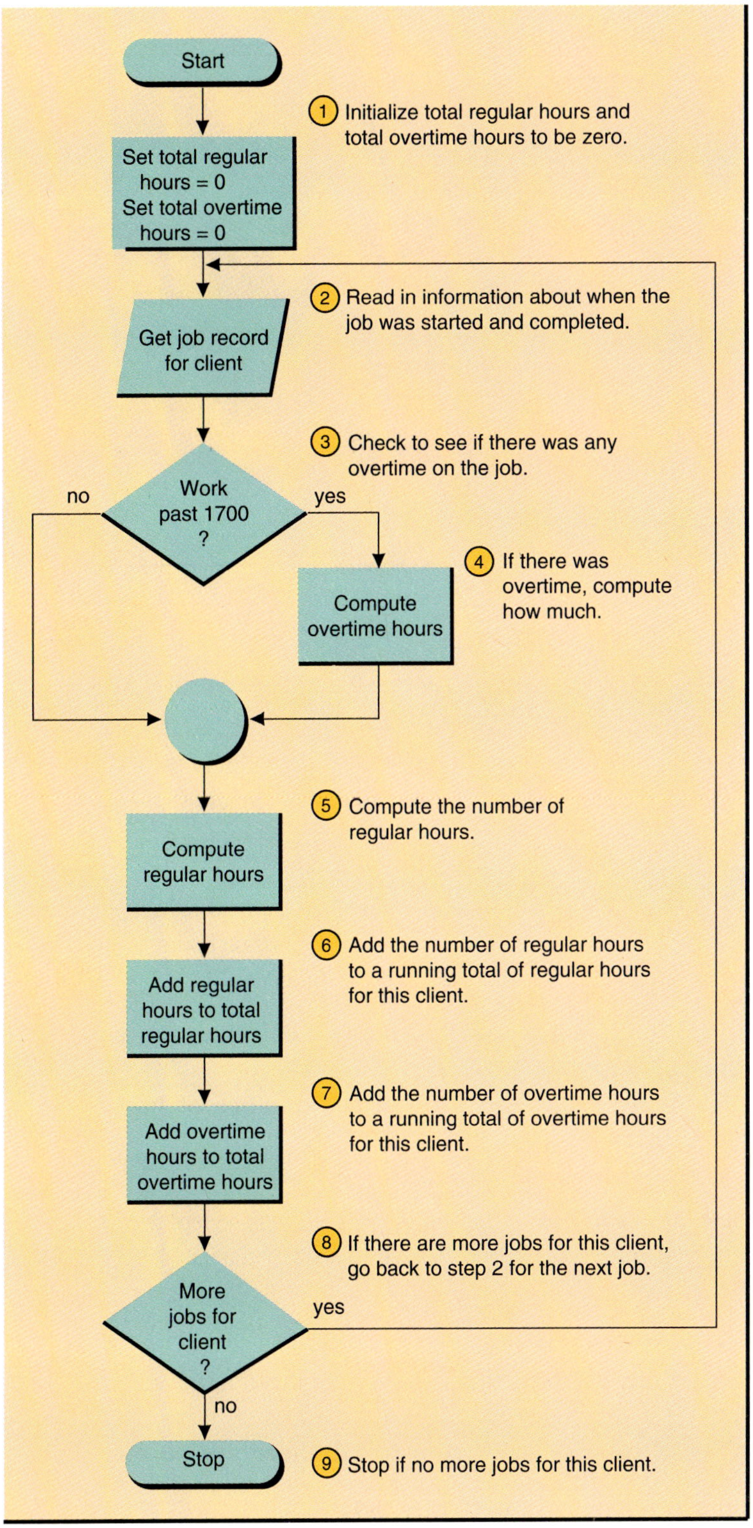

FIGURE 12-7

Flowchart symbols and example of a program flowchart for computing time worked.

Flowchart symbols

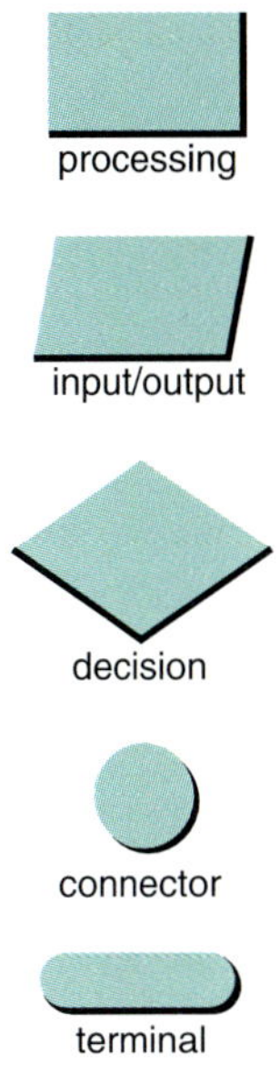

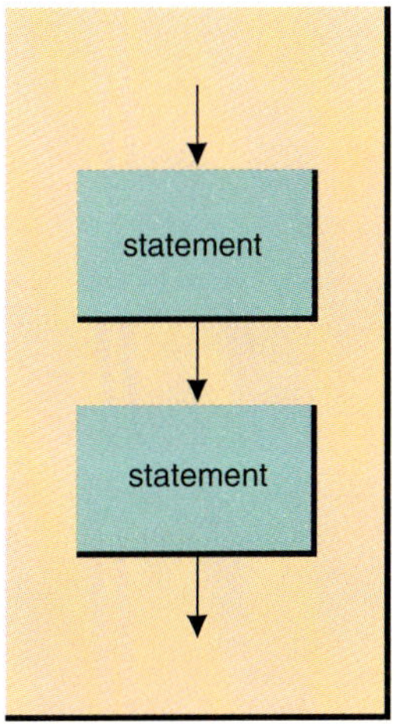

FIGURE 12-8

Sequence logic structure.

FIGURE 12-9
Selection (IF-THEN-ELSE) logic structure.

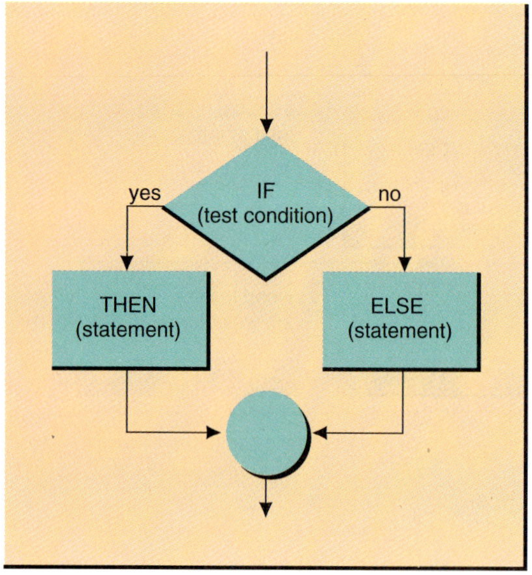

"Add overtime hours to total overtime hours." They logically follow each other. There is no question of "yes" or "no," of a decision suggesting other consequences.

- The **selection structure** occurs when a decision must be made. The outcome of the decision determines which of two paths to follow. (See Figure 12-9.) This structure is also known as an **IF-THEN-ELSE structure,** because that is how you can formulate the decision.

  Consider, for example, the selection structure in the "compute time" flowchart, which is concerned about computing overtime hours. (Refer back to Figure 12-7.) It might be expressed in detail as follows:

  IF hour finished for this job is later than or equal to 1700 hours (5:00 P.M.),
  THEN overtime hours equal the number of hours past 1700 hours,
  ELSE overtime hours equal zero.

- The **loop structure** describes a process that may be repeated as long as a certain condition remains true. The structure is called a "loop" or "iteration" because the program loops around (iterates or repeats) again and again.

The loop structure has two variations: *DO UNTIL* and *DO WHILE.* (See Figure 12-10.) The **DO UNTIL structure** is the most used form. An example is as follows.

DO read in job information UNTIL there are no more jobs.

An example of the **DO WHILE structure** is:

DO read in job information WHILE (that is, as long as) there are more jobs.

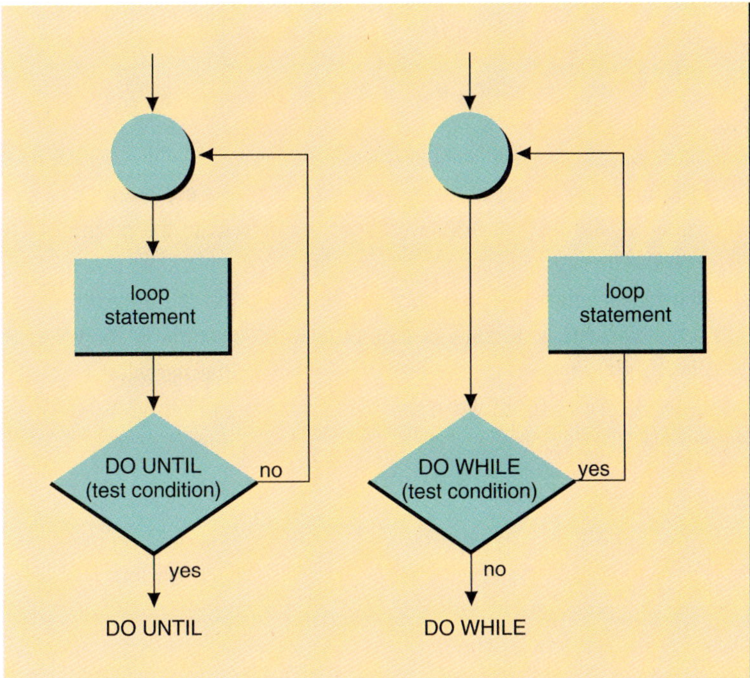

FIGURE 12-10
Loop logic structures: DO UNTIL and DO WHILE.

There is a difference between the two loop structures. You may have several statements that need to be repeated. If so, the decision when to *stop* repeating them can appear at the *beginning* of the loop (DO WHILE). Or, it can appear at the *end* of the loop (DO UNTIL). The DO UNTIL loop means that the loop statements will be executed at least once. This is because the loop statements are executed *before* you are asked whether to stop.

A summary of the structured programming techniques is presented in Figure 12-11.

The last thing to do before leaving the program design step is to document the logic of the design. This report typically includes pseudocode, flowcharts, and logic structures. Now you are ready for the next step, program code.

STRUCTURED PROGRAMMING TECHNIQUES

TECHNIQUE	DESCRIPTION
Top-down design	Major processing steps, called program modules, are identified
Pseudocode	A narrative expression of the logic of the program is written
Program flowcharts	Graphic representation of the steps needed to solve the programming problem is drawn
Logic structures	Three arrangements are used in program flowcharts to write structured programs

FIGURE 12-11
Summary of structured programming techniques.

Step 3: Program Code

"Coding" is the actual writing of the program, using a programming language.

Writing the program is called **coding.** Here you use the logic you developed in the program-design step to actually write the program. That is, you write out—using pencil and paper or typing on a computer keyboard—the letters, numbers, and symbols that make up the program. An example of the handwritten code for the "compute time" module is shown in Figure 12-12. This is the "program code" that instructs the computer what to do. Coding is what many people think of when they think of programming. As we've pointed out, however, it is only one of the six steps in the programming process.

The Good Program

What are the qualities of a good program? Above all, it should be reliable—that is, it should work under most conditions. It should catch obvious and common input errors. It should also be well documented and understandable by programmers other than the person who wrote it. After all, someone may need to make changes in the program in the future. The best way to code effective programs is to write so-called *structured programs,* using the logic structures described in Step 3.

Which Language?

An important decision is the selection of the programming language. There are hundreds of programming languages, but for microcomputers the most popular have been BASIC, Pascal, and C. We describe programming languages later in this

FIGURE 12-12
Example of handwritten code for computing the time worked.

```
begin
total_regular :=0;
total_overtime:=0;
while not eof(input_file)do
      begin
      readln(input_file,hour_in,minute_in,hour_out,minute_out):
      if (hour_out >=17) then
         overtime := (hour_out - 17) + (minute_out/60)
      else
         overtime := 0;
      regular := (hour_out - hour_in) +(minute_out-minute_in)/60)-overtime;

      total_regular := total_regular + regular;
      total_overtime := total_overtime - overtime;
      end;
end.
```

chapter. First you must determine the program's logic. Then you can write (code) it in whatever language you choose that is appropriate and available on your computer. A Pascal program for the "compute time" module is illustrated in Figure 12-13. The next step is testing, or debugging, the program.

Step 4: Program Test

"Debugging" is testing a program and correcting syntax and logic errors.

Debugging is a programmer's word for testing and then *eliminating* errors ("getting the bugs out"). It means running the program on a computer and then fixing the parts that do not work. (See Figure 12-14.) Programming errors are of two types: *syntax errors* and *logic errors.*

Syntax Errors

A **syntax error** is a violation of the rules of the programming language. For example, in the programming language called Pascal, the instruction "write In" is wrong. It is supposed to be "writeln." That is an example of a syntax error.

```
Program compute_time:

var
  input_file : text;
  total_regular,
  total_overtime,
  regular,
  overtime : real;
  hour_in,
  minute_in,
  hour_out,
  minute_out : integer;

begin
assign (input_file,'time.txt');
reset (input_file);

total_regular := 0;
total_overtime  := 0;
while not eof(input_file) do
  begin
  readln (input_file,hour_in,minute_in,hour_out,minute_out);
  if (hour_out >= 17) then
    overtime := (hour_out – 17) + (minute_out/60)
  else
    overtime := 0;
  regular := (hour_out-hour_in) + ((minute_out-minute_in)/60) – overtime;
  total_regular := total_regular + regular;
  total_overtime := total_overtime + overtime;
  end;

writeln('regular = ',total_regular);
writeln('overtime = ',total_overtime);
end.
```

FIGURE 12-13
The "compute time" program written in Pascal.

FIGURE 12-14
Debugging: testing and eliminating program errors using sample data.

Logic Errors

A **logic error** occurs when the programmer uses an incorrect calculation or leaves out a programming procedure. For example, a payroll program that did not compute overtime hours would have a logic error.

The Testing Process

Several methods have been devised for finding and removing both types of errors, as follows.

- **Desk checking:** In **desk checking,** a programmer sitting at a desk checks (proofreads) a printout of the program. The programmer goes through the listing line by line looking for syntax and logic errors.
- **Manual testing with sample data:** Both correct and incorrect data is run through the program—manually, not with a computer—to test for correct processing results.
- **Attempt at translation:** The program is run through a computer, using a translator program. The translator attempts to translate the written program from the programming language (such as Pascal) into the machine language. Before the program will run, it must be free of syntax errors. Such errors will be identified by the translating program.
- **Testing sample data on the computer:** After all syntax errors have been corrected, the program is tested for logic errors. Sample data is used to test the correct execution of each program statement.
- **Testing by a select group of potential users:** This is sometimes called *beta testing*. It is usually the final step in testing a program. Potential users try out the program and provide feedback.

Step 5: Program Documentation

"Documenting" means writing a description of the purpose and process of the program.

Documentation consists of written descriptions and procedures about a program and how to use it. It is not something done just at the end of the programming process. Documentation is carried on throughout all the programming steps. This documentation is typically within the program itself and in printed documents. In this step, all the prior documentation is reviewed and finalized. Documentation is important for people who may be involved with the program in the future. (See Figure 12-15.) These people may include the following:

FIGURE 12-15
Documentation: describing the program so that others can understand it.

- **Users:** Users need to know how to use the software. Some organizations may offer training courses to guide users through the program. However, other organizations may expect users to be able to learn a package just from the written documentation. Two examples of this sort of documentation are the manuals that accompany the software and the help option within most microcomputer applications.
- **Operators:** Documentation must be provided for computer operators. If the program sends them error messages, for instance, they need to know what to do about them.
- **Programmers:** As time passes, even the creator of the original program may not remember much about it. Other programmers wishing to update and modify it—that is, perform program maintenance—may find themselves frustrated without adequate documentation. This kind of documentation should include text and program flowcharts, program listings, and sample output. It might also include system flowcharts to show how the particular program relates to other programs within an information system.

Step 6: Program Maintenance

Programmers update software to correct errors, improve usability, standardize, and adjust to organizational changes.

The final step is **program maintenance.** As much as 75 percent of the total lifetime cost for an application program is for maintenance. (See Figure 12-16.) This activity is so commonplace that a special job title, *maintenance programmer,* exists.

The purpose of program maintenance is to ensure that current programs are operating error free, efficiently, and effectively. Activities in this area fall into two categories: operations and changing needs.

FIGURE 12-16
Maintenance: ensuring that the programs continue to operate efficiently and effectively.

Operations

Operations activities concern locating and correcting operational errors, making programs easier to use, and standardizing software using structured programming techniques. For properly designed programs these activities should be minimal.

Changing Needs

The category of changing needs is unavoidable. All organizations change over time, and their programs must change with them. Programs need to be adjusted for a variety of reasons, including new tax laws, new information needs, and new company policies.

Figure 12-17 summarizes the six steps of the programming process.

FIGURE 12-17
Summary of six steps in programming.

PROGRAMMING STEPS

STEP	PRIMARY ACTIVITY
1. Program specification	Determine program objectives, desired output, required input, and processing requirements
2. Program design	Use structured programming techniques
3. Program code	Select programming language; write the program
4. Program test	Perform desk check and manual checks; attempt translation; test using sample data; beta test with potential users
5. Program documentation	Write procedure for users, operators, and programmers
6. Program maintenance	Adjust for errors, inefficient or ineffective operations, nonstandard code, and changes over time

Improving Efficiency and Productivity

CASE tools automate the development process. Object-oriented software development changes the approach.

You hear about efficiency and productivity everywhere. They are particularly important for software development. Two resources that promise to help are *CASE tools* and *object-oriented software development.*

CASE Tools

Professional programmers are constantly looking for ways to make their work easier, faster, and more reliable. One tool we mentioned in the last chapter, CASE, is meeting this need. **CASE (computer-aided software engineering) tools** provide some automation and assistance in program design, coding, and testing. (See Figure 12-18.)

Object-Oriented Software Development

Traditional systems development is a careful, step-by-step approach focusing on the procedures needed to complete a certain objective. **Object-oriented software development** is a new approach. It focuses less on the tasks and more on defining the relationships between previously defined procedures or objects. **Object-oriented programming (OOP)** is a process by which a program is organized into objects. Each object contains both the data and processing operations necessary to perform a task. Let's explain what this means.

In the past, programs were developed as giant entities, from the first line of code to the last. This has been compared to building a car from scratch. Object-oriented programming is like building a car from prefabricated parts—carburetor, generator, fenders, and so on. Object-oriented programs use *modules* called "objects." Objects are reusable, self-contained components. Programs built with these objects assume that certain functions are the same. For example, many programs, from

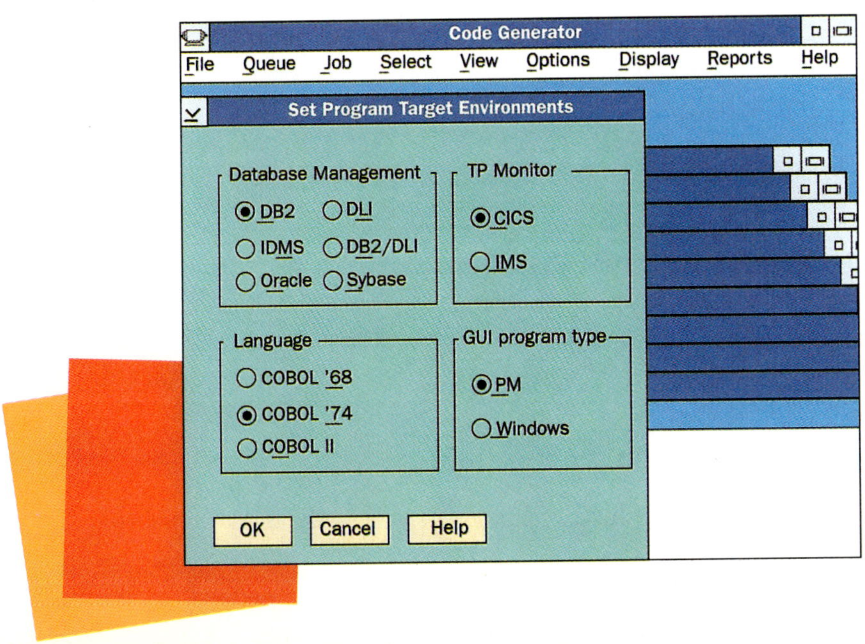

FIGURE 12-18
CASE tools: Sterling Software's Code Generator.

spreadsheets to database managers, have an instruction that will sort lists of names in alphabetical order. A programmer might use this module or object for alphabetizing in many other programs. There is no need to invent this activity anew every time. C++ is one of the most widely used object-oriented programming languages.

Some expect that object-oriented software development will improve productivity and efficiency tenfold. However, this will depend upon how many available objects are clearly defined, programmed, documented, and saved in libraries for later use.

Five Generations of Programming Languages

Languages are described as occurring in "generations," from machine languages to natural languages.

Computer professionals talk about **levels** or **generations of programming languages,** ranging from "low" to "high." Programming languages are called *lower level* when they are closer to the language the computer itself uses. The computer understands the 0s and 1s that make up bits and bytes. Programming languages are called *higher level* when they are closer to the language humans use—that is, for English speakers, more like English.

There are five generations of programming languages. These are (1) machine languages, (2) assembly languages, (3) procedural languages, (4) problem-oriented languages, and (5) natural languages.

Machine Languages: The First Generation

We mentioned earlier that a byte is made up of *bits,* consisting of 1s and 0s. These 1s and 0s may correspond to electricity's being on or off in the computer. They may also correspond to a magnetic charge's being present or absent on storage media such as disk or tape. From this two-state system have been built coding schemes that allow us to construct letters, numbers, punctuation marks, and other special characters. Examples of these coding schemes, as we saw, are ASCII and EBCDIC.

Data represented in 1s and 0s is said to be written in **machine language.** To see how hard this is to understand, imagine if you had to code this:

111100100111001111010010000100000111000000101011

Machine languages also vary according to make of computer—another characteristic that makes them hard to work with.

Assembly Languages: The Second Generation

Assembly languages have a clear advantage over the 1s and 0s of machine language because they use abbreviations or mnemonics. These are easier for human beings to remember. The machine language code we gave earlier could be expressed in assembly language as

ADD 210(8,13),02B(4,7)

This is still pretty obscure, of course, and so assembly language is also considered low-level.

Assembly languages also vary from computer to computer. With the third generation, we advance to high-level languages, many of which are considered **portable languages.** That is, they can be run on more than one kind of computer—they are "portable" from one machine to another.

High-Level Procedural Languages: The Third Generation

People are able to understand languages that are more like their own (e.g., English) than machine languages or assembly languages. These more English-like programming languages are called "high-level" languages. However, most people still require some training in order to use higher-level languages. This is particularly true of procedural languages.

Procedural languages are programming languages with names like BASIC, Pascal, C, COBOL, and FORTRAN. They are called "procedural" because they are designed to express the logic—the procedures—that can solve general problems. Procedural languages, then, are intended to solve *general* problems. COBOL, for instance, is used in all kinds of business applications, such as payroll and inventory control. It is fourth-generation languages, discussed next, that are intended to solve *specific* problems.

For a procedural language to work on a computer, it must be translated into machine language so that the computer understands it. Depending on the language, this translation is performed by either a *compiler* or an *interpreter.*

- A **compiler** converts the programmer's procedural language program, called the *source code,* into a machine language code, called the *object code.* This object code can then be saved and run later. Examples of procedural languages using compilers are the standard versions of Pascal, COBOL, and FORTRAN.
- An **interpreter** converts the procedural language one statement at a time into machine code just before it is to be executed. No object code is saved. An example of a procedural language using an interpreter is the standard version of BASIC.

What is the difference between using a compiler and using an interpreter? When a program is run, the compiler requires two steps. The first step is to convert the entire program's source code to object code. The second step is to run the object code. The interpreter, in contrast, converts and runs the program one line at a time. The advantage of a compiler language is that once the object code has been obtained, the program executes faster. The advantage of an interpreter language is that programs are easier to develop.

The principal procedural languages with which you may come in contact are as follows:

- **BASIC:** Short for *B*eginner's *A*ll-purpose *S*ymbolic *I*nstruction *C*ode, **BASIC** is a popular microcomputer language. Widely used on microcomputers and easy to learn, it is suited to both beginning and experienced programmers. It is also interactive—you and the computer communicate with each other directly during the writing and running of programs.

  Another version created by the Microsoft Corporation is Visual BASIC, which has been hailed as a programming breakthrough. Visual BASIC makes it easier for novice programmers, as well as professionals, to develop customized applications for Windows. The new language is expected to become quite popular for corporate, in-house development.

- **Pascal:** Another language that is widely used on microcomputers and easy to learn is **Pascal.** It is named after Blaise Pascal, a seventeenth-century French mathematician. This language has become quite popular in computer science educational programs. One advantage of Pascal is that it encourages programmers to follow structured coding procedures. It also works well for graphics. We showed an example of Pascal earlier. (Refer back to Figure 12-13.)
- **C/C++:** **C** is a general-purpose language that also works well with microcomputers. It is useful for writing operating systems, spreadsheet programs, database programs, and some scientific applications. Programs are portable: They can be run without change on a variety of computers. **C++** is a version of C that incorporates object-oriented technologies. It is popular with some software developers and promises to increase programmer productivity.
- **COBOL:** **COBOL**—which stands for *CO*mmon *B*usiness-*O*riented *L*anguage—is one of the most frequently used programming languages in business. Though harder to learn than BASIC, its logic is easier for a person who is not a trained programmer to understand. Writing a COBOL program is sort of like writing the outline for a term paper. The program is divided into four divisions. The divisions in turn are divided into sections, which are divided into paragraphs, then into statements.
- **FORTRAN:** Short for *FOR*mula *TRAN*slation, **FORTRAN** is a widely used scientific and mathematical language. It is very useful for processing complex formulas. Thus, many scientific and engineering programs have been written in this language.
- **Ada:** **Ada** is named after Augusta Ada, the English Countess of Lovelace who is regarded as the first programmer. Ada was developed under the sponsorship of the U.S. Department of Defense. Originally designed for weapons systems, it has commercial uses as well. Because of its structured design, modules (sections) of a large program can be written, compiled, and tested separately—before the entire program is put together.
- **Java:** **Java** is one of the newest and most exciting programming languages. Java programs called **applets** are widely used on the Internet to add animation and interest to Web pages. Unlike the programs written with other languages, a program written in Java can run on any system: Windows, Mac, or Unix. Recently Java has been used to develop general-application software. Some experts predict that Java will become the most widely used programming lanugage within the next few years.

Problem-Oriented Languages: The Fourth Generation

Third-generation languages are valuable, but they require training in programming. Problem-oriented languages, also known as *very high level languages,* require little special training on the part of the user.

Unlike general-purpose languages, **problem-oriented languages** are designed to solve specific problems. Some of these fourth-generation languages are used for very specific applications. For example, IFPS (interactive financial planning system) is used to develop financial models. Many consider Lotus 1-2-3 and dBASE to be flexible fourth-generation languages. This group also includes query languages and application generators:

- **Query languages:** **Query languages** enable nonprogrammers to use certain easily understood commands to search and generate reports from a database. An example is the commands used on an airline reservations system by clerks needing flight information.
- **Application generators:** An **application generator** contains a number of modules—logically related program statements—that have been preprogrammed to accomplish various tasks. An example would be a module that calculates overtime pay. The programmer can simply state which task is needed for a particular application. The application generator creates the program code by selecting the appropriate modules.

Natural Languages: The Fifth Generation

Natural languages are still being developed. They are designed to give people a more human ("natural") connection with computers. The languages are human languages: English, French, Japanese, or whatever. Researchers also hope that natural languages will enable a computer to *learn*—to "remember" information, as people do, and to improve upon it. Clearly, this area is extremely challenging.

The five generations of programming languages are summarized in Figure 12-19.

PROGRAMMING GENERATIONS

GENERATION:	SAMPLE STATEMENT
Machine First: Name	10010001
Second: Assembly	ADD 210(8, 13), 02B(4, 7)
Third: Procedural	Overtime: = 0
Fourth: Problem	FIND NAME = "JONES"
Fifth: Natural	IF patient is dizzy, THEN check temperature and blood pressure

FIGURE 12-19
Summary of five programming generations.

A Look at the Future

The Year 2000 Problem could cost $600 billion to fix and $2 trillion in legal fees.

The second millennium is just around the corner. Many look to the year 2000 as the beginning of exciting new and challenging opportunities. In programming and information systems circles, it represents a significant challenge. In fact, they have given this challenge a name—The Year 2000 Problem.

What is supposed to happen in the year 2000? Many experts say it could be chaos. They predict that millions of miscalculations on finance, scheduling, insurance, and accounting applications could be commonplace. Your credit cards, school loans, and other financial aid could suddenly be canceled. Social security checks could be stopped, federal assistance programs could be discontinued, and millions of applications programs could fail to execute.

The source of this potential problem began twenty years ago when programmers first standardized how computers would handle dates. Only two digits were typically used to represent years. For example, the year 1980 was recorded simply as 80. Since that time thousands of databases and millions of programs have been created using that standard. Many of them are still widely used today, and they work fine as long as the year's first two digits are 19.

Does this sound like a difficult problem to fix? The experts think so. One well respected industry source estimates that the costs to avoid this problem could reach $600 billion. The American Bar Association predicts legal costs of $2 trillion for related law suits. The federal government, state governments, and every major corporation have teams of programmers reviewing program code, assessing potential problems, and reprogramming.

What will actually happen in the year 2000? Will the programming problem be fixed in time? We'll have to wait and see.

KEY TERMS

Ada (266)
applets (266)
application generator (267)
assembly language (264)
BASIC (265)
C (266)
C++ (266)
CASE (computer-aided software engineering) tool (263)
COBOL (266)
coding (258)
compiler (265)
debugging (259)
desk checking (260)
DO UNTIL structure (256)
DO WHILE structure (256)
documentation (261)
FORTRAN (264)
generations of programming languages (256)
IF-THEN-ELSE structure (256)
interpreter (265)
Java (266)
levels of programming languages (264)
logic error (260)
logic structure (254)
loop structure (256)
machine language (264)
module (253)
natural languages (267)
object-oriented programming (OOP) (263)
object-oriented software development (263)
Pascal (266)
portable language (265)
problem-oriented languages (267)
procedural language (265)
program (249)
program analysis (250)
program definition (250)
program design (253)

program flowchart (254)
program maintenance (261)
programming (249)
program module (253)
program specification (250)
pseudocode (254)
query language (267)
selection structure (256)
sequence structure (254)
software development (249)
structured programming techniques (253)
syntax error (259)
top-down program design (253)

REVIEW QUESTIONS

True/False

1. A program is a list of instructions for the computer to follow to accomplish the task of processing data into information.
2. All documentation is performed in the last step in the programming.
3. CASE stands for Computer Association of Scientific Engineers.
4. A translator converts a programming language into machine language.
5. Assembly languages represent the first generation of programming languages.

Multiple Choice

1. Another name for application software is:
   a. application programs
   b. system software
   c. programming languages
   d. package software
   e. custom-made programs
2. The structured programming technique that graphically presents the detailed steps needed to solve the problem:
   a. top-down design
   b. pseudocode
   c. flowcharts
   d. logic structures
   e. object-oriented programming
3. The last thing to do before leaving the program design step:
   a. determine outputs
   b. document
   c. test
   d. select programming language
   e. code
4. The last step in programming:
   a. design
   b. analysis
   c. test
   d. maintenance
   e. coding
5. Translator that converts procedural languages one statement at a time into machine code before it is executed:
   a. BASIC
   b. interpreter
   c. Pascal
   d. query language
   e. compiler

Fill in the Blank

1. In program specification, you should specify ________ before inputs.
2. The logic structure ________ is used when a decision must be made.
3. ________ is another name for testing the program.
4. Unlike traditional software development, object-oriented development focuses on defining the ________ between procedures or objects.
5. ________ is the most frequently used language in business programming.

Open Ended

1. Describe the six steps involved in programming.
2. Identify and give an example for each of the three logic structures.
3. List and discuss the five generations of programming languages.
4. Explain the difference between a compiler and an interpreter.
5. Discuss the principal advantage(s) of natural languages if researchers are successful in developing them.

DISCUSSION QUESTIONS

1. *Pencil-and-paper programming:* Suppose you are the manager of a clothing store. Using just pencil and paper, see if you can devise the steps in a program that will do the following:
   a. Pay a sales bonus of 1 percent of total sales to salespeople who sell $50,000 worth of clothes.
   b. Pay a sales bonus of 5 percent of total sales to salespeople who sell $250,000 worth of clothes.
   c. Pay a sales bonus of 10 percent of total sales to salespeople who sell $500,000 worth of clothes.
2. *Programming the beginning of your day:* Flowcharts can be used to graphically present the sequence of steps involved in almost any activity. Different shapes and symbols are used to represent different kinds of activities: processing, input and output of data, decision-making, and starting and stopping. The lines and arrows connecting the shapes show the sequence of steps used to complete the activity. Create a flowchart that describes what you do each morning to get ready for the day.

on the web

Exercises and Explorations

1 Java

Java has been touted as the next great programming language, but it won't get far without real-world business applications. Find out what Java can do for you in the business world by visiting our Web site at http://www.magpie.org/essentials/chapter-12 to link to a site specializing in Java. Once connected to that site, print out the most informative Web page, and write a paragraph discussing the advantages and disadvantages of Java for business applications.

2 Active X

Microsoft developed Active X as a response to Java. To learn more about Active X, visit our Web site at http://www.magpie.org/essentials/chapter-12 to link to a site specializing in Active X. Once connected to that site, print out the table of contents for an *overview of Active X,* and write a paragraph on what Active X is and how it compares with Java.

3 The Year 2000 Problem

The coming of the year 2000 may present a problem to many computer users. Many programs are designed only for dates with years in the 1900s. To learn more about this potential problem, connect to the Hotbot search tool at http://news.hotbot.com/index.html and use the keywords "year 2000 problem." Print the first page of results, and write a paragraph clearly defining the problem and describing the programs that may be effected and how.

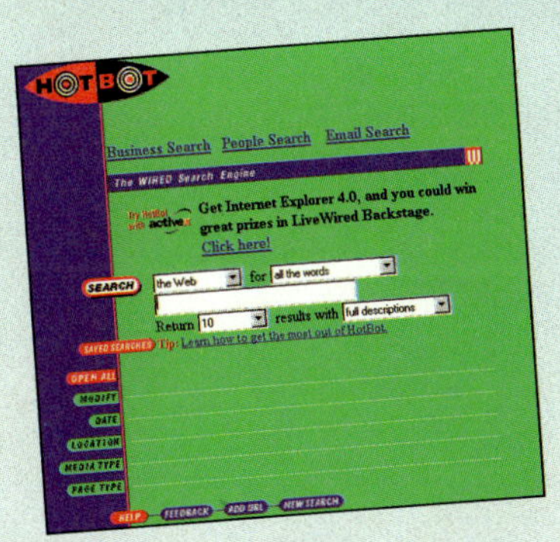

4 World Wide Weather

The fact that the weather is changing and is different all around the world makes it an ideal subject for the Internet. You can find out recent reports on the weather anywhere in the world. Visit visit our Web site at http://www.magpie.org/essentials/chapter-12 to link to the weather channel's site. Print the five-day forecast for your area. Write a paragraph describing how you and others might use this site.

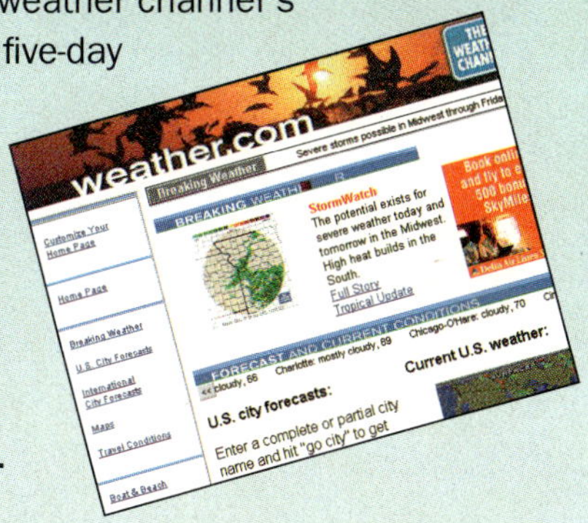

VISUAL SUMMARY

12 Programming and Languages

A *program* is a list of instructions for the computer to follow to do a task. The instructions are made up of statements written in a programming language (e.g., BASIC). *Programming* is a six-step procedure for producing that list.

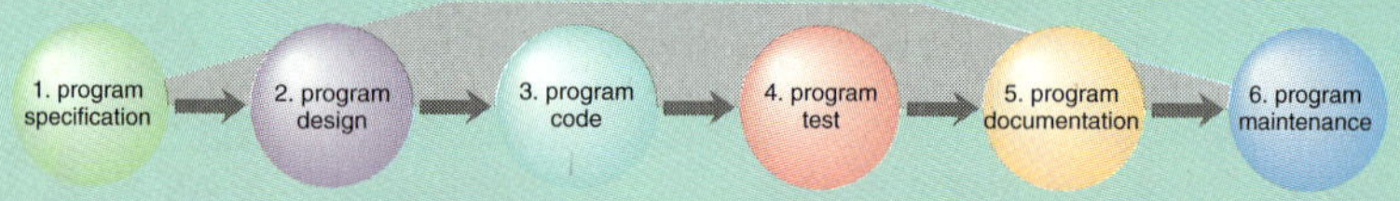

STEP 1: PROGRAM SPECIFICATION

Program definition, also called **program analysis,** consists of specifying five tasks:

- Determining program objectives by focusing on the specific problem to be solved.
- Determining the desired output before considering the required inputs.
- Determining the input data and the source of the data.
- Determining the processing requirements to use input to produce output.
- Documenting program objectives, outputs, inputs, and processing.

STEP 2: PROGRAM DESIGN

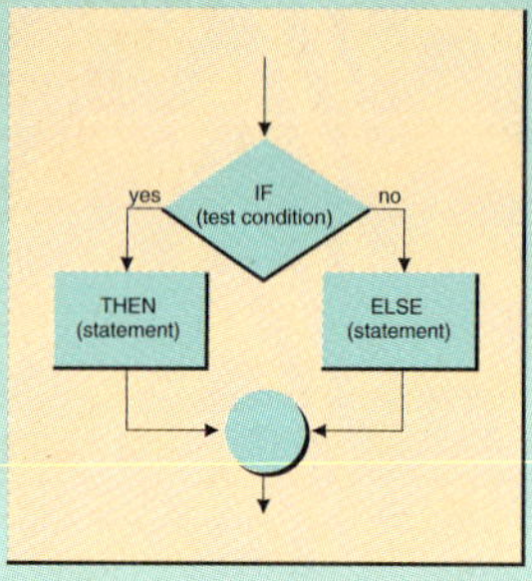

In **program design,** a solution is designed using structured programming techniques. (See table below.)

Three Logic Structures

- **Sequence**—one program statement followed by another.
- **Selection** (or **IF-THEN-ELSE**)—when a decision must be made.
- **Loop**—when process is repeated as long as a condition is true. May be either **DO UNTIL** or **DO WHILE.**

STEP 3: PROGRAM CODE

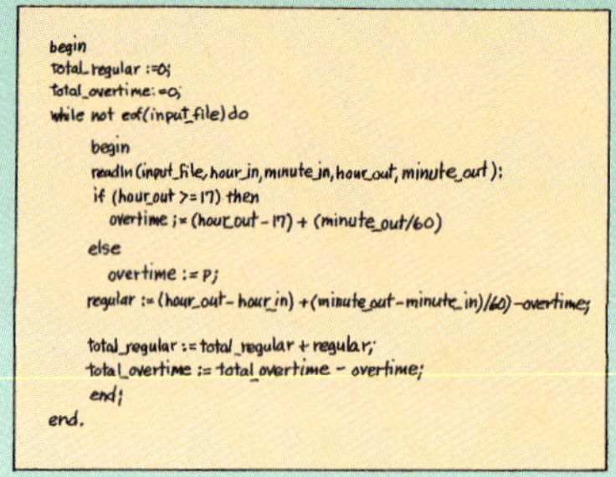

Coding is writing a program. There are several important aspects of writing a program. Two are:

- Program quality—good programs are structured using logic structures.
- Language selection—a **programming language** should be chosen that is appropriate for the programming problem and the computer.

STRUCTURED PROGRAMMING TECHNIQUES

TECHNIQUE	DESCRIPTION
Top-down design	Major processing steps, called program modules, are identified
Pseudocode	A narrative expression of the logic of the program is written
Program flowcharts	Graphic representation of the steps needed to solve the programming problem is drawn
Logic structures	Three arrangements are used in program flowcharts to write structured programs

Two resources that promise to improve software development efficiency and productivity are: CASE (computer-aided software engineering) and object-oriented software development. **CASE** tools provide some automation and assistance in program design, coding, and testing. **Object-oriented software development** is a new approach that focuses less on the tasks and more on defining the relationships between previously defined procedures or objects.

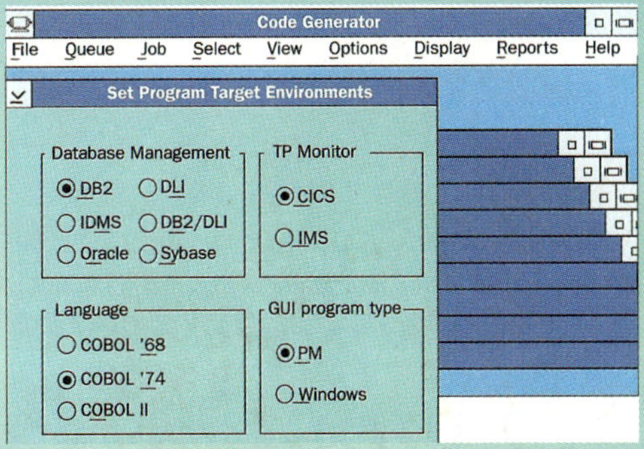

STEP 4: PROGRAM TEST

Debugging consists of testing and eliminating the **syntax errors** (violation of rules of programming language) and **logic errors** (incorrect calculations or procedures). Debugging methods consist of:

- **Desk checking**—careful reading of a printout of the program.
- **Manual testing**—using sample data to test for correct processing results.
- **Attempt at translation**—running the program through a computer, using a translator program.
- **Testing sample data**—testing the program for logic errors on a computer, using sample data.
- **Testing by users**—*beta testing* by selected users is the final step.

STEP 5: PROGRAM FINALIZED DOCUMENTATION

Documentation consists of a written description of the program and the procedures for running it for users, operators, and programmers during **program maintenance**—modifying or updating of the program.

- Users need to know how to use the program and to input the data to produce correct results.
- Operators need to know how to execute the program and to recognize and correct errors.
- Programmers need to be able to explain how the program works and to maintain the program in the future.

STEP 6: PROGRAM MAINTENANCE

Maintenance is the final step in the programming process. It is to ensure efficient and effective ongoing operation of the program.

Two major categories of activities in program maintenance are:

- Operations activities to locate and correct errors, improve usability, and standardize software.
- Activities related to the changing needs of the organization that often require programs to be modified.

PROGRAMMING GENERATIONS

GENERATION	NAME	SAMPLE STATEMENT
First	Machine	10010001
Second	Assembly	ADD 210(8, 13),02B(4, 7)
Third	Procedural	Overtime: = 0
Fourth	Problem	FIND NAME = "JONES"
Fifth	Natural	IF patient is dizzy, THEN check temperature and blood pressure

Workplace Issues: Ergonomics, Privacy, Security, and the Environment

The tools and products of the information age do not exist in a world by themselves. As we said in Chapter 1, a computer system consists not only of software, hardware, data, and procedures but also of *people.* Because of people, computer systems may be used for both good and bad purposes. In this chapter we examine what some of the people issues are.

COMPETENCIES

After you have read this chapter, you should be able to:

1. Describe ergonomics and how it helps avoid physical and mental risks.
2. Describe the four ethical issues: privacy, accuracy, property, and access.
3. Discuss the privacy issues raised by the presence of large databases, electronic networks, the Internet, and the Web.
4. List the major laws on privacy.
5. Explain the effects of computer crimes, including the spreading of computer viruses.
6. Describe other hazards to the computer.
7. Discuss security measures that may be taken.
8. Discuss what the computer industry is doing to help protect the environment.
9. Discuss what you can do to help protect the environment.

There are more than 200 million microcomputers in use today. Millions of American workers use these machines every day for hours at a time. What are the consequences of the widespread presence of this technology? We consider some of the effects below.

Ergonomics

Ergonomics helps computer users take steps to avoid physical and mental health risks and to increase productivity.

Even though the cost of computers has decreased significantly, they are still expensive. Why have them, then, unless they can make workers more effective? Ironically, there are certain ways in which computers may actually make people *less* productive. Many of these problems will most likely affect workers in data entry–intensive positions, such as clerks and word processor operators. However, they may also happen to anyone whose job involves heavy use of the computer. As a result, there has been great interest in a field known as ergonomics.

Ergonomics (pronounced "er-guh-*nom*-ix") is defined as the study of human factors related to computers. It is concerned with fitting the job to the worker rather than forcing the worker to contort to fit the job. As computer use has increased, so has interest in ergonomics. People are devising ways that computers can be designed and used to increase productivity and avoid health risks.

Physical Health Matters

Sitting in front of a screen in awkward positions for long periods may lead to physical problems. These can include eyestrain, headaches, and back pain. Users can alleviate these problems by taking frequent rest breaks and by using well-designed computer furniture. Some recommendations by ergonomic experts for the ideal setup for a microcomputer are illustrated in Figure 1.

The physical health matters related to computers that have received the most attention recently are the following.

- **Avoiding eyestrain and headache:** Our eyes were made for most efficient seeing at a distance. However, monitors require using the eyes at closer range for a long time, which can create eyestrain, headaches, and double vision.

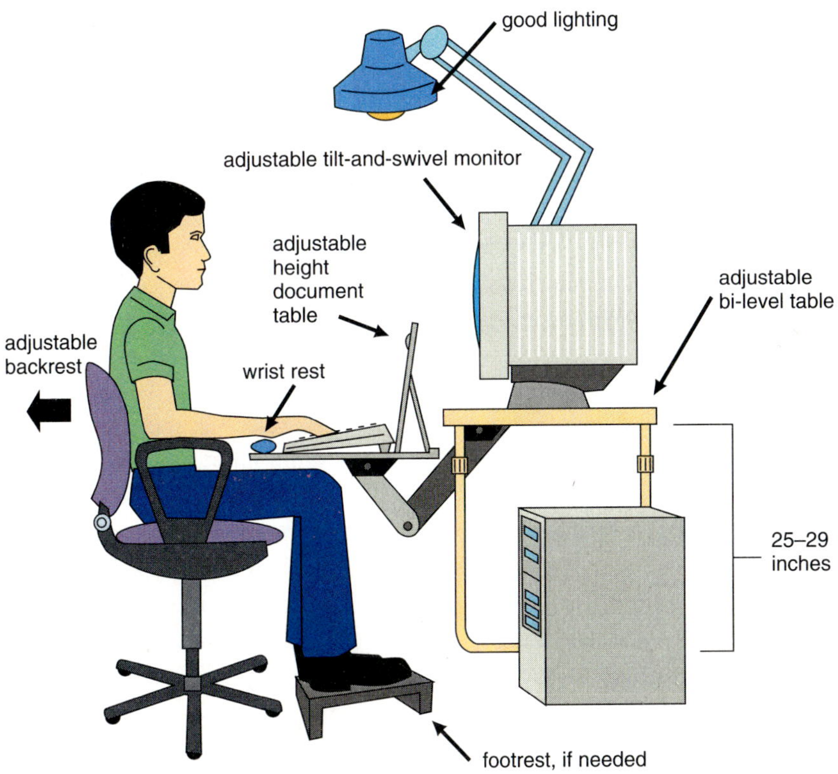

FIGURE 1
Recommendations for the ideal microcomputer work environment.

To make the computer easier on the eyes, take a 15-minute break every hour or two. Avoid computer screens that flicker. Keep computer screens away from windows and other sources of bright light to minimize reflected glare on the screen. Special antiglare screen coatings and "glare shields" are also available. Make sure the screen is three to four times brighter than room light. Keep everything you're focusing on at about the same distance. For example, the computer screen, keyboard, and a document holder containing your work might be positioned about 20 inches away. Clean the screen of dust from time to time.

- **Avoiding back and neck pain:** Many people work at monitors and keyboards that are in improper positions. The result can be pains in the back and neck.

  To avoid such problems, make sure equipment is adjustable. You should be able to adjust your chair for height and angle, and the chair should have good back support. The table on which the monitor stands should also be adjustable, and the monitor itself should be of the tilt-and-swivel kind. The monitor should be at eye level or slightly below eye level. Keyboards should be detachable. Document holders should be adjustable.

- **Avoiding effects of electromagnetic fields:** Like many household appliances, monitors generate invisible electromagnetic field (EMF) emissions, which can pass through the human body. Some observers feel that there could be a connection between these EMF emissions and possible miscarriages (and even some cancers). A study by the government's National Institute of Occupational Safety and Health found no statistical relationship between monitors and miscarriages. Even so, several companies have introduced low-emission monitors. They state that no health or safety problems exist with older monitors; rather, they are merely responding to market demands.

  One recommendation is that computer users should follow a policy of "prudent avoidance" in reducing their exposure to EMF emissions. They should try to sit about 2 feet or more from the computer screen and 3 feet from neighboring terminals. The strongest fields are emitted from the sides and backs of terminals. Pregnant women should be particularly cautious and are encouraged to consult with their physician.

- **Avoiding repetitive strain injury:** Data-entry operators may make as many as 23,000 keystrokes a day. Some of these workers and other heavy keyboard users have fallen victim to a disorder known as repetitive strain injury.

  Repetitive strain injury (RSI)—also called **repetitive motion injury** and **cumulative trauma disorder**—is the name given to a number of injuries. These result from fast, repetitive work that can cause neck, wrist, hand, and arm pain. RSI is by far the greatest cause of workplace illnesses in private industry. Some RSI sufferers are slaughterhouse, textile, and automobile workers, who have long been susceptible to the disorder. One particular type of RSI, **carpal tunnel syndrome,** found among heavy computer users, consists of damage to nerves and tendons in the hands. Some victims report the pain is so intense that they cannot open doors or shake hands and that they require corrective surgery.

Before the computer, typists would stop to change paper or make corrections, thus giving themselves short but frequent rest periods. Ergonomically correct keyboards have recently been developed to help make up for this lack of rest periods. (See Figure 2.) But, in addition, because RSI is caused by repetition and a fast work pace, you should remember to take frequent short rest breaks. Experts also advise getting plenty of sleep and exercise, losing weight, sitting up straight, and learning stress-management techniques.

FIGURE 2
Ergonomic keyboard: ERGO from Acer Peripherals, Inc.

Mental Health Matters

Computer technology offers not only ways of improving productivity but also some irritants that may be counterproductive.

- **Avoiding noise:** Computing can be quite noisy. Voice input and output can be distracting for coworkers. Working next to an impact printer for several hours can leave one with ringing ears. Also, users may develop headaches and tension from continual exposure to the high-frequency, barely audible squeal produced by computer monitors and cooling fans inside the system unit. This is particularly true for women, who hear high-frequency sounds better than men do. They may be affected by the noise even when they are not conscious of hearing it.

  Acoustical tile and sound-muffling covers are available for reducing the noise from coworkers and impact printers. However, there appears to be no immediate solution for abating the noise from monitors.

- **Avoiding stress from excessive monitoring:** Research shows that workers whose performance is monitored electronically suffer more health problems than do those watched by human supervisors. For instance, a computer may monitor the number of keystrokes a data-entry clerk completes in a day. It might tally the time a customer-service person takes to handle a call. The company might then decide to shorten the time allowed and to continue monitoring the employees electronically. By so doing, it may force a pace leading to physical, RSI-type problems and mental health difficulties. One study found that electronically monitored employees reported more boredom, higher tension, extreme anxiety, depression, anger, and severe fatigue.

  Recently it has been shown that electronic monitoring actually is not necessary. For instance, both Federal Express and Bell Canada replaced electronic monitoring with occasional monitoring by human managers. They found that employee productivity stayed up and even increased.

A new word—*technostress*—has been proposed to describe the stress associated with computer use that is harmful to people. Technostress is the tension that arises when we have to unnaturally adapt to computers rather than having computers adapt to us.

Design with People in Mind

Electronic products from microwave ovens to VCRs to microcomputers offer the promise of more efficiency and speed. Often, however, the products are so overloaded with features that users cannot figure them out. Because a microprocessor chip handles not just one operation but several, manufacturers feel obliged to pile on the "bells and whistles." Thus, many home and office products, while being fancy technology platforms, are difficult for humans to use.

A recent trend among manufacturers is deliberately stripping down the features offered, rather than to constantly do all that is possible. In appliances, this restraint is shown among certain types of high-end audio equipment, which come with fewer buttons and lights. In computers, there are similar trends. Surveys show that consumers want "plug and play" equipment—machines that they can simply turn on and quickly start working. Thus, computers are being made easier to use, with more menus, windows, and use of icons and pictures.

Similar attempts at designing computers for ease of human use are found in other areas. For example, psychologists have found that workers regard expert systems—the complex programs that emulate human experts—much as they would human expertise. To be trusted by humans, the programs must contain procedures that are very close to the logic processes used by experts. That is, they must appear to think like humans in order to be acceptable.

Privacy

Every computer user should be aware of ethical matters, including how databases and networks are used and the major privacy laws.

What do you suppose controls how computers can be used? You probably think first of laws. Of course that is right, but technology is moving so fast that it is very difficult for our legal system to keep up. The essential element that controls how computers are used today is ethics.

Ethics, as you may know, are standards of moral conduct. *Computer ethics* are guidelines for the morally acceptable use of computers in our society. There are four primary computer ethics issues:

- **Privacy** concerns the collection and use of data about individuals.
- **Accuracy** relates to the responsibility of those who collect data to ensure that the data is correct.
- **Property** relates to who owns data and rights to software.
- **Access** relates to the responsibility of those who have data to control who is able to use that data.

We are all entitled to ethical treatment. This includes the right to keep personal information, such as credit ratings and medical histories, from getting into the wrong hands. Many people worry that this right is severely threatened. Let us see what some of the concerns are.

Use of Large Databases

Large organizations are constantly compiling information about us. For instance, our social security numbers are now used routinely as key fields in databases for organizing our employment, credit, and tax records. Indeed, even children are now required to have social security numbers. Shouldn't we be concerned that cross-referenced information might be used for the wrong purposes?

Every day, data is gathered about us and stored in large databases. For example, for billing purposes, telephone companies compile lists of the calls we make, the numbers called, and so on. A special telephone directory (called a *reverse directory*) lists telephone numbers followed by subscriber names. Using it, government authorities and others could easily get the names, addresses, and other details about the persons we call. Credit card companies keep similar records. Supermarket scanners in grocery checkout counters record what we buy, when we buy it, how much we buy, and the price. (See Figure 3.) Publishers of magazines, newspapers, and mail-order catalogs have our names, addresses, phone numbers, and what we order.

FIGURE 3
Large organizations are constantly compiling information about us, such as the kinds of products we buy.

A vast industry of data gatherers or "information resellers" now exists that collects such personal data. They then sell it to direct marketers, fund-raisers, and others. Even government agencies contribute; some state motor vehicle departments sell the car registration data they collect. Database companies have been able to collect names, addresses, and other information on about 80 percent of American households. The average person is on 100 mailing lists and 50 databases, according to some privacy experts.

In such ways, your personal preferences and habits become marketable commodities. This raises two areas of concern.

- **Spreading information without personal consent:** How would you feel if your name and your taste in movies were made available nationwide? For a while, Blockbuster, a large video rental company, considered doing just this. What if a great deal of information about your shopping habits—collected about you without your consent—was made available to any microcomputer user who wanted it? Before dropping the project, Lotus Development Corporation and Equifax Inc. planned to market disks containing information on 120 million American consumers. (Lotus claimed it was providing only small businesses with the same information currently available to larger organizations.) Finally, how would you feel if your employer were using your *medical* records to make decisions about placement, promotion, and firing? A University of Illinois survey found that half the Fortune 500 companies were using employee medical records for that purpose.
- **Spreading inaccurate information:** How *accurate* is the information being circulated? Mistakes that creep into one computer file may find their way into other computer files. For example, credit records may be in error. Moreover, even if you

correct an error in one file, the correction may not be made in other files. Indeed, erroneous information may stay in computer files for years. It's important to know, therefore, that you have some recourse. The law allows you to gain access to those records about you that are held by credit bureaus. Under the Freedom of Information Act (described shortly), you are also entitled to look at your records held by government agencies. (Portions may be deleted for national security reasons.)

Use of Private Networks

Suppose you use your company's electronic mail system to send a coworker an unflattering message about your supervisor. Later you find the boss has been spying on your exchange. Or suppose you are a subscriber to an online electronic bulletin board. You discover that the company that owns the bulletin board screens all your messages and rejects those it deems inappropriate. Both these cases have actually happened.

The first instance, of firms eavesdropping on employees, has inspired attempts at federal legislation. One survey revealed that over 20 percent of businesses search employees' electronic mail and computer files. Currently this is legal. One proposed law would not prohibit electronic monitoring but would require employers to provide prior written notice. They would also have to alert employees during the monitoring with some sort of audible or visual signal. The second instance, in which online information services restrict libelous, obscene, or otherwise offensive material, exists with most commercial services. In one case, the Prodigy Information Service terminated the accounts of eight members who had been using the electronic mail system to protest Prodigy's rate hikes.

Prodigy executives argued that the U.S. Constitution does not give members of someone's private network the right to express their views without restrictions. Opponents say that the United States is becoming a nation linked by electronic mail. Therefore, there has to be fundamental protection for users against other people reading or censoring their messages.

Use of the Internet and the Web

When you send e-mail on the Internet or browse the Web, do you have any concerns about privacy? Most people do not. They think as long as they are selective about disclosing their name or other personal information, then little can be done to invade their personal privacy. Experts call this the *illusion of anonymity* that the Internet brings.

As discussed earlier, it is a common practice in many organizations to monitor e-mail content on messages sent within their private electronic networks. Likewise, for some unscrupulous individuals, it is also a common practice to eavesdrop or snoop into the content of e-mail sent across the Internet.

Furthermore, when you browse the Web, your activity is monitored. Whenever you visit a Web site, your browser stores critical information onto your hard disk, typically without your permission or knowledge. For example, your browser creates a **history file** that includes the location of every site visited by your computer system. Addtionally, many Web sites have specialized programs called **cookies** that

PROTECT YOURSELF

Encryption	Encrypt or code sensitive e-mail using special encryption programs
Anonymous remailer	Shield your identity by using an anonymous remailer or special Web site that forwards your e-mail without disclosing your identity
Cookies	Use the newer browsers that allow you to block Web sites from depositing cookies on your hard disk
Providers	Instruct your service provider or whoever you use to link to the Internet not to sell your name or any other personal information
Confidential	Never disclose your telephone number, password, or other private information to strangers

FIGURE 4

Measures to protect your personal privacy.

record how often you visit a site, what you do there, and any other information that you provide, such as credit card numbers. Although these programs are intended to better provide service to you when you revisit a Web site, you may consider some of this information private, and you may not like others saving this information on your hard disk.

Recently, companies have been created that specialize in monitoring Internet and Web site activities. Many of these firms sell e-mail mailing lists and individualized personal profiles without obtaining permission. How can you protect yourself? See Figure 4 for some suggestions.

The Major Laws on Privacy

Some federal laws governing privacy matters (summarized in Figure 5) are as follows:

- **Fair Credit Reporting Act:** The **Fair Credit Reporting Act of 1970** is intended to keep inaccuracies out of credit bureau files. Credit agencies are barred from sharing credit information with anyone but authorized customers. Consumers have the right to review and correct their records and to be notified of credit investigations for insurance and employment.

  Drawback: Credit agencies may share information with anyone they reasonably believe has a "legitimate business need." Legitimate is not defined.
- **Freedom of Information Act:** The **Freedom of Information Act of 1970** gives you the right to look at data concerning you that is stored by the federal government.

  Drawback: Sometimes a lawsuit is necessary to pry data loose.
- **Privacy Act:** The **Privacy Act of 1974** is designed to restrict federal agencies in the way they share information about American citizens. It prohibits federal information collected for one purpose from being used for a different purpose.

  Drawback: Exceptions written into the law permit federal agencies to share information anyway.

FIGURE 5

Summary of privacy laws.

PRIVACY LAWS

LAW	PROTECTION
Fair Credit Reporting Act	Gives right to review and correct personal credit records; restricts sharing of personal credit histories
Freedom of Information Act	Gives right to see personal files collected by federal agencies
Privacy Act	Prohibits use of federal information for purposes other than original intent
Right to Financial Privacy Act	Limits federal authority to examine personal bank records
Computer Fraud and Abuse Act	Allows prosecution of unauthorized access to computers and databases
Electronic Communications Privacy Act	Protects privacy on public electronic-mail systems
Video Privacy Protection Act	Prevents sale of video-rental records
Computer Matching and Privacy Protection Act	Limits government's authority to match individual's data

- **Right to Financial Privacy Act:** The **Right to Financial Privacy Act of 1979** sets strict procedures that federal agencies must follow when seeking to examine customer records in banks.

  Drawback: The law does not cover state and local governments.

- **Computer Fraud and Abuse Act:** The **Computer Fraud and Abuse Act of 1986** allows prosecution of unauthorized access to computers and databases.

  Drawback: The act is limited in scope. People with legitimate access can still get into computer systems and create mischief without penalty.

- **Electronic Communications Privacy Act:** The **Electronic Communications Privacy Act of 1986** protects the privacy of users on public electronic-mail systems.

  Drawback: The act is limited to public electronic communications mail systems. It does not cover communication within an organization's internal electronic communications.

- **Video Privacy Protection Act:** The **Video Privacy Protection Act of 1988** prevents retailers from selling or disclosing video-rental records without customer consent or a court order.

  Drawback: The same restrictions do not apply to even more important files, such as medical and insurance records.

- **Computer Matching and Privacy Protection Act:** The **Computer Matching and Privacy Protection Act of 1988** sets procedures for computer matching or searching of federal data. Such matching can be for verifying a person's eligibility for federal benefits or for recovering delinquent debts. Individuals are given a chance to respond before the government takes any adverse action against them.

  Drawback: Many possible computer matches are not affected, including those done for law-enforcement or tax reasons.

- **Communications Decency Act:** The **Communications Act of 1996** made it a federal crime to publish obscene material that could be seen by minors over the Internet.

  Drawback: The act is viewed by many as unclear, too broad, and an infringement on free-speech rights.

Currently, privacy is primarily an *ethical* issue, for many records stored by nongovernment organizations are not covered by existing laws. Yet individuals have shown that they are concerned about controlling who has the right to personal information and how it is used. A Code of Fair Information Practice is summarized in Figure 6. The code was recommended in 1977 by a committee established by former Secretary of Health, Education and Welfare Elliott Richardson. It has been adopted by many information-collecting businesses, but privacy advocates would like to see it written into law.

FAIR INFORMATION PRACTICE CODE

PRINCIPLE	DESCRIPTION
No secret databases	There must be no record-keeping systems containing personal data whose very existence is kept secret.
Right of individual access	Individuals must be able to find out what information about them is in a record and how it is used.
Right of consent	Information about individuals obtained for one purpose cannot be used for other purposes without their consent.
Right to correct	Individuals must be able to correct or amend records of identifiable information about them.
Assurance of reliability and proper use	Organizations creating, maintaining, using, or disseminating records of identifiable personal data must make sure the data is reliable for its intended use. They must take precautions to prevent such data from being misused.

FIGURE 6
Principles of the Code of Fair Information Practice.

Security

Threats to computer security are computer crimes, including viruses, electronic break-ins, and natural and other hazards. Security measures consist of encryption, restricting access, anticipating disasters, and making backup copies.

We are all concerned with having a safe and secure environment to live in. We are careful to lock our car doors and our homes. We are careful about where we walk at night and who we talk to. This is physical security. What about computer security? Does it matter if someone gains access to personal information about you? What if someone learns your credit card number or your checking account number? What if a mistake is made and your credit history shows a number of large unpaid loans? What if all your school records are lost? These are just a few of the reasons to be concerned about computer security.

Threats to Computer Security

Keeping information private depends on keeping computer systems safe from criminals, natural hazards, and other threats.

COMPUTER CRIMINALS A **computer crime** is an illegal action in which the perpetrator uses special knowledge of computer technology. Computer criminals are of four types:

- **Employees:** The largest category of computer criminals consists of those with the easiest access to computers—namely, employees. (See Figure 7.) Sometimes the employee is simply trying to steal something from the employer—equipment, software, electronic funds, proprietary information, or computer time. Sometimes the employee may be acting out of resentment and is trying to "get back" at the company.

FIGURE 7
The experts reply: Whom do you consider to be a threat against your network?

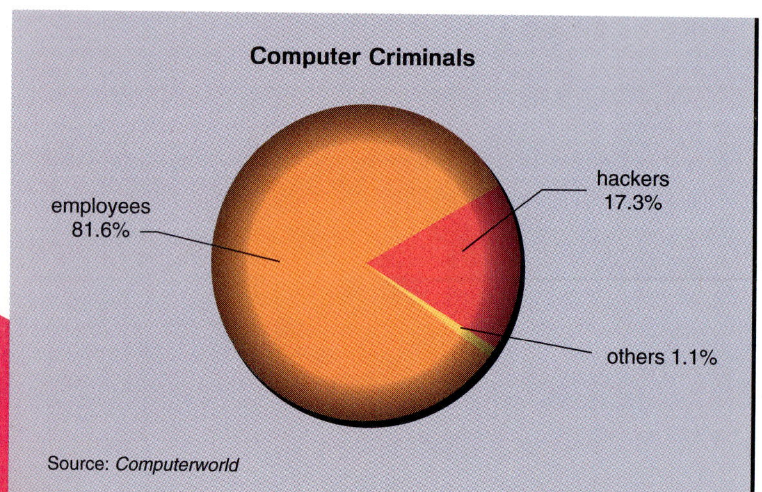

- **Outside users:** Not only employees but also some suppliers or clients may have access to a company's computer system. Examples are bank customers who use an automatic teller machine. Like employees, these authorized users may obtain confidential passwords or find other ways of committing computer crimes.
- **"Hackers" and "crackers":** Some people think of these two groups as being the same, but they are not. **Hackers** are people who gain unauthorized access to a computer system for the fun and challenge of it. **Crackers** do the same thing but for malicious purposes. They may intend to steal technical information or to introduce what they call a "bomb"—a destructive computer program—into the system.
- **Organized crime:** Organized crime has discovered that computers can be used just like legitimate business people use them, but for illegal purposes. For example, computers are useful for keeping track of stolen goods or illegal gambling debts. In addition, counterfeiters and forgers use microcomputers and printers to produce sophisticated-looking documents such as checks and driver's licenses.

COMPUTER CRIME Computer crime can take various forms, as follows.

- **Damage:** Disgruntled employees sometimes attempt to destroy computers, programs, or files. For example, in a crime known as the **Trojan horse program,** instructions are written to destroy or modify software or data.

  In recent years, computer viruses have gained wide notoriety. **Viruses** are programs that "migrate" through networks and operating systems and attach themselves to different programs and databases. (See Figure 8.) Creating and knowingly spreading a virus is a federal offense punishable under the Computer Abuse Amendments Act of 1994.

FIGURE 8
How a computer virus can spread.

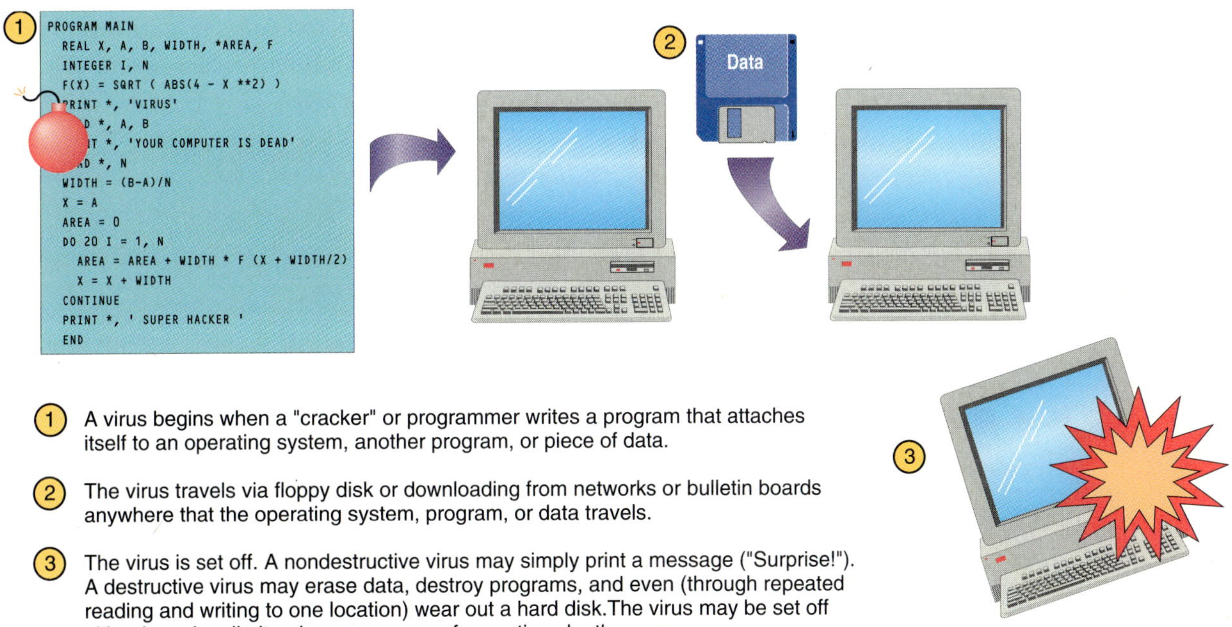

A variant on the virus is the **worm.** This destructive program fills a computer system with self-replicating information, clogging the system so that its operations are slowed or stopped. The most infamous is known as the Internet Worm. In 1988, it traveled across North America, stopping thousands of computers along its way.

Viruses typically find their way into microcomputers through copied floppy disks or programs downloaded from electronic bulletin boards. Because viruses can be so serious—certain "disk-killer" viruses can destroy all the information on one's system—computer users are advised to exercise care in accepting new programs and data from other sources. (See Figure 10.). See Figure 9 for a list of the viruses you are most likely to encounter.

Detection programs called *virus checkers* are available to alert users when certain kinds of viruses enter the system. Unfortunately, new viruses are being developed all the time, and not all viruses can be detected. There are recommended procedures to reduce the risk of catching a computer virus and to minimize its potential damage.

- **Theft:** Theft can take many forms—of hardware, of software, of data, of computer time. Thieves steal equipment, of course, but there are also "white-collar crimes." Thieves steal data in the form of confidential information such as preferred client lists. They also use (steal) their company's computer time to run another business.

Unauthorized copying—a form of theft—of programs for personal gain is called **software piracy.** According to the **Software Copyright Act of 1980,** it is legal for a program owner to make only his or her own backup copies of that program. *It's important to note that none of these copies may be legally resold or given away. This may come as a surprise to students who copy software from a friend, but that's the law.*

Pirated software accounts for 40 percent of software used in the United States. The incidence of pirated software is even higher overseas in such countries as Italy (82 percent) and Thailand (92 percent). Penalties for violating this law are payment of monetary damages to the developer of the program and even prison terms.

FIGURE 9
Commonly encountered viruses.

COMMON VIRUSES

AntiCMOS	changes disk drive designation letters and blocks access to hard disk and / or CD ROM drives
Concept	displays messages on monitor and / or rearranges words in text documents
Form.A	strikes on the 18th of the month, makes keys beep, displays messages on monitor, can destroy files
Parity Boot	displays "Parity Error" and locks up PC until restarted
Stone.Empire.Monkey	blocks access to files

FIGURE 10
How to prevent computer viruses and minimize damage.

VIRUS PROTECTION

STEP	ACTION
1	Make backup copies of your data on a frequent basis
2	Protect data on your floppy disks by using write-protect tabs
3	Turn off your microcomputer when you're not using it
4	Don't use master disk to install software programs; make a working copy and store the master
5	Avoid downloading computer games from electronic bulletin boards
6	Limit your use of "shareware" programs and check for viruses before running
7	Do not loan out your utility or other software programs
8	Run a virus protection program frequently
9	Update your virus protection program regularly

- **Manipulation:** Finding entry into someone's computer network and leaving a prankster's message may seem like fun, which is why hackers do it. It is still against the law. Moreover, even if the manipulation seems harmless, it may cause a great deal of anxiety and wasted time among network users.

  The Computer Fraud and Abuse Act of 1986 makes it a crime for unauthorized persons even to *view*—let alone copy or damage—data using any computer across state lines. It also prohibits unauthorized use of any government computer or computer used by any federally insured financial institution. Offenders can be sentenced to up to 20 years in prison and fined up to $100,000.

  Of course, using a computer in the course of performing some other crime, such as selling fraudulent products, is also illegal.

OTHER HAZARDS There are plenty of other hazards to computer systems and data besides criminals. They include the following:

- **Natural hazards:** Natural forces include fires, floods, wind, hurricanes, tornadoes, and earthquakes. Even home computer users should store backup disks of programs and data in safe locations in case of fire or storm damage.
- **Civil strife and terrorism:** Wars, riots, and other forms of political unrest are real risks in some parts of the world. Even people in developed countries, however, must be mindful that acts of sabotage are possible.
- **Technological failures:** Hardware and software don't always do what they are supposed to do. For instance, too little electricity, caused by a brownout or blackout, may cause the loss of data in primary storage. Too much electricity, as when lightning or other electrical disturbance affects a power line, may cause a **voltage surge,** or **spike.** This excess of electricity may destroy chips or other electronic components of a computer.

  Most microcomputer users buy a **surge protector,** a device that separates the computer from the power source of the wall outlet. When a voltage surge occurs, it activates a circuit breaker in the surge protector, protecting the computer system.

Another technological catastrophe is when a hard-disk drive suddenly "crashes," or fails, perhaps because it has been bumped inadvertently. If the user has forgotten to make backup copies of data on the hard disk, data may be lost.

- **Human errors:** Human mistakes are inevitable. Data-entry errors are probably the most commonplace. Programmer errors also occur frequently. Some mistakes may result from faulty design, as when a software manufacturer makes a deletion command closely resembling another command. Some errors may be the result of sloppy procedures. One such example occurs when office workers keep important correspondence under filenames that no one else in the office knows.

FIGURE 11
Disasters—both natural and manmade—can play havoc with computers.

Measures to Protect Computer Security

Security is concerned with protecting information, hardware, and software. They must be protected from unauthorized use as well as from damage from intrusions, sabotage, and natural disasters. (See Figure 11.) Considering the numerous ways in which computer systems and data can be compromised, we can see why security is a growing field. Some of the principal aspects are as follows.

ENCRYPTING MESSAGES Whenever information is sent over a network, the possibility of unauthorized access exists. The longer the distance the message has to travel, the higher the security risk is. For example, an e-mail message on a LAN meets a limited number of users operating in controlled environments such as offices. An e-mail message traveling across the country on the National Information Highway affords greater opportunities for the message to be intercepted.

Businesses have been **encrypting,** or coding, messages for years. They have become so good at it that some law enforcement agencies are unable to "wire-tap" messages from suspected criminals. Some federal agencies have suggested that a standard encryption procedure be used so that law enforcement agencies can monitor suspected criminal communications. The government is encouraging businesses that use the National Information Highway to use a special encryption program. This program is available on a processor chip called the Clipper chip and is also known as the Key Escrow chip.

Individuals are also using encryption programs to safeguard their private communications. One of the most widely used personal encryption programs is Pretty Good Privacy. (See Figure 12.)

RESTRICTING ACCESS Security experts are constantly devising ways to protect computer systems from access by unauthorized persons. Sometimes security is a matter of putting guards on company computer rooms and checking the identification of everyone admitted. Oftentimes it is a matter of being careful about assigning passwords to people and of changing them when people leave a company. *Passwords,* you'll remember, are secret words or numbers that must be keyed into a computer system to gain access. In some "dial-back" computer systems, the user telephones the computer, punches in the correct password, and hangs up. The computer then calls back at a certain preauthorized number.

Most major corporations today use special hardware and software called **firewalls** to control access to their internal computer networks. These firewalls act as

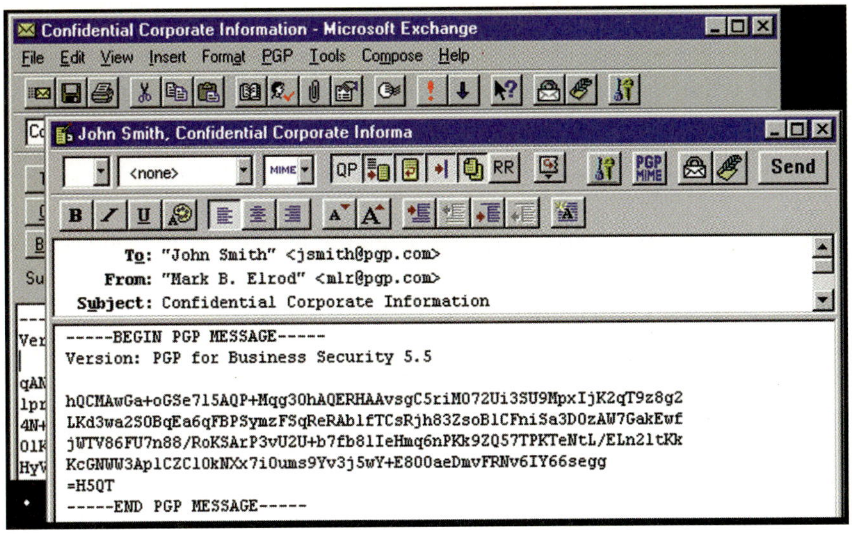

FIGURE 12
Pretty Good Privacy Web site.

a security buffer between the corporation's private network and all external networks, including the Internet. All electronic communications coming into and leaving the corporation must be evaluated by the firewall. Security is maintained by denying access to unauthorized communications.

ANTICIPATING DISASTERS Companies (and even individuals) that do not make preparations for disasters are not acting wisely. **Physical security** is concerned with protecting hardware from possible human and natural disasters. **Data security** is concerned with protecting software and data from unauthorized tampering or damage. Most large organizations have a **disaster recovery plan** describing ways to continue operating until normal computer operations can be restored.

Hardware can be kept behind locked doors, but often employees find this restriction a hindrance, so security is lax. Fire and water (including the water from ceiling sprinkler systems) can do great damage to equipment. Many companies therefore will form a cooperative arrangement to share equipment with other companies in the event of catastrophe. Special emergency facilities called **hot sites** may be created if they are fully equipped computer centers. They are called **cold sites** if they are empty shells in which hardware must be installed.

BACKING UP DATA Equipment can always be replaced. A company's *data,* however, may be irreplaceable. Most companies have ways of trying to keep software and data from being tampered with in the first place. They include careful screening of job applicants, guarding of passwords, and auditing of data and programs from time to time. The safest procedure, however, is to make frequent backups of data and to store them in remote locations.

SECURITY FOR MICROCOMPUTERS If you own a microcomputer system, there are several procedures to follow to keep it safe:

- **Avoid extreme conditions:** Don't expose the computer to extreme conditions. Direct sun, rain from an open window, extreme temperatures, cigarette smoke, and spilled drinks or food are harmful to microcomputers. Clean your equipment regularly. Use a surge protector to protect against voltage surges.
- **Guard the computer:** Put a cable lock on the computer. If you subscribe or belong to an online information service, do not leave passwords nearby in a place accessible by others. Etch your driver's license number or social security number into your equipment. That way it can be identified in the event it is recovered after theft.
- **Guard programs and data:** Store disks properly, preferably in a locked container. Make backup copies of all your important files and programs. Store copies of your files in a different—and safe—location from the site of your computer.

See Figure 13 for a summary of the different measures to protect computer security.

COMPUTER SECURITY

MEASURE	DESCRIPTION
encrypting	coding all messages sent over a network
restricting	limiting access to authorized persons using such measures as passwords, dial-back systems, and biometrics
anticipating	preparing for disasters by ensuring physical security and data security through a disaster recovery plan
backing up	routinely copying data and storing at a remote location
securing	protecting microcomputer by avoiding extreme conditions, guarding the computer, programs, and data.

FIGURE 13
Measures to protect computer security.

The Environment

Computer industry has responded to the Energy Star program with the Green PC. You can help by conserving, recycling, and educating.

What do you suppose is the greatest user of electricity in the workplace? Microcomputers are. They account for 5 percent of the electricity used. If current trends continue, this will increase to 10 percent by the year 2000. Increased power production translates to increased air pollution, depletion of nonrenewable resources, and other environmental hazards.

The Environmental Protection Agency (EPA) has created the **Energy Star** program to discourage waste in the microcomputer industry. Along with over 50 manufacturers, the EPA has established a goal of reducing power requirements for system units, monitors, and printers. The industry has responded with the concept of the **Green PC.** (See Figure 14.)

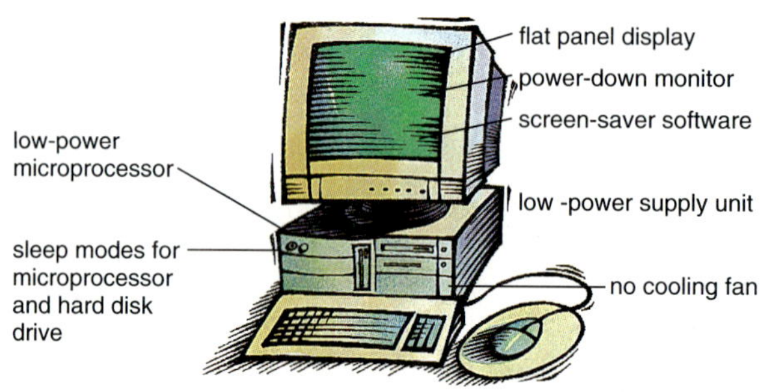

FIGURE 14
The Green PC.

The Green PC

The basic elements of the Green PC are:

- **System Unit:** Using existing technology from portable computers, the system unit: (1) uses an energy-saving microprocessor that requires less power, (2) employs microprocessor and hard-disk drives that shift to an energy-saving or sleep mode when not in operation, (3) replaces the conventional supply unit with an adapter that requires less electricity, and (4) eliminates the cooling fan.

- **Display:** Displays have been made more energy efficient by using: (1) flat panels that require much less energy than the traditional monitors, (2) special power-down monitors that automatically reduce power consumption when not in use, and (3) screen-saver software that clears the display whenever it is not in use.
- **Manufacturing:** Computer manufacturers such as Intel, Apple, Compac, and others are using less harmful chemicals in production. Particular attention is given to **chlorofluorocarbons (CFCs)** in solvents and cleaning agents. (CFCs can travel into the atmosphere and are suspected by some in the scientific community to deplete the earth's ozone layer.) Toxic nickel and other heavy metals are being eliminated or reduced in the manufacturing processes.

Of course, not all of these technologies and manufacturing processes are used for all microcomputers. But more and more of them are.

Personal Responsibility

There are some things that you, as a computer user, can do to help protect the environment. Some of these include:

- **Conserve:** The EPA estimates that 30 to 40 percent of computer users leave their machines running days, nights, and weekends. When through working for the day, turn off all computers and other energy-consuming devices. The EPA also estimates that 80 percent of the time a monitor is on, no one is looking at it. Use screen-saver programs that blank the computer screen after 3 to 5 minutes of inactivity.
- **Recycle:** U.S. businesses use an enormous amount of paper each year—a pile 48,900 miles high. Much of that, as well as the paper we throw out at home, can be recycled. Other recyclable items include computer boxes, packaging material, printer cartridges, and floppy disks.
- **Educate:** Be aware and learn more about ecological dangers of all types. Make your concerns known to manufacturers and retail agencies. Support ecologically sound products.

A Look at the Future

New legislation will be needed to define access to government files and to regulate government interference in free speech in the new electronic world.

Technology often has a way of outracing existing social and political institutions. For instance, citizens have a right to request government records under the Freedom of Information Act. But even in its most recent amendment, in 1986, the act does not mention "computer" or define the word "record." Can the government therefore legally deny, as one agency did, a legitimate request for data on corporate compliance with occupational safety and health laws? *Access laws* lag behind even as the government collects more information than ever.

In addition, there has been a rise in computer-related crimes. These include bank and credit card fraud, viruses, and electronic break-ins of government and private computer systems. Law-enforcement agencies continue to crack down on these computer operators. Yet they may also be jeopardizing the rights of computer users who are not breaking the law. Such users may be suffering illegal searches and violation of constitutional guarantees of free speech. However, it is unclear how the First Amendment protects speech and the Fourth Amendment protects against searches and seizures in this electronic world.

One professor of constitutional law has proposed a new amendment to the Constitution. This amendment would extend the other freedoms in the Bill of Rights, those on free speech and search and seizure restrictions. Under this amendment, all new technology and mediums for generating, storing, and altering information would be covered.

KEY TERMS

access (WI5)
accuracy (WI5)
carpal tunnel syndrome (WI3)
chlorofluorocarbon (CFC) (WI18)
cold site (WI16)
Communications Act of 1996 (WI10)
computer crime (WI11)
Computer Fraud and Abuse Act of 1986 (WI9)
Computer Matching and Privacy Protection Act of 1988 (WI10)
cookies (WI7)
cracker (WI12)
cumulative trauma disorder (WI3)
data security (WI16)
disaster recovery plan (WI16)
Electronic Communications Privacy Act of 1986 (WI9)
encrypting (WI15)
Energy Star (WI17)
ergonomics (WI2)
ethics (WI5)
Fair Credit Reporting Act of 1970 (WI8)
firewall (WI15)
Freedom of Information Act of 1970 (WI8)
Green PC (WI17)
hacker (WI12)
history file (WI7)
hot site (WI16)
physical security (WI16)
privacy (WI5)
Privacy Act of 1974 (WI8)
property (WI5)
repetitive motion injury (WI3)
repetitive strain injury (RSI) (WI3)
Right to Financial Privacy Act of 1979 (WI9)
security (WI15)
Software Copyright Act of 1980 (WI13)
software piracy (WI13)
spike (WI14)
surge protector (WI14)

Trojan horse program (WI12)
Video Privacy Protection Act of 1988 (WI9)
virus (WI12)
voltage surge (WI14)
worm (WI13)

REVIEW QUESTIONS

True/False

1. Most people who use computers are mid-level managers.
2. Electromagnetic field (EMF) emissions can travel through a person's body.
3. Our legal system is the essential element used to control computers today.
4. Over 20 percent of businesses search through employees' electronic messages and computer files.
5. A Trojan horse is a virus that keeps replicating itself until the computer system's operations are slowed or stopped.

Multiple Choice

1. The study of human factors related to computers:
   a. data analysis
   b. human system performance
   c. ergonomics
   d. expert analysis
   e. personal design
2. A repetitive strain injury that causes damage to nerves and tendons in hands:
   a. RSI
   b. carpal tunnel syndrome
   c. EMF
   d. hacker
   e. virus
3. The ethical issue that deals with the responsibility to control the availability of data:
   a. privacy
   b. accuracy
   c. property
   d. ownership
   e. access
4. The largest category of computer criminals:
   a. students
   b. hackers
   c. outside users
   d. employees
   e. database managers
5. The computer industry's response to the Energy Star program is the:
   a. Green PC
   b. multimedia PC
   c. flat-panel display
   d. Fair Credit Reporting Act
   e. network encryption standard

Fill in the Blank

1. The new word __________ is used to describe harmful stress associated with computer use.
2. Computer __________ are guidelines for the morally acceptable use of computers in our society.
3. A common security measure for business is __________ or coding messages.
4. People who gain unauthorized access to a computer system for fun and challenge are called __________.

5. __________ __________ is the unauthorized copying of programs for personal gain.

Open Ended

1. What kind of activities can you perform to avoid computer-related eyestrain, headaches, and back and neck pain?
2. Describe some mental health problems associated with frequent computer use.
3. What are four types of computer criminals?
4. How are computers a threat to your privacy? Discuss what you can do to better ensure your privacy.
5. How are computers a threat to the environment? Discuss three things you can do to protect the environment.

DISCUSSION QUESTIONS AND PROJECTS

1. *Your credit record:* If you or some member of your family presently own a credit card—oil company, department store, Visa, MasterCard—you can determine your credit rating. The law allows credit card holders access to credit records in order to determine their rating and to correct any errors. This is an important right, because your credit rating determines your eligibility for loans in the future.

   To request a free copy of your credit record, available once per year, write to TRW, P.O. Box 2350, Chatsworth, CA 91313-2350. Include your full name, addresses for the past five years with dates and zip codes, social security number, date of birth, and your spouse's name if you're married. Also include a photocopy of your driver's license or a utility bill showing your present name and address. Allow about four weeks for delivery. Once you have your report, look it over and let TRW know of any inaccuracies.

2. *Your national identification number:* One characteristic of many dictatorships is that all citizens are made to carry "papers." These are a kind of internal passport, each with its own number. They enable the government to keep track of—and regulate—one's travel, employment, and so on. In the United States, the founding fathers were deeply concerned about the government's having tyranny over its citizens. Thus, internal papers have never been required.

   Unfortunately, the social security number, or SSN, has been stretched to cover purposes for which it was never intended. It has become a national identification number that, once given out, never goes away. It can be a person's student ID, tax number, military ID, medical insurance number, criminal file number, and credit number. Every time you scrawl the number on a credit or job application or other form, it becomes available to thousands of people you don't know. It will be available to anyone with access to a legal database.

   Discuss with classmates or write an essay on your worst scenario of what could happen to you because of the easy availability of your SSN.

on the web

Exercises and Explorations

1 Pretty Good Privacy

Pretty Good Privacy is the most popular encryption software available. It offers military-grade encryption for free. Learn more about your privacy rights and needs by visiting our Web site at http://www.magpie.org/essentials/chapter-WI to link to a site specializing in encryption software. Once connected to that site, print out the Web page that discusses your privacy rights on the Internet. Write a paragraph discussing individual privacy rights in the workplace and in regard to the government.

2 Computer Viruses

Computer viruses can strike anytime and can create serious problems. To learn more about them, visit our Web site at http://www.magpie.org/essentials/chapter-WI to link to a site specializing in computer viruses. Once connected to that site, look for an *info library on viruses,* and find a list of the most *common viruses*. Print out the list. Select three of the viruses from the list, and write a paragraph describing what each could do and what effect it could have on a major corporation.

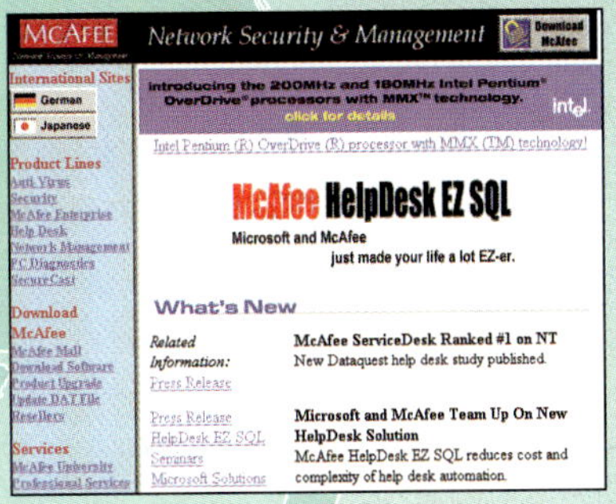

3 Crime on the Internet

Just like any community, the Internet community has crime. The best way to fight it is to know more about it. Visit the Infoseek site at http://guide.infoseek.com, and search with keywords such as "internet crime," "email fraud," and "web police." Print a copy of the first page of the results of your search. Explore one or more of the sites, and write a paragraph describing one type of computer crime and what we can do to fight against it.

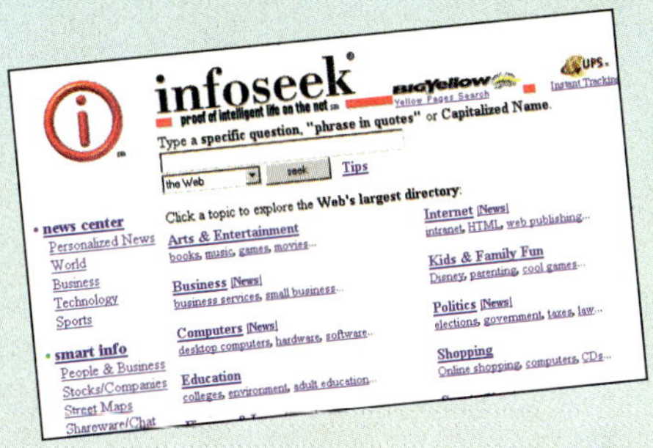

4 Sports

The Web is one of the best resources for the latest sports information. Visit our Web site at http://www.magpie.org/essentials/chapter-WI to link to one of the best known sports sites. Once connected to that site, print out an article that interests you, and write a paragraph summarizing it.

VISUAL SUMMARY

Workplace Issues: Ergonomics, Privacy, Security, and the Environment

One-third of Americans use a computer at work. Thus, there are many "people issues" connected with computers.

ERGONOMICS

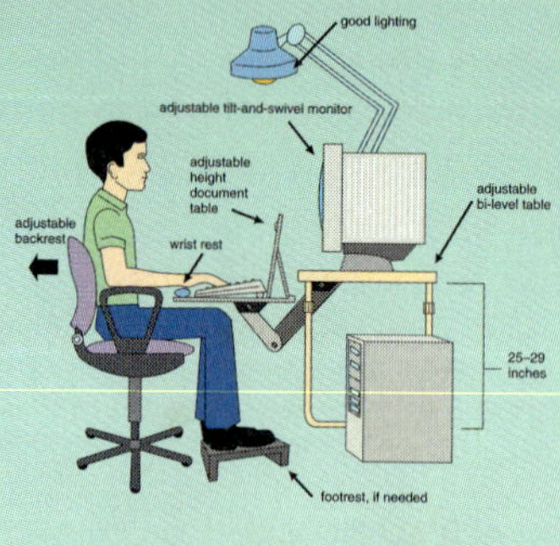

Users should take steps to increase productivity and avoid physical and mental health risks. **Ergonomics** is the study of human factors related to computers.

Physical Health Matters

Some computer-associated physical health matters that can be avoided:

- Eyestrain and headache: Take frequent breaks, avoid glare on monitor screen.
- Back and neck pains: Use adjustable chairs, tables, monitor stands, keyboards.
- Electromagnetic fields: May lead to miscarriages, but not proven. Sit 2 feet from screen, 3 feet from adjacent computers.
- **Repetitive strain injury (RSI):** Also known as **repetitive motion injury** and **cumulative trauma disorders,** RSIs are neck, wrist, hand, and arm injuries resulting from fast, repetitive work. **Carpal tunnel syndrome,** damage to nerves and tendons in hands, afflicts heavy keyboard users. Avoidance consists of frequent, short rest breaks.

Mental Health Matters

Irritations consist of:

- Noise from clattering printers and high-frequency squeal from monitors.
- Stress from excessive monitoring.

Design with People in Mind

Computers are being designed for easier use.

PRIVACY

Computer ethics are guidelines for moral computer use. Four computer ethics issues are: privacy, accuracy, property, and access.

Use of Large Databases

Large databases are constantly compiling information about us. A vast industry of data gatherers or "information resellers" collects data about us and sells it to direct marketers and others.

Use of Networks

Some information networks have been used to eavesdrop on employees or to restrict members' messages.

Use of the Internet and the Web

All Internet Web communications are subject to eavesdropping. Browsers record your activities in **history files. Cookies** deposited by Web sites collect information about you.

Major Laws on Privacy

There are numerous federal laws governing privacy matters; however, each has drawbacks that make enforcement difficult.

VIRUS PROTECTION

STEP	ACTION
1	Make backup copies of your data on a frequent basis
2	Protect data on your floppy disks by using write-protect tabs
3	Turn off your microcomputer when you're not using it
4	Don't use master disk to install software programs; make a working copy and store the master
5	Avoid downloading computer games from electronic bulletin boards
6	Limit your use of "shareware" programs and check for viruses before running
7	Do not loan out your utility or other software programs
8	Run a virus protection program frequently
9	Update your virus protection program regularly

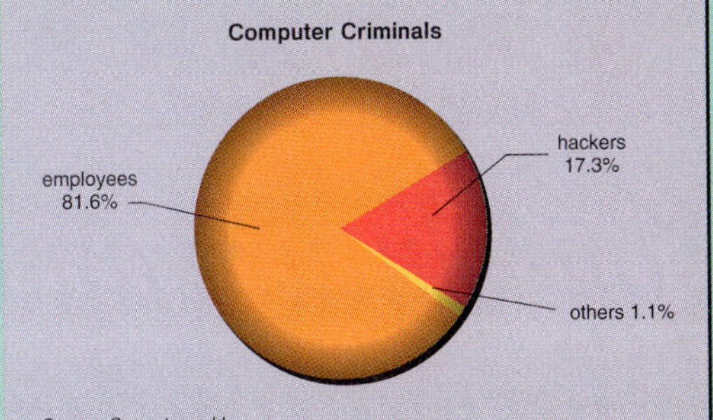

Source: *Computerworld*

SECURITY

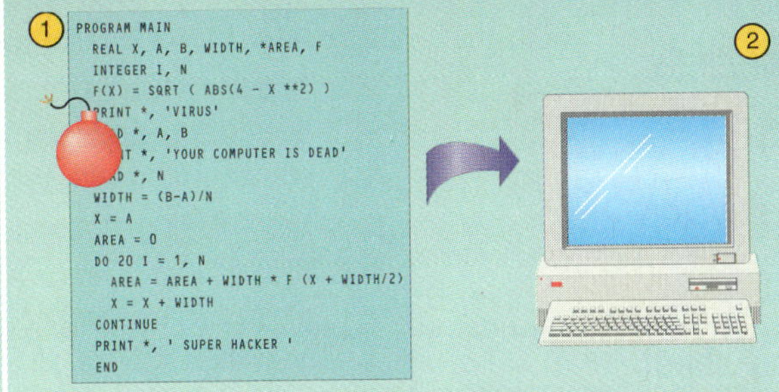

There is a variety of sources that threaten computer security. There is also a variety of protective measures.

Threats to Computer Security

Keeping information private depends on keeping computer systems safe from:

- Computer criminals—can be employees, outside users, **hackers/crackers,** and organized-crime members.
- Computer crime—can be damage caused by computer **viruses,** theft, and manipulation, as in the unauthorized entry to a computer system for fun.
- Other hazards—include natural forces, civil strife, terrorism, technological failures, and human errors.

Measures to Protect Computer Security

Security of information, hardware, and software can be improved by:

- Restricting access through passwords and biometrics.
- Anticipating disasters by providing physical security for hardware and data security for software and data.
- Backing up data frequently and storing it in safe locations.
- Providing **security for microcomputers** by avoiding extreme conditions and guarding the computer, software, and data.

ENVIRONMENT

Microcomputers are the greatest users of electricity in the workplace. The **Environmental Protection Agency (EPA)** has established the **Energy Star** program to encourage efficient use of energy by the computer industry. The industry has responded with the concept of the Green PC.

The Green PC

Basic elements of the Green PC include:

- Systems units that use energy-saving microprocessors, have sleep-mode capability, are more energy-efficient, and eliminate cooling fans.
- Display units that are made more efficient by replacing CRT displays with flat panels, using special power-down monitors, and using screen-saver software.
- Manufacturing that eliminates or reduces the use of harmful chemicals such as **chlorofluorocarbons (CFCs),** nickel, and other heavy metals.

Personal Responsibility

You can help protect the environment from computer-related activities by:

- Conserving energy by turning off computer systems at the end of the workday and using screen-saver software to blank computer screens after 3 to 5 minutes of inactivity.
- Recycling paper, computer boxes, packaging materials, printer cartridges, and floppy disks.
- Educating yourself and others about ecological dangers of all types. Making sure your concerns are known by supporting ecologically sound products.

Your Future and Information Technology

Throughout this book, we have emphasized practical subjects that are useful to you now or will be very soon. Accordingly, this final chapter is not about the far future of, say, 10 years from now. Rather, it is about the near future—about developments whose outlines we can already see. It is about how organizations adapt to technological change. It is also about what you as an individual can do to keep your computer competency up to date.

COMPETENCIES

After you have read this chapter, you should be able to:

1. **Explain why it's important to have an individual strategy in order to be a "winner" in the information age.**
2. **Describe how technology is changing the nature of competition.**
3. **Discuss three ways people may react to new technology.**
4. **Describe how you can use your computer competence to stay current and to take charge of your career.**
5. **Discuss what systems analysts, programmers, technical writers, network managers, and computer trainers do.**

Are the times changing any faster now than they ever have? It's hard to say. People who were alive when radios, cars, and airplanes were being introduced certainly lived through some dramatic changes. Has technology made our own times even more dynamic? Whatever the answer, it is clear we live in a fast-paced age. The challenge for you as an individual is to devise ways to stay current.

Changing Times

To be a winner in the information revolution, you need an *individual* strategy.

Most businesses have become aware that they must adapt to changing technology or be left behind. Many organizations are now making formal plans to keep track of technology and implement it in their competitive strategies. For example, banks have found that automated teller machines (ATMs) are vital to retail banking. (See Figure 1.) Not only do they require fewer human tellers, but they can also be made available 24 hours a day. More and more banks

FIGURE 1
Automatic teller machines are examples of technology used in business strategy.

are also trying to go electronic, doing away with paper transactions wherever possible. Thus, ATM cards can now be used in certain places to buy gas or groceries. Many banks are also trying to popularize home banking, so that customers can use microcomputers for certain financial tasks. In addition, banks are exploring the use of some very sophisticated application programs. These programs will accept cursive writing (the handwriting on checks) directly as input, verify check signatures, and process the check without human intervention.

Clearly, such changes do away with some jobs—those of many bank tellers and cashiers, for example. However, they create opportunities for other people. New technology requires people who are truly capable of working with it. These are not the people who think every piece of equipment is so simple they can just turn it on and use it. Nor are they those who think each new machine is a potential disaster. In other words, new technology needs people who are not afraid to learn it and are able to manage it. The real issue, then, is not how to make technology better. Rather, it is how to integrate the technology with people.

You are in a very favorable position compared with many other people in industry today. After reading the previous chapters, you have learned more than just the basics of hardware, software, and connectivity. You have learned the most *current* technology. You are therefore able to use these tools to your advantage—to be a winner.

How do you become and stay a winner? In brief, the answer is: You must form your own individual strategy for dealing with change. First let us look at how businesses are handling technological change. Then let's look at how people are reacting to these changes. Finally, we will offer a few suggestions that will enable you to keep up with—and profit by—the information revolution.

Technology and Organizations

Technology changes the nature of competition by introducing new products, new enterprises, and new relationships among customers and suppliers.

Technology can introduce new ways businesses compete with each other. Some of the principal changes are as follows.

FIGURE 2
The Sabre reservations system used by American Airlines.

New Products

Technology creates products that operate faster, are priced cheaper, are often of better quality, or are wholly new. Indeed, new products can be custom tailored to a particular customer's needs. For example, financial services company Merrill Lynch took advantage of technology to launch a cash management account. This account combines information on a person's checking, savings, credit card, and securities accounts into a single monthly statement. It automatically sets aside "idle" funds into interest-bearing money market funds. The result is that customers can get a complete picture of their financial condition at one time. However, even if they don't pay much attention to their statements, their surplus funds are invested automatically.

New Enterprises

Information technology can build entire new businesses. An example is the availability of the facsimile (fax) machine business. Now chains of quick-print and photocopying shops offer fax services. You can send a fax message to, or receive one from, nearly anywhere in the United States.

A company may use its extra information systems capability to develop new services for customers outside the area it serves directly. For example, American Airlines has a reservations system called Sabre that lists the flight schedules of every major airline in the world. Travel agents with online access to Sabre pay American a fee for every reservation made on Sabre for other airlines. (See Figure 2.)

New Customer and Supplier Relationships

Businesses that make their information systems easily available may make their customers less likely to take their business elsewhere. For instance, Federal Express, the overnight package delivery service, does everything possible to make its customers dependent on it. Upon request, customers receive airbills with their name, address, and account number preprinted on them, making shipping and billing easier. Package numbers are scanned into the company's information system, so that they can be tracked from pickup point to destination. (See Figure 3.) Thus, apprehensive customers can be informed very quickly of the exact location of their package as it travels toward its destination.

FIGURE 3
Federal Express couriers scan bar codes on every package, transferring customer and delivery data to a worldwide network that can be closely monitored by customer service agents.

Technology and People

People may be cynical, naïve, or frustrated in response to technology.

Clearly, recent technological changes, and those sure to come in the near future, will produce some upheavals in the years ahead. How should we be prepared for them?

People have different coping styles when it comes to technology. It has been suggested, for instance, that people react to the notion of microcomputers in business in three ways. These ways are *cynicism, naïveté,* and *frustration.*

Cynicism

The cynic feels that, for a manager at least, the idea of using a microcomputer is overrated. (See Figure 4.) Learning and using it take too much time, time that could be delegated to someone else. Doing spreadsheets and word processing, according to the cynic, are tasks that managers should understand. However, the cynic feels that such tasks take time away from a manager's real job of developing plans and setting goals for the people being supervised.

FIGURE 4
The cynic: "These gadgets are overrated."

FIGURE 5
The naïve: "Let the computer make the decision."

Cynics may express their doubts openly, especially if they are top managers. Or they may only pretend to be interested in microcomputers, when actually they are not interested at all.

Naïveté

Naïve people are those who are unfamiliar with computers. Thus, they may think computers are magic boxes capable of solving all kinds of problems that computers really can't handle. (See Figure 5.) In contrast, some naïve persons are actually quite familiar with computers. However, such people underestimate the difficulty of changing computer systems or of generating information.

FIGURE 6
The frustrated: "This stuff doesn't make sense half the time."

Frustration

The frustrated person may already be quite busy and may hate having to take time to learn about microcomputers. Such a person feels it is an imposition to have to learn something new. Often she or he is too impatient to try to understand the manuals explaining what hardware and software are supposed to do. The result, therefore, is continual frustration. (See Figure 6.) Some people are frustrated because they try to do too much. Or they're frustrated because they find manuals difficult to understand. Oftentimes they feel stupid when actually the manuals are at fault.

Cynicism, naïveté, and frustration are not just confined to microcomputers, of course. They apply to all new technology. Do you see yourself reacting in any of these ways? They are actually commonplace responses—part of just being human. Knowing which, if any, of these reactions characterize you or those around you may be helpful. It can help you survive and react in positive ways in organizational life.

How You Can Be a Winner

Individuals need to stay current, develop specialties, and be alert to organizational changes and opportunities for innovation.

So far we have described how progressive organizations are using technology in the information age. Now let's concentrate on you as an individual. How can you stay ahead? Here are some ideas.

Stay Current

Whatever their particular line of work, successful professionals keep up both with their own fields and with the times. We don't mean you should try to become a computer expert and read a lot of technical magazines. Rather, you should concentrate on your profession and learn how computer technology is being used within it.

Every field has trade journals, whether the field is interior design, personnel management, advertising, or whatever. Most such journals regularly present articles about the uses of computers. It's important that you also belong to a trade or industry association and go to its meetings. Many associations sponsor seminars and conferences that describe the latest information and techniques. Another way to stay current is by participating electronically with interest groups on the Internet.

Maintain Your Computer Competence

Actually, you should try to stay *ahead* of the technology. Books, journals, and trade associations are the best sources of information about new technology that applies to your field. The general business press—*Business Week, Fortune, Inc., The Wall Street Journal,* and the business section of your local newspaper—also carries computer-related articles.

However, if you wish, you can subscribe to a magazine that covers microcomputers and information more specifically. Examples are *InfoWorld, PC World,* and *MacWorld.* You may also find it useful to look at newspapers and magazines that cover the computer industry as a whole. An example of such a periodical is *ComputerWorld.*

Develop Professional Contacts

Besides being members of professional associations, successful people make it a point to maintain contact with others in their field. They stay in touch by telephone and letter and go to lunch with others in their line of work. Doing this lets them learn what other people are doing in their jobs. It tells them what other firms are doing and what tasks are being automated. Developing professional contacts can keep you abreast not only of new information but also of new job possibilities. (See Figure 7.) It also offers social benefits. An example of a professional organization found in many areas is the local association of realtors.

Develop Specialties

Develop specific as well as general skills. You want to be well-rounded within your field, but certainly not a "jack of all trades, master of none." Master a trade or two *within* your profession. At the same time, don't become identified with a specific technological skill that might very well become obsolete.

The best advice is to specialize to some extent. However, don't make your specialty so tied to technology that you'll be in trouble if the technology shifts. For example, if your career is in marketing or graphics design, it makes sense to learn about desktop publishing. (See Figure 8.) That way you can learn to make high-quality, inexpensive graphics layouts. It would not make as much sense for you to

FIGURE 7
Professional organizations and contacts help you keep up in your field.

become an expert on, say, the various types of monitors used to display the graphics layouts, because such monitors are continually changing.

Expect to take classes during your working life to keep up with developments in your field. Some professions require more keeping up than others—a computer specialist, for example, compared to a human resources manager. Whatever the training required, always look for ways to adapt and improve your skills to become more productive and marketable. There may be times when you are tempted to start all over again and learn completely new skills. However, a better course of action is to use emerging technology to improve your present base of skills. This way you can build on your current strong points and then branch out to other fields from a position of strength.

Be Alert for Organizational Change

Every organization has formal lines of communication—for example, supervisor to middle manager to top manager. However, there is also the *grapevine*—informal lines of communication. (See Figure 9.) Some service departments will serve many layers of management and be abreast of the news on all levels. For instance, the art director for advertising may be aware of several aspects of a companywide

FIGURE 8
Desktop publishing: a good specialty to develop for certain careers.

FIGURE 9
Informal communication can alert you to important organizational changes.

marketing campaign. Secretaries and administrative assistants know what is going on in more than one area.

Being part of the office grapevine can alert you to important changes—for instance, new job openings—that can benefit you. However, you always have to assess the validity of what you hear on the grapevine. Moreover, it's not advisable to be a contributor to "office gossip." Behind-the-back criticisms of other people have a way of getting back to the person criticized.

Be especially alert for new trends within the organization—about future hiring, layoffs, automation, mergers with other companies, and the like. Notice which areas are receiving the greatest attention from top management. One tip-off is to see what kind of outside consultants are being brought in. Independent consultants are usually invited in because a company believes it needs advice in an area with which it has insufficient experience.

Look for Innovative Opportunities

You may understand your job better than anyone—even if you've only been there a few months. Look for ways to make it more efficient. How can present procedures be automated? How can new technology make your tasks easier? Discuss your ideas with your supervisor, the training director, or the head of the information systems department. Or discuss them with someone else who can see that you get the recognition you deserve. (Coworkers may or may not be receptive and may or may not try to take credit themselves.)

A good approach is to present your ideas in terms of *saving money* rather than "improving information." (See Figure 10.) Managers are generally more impressed with ideas that can save dollars than with ideas that seem like potential breakthroughs in the quality of decisions.

In general, it's best to concentrate on the business and organizational problems that need solving. Then look for a technological way of solving them. That is, avoid becoming too enthusiastic about a particular technology and then trying to make it fit the work situation.

FIGURE 10
Present your ideas as saving money rather than "improving information."

Consider a Career in Information Systems

Five careers to consider are systems analyst, programmer, technical writer, network manager, and computer trainer.

To be a winner does not necessarily mean having a career in information systems. There are, however, several jobs within information systems that you might like to consider. Some are *systems analyst, programmer, technical writer, network manager,* and *computer trainer.*

Systems Analyst

The occupation of **systems analyst** is one of the fastest growing and is expected to almost double by the year 2005. As a systems analyst, you would work with other individuals within an organization to evaluate their information needs, design computer software and hardware to meet those needs, and then implement the information systems.

Programmer

Another high-demand profession is that of **programmer.** Programmers typically work closely with a systems analyst to either create new software or to revise existing programs. As a programmer you likely would use programming languages like C++ and Java.

Technical Writer

Technical writers explain in writing how a computer program works. As a technical writer you would likely work closely with systems analysts and users to document an information system and to create clearly written user manuals.

FIGURE 11
Network managers monitor and develop new communication systems.

Network Manager

Nearly all information systems within an organization are connected by networks. **Network managers** ensure that existing information and communication systems are operating effectively and that new communication systems are implemented as needed. (See Figure 11.) The importance of this occupation within most organizations is increasing dramatically as the Internet plays a larger role in corporate communications. As a network manager, you would also be responsible for ensuring computer security and individual privacy.

Computer Trainer

One of the most important steps in creating a new information system is to prepare and train users. As a **computer trainer,** you would provide classes for users giving them an opportunity to explore a new system, to ask questions, and to try out common tasks. (See Figure 12.)

FIGURE 12
Computer trainers teach others about new systems and software.

A Look at the Future: The Rest of Your Life

Being computer competent means taking positive control.

This is not the end; it is the beginning. Being a skilled computer end user—being computer competent—is not a matter of thinking "Some day I'll . . ." ("Some day I'll have to learn all about that.") It is a matter of living in the present and keeping an eye on the future. It is also a matter of having the discipline to keep up with the prevailing technology. It is not a matter of focusing on vague "what ifs." It is a matter of concentrating on your goals and learning how the computer can help you achieve them. Being an end user, in short, is not about trying to avoid failure. Rather, it is about always moving toward success—about taking control over the exciting new tools available to you.

KEY TERMS

computer trainer (YF10)
network manager (YF9)
programmer (YF9)
systems analyst (YF9)
technical writer (YF9)

REVIEW QUESTIONS

True/False

1. Most businesses are making formal plans to track and to implement technology into their competitive strategies.
2. Businesses never allow customers access to their information systems.
3. In all fields, successful professionals have to be experts in their own field as well as in computer technology.
4. *InfoWorld, PC World,* and *MacWorld* are magazines that specifically cover microcomputers and information.
5. The office grapevine can be a good source to alert you to organizational changes.

Multiple Choice

1. The real issue with new technology is:
   a. how to make it better
   b. which printer is better
   c. how to control it
   d. how to integrate it with people
   e. managing its impact on government
2. By giving their customers access to their package tracking information system, Federal Express is developing new:
   a. global computer facilities
   b. customer and supplier relationships
   c. airline reservation procedures
   d. serious security problems
   e. government delivery systems
3. The type of person who underestimates the difficulty of changing computer systems or of generating information is:
   a. a cynic
   b. frustrated
   c. naïve
   d. a losere.
   e. a winner
4. By staying in touch with others in your field, you are:
   a. developing professional contacts
   b. staying current
   c. developing specialties
   d. maintaining computer competence
   e. being alert to organizational changes
5. A good idea is to present your innovative ideas:
   a. in terms of improving decision making
   b. to coworkers
   c. in terms of improving information
   d. to the union chief
   e. in terms of saving money

Fill in the Blank

1. ATM cards, home banking, and programs to analyze cursive writing are examples of how some banks are looking to use technology in their competitive __________ .
2. The person who thinks that microcomputers are overrated can be classified as a __________ .
3. Reading trade journals about the use of technology is a good way to stay __________ .
4. __________ is another name for the informal lines of communication within an organization.
5. Being computer competent means taking __________ control.

Open Ended

1. How do you become and stay a winner in the information age?
2. Give an example of how technology can change the nature of competition.
3. What are the three responses or attitudes that people are apt to have when confronted by new technology?
4. Name six strategies individuals should follow in order to be successful in the information age.
5. What periodicals might you read in order to keep current on changes in microcomputer technology?

DISCUSSION QUESTIONS AND PROJECTS

1. *Volunteering your computer skills:* What would you do if you had an old but still useful microcomputer? It might not be something you want or even something you can sell. Still, someone can benefit from it. There are several groups that collect donated hardware and software for nonprofit organizations, such as conservation, veterans, arts, and child-care groups.

   These groups also provide volunteers to assist nonprofits in learning to use their new systems. Perhaps this is a case where you can lend your own experience to a good cause. Contact one of the following or a similar organization, which you may learn about through local computer users' groups, to see how you can help:

   a. *Boston:* CONNECT, Technical Development Corporation, 30 Federal St., 5th floor, Boston, MA 02110 (telephone: 617-728-9151).
   b. *Chicago:* Information Technology Resource Center, 59 East Van Buren, Suite 2020, Chicago, IL 60605-1219 (telephone: 312-939-8050).
   c. *Dallas:* Technology Learning Center, Center for Nonprofit Management, 2900 Live Oak St., Dallas, TX 75204 (telephone: 214-823-8097).
   d. *New York:* Nonprofit Computer Exchange, Fund for the City of New York, 121 Sixth Ave., 6th floor, New York, NY 10013 (telephone: 212-925-5101).
   e. *San Francisco:* CompuMentor, 89 Stillman St., San Francisco, CA 94107 (telephone: 415-512-7784).

2. *Being careful about technology predictions:* Technology forecasts have a way of often being so wide of the mark that in looking back we may wonder how the experts could have erred so badly. For instance, nuclear-powered airplanes, household robots, and widespread use of electric cars have never realized the rosy promises of the forecasters.

   Editor Herb Brody in *Technology Review* suggests some guidelines for reducing erroneous predictions. Among them are the following.

- Be wary of forecasts based on information from vested interests, such as technology developers needing financing, who may in turn exert undue influence on market-forecasting firms, the news media, and investors.
- Expect existing technologies to keep on improving, but don't expect people to abandon what they have for something only somewhat better.
- Expect truly revolutionary technologies to take 10 to 25 years to gain widespread use.

Given these guidelines, describe some future uses and assess the popularity you would expect for the following: neural-network computers; pen-based computers; shirt-pocket telephones; hypermedia; computer-generated virtual realities; flat-panel display TVs to hang on living-room walls.

on the web

Exercises and Explorations

1 Computer Innovations

It is important to stay current with computer innovations in order to maintain your computer competency. To obtain help with this task, visit our Web site at http://www.magpie.org/essentials/chapter-YF to link to a commercial news service site. Once connected to that site, look for articles relating to *technology.* Print out one article and write a paragraph summarizing it.

2 JobWeb

The Internet could be important in finding your next job. Visit our Web site at http://www.magpie.org/essentials/chapter-YF to link to one of the Web's largest employment resource pages. Once connected to that site, conduct a search for *jobs* in your field or interest. Print out the first page of results. Write a paragraph describing the value of this site and discussing how you might use the Web in the future when searching for a job.

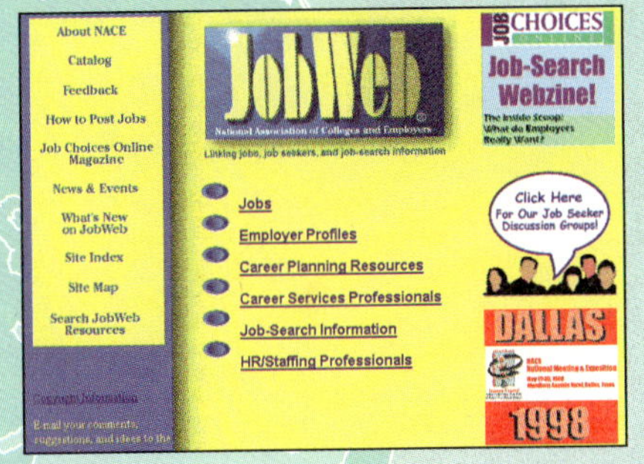

3 Job Hunting

The Web is a good tool to learn how to look for a job. Visit the Yahoo site at http://www.yahoo.com, and explore the category of "Business and Economy Employment" and using the keywords "resume," "job hunting," and "employment." Print out the first page of results from your search. Write a paragraph summarizing the most useful advice and information you found.

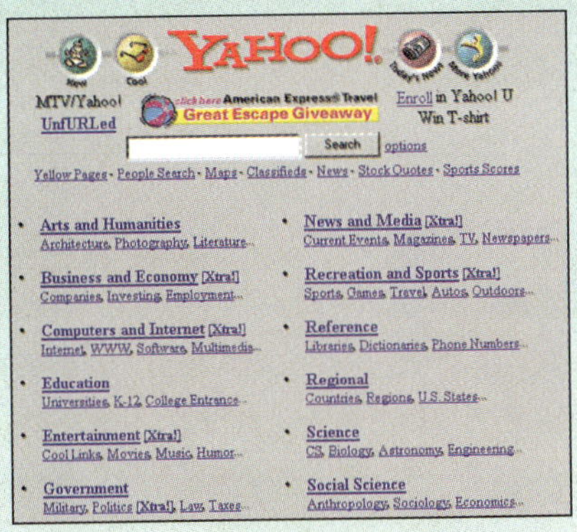

4 Motion Pictures

Selecting movies and movie theaters can be a real hassle. The Web can tell you which movies are being offered at your local theaters and can provide their show times and movie reviews. Visit our Web site at http://www.magpie.org/essentials/chapter-YF to link to one of these motion picture sites. Once you have connected to that site, find a movie playing at a theater near you that you might like to see. Print out the show time for today. Check out one or more reviews on the movie, and write a paragraph summarizing your findings.

VISUAL SUMMARY

Your Future and Information Technology

Being a winner in the information revolution means devising an individual strategy for dealing with change.

TECHNOLOGY AND ORGANIZATIONS

Technology can introduce new ways for businesses to compete with each other.

New Products

Technology creates products that operate faster, are priced more cheaply, are often of better quality, or are wholly new. New products can be custom-tailored to a particular customer's needs.

New Enterprises

Technology can build entire new businesses (e.g., an airline charges travel agents for using its reservations system for making reservations on other airlines).

New Customer and Supplier Relationships

Businesses that make their information systems easily available may make their customers less likely to take their business elsewhere (e.g., overnight delivery services closely track packages and bills).

TECHNOLOGY AND PEOPLE

Three common reactions to the prospect of new technology are:

Cynicism

The cynics feel that new technology is overrated and too troublesome to learn.

Naïveté

The naïve believe that technology can solve problems it cannot.

Frustration

The frustrated are impatient and irritated about taking time to learn new technology.

Being a skilled computer end user—being computer competent—is a matter of living in the present and keeping an eye on the future. It is a matter of concentrating on your goals and learning how the computer can help you achieve them.

HOW YOU CAN BE A WINNER

Six ongoing activities that can help you be successful are as follows:

Stay current

read trade journals and the general business press, join professional associations, and participate in interest groups on the Internet

Maintain computer competence

stay current with technology by being alert for computer related articles

Develop personal contacts

stay active in your professoin and meet people in your field

Develop specialties

develop specialties within your filed, master an essential skill

Be alert for organizational change

use informal lines of communication

Look for innovative opportunities

present your ideas as saving money

CAREERS IN INFORMATION TECHNOLOGY

To be a winner does not mean you have to have a career in information systems. Five careers to consider:

Systems Analyst

Systems analysts, determine needs, design systems and implement them.

Programmer

Programmers create new software and revise existing programs.

Technical Writer

Technical writers create documents to explain how systems work.

Network Manager

Network managers monitor existing networks and implement new ones.

Computer Trainer

Computer trainers present classes on new systems.

Guide to the Internet and the World Wide Web

How to Surf the Net

Want to communicate with a friend across town, in another state, or even in another country? Perhaps you would like to send a drawing, a photo, or just a letter. Looking for travel or entertainment information? Perhaps you're researching a term paper or exploring different career paths. Where do you start? For these and other information-related activities, try the Internet and the World Wide Web. They are the 20th-century information resources designed for all of us to use.

The Internet is like a highway that connects you to millions of other people and organizations. Unlike typical highways that move people and things from one location to another, the Internet moves your *ideas* and *information*. Rather than moving through geographic space, you move through **cyberspace**—the space of electronic movement of ideas and information. In this guide, we describe the Internet and how you can get onto it. We describe the World Wide Web and how to use it to search for and retrieve information.

The Internet: Access, E-Mail, Discussion Groups, and Services

The Internet is a giant worldwide network. Popular uses include communicating, shopping, researching, and entertainment.

The Internet is a giant worldwide network. It connects computer systems located throughout the world that are willing to share their resources. The Internet has created a cooperative society that forms a virtual community stretching from one end of the globe to the other. (See Figure 1.)

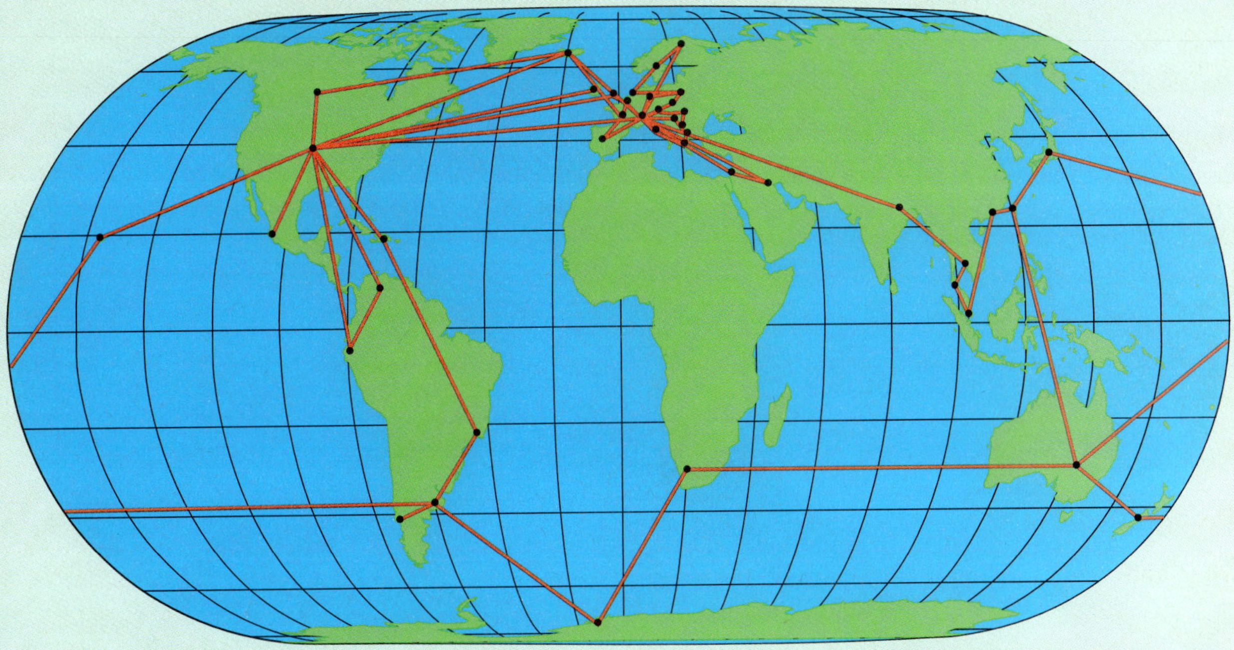

FIGURE 1
Internet connections around the world.

The Internet's origin can be traced back to 1969, when the United States government funded a major research project on computer networking. A national computer network called **ARPANET (Advanced Research Project Agency Network)** was developed. It was used by government and military agencies to communicate and share computer resources with researchers working on national security projects.

From these military and research beginnings, the Internet has evolved as a tool for all of us to use. Every day more than 30 million people in over 50 countries use the Internet. By the year 2000, over a billion users from every country in the world are expected to be connected to the Internet. (See Figure 2.)

To access the Internet, you connect to one of the computer systems already on it. After you connect to one, you can easily connect to another. You move electronically from one computer system to another, from one site to another, and often from one country to another—all within seconds. What makes the Internet so remarkable is the incredible speed and efficiency with which these connections are made. Once you are on the Internet it seems like you are on a single giant computer that branches all over the world.

FIGURE 2
Internet use—past, present, and future.

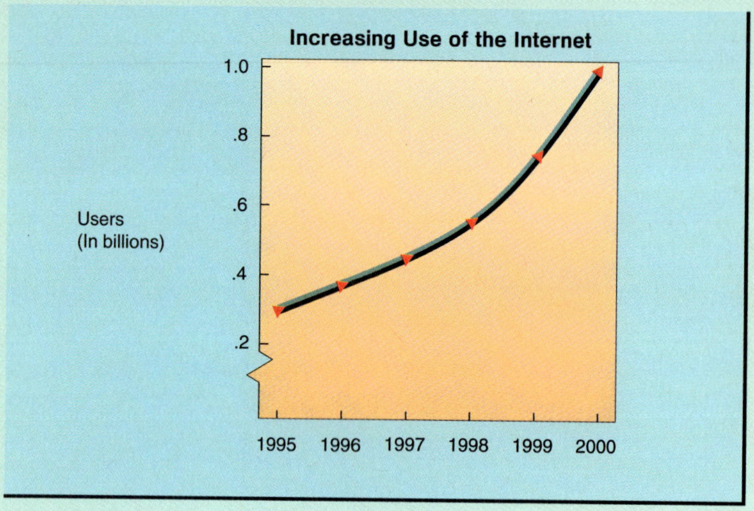

Internet Applications

What Can You Do on the Internet? There are any number of uses for the Internet. The most common are

- **Communicating:** Sending and receiving e-mail is the most popular Internet activity. You can send and receive e-mail to and from your friends and family located almost anywhere in the world. You can join and listen to discussions and debates on a wide variety of special-interest topics.
- **Shopping:** One of the fastest-growing applications is electronic commerce. You can visit a cyber mall to windowshop at the best stores, look for the latest fashions, search for bargains, and make purchases. (See Figure 3.)

FIGURE 3
The Internet Mall Web site.

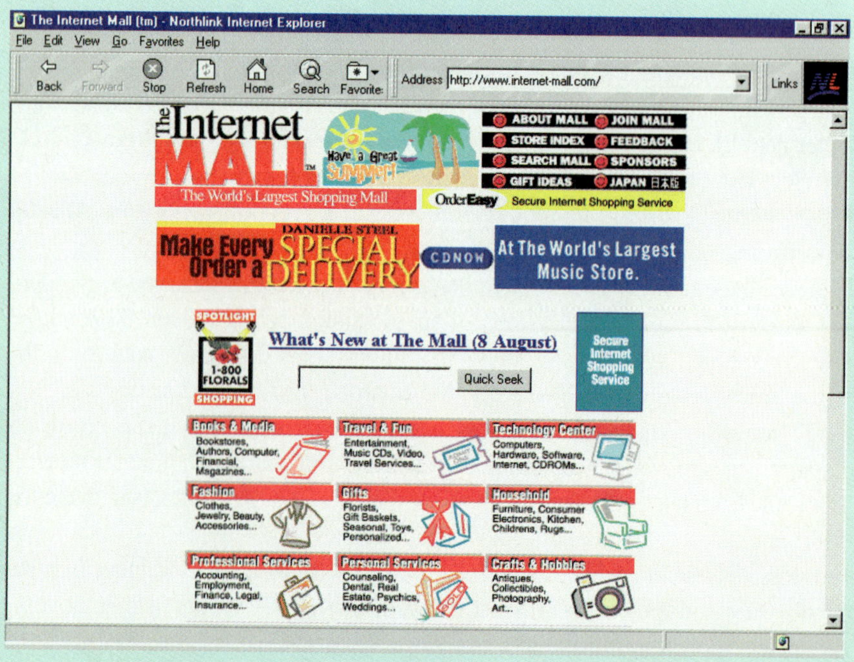

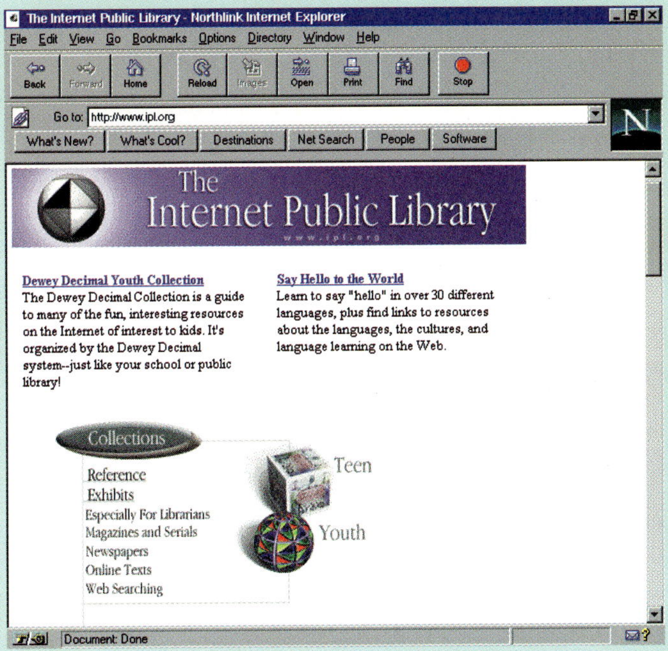

FIGURE 4
The Internet Public Library Web site.

- **Researching:** How would you like to have one of the world's largest libraries available from home? Well, you can have several of them. (See Figure 4.)
- **Entertainment:** Do you like music, the movies, reading, or playing computer games? You'll find them all on the Internet waiting for you to locate and enjoy.

Where should you begin to learn more about how to use and to surf the Internet? First, you should gain access to or get onto the Internet. Then, explore the applications and use the available Internet services. The following sections of this guide will help you do just that.

Access

Providers give access to the Internet. Internet connections are either direct, SLIP and PPP, or by terminal connection. Protocols are rules for exchanging information between computers.

The Internet and the telephone system are similar—you can connect to the Internet much like you connect a phone to the telephone system. Once you are on the Internet, your computer becomes an extension of what seems like a giant computer—a computer that branches all over the world.

Providers

The most common way to access the Internet is through a **provider** or **host computer.** The providers are already connected to the Internet and provide a path or connection for individuals to access the Internet. There are two widely used providers.

- **College and universities:** Most colleges and universities provide free access to the Internet through their local area networks. You may be able to access the Internet through your school or through other local colleges and universities.
- **Internet service providers:** An **Internet service provider (ISP)** offers access to the Internet for a fee. The best known national Internet service providers are AT&T WorldNet, MindSpring, Netcom, and Sprynet. Local providers are also available in many areas at a slightly lower cost.
- **Online services providers:** The most widely used source for access to the Internet is through **online services providers.** Like Internet service providers, they provide access to the Internet. Additionally, online services providers offer a variety of other services as well. The best known are America Online (AOL), CSi (formerly known as CompuServe), MSN (Microsoft Network), and Prodigy. (See Figure 5.)

Connections

To gain access to the Internet, you must have a connection. This connection can be made either directly to the Internet or indirectly through a provider. There are three types of connections:

- **Direct or dedicated:** To have the most efficient access to all the functions on the Internet, you need a direct or dedicated link. Individuals rarely have direct connections because they are quite expensive. However, many organizations such as colleges, universities, service providers, and corporations do have direct links.

  The primary advantages of a direct link are complete access to Internet functions, ease of connection for individual users, and fast response and retrieval of information. The primary disadvantage is cost.

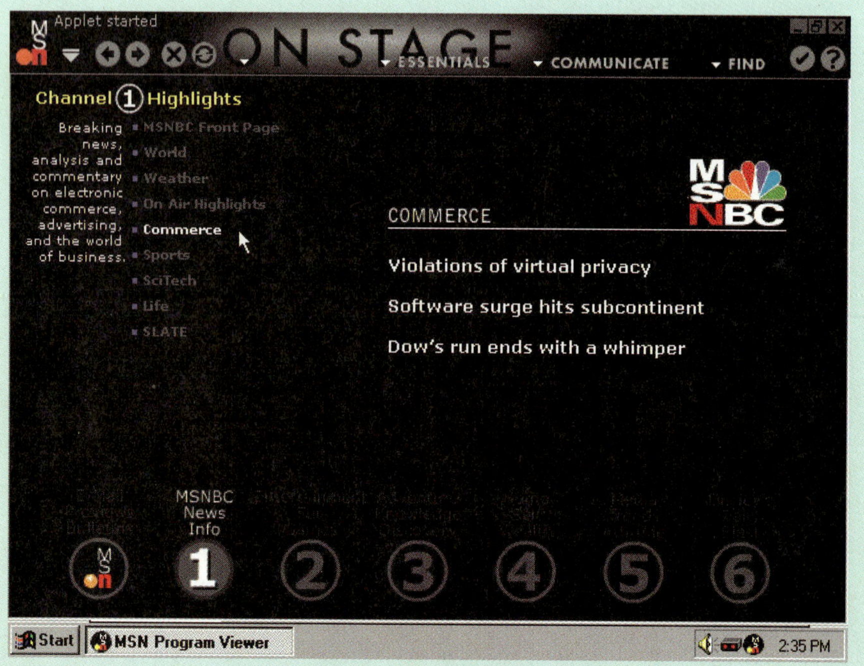

FIGURE 5
Online Service Provider.

- **SLIP and PPP:** Using a high-speed modem and standard telephone lines, you can connect to a provider that has a direct connection to the Internet. This type of connection requires special software such as **SLIP (serial line Internet protocol)** or **PPP (point-to-point protocol).** Using this type of connection, your computer becomes part of a client/server network. The provider or host computer is the server providing access to the Internet. Your computer is the client. Using special client software, your computer is able to communicate with server software running on the provider's computer and on other Internet computers.

  This type of connection is widely used by end users to connect to the Internet. It provides a high level of service at a lower cost than a direct or dedicated connection. Of course, it is somewhat slower and may not be as convenient.
- **Terminal connection:** Another way to access the Internet using a high-speed modem and standard telephone lines is called a **terminal connection.** Using this type of connection, your computer becomes a part of a terminal network. Unlike with a SLIP or PPP connection, your computer's operations with a terminal connection are very limited. Your computer simply displays the communication that occurs between the provider and the other computers on the Internet. Compared to a SLIP or PPP connection, terminal connection is less expensive but not as fast or convenient.

For a summary of the typical costs and users of the three types of connections, see Figure 6.

TCP/IP

When information is sent over the Internet, it usually travels through numerous interconnected networks. Before a message is sent, it is broken down into small parts called **packets.** Each packet is then sent separately over the Internet, possibly traveling different routes to one common destination. At the receiving end, the packets are reassembled into the correct order. *Protocols* control how the messages are broken down, sent, and reassembled. They govern how and when computers talk to one another. The standard protocol for the Internet is called **TCP/IP (transmission control protocol/Internet protocol).**

USERS AND CONNECTION COSTS

CONNECTION	USER	COST
Direct/Dedicated	Medium to large company	$4,000 to $15,000 per year
SLIP/PPP	Individual or small company	$20 to $200 per year plus hourly charges
Terminal connection	Individual	$0 to $50 per year

FIGURE 6
Typical user and connection costs.

E-Mail

An e-mail message has three basic elements. Internet addresses use the domain name system. E-mail etiquette is called netiquette.

E-mail is a way of sending an electronic letter or message between individuals or computers. It is like an answering machine in that you can receive messages even when you are not home. Unlike an answering machine, e-mail can contain text, graphics, and images as well as sound. E-mail can also be used to communicate with more than one person at a time, to conveniently schedule meetings, to keep current on important events, and much more.

Sending and receiving e-mail is by far the most common Internet activity. You can communicate with anyone in the world who has an Internet address or e-mail account with a system connected to the Internet. E-mail programs such as Pine, Elm, and Eudora automate the process of creating, sending, reading, and receiving messages.

Suppose that you have a friend, Dan Coats, who is going to the University of Southern California. You and Dan have been calling back and forth at least once a week for the past month. Your telephone bill has skyrocketed. Fortunately, you both have Internet e-mail accounts through your schools. To save money, you and Dan agree to communicate via the Internet instead of the telephone. After exchanging e-mail addresses, you are ready to send your first Internet e-mail message to Dan.

Basic Elements

A typical e-mail message has three basic elements: header, message, and signature. (See Figure 7.) The header appears first and typically includes the following information.

FIGURE 7
Basic elements of an e-mail message.

header —
To: dcoats@usc.edu
From: [your Internet address]
Subject: First e-mail to Chris
Attachment: BUDGET.XLS

message —
Chris, this Internet stuff is really something. We should save a lot on telephone bills. I figure at least $20.00 a month. Remember the Excel spreadsheet we used this past summer to estimate our college expenses? I just revised it to reflect lower telephone expenses. It is attached in the file BUDGET.XLS.

I just talked to Joe. Unfortunately, his school does not have an Internet connection. However, he is going to subscribe to America Online so he can e-mail us. Of course, it will cost him more because he'll have to pay an online service fee. But, he figures he will still save money.

Another thing I like about this e-mail … we don't have to schedule our calls so that we are both available at the same time. Plus we can send e-mail messages anytime we want at almost no cost.

signature — [your name, address, and telephone number]

- **To line:** The e-mail address for the person who is to receive the letter.
- **From line:** The address of the person sending the e-mail. It follows the To line.
- **Subject line:** A one-line description of the message, used to present the topic of the message. Subject lines typically are displayed when a person checks his or her mailbox.
- **Attachment line:** Many e-mail programs allow you to attach files such as documents and worksheets. If a message has an attachment, the file name appears on the attachment line.

The letter or message comes next. It is typically short and to the point. Finally, the signature line provides additional information about the sender. Typically, this information includes the sender's name, address, and telephone number.

Addresses

One of the most important elements of an e-mail message is the address of the person who is to receive the letter. The Internet uses an addressing method known as the **domain name system (DNS)** to assign names and numbers to people and computers. This system divides an address into three parts. (See Figure 8.)

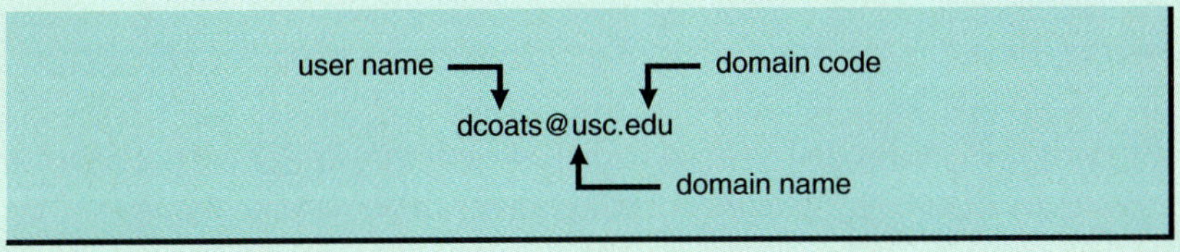

FIGURE 8
Parts of an Internet address.

Internet addresses typically are read backwards. The last part of the address is the **domain code,** which identifies the geographical description or organizational identification. For example, *edu* in Figure 8 indicates an address at an educational and research institution. (See Figure 9.)

Separated from the domain code by a dot (.) is the **domain name.** It is a reference to the particular organization. In this case, *usc* represents the University of Southern California. Separated from the domain name by an "at" (@) symbol, the **user name** identifies a unique person or computer at the listed domain. The address shown in Figure 10 is for Dan Coats (dcoats) at the University of Southern California (USC), which is an education and research institution (edu).

DOMAIN CODES

DOMAIN	IDENTIFICATION
com	Commercial
edu	Educational and research
org	Other organizations
net	Major network centers
gov	Government

FIGURE 9
Commonly used Internet domain codes.

Netiquette

Netiquette refers to the etiquette you should observe when using e-mail. Remember that you are communicating with people, not computers—these people have the same feelings and sensibilities that you do. (See Figure 10.)

FIGURE 10
E-mail etiquette.

NETIQUETTE

1. Don't send abusive, threatening, harassing, or bigoted messages. You could be held criminally liable for what you write.
2. DO NOT TYPE YOUR MESSAGES IN ALL UPPERCASE CHARACTERS! This is called shouting and is perceived as very harsh. Use a normal combination of upper- and lowercase characters. Sometimes all lowercase is perceived as too informal or timid.
3. Keep line length to 60 characters or less so your messages can be comfortably displayed on most monitors.
4. Before sending a message, carefully check the spelling, punctuation, and grammar. Also think twice about the content of your message. Once it is sent, you can't get it back.

Discussion Groups

Mailing lists send e-mail to all members. Newsgroups use the Usenet. Lurk before you contribute.

You can also use e-mail to communicate with people you do not know but with whom you wish to share ideas and interests. You can participate in discussions and debates that range from general topics like current events and movies to specialized forums like computer troubleshooting and Star Trek.

Mailing Lists

Mailing lists are one type of discussion group available on the Internet. Members of a mailing list communicate by sending messages to a **list address.** Each message is then copied and sent via e-mail to every member of the mailing list.

There are thousands of different mailing lists. To participate in one, you must first subscribe by sending an e-mail request to the mailing list **subscription address.** (See Figure 11.) Once you are a member of a list, you can expect to receive e-mail from others on the list. You may find the number of messages to be overwhelming. If you want to cancel a mailing list, send an e-mail request to "unsubscribe" to the subscription address.

FIGURE 11
Seven popular mailing lists.

MAILING LISTS

DESCRIPTION	SUBSCRIPTION ADDRESS
Alanis Morrissette fans	cantnot-request@smoe.org
Jimi Hendrix fans	hey-joe-request@inslab.uky.edu
Motorcycle enthusiasts	harleys-request@think.age.on.ca
Sports enthusiasts	listproc@u.washington.edu-Pac-10
Star Wars fans	majordomo@peak.org
The Artist formerly known as Prince	igot@ns.sympatico.ca
Truck enthusiasts	fordtrucks80up-request@lofcom.com

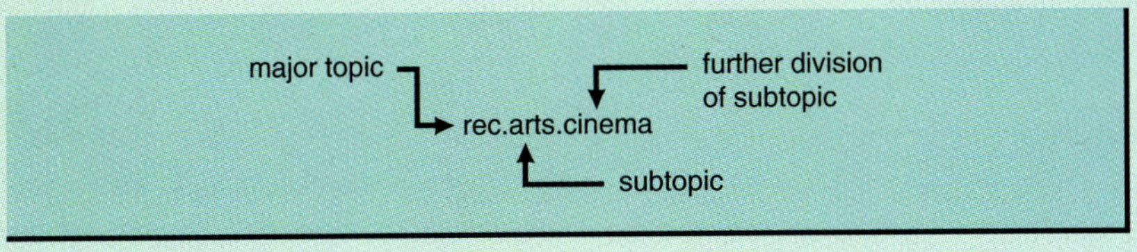

FIGURE 12
Newsgroup hierarchy.

Newsgroups

Newsgroups are the most popular type of discussion group. Unlike mailing lists, **newsgroups** use a special network of computers called the **UseNet.** Each of these computers maintains the newsgroup listing. There are over 10,000 different newsgroups organized into major topic areas that are further subdivided into hierarchies.

This hierarchy system is similar to the domain name system. For example, the newsgroup specializing in motion picture discussions is categorized under the major topic *rec* (for "recreational"), then the subtopic *arts,* and then the further subdivision *cinema.* (See Figure 12.)

Contributions to a particular newsgroup are sent to one of the computers on the UseNet. This computer saves the messages on its system and periodically shares all its recent messages with the other computers on the UseNet. Unlike mailing lists, a copy of each message is not sent to each member of a list. Rather, interested individuals check contributions to a particular newsgroup, reading only those of interest.

There are thousands of newsgroups covering a wide variety of topic areas. (See Figure 13.)

Chat Groups

Chat groups are becoming a very popular type of discussion group. While mailing lists and newsgroups rely on e-mail, chat groups allow direct "live" communication. To participate, you join a chat group, select a **channel** or topic, and communicate live with others by typing words on your computer. Other members of your channel immediately see those words on their computers and can respond in the same manner.

NEWSGROUPS

DESCRIPTION	NEWSGROUPS
Aerobics fitness	misc.fitness.aerobics
Beatles	rec.music.beatles
Cinema	rec.arts.movies
Mountain biking	rec.bicycles.off-road
Investing	misc.invest
Reading	rec.arts.books
Computer Games	alt.binaries.games.discussion
Music	rec.music.funky

FIGURE 13
Popular newsgroups.

FIGURE 14
Selected discussion group terms.

DISCUSSION GROUP TERMS

TERM	DESCRIPTION
Lurking	Reading news but not joining in to contribute
FAQ	Frequently asked question
Flaming	Insulting, putting-down, or attacking
RFD	Request for discussion
Saint	Someone who aids new users by answering questions
Thread	A sequence of ongoing messages on the same subject
Wizard	Someone who has comprehensive knowledge about a subject

By far the most popular chat service is called Internet Relay Chat (IRC). To participate, you need access to a server or computer that supports IRC. This is done using special chat client software. This software is available free from several locations on the Internet. Using the chat client software, you log on to the server, select a channel or topic in which you are interested, and begin chatting.

Lurking

Before you submit a contribution to a discussion group, it is recommended that you observe or read the communications from others. This is called **lurking.** (See Figure 14.)

By lurking, you can learn about the culture of a discussion group. For example, you can observe the level and style of the discussions. You may decide that a particular discussion group is not what you were looking for—in which case, unsubscribe. If the discussions are appropriate and you wish to participate, try to fit into the prevailing culture. Remember that your contributions will likely be read by hundreds of people.

Services

Telnet runs programs on remote computers. FTP transfers files. Gopher provides menus for available resources. WAIS maintains lists of key words and phrases. The Web provides a multimedia interface to available resources.

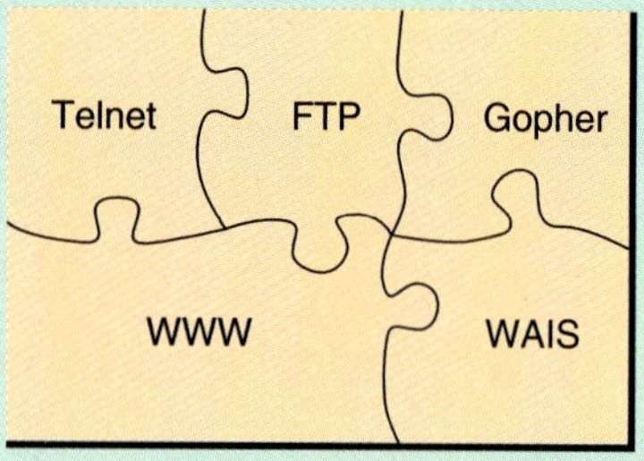

FIGURE 15
Internet services.

There are numerous services available on the Internet. Five commonly used services are Telnet, FTP, Gopher, WAIS, and the Web. (See Figure 15.)

Telnet

Many computers on the Internet will allow you to connect to them and to run selected programs on them. **Telnet** is the Internet service that allows you to connect to another computer (host) on the Internet and log on to that computer as if you were a terminal in the next room. There are hundreds of computers on the Internet that you can connect to. Some allow limited free access, and others charge fees for their use.

FTP

FTP (file transfer protocol) is an Internet service for transferring files. Many computers on the Internet allow you to copy files to your computer. This is called **downloading.** Using FTP you can also copy files from your computer to another computer on the Internet. This is called **uploading.**

Gopher

Gopher is a software application that provides menu-based search and retrieval functions for a particular computer site. It was originally developed at the University of Minnesota in 1991. Internet **Gopher sites** are computers that provide menus describing their available resources and direct links to the resources. Essentially, these menus are a "table of contents" for organizing and locating information. In addition, these sites typically handle transferring of files (FTP) and connecting to other computers (Telnet).

WAIS

Another search tool, **WAIS (wide area information server)** (pronounced "wayz"), extends the search capabilities of Gopher. It creates its lists of available resources by investigating menu options from various Gopher sites, then examines documents and maintains an extensive list of key words and phrases. A WAIS search on a topic is more thorough and provides more specific references. There are hundreds of WAIS sites available. Each site generally maintains information on a single subject.

The Web

The Internet service receiving the most attention today is the **Web.** It is the topic of our next section. It is easy to get the Internet and the Web confused. They are not the same thing. The Internet is the actual physical network. It is made up of wires, cables, and satellites. It connects computers and resources throughout the world. The Web is a multimedia interface to resources available on the Internet.

See Figure 16 for a summary of Internet services.

INTERNET SERVICES

Telnet	Runs programs on remote computers
FTP	Uploads and downloads files
Gopher	Provides menus for available resources for one computer site
WAIS	Maintains lists of key words and phrases for several computer sites
Web	Uses a multimedia interface to link to resources located worldwide

FIGURE 16
Internet Services.

World Wide Web: Browsers, Pages, Search Tools, and Web Utilities

Browsers connect to the Web. Web pages contain information and hypertext links. Search tools locate information. Web utilities include plug-ins and helper applications.

The largest, most exciting, and fastest growing Internet service is the **World Wide Web,** also known as **WWW** and the **Web.** It was introduced in 1992 at CERN, the Center for European Nuclear Research in Geneva, Switzerland. Today, the Web is widely used for entertainment, shopping, research, and any number of other things. To effectively use the Web, you need to understand browsers, Web pages, search tools, and Web utilities.

Browsers

Browsers connect to Web sites using ULR addresses.

The Web is accessed through your computer using special software known as **browsers.** This software connects you to remote computers, opens and transfers files, displays text and images, and provides in one tool an uncomplicated interface to the Internet and WWW documents. Three well-known browsers are Netscape Navigator, Microsoft Internet Explorer, and NCSA Mosaic. (See Figure 17.)

FIGURE 17
Netscape Navigator.

URL

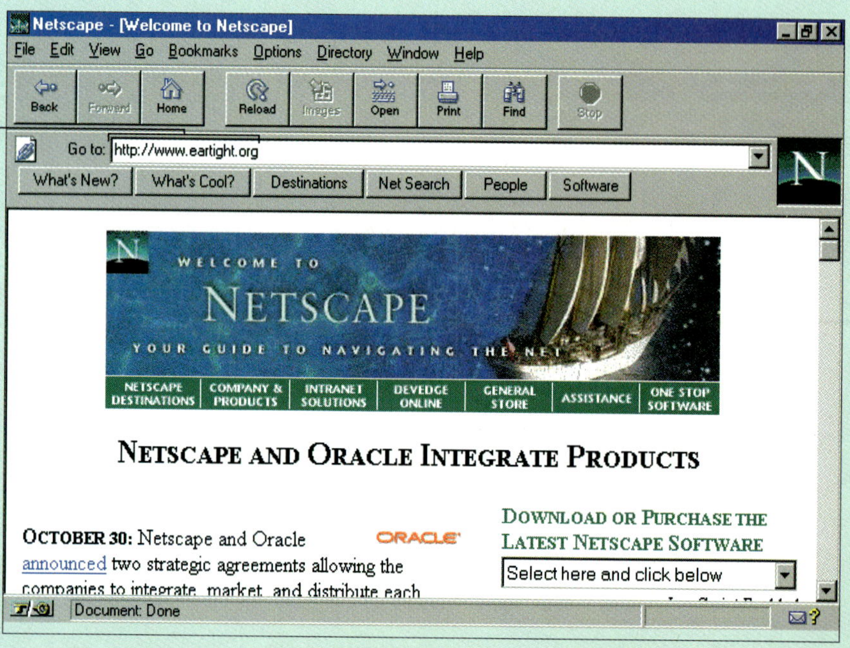

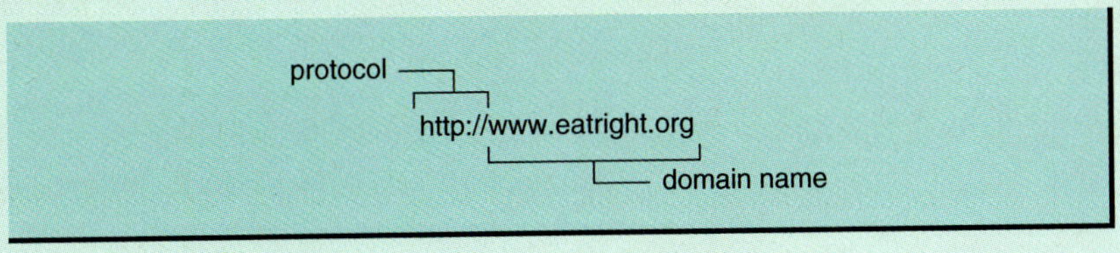

FIGURE 18
Two basic parts of a URL.

Uniform Resource Locators

In order for browsers to connect to other resources, the location or address of the resources must be specified. These addresses are called **uniform resource locators (URLs).** (See Figure 17.)

All URLs have at least two basic parts. (See Figure 18.) The first part presents the protocol used to connect to the resource. The protocol *http://*, shown in Figure 18, is by far the most common. The second part presents the domain name or the name of the server where the resource is located. In Figure 18 the server is identified as *www.eatright.org*. (Many URLs have additional parts specifying directory paths, file names, and pointers.)

The URL *http://www.eatright.org* connects your computer to a computer that provides information about healthy eating. These informational locations on the Web are called **Web sites.**

Web Pages

Browsers interpret HTML documents to display Web pages.

Once the browser has connected to a Web site, a document file is sent to your computer. This document contains **HTML (Hypertext Markup Language)** commands. (See Figure 19.)

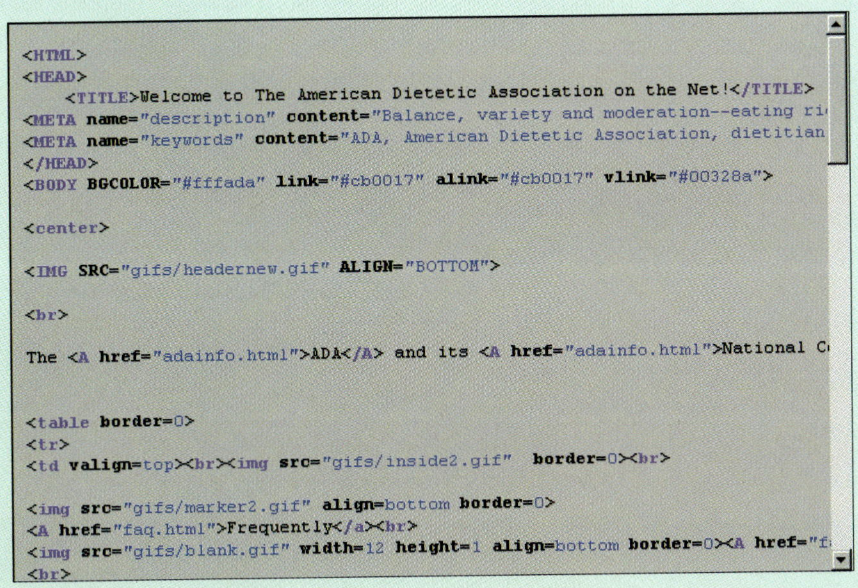

```
<HTML>
<HEAD>
    <TITLE>Welcome to The American Dietetic Association on the Net!</TITLE>
<META name="description" content="Balance, variety and moderation--eating ri
<META name="keywords" content="ADA, American Dietetic Association, dietitian
</HEAD>
<BODY BGCOLOR="#fffada" link="#cb0017" alink="#cb0017" vlink="#00328a">

<center>

<IMG SRC="gifs/headernew.gif" ALIGN="BOTTOM">

<br>

The <A href="adainfo.html">ADA</A> and its <A href="adainfo.html">National C


<table border=0>
<tr>
<td valign=top><br><img src="gifs/inside2.gif"  border=0><br>

<img src="gifs/marker2.gif" align=bottom border=0>
<A href="faq.html">Frequently</a><br>
<img src="gifs/blank.gif" width=12 height=1 align=bottom border=0><A href="f
<br>
```

FIGURE 19
HTML commands.

The browser interprets the HTML commands and displays the document as a **Web page.** Typically, the first page at a Web site is referred to as the home page. (See Figure 20.) The **home page** presents information about the site along with references and **hyperlinks,** or connections to other documents that contain related information—text files, graphic images, audio, and video clips.

These documents may be located on a nearby computer system or one located halfway around the world. The references appear as underlined and colored text and/or images on the Web page. To access the referenced material, all you do is click on the highlighted text or image. A link is automatically made to the computer containing the material, and the referenced material appears.

Applets and Java

Web pages can also contain links to special programs called **applets** written in a programming language called **Java.** These programs can be quickly downloaded and run by most browsers. Java applets are widely used to add interest and activity to a Web site by presenting animation, displaying graphics, providing interactive games, and much more.

Search Tools

Indexes are organized by categories. Search engines are organized like a database.

The Web is a massive collection of interrelated Web pages. With so much available information, locating the precise information you need can be difficult. Fortunately, a number of **search tools** have been developed and are avail-

FIGURE 20
The American Dietetic Association Web site.

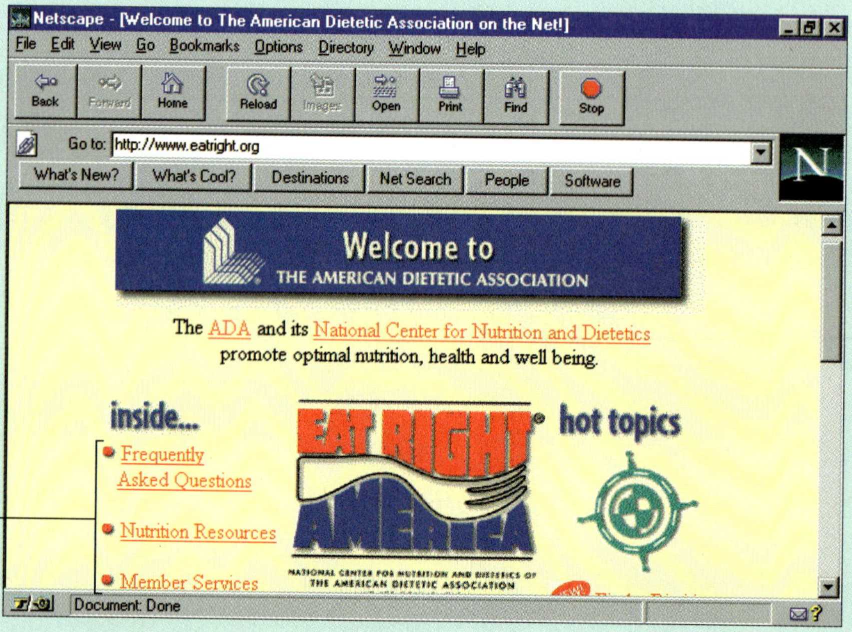

hyperlinks

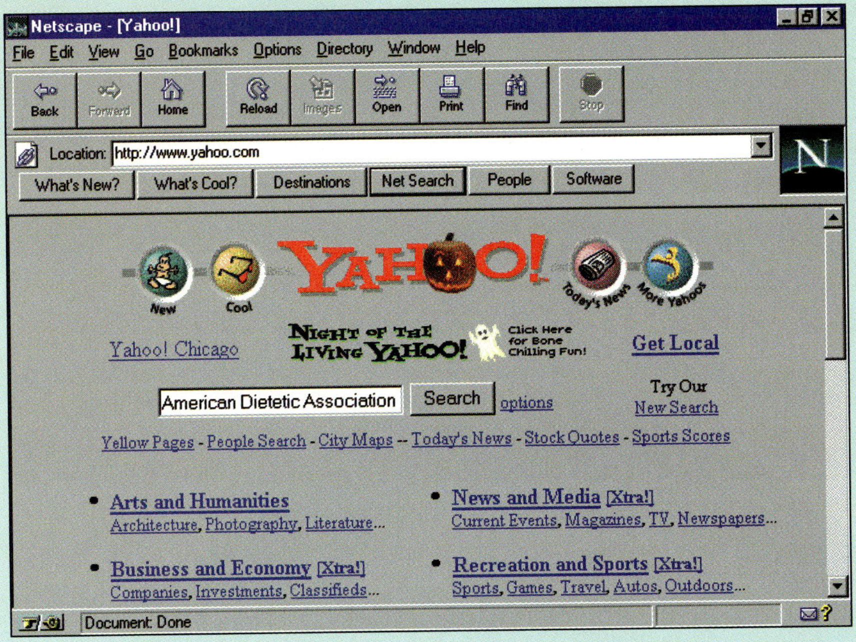

FIGURE 21
Yahoo! home page.

able to you by visiting their Web sites. There are basically two types: indexes and search engines.

Indexes

Indexes, also known as **Web directories,** are organized by categories such as art, computers, entertainment, news, science, sports, and so on. Each category is further organized into subcategories. Using your browser, you select a category and continue to select subcategories until your search has been narrowed and a list of relevant documents appears. By selecting a document, you cause the appropriate links to be made and the document appears. The best known and most widely used index is Yahoo! (See Figure 21.)

Search Engines

Search engines are also known as **Web crawlers** and **Web spiders.** Information is not organized by major categories. Rather, search engines are organized like a database, and you search through them by entering key words and phrases. These databases are maintained by special programs called **agents, spiders,** or **bots.** They automatically search for new information on the Web and update the databases. Three widely used search engines are Hotbot, WebCrawler, and Alta Vista.

Locating Information

If you are looking for some general information about a topic, use an index first. For example, if you are planning a trip to Peru and want to learn more about the country, you should use an index like Yahoo. If you are looking for more specific

FIGURE 22
Tips for searching.

SEARCHING TIPS

Precision	use specific descriptive key words as opposed to general ones
Multiple words	use more than one word or synonyms
Essentials only	leave out non-essential words like prepositions and articles
Operators	use advanced search operators such as AND, OR, and NOT to combine key words or to eliminate others

information, use a search engine. For example, if you want to know the locations of the ancient Inca ruins in Peru, you should start with a search engine like HotBot. For some more tips on using search tools to find information on the Web, see Figure 22.

Web Utilities

Plug-ins are automatically loaded by your browser. Helper applications are independent programs executed from your browser.

Web utilities are programs that work with a browser to increase your speed, productivity, and capabilities. Many utilities are found in the latest versions of browsers, and others are available free or for a nominal charge. There are two categories of utilities: plug-ins and helper applications.

Plug-ins

Plug-ins are programs that are automatically loaded and operate as a part of your browser. Many Web sites require one or more plug-ins to fully experience their content. Some widely used plug-ins include:

- Shockwave from Macromedia, used for a variety of Web-based games, live concerts, and dynamic animations. (See Figure 23.)
- Quicktime from Apple, required by over 20,000 Web sites to display video and play audio.
- Live 3-D from Netscape, displaying three-dimensional graphics and used in sites displaying virtual reality.

Helper Applications

Also known as **add-ons, helper applications** are independent programs that can be executed or launched from your browser. There are hundreds of helper applications, most of them designed to maximize your efficiency. Four of the most common types are off-line search utilities, information pushers, off-line browsers, and filters.

- **Off-line browsers:** In order for a Web page to appear on your screen, its HTML document has to be downloaded from the Web site to your computer and executed.

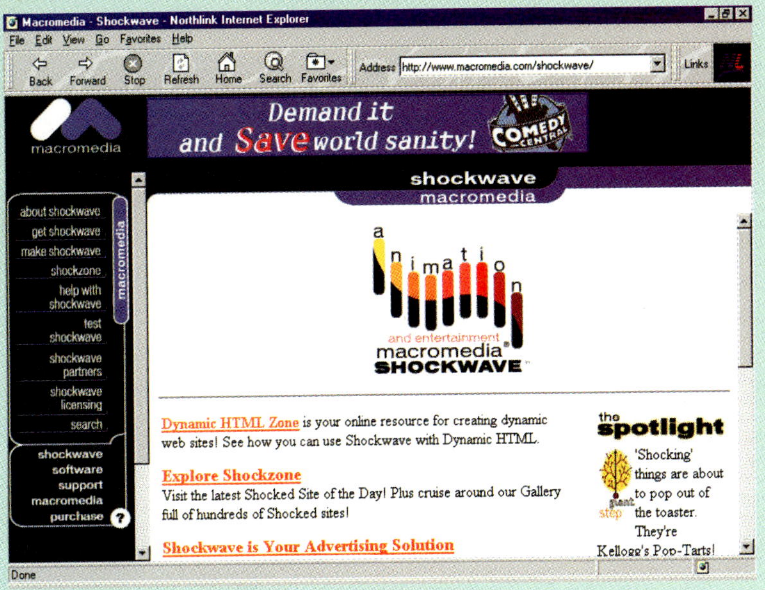

FIGURE 23
Plug-in: Macromedia's Shockwave Web site.

When the Internet is busy and/or the document is large, you spend a fair amount of time waiting. **Off-line browsers,** also known as **Web-downloading utilities** and **pull products,** offer a solution.

An off-line browser is a program that automatically connects to selected Web sites, downloads HTML documents, and saves them to your hard disk. You can view the Web pages later without being connected to the Internet and without waiting for documents to be downloaded. Two popular off-line browsers are InContext FlashSite and Teleport Pro. (See Figure 24.)

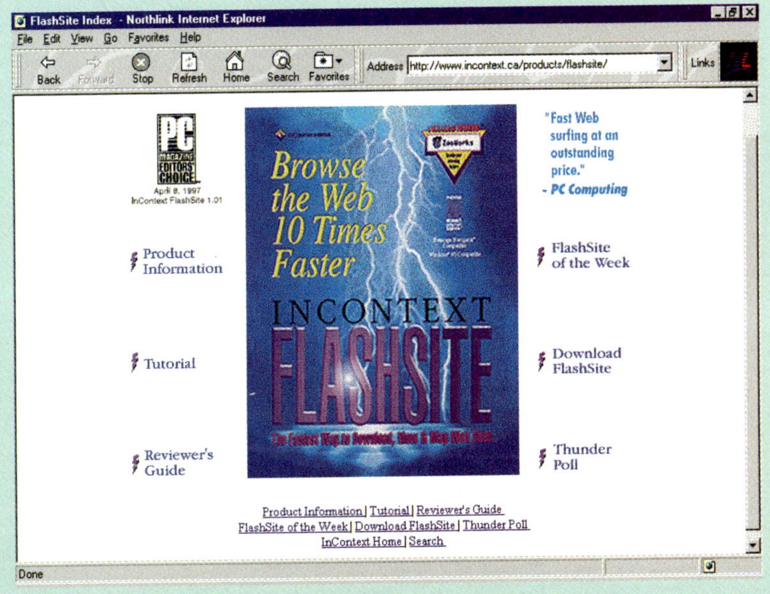

FIGURE 24
Off-line browser: In Context Flash site.

- **Information pushers:** Imagine a personalized newspaper containing only those articles that interested you the most. That is the basic idea behind **information pushers,** which are also known as **Web Broadcasters** and **push products.** You select topic areas known as *channels* that you are interested in. The information pusher automatically gathers information on your topics and sends it to your hard disk where you can read it whenever you want. Three well-known information pushers are PointCast Network and BackWeb. (See Figure 25.)
- **Off-line search utilities:** One way to research a topic is to visit the Web site for several individual indices and search engines. At each site, the search instructions are entered, and the search begins. After a few moments (or longer, depending on the particular search and the level of activity on the Internet), a list appears. This process can be quite time-consuming, and duplicate responses from the different search tools are inevitable. **Off-line search utilities,** also known as **metasearch programs,** offer a solution.

  An off-line search utility is a program that automatically submits your search request to several indices and search engines. It receives the results, sorts them, eliminates duplicates, and creates an index for your review. Three popular off-line search utilities are Internet FastFind, WebCompass, and EchoSearch.
- **Filters:** The Internet is an interesting and multifaceted arena. But one of those facets is a dark and seamy one. Parents, in particular, are concerned about children roaming unrestricted across the Internet. **Filter** programs allow parents

FIGURE 25
Information pusher: BackWeb.

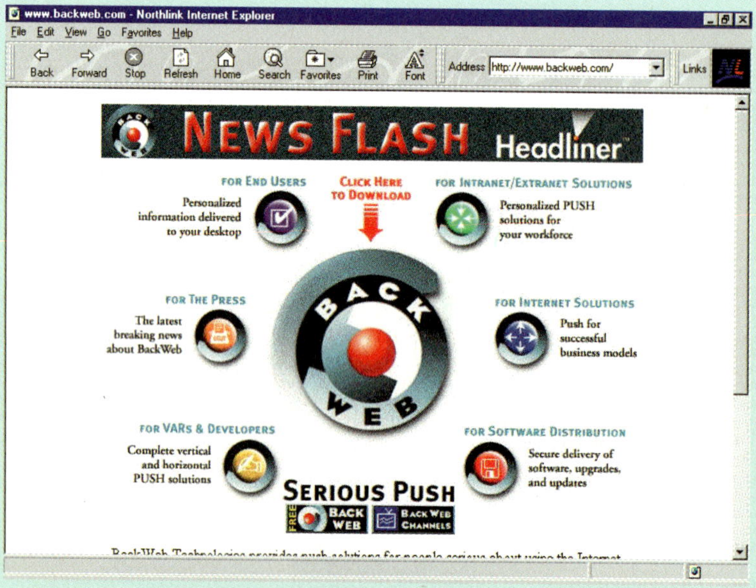

as well as organizations to block out selected sites and set time limits. Additionally, these programs can monitor use and generate reports detailing the total time spent on the Internet, and time spent at individual Web sites, chat groups, and newsgroups. Three well-known filters are Cyber patrol, Cybersitter, and Net Nanny. (See Figure 26.)

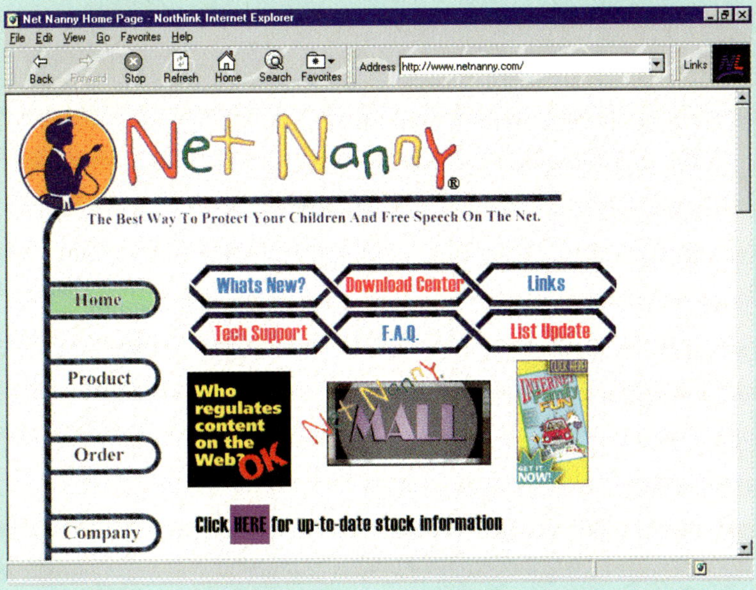

FIGURE 26
Filter: Net Nanny Web site.

A Look at the Future

Internet2 will be a private high-performance Internet.

Have you ever been unable to connect to the Internet? Have you ever had a long wait before a Web page or a graphic appeared on your screen? Almost all of us have experienced busy servers and slow access. Unfortunately, Internet service is expected to get worse. For organizations that depend on the Internet to reach customers and conduct other business activities, this trend is very concerning.

To address this concern, a separate private Internet called Internet2 is being developed. It will be a high-speed network capable of dazzling feats that far exceed today's Internet capabilities. Expected to be fully operational by 2002, Internet2 will have limited access to those willing to pay more to get more. Access to today's Internet will remain public and available for a nominal fee.

The primary beneficiaries of Internet2 will be federal agencies and major corporations. Each will pay an annual fee of $500,000 for access to this network that combines high performance with tightly controlled security. One of the first to take advantage of Internet2 will be online publishers of books, photographs, and original artwork. Advanced virtual reality interfaces, called nanomanipulators, are expected to be available. Researchers from different parts of the world will be able to share devices such as atomic microscopes and to jointly study, experience, and move within realistic virtual subatomic environments.

Will moving power users to Internet2 increase the performance of the public Internet? We will have to wait and see.

KEY TERMS

add-on (IG19)
agents (IG17)
applets (IG16)
ARPANET (Advanced Research Project Agency Network) (IG2)
bots (IG18)
browser (IG14)
channel (IG11)
chat groups (IG11)
cyberspace (IG1)
domain code (IG9)
domain name (000)
domain name system (DNS) (IG9)
downloading (IG13)
e-mail (IG7)
filter (IG21)
FTP (file transfer protocol) (IG13)
Gopher (IG13)
Gopher site (IG13)
helper application (IG19)
home page (IG16)
host computer (IG3)
HTML (Hypertext Markup Language) (IG16)
hyperlinks (IG16)
indexes (IG17)
information pusher (IG20)
Internet service provider (ISP) (IG4)
Java (IG16)
list address (IG10)
lurking (IG12)
mailing list (IG10)

metasearch program (IG20)
netiquette (IG10)
newsgroup (IG10)
off-line browser (IG20)
off-line search utility (IG20)
online services provider (IG5)
packet (IG7)
plug-in (IG19)
PPP (point-to-point protocol) (IG6)
provider (IG3)
pull product (IG20)
push product (IG20)
search engines (IG17)
search tools (IG17)
SLIP (serial line internet protocol) (IG6)
spiders (IG17)
subscription address (IG10)
TCP/IP (transmission control protocol/internet protocol) (IG7)
Telnet (IG13)
terminal connection (IG7)
uniform resource locator (URL) (IG15)
uploading (IG13)
UseNet (IG10)
user name (IG9)
WAIS (wide area information server) (IG13)
Web Broadcaster (IG18)
Web crawlers (IG17)
Web directories (IG17)
Web-downloading utilities (IG20)
Web page (IG16)
Web site (IG15)
Web spiders (IG17)
World Wide Web, WWW, the Web (IG13, IG14)

REVIEW QUESTIONS

True/False

1. The Internet is a huge network that connects computers worldwide.
2. Newsgroups use a special network of computers called the NewsNet.
3. Gopher is a software application that surveys resources from several computer sites.
4. URLs are used to route e-mail.
5. Spiders are special programs that automatically search for new information on the Web.

Multiple Choice

1. If you wanted to windowshop on the Internet, you would visit a:
   a. chat group.
   b. Gopher.
   c. Telnet.
   d. cyber mall.
   e. FTP.

2. In an e-mail message, the ________ provides additional information about the sender.
   a. header
   b. closing
   c. signature
   d. message
   e. greeting
3. The most popular chat service is:
   a. Talk today.
   b. Internet relay chat.
   c. browser.
   d. Yahoo!
   e. Internet Explorer.
4. The Web is accessed using a:
   a. browser.
   b. newsgroup.
   c. WAIS.
   d. Gopher.
   e. search tool.
5. Yahoo! is a:
   a. Gopher site.
   b. browser.
   c. chat group.
   d. home page.
   e. search tool.

Fill in the Blank

1. ________ is the electronic movement of ideas and information.
2. SLIP and ________ connections are widely used to access the Internet.
3. The three parts of an Internet address are user name, domain name, and ________.
4. Off-line search utilities, information pushers, off-line browsers, and filters are ________ ________.
5. ________ is an Internet service that runs programs on remote computers.

Open-Ended

1. How is a message sent over the Internet using TCP/IP?
2. Discuss five frequently used Internet services.
3. What are browsers?
4. What are the two types of Internet search tools?
5. What are Web utilities and what do they do?

DISCUSSION QUESTIONS AND PROJECTS

1. *Going on an Internet scavenger hunt:* Use the Internet to find information about the following topics. (Record the URLs where you found the information, and write a short description of your findings.)
   a) Hotels in London
   b) Cast members for one of your favorite television programs
   c) MTV's news for this week
   d) Employment opportunities in a career of your choice
   e) Painting of the Mona Lisa
   f) The weather conditions for your city (or the nearest large city)

The Internet and the World Wide Web

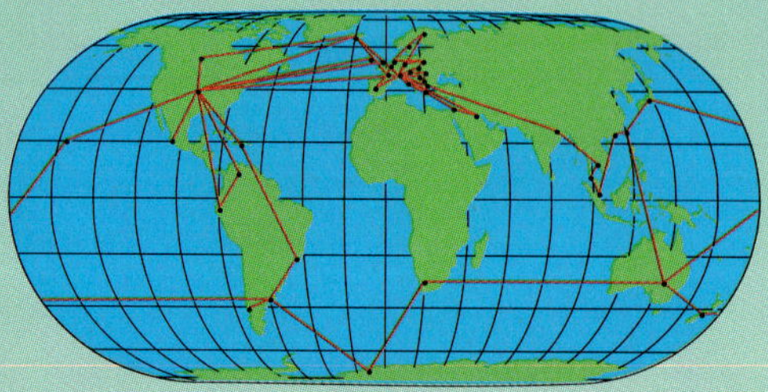

The Internet is the roadway for ideas and information through **cyberspace.** It is a giant world-wide computer network.

ACCESS

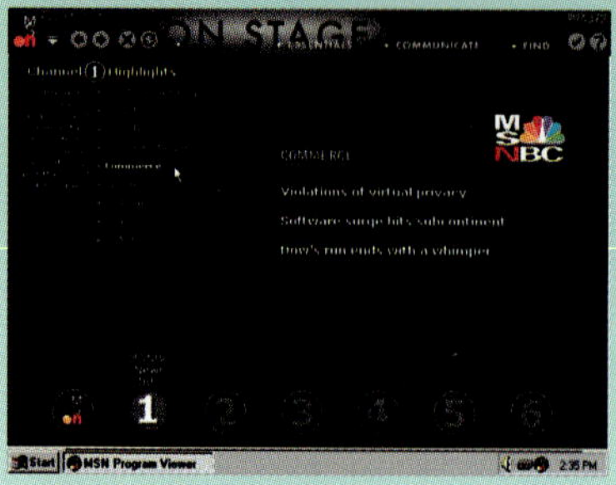

Providers

The most common access is through a **provider** or **host computer.** Three widely used providers:

- Most colleges or universities provide free access to their students.
- **Internet service providers (ISPs)** provide access for a fee.
- Online services providers provide access plus additional services.

Connections

To access the Internet, you need to connect to a provider. Three types:

- **Direct** or **dedicated** lines directly connect to the Internet through expensive high-speed lines.
- **SLIP** and **PPP** connections use high-speed modems. They are widely used by individuals.
- **Terminal connections** also use high-speed modems but are not as fast or convenient as SLIP or PPP connections.

TCP/IP

TCP/IP (transmission control protocol/ Internet protocol) is the standard protocol of the Internet.

E-MAIL

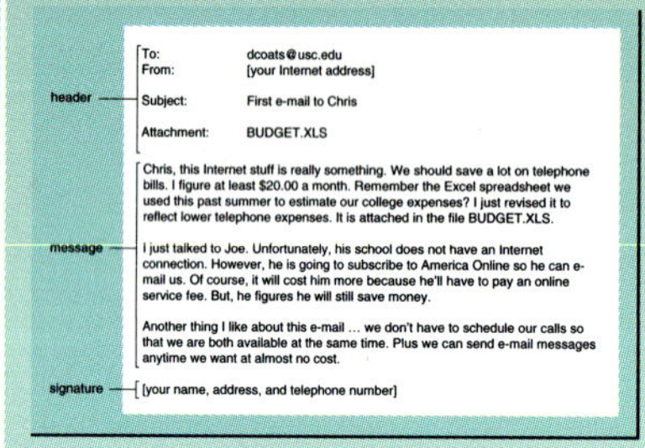

Basic Elements

An e-mail message has three basic elements:

- The **header** includes To, From, Subject, and Attachment lines
- The **message** is short and to the point
- The **signature** provides additional sender information

Addresses

The Internet uses the **domain name system (DNS)** addressing system.

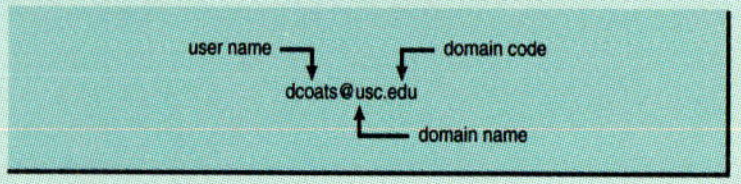

Netiquette

Netiquette is the accepted rules of etiquette when using the Internet.

DISCUSSION GROUPS

DISCUSSION GROUP TERMS

TERM	DESCRIPTION
Lurking	Reading news but not joining in to contribute
FAQ	Frequently asked question
Flaming	Insulting, a putting-down, or attacking
RFD	Request for discussion
Saint	Someone who aids new users by answsering questions
Thread	A sequence of ongoing messages on the same subject
Wizard	Someone who has comprehensive knowledge about a subject

Mailing Lists

Mailing lists send all messages to each member of a **list address.** You can subscribe and unsubscribe to a list by sending a request to the **subscription address.**

Newsgroups

Newgroups use a special network, **UseNet,** on which discussions are organized into topic areas and hierarchies.

Chat Groups

Chat groups allow direct "live" communication on selected topics or **channels. Internet Rely Chat (IRC)** is the most popular chat service.

Lurking

Lurking means to observe before contributing to a discussion.

INTERNET SERVICES

Telnet	Runs programs on remote computers
FTP	Uploads and downloads files
Gopher	Provides menus for available resources for one computer site
WAIS	Maintains lists of key words and phrases for several computer sites
Web	Uses hyperlinks to interrelated Web pages located worldwide

WORLD WIDE WEB

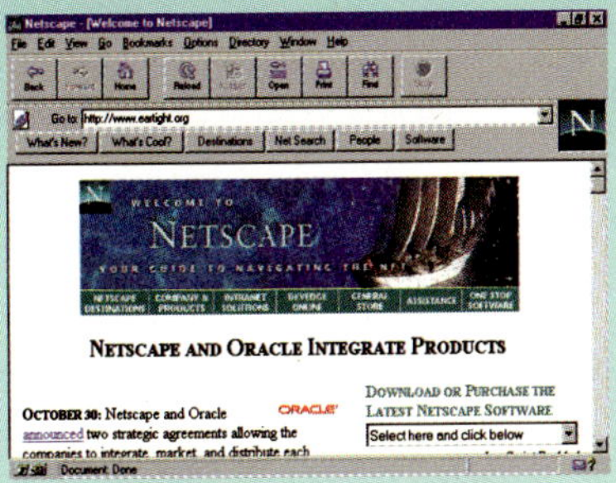

World Wide Web

The **World Wide Web** is also known as the **WWW** and the **Web.** It is widely used for entertainment, shopping, researching, and many other things.

Browsers

Browsers are programs that can access remote computers, open and transfer files, display text and images, and provide an interface to the Internet and the Web.

- **Uniform Resource Locators (URLs)** are addresses of available resources.

- **Web sites** are informational locations on the Web.

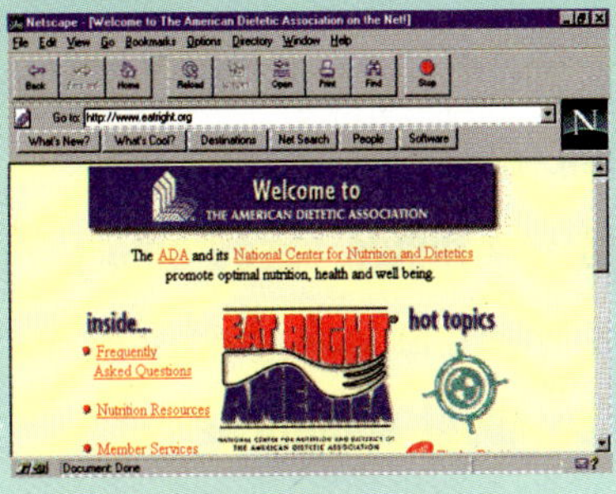

Web Pages

Web pages are created with **HTML (Hypertext Markup Language).** Browsers interpret HTML commands and display Web pages.

- **Home pages** are the first page at a Web site.
- **Java** is a programming language for creating special programs called **applets.** These programs are used to add interest and activity to a Web site.

Search Tools

Search tools are used to locate information on the Web. There are two basic types:

- **Indexes** are organized by categories. Searching involves moving from category to subcategories.
- **Search engines** are organized like databases. Searching involves specifying key words and phrases.

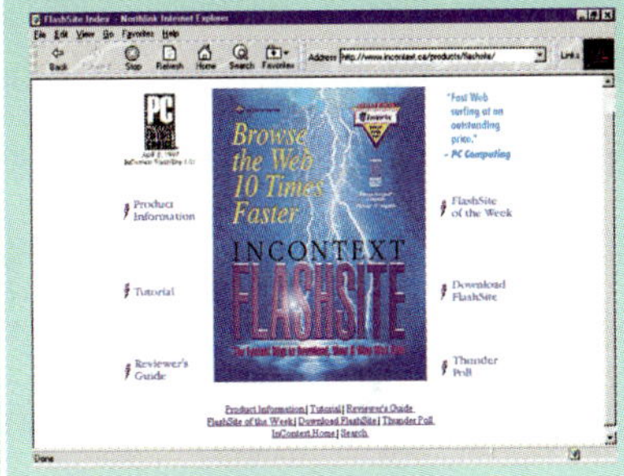

Web Utilities

Web utilities increase the performance of browsers. Two types:

- **Plug-ins** are automatically loaded. Widely used plug-ins include Shockwave from Macromedia, Quicktime from Apple, Live 3-D from Netscape.
- **Helper applications** are independent applications. There are four basic types:

HELPER APPLICATIONS

Off-line browsers	automatically connect to Web sites and download HTML documents for later viewing, also known **as Web-downloading utilities** and **pull products**
Information Pushers	automatically collect information on selected topics to be read later, also known as **Web Broadcasters** and **push products**
Off-line search utilities	automatically submit search requests to several indices and search engines, also known as **metasearch programs**
Filters	block out seleted sites and set connection time limits

The Buyer's Guide:

How to Buy Your Own Microcomputer System

Some people make snap judgments about some of the biggest purchases in their lives: cars, college educations, houses. People have been known to buy things based solely on an ad, a brief conversation, or a one-time look. And they may be making an impulsive decision about something costing thousands of dollars. Who is to blame, then, if they are disappointed later? They simply didn't take time to check it out.

The same concerns apply in buying a microcomputer system. You can make your choice on the basis of a friend's enthusiasm or a salesperson's promises. Or you can proceed more deliberately, as you would, say, in looking for a job.

Four Steps in Buying a Microcomputer System

The following is not intended to make buying a microcomputer an exhausting experience. Rather, it is to help you clarify your thinking about what you need and can afford.

The four steps in buying a microcomputer system are presented on the following pages. We divided each step into two parts on the assumption that your needs may change, but so may the money you have to spend on a microcomputer. For instance, later in your college career or after college graduation, you may want a far more powerful computer system than you need now. At that point you may have more money to spend. Or you may not need to spend money at all, if your employer provides you with a computer.

Step 1: What Needs Do I Want a Computer to Serve?

The trick is to distinguish between your needs and your wants. Sure, you *want* a cutting-edge system powerful enough to hold every conceivable record you'll ever need. And you want a system fast enough to process them all at the speed of light. But do you *need* this? Your main concern is to address the two-part question:

- What do I need a computer system to do for me today?
- What will I need it to do for me in another year or two?

The questionnaire at the end of this guide will help you determine the answers to both questions.

Suggestions

The first thing to establish is whether you need a computer at all. Some colleges offer computer facilities at the library or in some dormitories. Or perhaps you can borrow a roommate's. The problem, however, is that when you are up against a term-paper deadline, many others may be also. Then the machine you want may not be available. Perhaps all you need is a network computer or an Internet terminal. To determine the availability of campus computers and network support, call the computer center or the dean of students' office.

Another matter on which you might want advice is what type of computer is popular on campus. Some schools favor Apple Macintoshes, others favor IBMs or IBM-compatibles. If you own a system that's incompatible with most others on campus, you may be stuck if your computer breaks down. Ask someone knowledgeable who is a year or two ahead of you if your school favors one system over another.

Finally, look ahead and determine whether your major requires a computer. Business and engineering students may find one a necessity, physical education and drama majors less so. Your major may also determine the kind of computer that's best. A journalism major may want an IBM or IBM-compatible notebook that can be set up anywhere. An architecture major may want a powerful desktop Macintosh with a LaserWriter printer that can produce elaborate drawings. Ask your academic advisor for some recommendations.

Example

Suppose you are a college student beginning your sophomore year, with no major declared. Looking at the courses you will likely take this year, you decide you will probably need a computer mainly for word processing. That is, you need a system that will help you write short (10- to 20-page) papers for a variety of courses.

By this time next year, however, you may be an accounting major. Having talked to some juniors and seniors, you find that courses in this major, such as financial accounting, will require you to use elaborate spreadsheets. Or maybe you will be a fine arts or architectural major. Then you may be required to submit projects for which drawing and painting desktop publishing software would be helpful. Or perhaps you will be out in the job market and will be writing application letters and résumés. In that case, you'll want them to have a professional appearance.

Step 2: How Much Money Do I Have to Spend on a Computer System?

When you buy your first computer, you are not necessarily buying your last. Thus, you can think about spending just the bare-bones amount for a system that meets your needs while in college. Then you might plan to get another system later on. After all, most college students who own cars (quite often used cars) don't consider those the last cars they'll own. Of course, if you can afford it, buy an expensive system. That way, your computer will handle any kind of work required in your major and even after graduation.

You know what kind of money you have to spend. Your main concern is to answer this two-part question:

- How much am I prepared to spend on a computer system today?
- How much am I prepared to spend in another year or two?

The questionnaire at the end of this guide asks you this.

Suggestions

You can probably buy a used computer of some sort for under $400 and a printer for under $100. On the other hand, you might spend $1500 to $4500 on a new state-of-the-art system. When upgraded, this computer could meet your needs for the next five years.

There is nothing wrong with getting a used system, if you have a way of checking it out. For a reasonable fee, a computer-repair shop can examine it prior to your purchase. Look at newspaper ads and notices on campus bulletin boards for good buys on used equipment. Also try the Internet. Often the sellers will include a great deal of software and other items (disks, reference materials) with the package. If you stay with recognized brands such as Apple, IBM, Compaq, or Dell, you probably won't have any difficulties. The exception may be with printers, which, since they are principally mechanical devices, may get a lot of wear and tear. This is even more reason to tell the seller you want a repair shop to examine the equipment before you buy.

If you're buying new equipment, be sure to look for student discounts. Most college bookstores, for instance, offer special prices to students. Mail-order houses also steeply discount their products. These firms run ads in such periodicals as *Computer Shopper* (sold on newsstands) and other magazines as well as the Internet. However, using mail and telephone for repairs and support can be a nuisance. Often you can use the prices advertised by a mail-order house to get local retail computer stores to lower their prices.

Example

Perhaps you have access to a microcomputer at the campus student computing center, the library, or the dormitory. Or you can borrow a friend's. However, this computer isn't always available when it's convenient for you. Moreover, you're not only going to college but also working, so both time and money are tight. Having your own computer would enable you to write papers when it's convenient for you. Spending more than $500 might cause real hardship, so a new microcomputer system may be out of the question. You'll need to shop the newspaper classified ads or the campus bulletin boards to find a used but workable computer system.

Or, maybe you can afford to spend more now—say, between $1000 and $2000—but probably only $500 next year. By this time next year, however, you'll know your major and how your computer needs have changed. For example, if you're going to be a finance major, you need to have a lot more computer memory (primary storage). This will hold the massive amounts of data you'll be working with in your spreadsheets. Or maybe you'll be an architecture major or graduating and looking for a job. In that case, you'll need a laser printer to produce attractive-looking designs or application letters. Thus, whatever system you buy this year, you'll want to upgrade it next year.

Step 3: What Kind of Software Will Best Serve My Needs?

Most computer experts urge that you determine what software you need before you buy the hardware. The reasoning here is that some hardware simply won't run the software that is important to you. This is certainly true once you get into *sophisticated* software. Examples include specialized programs available for certain professions (such as certain agricultural or retail-management programs). However, if all you are interested in today are the basic tools of software—word processing, spreadsheet, and communications programs—these are available for nearly all microcomputers. The main caution is that some more recent versions of application software won't run on older hardware. Still, if someone offers you a free computer, don't say no "because I have to decide what software I need first." You will no doubt find it sufficient for many general purposes, especially during the early years in college.

That said, you are better served if you follow step 3 after step 2—namely, finding the answers to the two-part question:

- What kind of software will best serve my needs today?
- What kind will best serve my needs in another year or two?

The questionnnaire at the end of this guide may help you determine your answers.

Suggestions

No doubt some kinds of application software are more popular on your campus—and in certain departments on your campus—than others. Are freshman and sophomore students mainly writing their term papers in Word, WordPerfect, or Ami Pro? Which spreadsheet is most often used by business students: Excel, Lotus 1-2-3, or Quattro Pro? Which desktop publishing program is most favored by graphic arts majors: PageMaker, Ventura Publisher, or First Publisher? Do many students use their microcomputers to access the Internet, and, if so, which communications software is the favorite? Do engineering and architecture majors use their own machines for CAD/CAM applications? Start by asking other students and your academic advisor.

If you're looking to buy state-of-the-art software, you'll find plenty of advice in various computer magazines. Several of them rate the quality of newly issued programs. Such periodicals include *InfoWorld, PC World, PC/Computing,* and *MacWorld.*

Example

Suppose you determine that all you need is software to help you write short papers. In that case, nearly any kind of word processing program would do. You could even get by with some older versions or off-brand kinds of word processing software. This might happen if such software was included in the sale of a used microcomputer that you bought at a bargain price.

But will this software be sufficient a year or two from now? Looking ahead, you guess that you'll major in theater arts, and minor in screenwriting, which you may pursue as a career. At that point a simple word processing program won't do. You learn from juniors and seniors in that department that screenplays are written using special screenwriting programs. This is software that's not available for some computers. Or, as an advertising and marketing major, you're expected to turn word-processed promotional pieces into brochures. For this, you need desktop publishing software. Or, as a physics major, you discover you will need to write reports on a word processor that can handle equations. This requires a machine with a great deal of memory. In short, you need to look at your software needs not just for today but also for the near future. You especially want to consider what programs will be useful to you in building your career.

Step 4: What Kind of Hardware Will Best Serve My Needs?

A bare-bones hardware system might include a three-year-old desktop or portable computer with a 3½-inch floppy disk drive and a hard-disk drive. It should also include a monitor and a printer. With a newer system, the sky's the limit. On the one hand, as a student—unless you're involved in some very specialized activities—it's doubtful you'll really need such things as voice-input devices, touch screens, scanners, and the like. On the other hand, you will probably need speakers and a CD-ROM or DVD-ROM drive. The choices of equipment are vast.

As with the other steps, the main task is to find the answers to a two-part question:

- What kind of hardware will best serve my needs today?
- What kind will best serve my needs in another year or two?

There are several questions on the questionnaire at the end of this guide to help you determine answers to these concerns.

Suggestions

Clearly, you should let the software be your guide in determining your choice of hardware. Perhaps you've found that the most popular software in your department runs on a Macintosh rather than an IBM-compatible. If so, that would seem to determine your general brand of hardware.

Whether you buy IBM or Macintosh, a desktop or a portable, we suggest you get a 3½-inch floppy disk drive, a hard-disk drive with at least 2 gigabytes of storage, a CD-ROM or DVD-ROM drive, at least 32 megabytes of memory, and an ink-jet printer.

As with software, several computer magazines not only describe new hardware but also issue ratings. See *InfoWorld, PC World,* and *MacWorld,* for example.

Example

Right now, let's say, you're mainly interested in using a computer to write papers, so almost anything would do. But you need to look ahead.

Suppose you find that WordPerfect seems to be the software of choice around your campus. You find that WordPerfect 5.0 will run well on a 486 machine with 4 megabytes of memory and a 120-megabyte hard disk. A near-letter-quality dot-matrix printer will probably be acceptable for most papers. Although this equipment is now outdated, you find from looking at classified ads that there are many such used machines around. Plus, they cost very little—well under $500 for a complete system.

If you're a history or philosophy major, maybe this is all the hardware and software you need. Indeed, this configuration may be just fine all the way through college. However, some majors, and the careers following them, may require more sophisticated equipment. Your choice then becomes: Should I buy an inexpensive system now that can't be upgraded, then sell it later and buy a better one? Or should I buy at least some of the components of a good system now and upgrade it over the next year or so?

As an advertising major, you see the value of learning desktop publishing. This will be a useful if not essential skill once you embark on a career. In exploring the software, you learn that Word includes some desktop publishing capabilities. However, the hardware you previously considered simply isn't sufficient. Morever, you learn from reading about software and talking to people in your major that there are better desktop publishing programs. Specialized desktop publishing programs like Ventura Publisher are considered more versatile than Word. Probably the best software arrangement, in fact, is to have Word as a word processing program and Ventura Publisher running under Windows for a desktop publishing program.

To be sure, the campus makes computers that will run this software available to students. If you can afford it, however, you're better off having your own. Now, however, we're talking about a major expense. A computer running a Pentium MMX microprocessor, with 32 megabytes of memory, a 3½-inch disk drive, a CD-ROM disk drive, and a 3.2-gigabyte hard disk, plus a modem, color monitor, and laser printer, could cost in excess of $2000.

Perhaps the best idea is to buy now, knowing how you would like your system to grow in the future. That is, you will buy a microcomputer with a Pentium MMX microprocessor. But at this point, you will buy only an ink-jet printer and not buy a CD-ROM drive. Next year or the year following, you might sell off the less sophisticated peripheral devices and add a CD-ROM drive and a laser printer.

Developing a Philosophy About Computer Purchasing

It's important not to develop a case of "computer envy." Even if you bought the latest, most expensive microcomputer system, in a matter of months, something better will come along. Computer technology is still in a very dynamic state, with more powerful, versatile, and compact systems constantly hitting the marketplace. So what if your friends have the hottest new piece of software or hardware? The main question is: Do you need it to solve the tasks required of you or to keep up in your field? Or can you get along with something simpler but equally serviceable?

The Buyer's Guide: How to Buy Your Own Microcomputer System

To help clarify your thinking about buying a microcomputer system, complete the questionnaire below by checking the appropriate boxes.

NEEDS

What do I need a computer system to do for me today? In another year or two?

I wish to use the computer for:

	Today	1–2 years
Word processing—writing papers, letters, memos, or reports	❑	❑
Business or financial applications—balance sheets, sales projections, expense budgets, or accounting problems	❑	❑
Record-keeping and sorting—research bibliographies, scientific data, or address files	❑	❑
Graphic presentations—of business, scientific, or social science data	❑	❑
Online information retrieval—to campus networks, service providers, or the Internet	❑	❑
Publications, design, or drawing—for printed newsletters, architectural drawing, or graphic arts	❑	❑
Multimedia—for video games, viewing, creating, presenting, or research	❑	❑
Other—(Specify): ___________	❑	❑

BUDGET

How much am I prepared to spend on a system today? In another year or two?

I can spend:

	Today	1–2 years
Under $500	❑	❑
Up to $1000	❑	❑
Up to $1500	❑	❑
Up to $2000	❑	❑
Up to $2500	❑	❑
Over $3000 (specify) ___________	❑	❑

BUYING A MICROCOMPUTER SYSTEM

STEP	QUESTIONS
1	*My Needs:* What do I need a computer system to do for me today? In another year or two?
2	*My Budget:* How much am I prepared to spend on a system today? In another year or two?
3	*My Software:* What kind of software will best serve my needs today? In another year or two?
4	*My Hardware:* What kind of hardware will best serve my needs today? In another year or two?

SOFTWARE

What kinds of software will best serve my needs today? In another year or two?

The application software I need includes:

	Today	1–2 years
Word processing—Word, WordPerfect, Word Pro, or other (specify): ____________	❑	❑
Spreadsheet—Excel, Lotus 1-2-3, Quattro Pro, or other (specify): ____________	❑	❑
Database—Access, dBASE, Paradox, Approach, or other (specify): ____________	❑	❑
Presentation Graphics—PowerPoint, Freelance, Corel Presentations, or other (specify): ____________	❑	❑
PIM—Organizer, Outlook, or other (specify): ____________	❑	❑
Browsers—Netscape Navigator, Microsoft Internet Explorer, or NCSA Mosaic	❑	❑
Other—integrated packages, software suites, graphics, multimedia, Web Publishers, CAD/CAM, other (specify): ____________	❑	❑

The system software I need:

	Today	1–2 years
Windows 95	❑	❑
Windows 98	❑	❑
Windows NT	❑	❑
OS/2	❑	❑
Macintosh	❑	❑
Unix	❑	❑
Other (specify): ____________	❑	❑

HARDWARE

What kinds of hardware will best serve my needs today? In another year or two?

The hardware I need includes:

	Today	1–2 years
Microprocessor—Pentium MMX, Pentium Pro, Pentium II 68040, Power PC, other (specify): ____________	❑	❑
Memory—(specify amount): ____________	❑	❑
Monitor—monochrome, color, size, (specify): ____________	❑	❑
Floppy disk drives—3½″ and/or 5¼″ (specify size of drive): ____________	❑	❑
Optical disk drive—CD-ROM, DVD-ROM, WORM, erasable (specify type, speed, and capacity): ____________	❑	❑
Hard-disk drive—(specify capacity): ____________	❑	❑
Portable computer—laptop, notebook, subnotebook, personal digital assistant (specify): ____________	❑	❑
Printer—ink-jet, laser, dot-matrix, color (specify): ____________	❑	❑
Other—modem, speakers, fax, surge protector (specify): ____________	❑	❑

Glossary

Access: Refers to the responsibility of those having data to control who is able to use that data.

Access arm: The arm that holds the read-write head and moves back and forth over the surface of a disk.

Access time: The period between the time the computer requests data from a secondary storage device and the time the transfer of data is completed.

Accounts payable: The activity that shows the money a company owes to its suppliers for the materials and services it has received.

Accounts receivable: The activity that shows what money has been received or is owed by customers.

Accuracy: Relates to the responsibility of those who collect data to ensure that the data is correct.

Active-matrix monitor: Monitor in which each pixel is independently activated. More colors with better clarity can be displayed.

Ada: Procedural language named after an English countess regarded as the first programmer; was originally designed for weapons systems but has commercial uses as well. Because of its structured design, modules of a large program can be written, compiled, and tested separately before the entire program is put together.

Adapter card: *See* Expansion board

Add-on: *See* Helper applications

Address: Location in main memory in which characters of data or instructions are stored during processing.

Agent: Program for updating search engine. Also called bot and spider.

Alignment: Refers to even margins in a document; may be left or right.

ALU: *See* Arithmetic-logic unit

American Standard Code of Information Interchange: *See* ASCII

Analog signal: Signal that represents a range of frequencies, such as the human voice.

Analytical graphs: Form of graphics used to put numeric data into forms that are easier to analyze, such as bar charts, line graphs, and pie charts.

Animation: Feature involving special visual and sound effects.

Applets: Java programs used on Web pages.

Application generator: Software with modules that have been preprogrammed to accomplish various tasks, such as calculation of overtime pay.

Application software: Software that can perform useful work, such as word processing, cost estimating, or accounting tasks.

Arithmetic-logic unit (ALU): The part of the CPU that performs arithmetic and logical operations.

Artificial intelligence(AI): A field of computer science that attempts to develop computer systems that can mimic or simulate human thought processes and actions.

Artificial reality: *See* Virtual reality

ASCII (American Standard Code for Information Interchange): Binary coding scheme widely used on all computers, including microcomputers.

Assembly language: Second generation of programming languages. These languages use abbreviations for program instructions.

Asynchronous communications port: *See* Serial port

Asynchronous transmission: Method whereby data is sent and received one byte at a time.

Automated design tool: Software package that evaluates hardware and software alternatives according to requirements given by the systems analyst.

Backup: Duplicate copy of a disk or program.

Backup tape cartridge unit: *See* Magnetic tape streamer

Bandwidth: Bit-per-second transmission capability of a channel.

Bar code: Code consisting of vertical zebra-striped marks printed on product containers; read with a bar-code reader.

Bar-code reader: Photoelectric scanner that reads bar codes for processing.

BASIC (Beginner's All-purpose Symbolic Instruction Code): Easy-to-learn procedural programming language widely used on microcomputers.

Basic input-output system: Type of system software consisting of programs that interpret keyboard characters or transmit characters to monitor or disk.

Batch processing: Processing performed all at once on data that has been collected over several days.

Baud rate: Communication speed; the number of changes in the electrical state in the line per second. At low speeds, baud rate is equal to bits per second (bps), but at higher speeds it is not.

BBS: *See* Electronic bulletin board system

Binary system: Numbering system in which all numbers consist of only two digits—0 and 1.

Bit (binary digit): A 0 or 1 in the binary system.

Bitmap file: Graphic file in which image is made up of thousands of dots (pixels).

Booting: Loading the operating system from hard or floppy disk into memory when the computer is turned on.

Bootstrap loader: Program that is stored permanently in the computer's electronic circuitry. When the computer is turned on, the bootstrap loader obtains the operating system from a hard or floppy disk and loads it into memory.

Bot: *See* Agent

Broadband: Bandwidth that includes microwave, satellite, coaxial cable, and fiber-optic channels. It is used for very high-speed computers.

Browser: Special Internet software that allows users to effortlessly jump from one computer's resources to another computer's resources.

Bus (bus line): Electronic data roadway, connecting the parts of the CPU to each other and linking the CPU with other important hardware, along which bits travel. Also, the common connecting cable in a bus network.

Bus network: Network in which all communications travel along a common path. Each device in the network handles its own communications control. There is no host computer or file server.

Byte: Unit consisting of eight bits. There are 256 possible bit combinations in a byte.

C: General-purpose procedural language originally designed for writing operating systems. Widely used and portable.

C++: One of the most widely used object-oriented programming languages.

Cable modem: Allows all digital communication; speed of 27 million bps.

Cache memory: Area of random-access memory (RAM) set aside to store the most frequently accessed information. Acts as a temporary high-speed holding zone between memory and CPU.

CAD: *See* Computer-aided design

CAM: *See* Computed-aided manufacturing

Carpal tunnel syndrome: Disorder found among frequent computer users, consisting of damage to nerves and tendons in the hands. *See also* Repetitive stress injury

CASE tool: *See* Automated design tool

Cathode-ray tube (CRT): Desktop-type monitor built in the same way as a television set. The most common type of monitor for the office and the home. These monitors are typically placed directly on the system unit or on the top of the desk.

CD-R: Optical disk that can be written to once. After that it can be read many times without deterioration and cannot be written on or erased.

CD-ROM (compact disk read-only memory): Optical disk that allows data to be read but not recorded.

CD-RW (compact disk rewriteable): Optical disk that is not permanently altered when data is recorded.

Cell: Intersection of a row and a column in a spreadsheet. A cell holds a single unit of information.

Cell address: Position of a cell in a spreadsheet.

Cell pointer: Indicator for where data is to be entered or changed in a spreadsheet.

Central processing unit (CPU): Part of the computer that holds data and program instructions for processing the data. The CPU consists of the control unit and the arithmetic-logic unit. In a microcomputer, the CPU is on a single electronic component, the microprocessor chip.

Character-based interface: Arrangement in DOS in which users issue commands by typing or selecting items from a menu.

Checklist: List of questions that helps in guiding the systems analyst and end user through key issues for the present system.

Child node: A node one level below the node being considered in a hierarchical database or network.

Chip: A tiny circuit board etched on a small square of sandlike material called silicon.

Chlorofluorocarbon (CFC): Toxic chemical found in solvents and cleaning agents. A chlorofluorocarbon can travel into the atmosphere and deplete the earth's ozone layer.

CISC (complex instruction set computer) chip: The most common type of microprocessor that has thousands of programs written specifically for it.

Client/server network system: Network in which one powerful computer coordinates and supplies services to all other nodes on the network. Server nodes coordinate and supply specialized services, and client nodes request the services.

Clip art: Graphics enhancement that enables the user to include available graphic images in a document.

Closed architecture: Computer manufactured in such a way that users cannot easily add new devices.

Coaxial cable: High-frequency transmission cable that replaces the multiple wires of telephone lines with a single solid-copper core.

COBOL (Common Business-Oriented Language): Procedural language most frequently used in business.

Coding: Actual writing of a program.

Cold site: Special emergency facility in which hardware must be installed but which is available to a company in the event of a disaster to its computer system. *Compare* Hot site

Collaborative technology: *See* Groupware

Column: Part of the grid of a spreadsheet. Columns are labeled across the top.

Command line interface: *See* Character-based interface

Common operational database: Integrated collection of records that contain details about the operations of a company.

Common user database: Company database that contains selected information both from the common operational database and from outside (proprietary) databases.

Communications Act of 1996: Made it a federal crime to publish obscene material that could be seen by minors on Internet.

Company database: Collection of integrated records shared throughout a company or other organization.

Compiler: Software that converts the programmer's procedural-language program (source code) into machine language (object code).

Computer: Electronic device that can follow instructions to accept input, process that input, and produce information.

Computer-aided design (CAD): Type of program that manipulates images on a screen.

Computer-aided manufacturing (CAM): Type of program that controls automated factory equipment, including machine tools and robots.

Computer-aided software engineering (CASE) tool: *See* Automated design tool

Computer competent: Being able to use a computer to meet one's information needs.

Computer crime: Illegal action in which a perpetrator uses special knowledge of computer technology. Criminals may be employees, outside users, hackers and crackers, and organized crime members.

Computer Fraud and Abuse Act of 1986: Law allowing prosecution of unauthorized access to computers and databases.

Computer Matching and Privacy Protection Act of 1988: Law setting procedures for computer matching of federal data for verifying eligibility for federal benefits or for recovering delinquent debts.

Computer network: Communications system connecting two or more computers and their peripheral devices.

Computer program: *See* Software

Computer trainer: Computer professional who provides classes to instruct users.

Computer virus: Hidden instructions that migrate through networks and operating systems and become embedded in different programs. They may be designed to destroy data or simply to display messages.

Connectivity: Capability of the microcomputer to use information from the world beyond one's desk. Data and information can be sent over telephone or cable lines and through the air.

Context-sensitive help: Feature of most application software that locates and displays reference information directly related to the task the user is performing.

Continuous speech recognition system: Voice-recognition system used to control a microcomputer's operations and to issue commands to special application programs.

Controller card: *See* Expansion board

Control unit: Section of the CPU that tells the rest of the computer how to carry out program instructions.

Conventional memory: First 640 kilobytes of RAM.

Conversion: *See* Systems implementation

Cookies: Programs that record information on Web site visitors.

Copy: Duplicate; in word processing, moving selected portions of text from one location to another.

CPU: *See* Central processing unit

CRT monitor: *See* Cathode-ray tube (CRT) monitor

Cumulative-trauma disorder: *See* Repetitive strain injury

Cursor: Blinking symbol on the screen that shows where data may be entered.

Cursor control keys: Special keys that are used to move the cursor.

Custom-made software: Software designed by a professional programmer for a particular purpose.

Custom program: *See* Custom-made software

Cut: In word processing, this command removes a portion of highlighted text to be moved from the screen.

Cyberspace: The space of electronic movement of ideas and information.

Data: Raw, unprocessed facts that are input to a computer system.

Database administrator (DBA): Person in a large organization who determines the structure of the large databases and evaluates the performance of the database management system.

Database file: File containing highly structured and organized data.

Database management system (DBMS): *See* Database manager

Database manager: Software package used to set up, or structure, a database.

Data communications system: Electronic system that transmits data over communications lines from one location to another.

Data compression/decompression: Method of improving performance by reducing the amount of space required to store data and programs. In data compression, data is scanned for ways to reduce the amount of required storage as it is entered. One way is to search for repeating patterns, which are replaced with a token, leaving enough so that the original can be rebuilt or decompressed.

Data dictionary: Dictionary containing a description of the structure of the data in a database.

Data flow diagram: Diagram showing the data or information flow within an information system.

Data processing system (DPS): Transaction processing system that keeps track of routine operations and records these events in a database.

Data security: Protection of software and data from unauthorized tampering or damage.

DAT drive: *See* Digital audiotape (DAT) drive

DBA: *See* Database administrator

Debugging: Programmer's word for testing and then eliminating errors in a program.

Decision model: Strategic, tactical, or operational model that gives the decision support system its analytical capabilities.

Decision support system (DSS): Flexible tool for analysis that helps managers make decisions about unstructured problems, such as the effect of events and trends outside the organization.

Decision table: Table showing the decision rules that apply when certain conditions occur and what action should take place as a result.

Demand report: The opposite of a scheduled report. A demand report is produced on request.

Demodulation: Process performed by a modem in converting analog signals to digital signals.

Desk checking: Process of checking out a computer program by studying the program listing line by line, looking for syntax and logic errors.

Desktop computer: Computer small enough to fit on top or along the side of a desk and yet too big to carry around.

Desktop manager: *See* Personal information manager (PIM)

Desktop publishing: Program that allows you to mix text and graphics to create publications of professional quality.

Diagnostic routine: Program stored in the computer's electronic circuitry that starts up when the machine is turned on. It tests the primary storage, the CPU, and other parts of the system.

Dialog box: Box that frequently appears on the screen after selecting a command from a pull-down menu. It is used to specify additional command options.

Dial-up connection: Method of accessing the Internet using a high-speed modem and standard telephone lines.

Digital audiotape (DAT) drive: Backup technology that uses 2- by 3-inch cassettes that store 1.3 gigabytes or more.

Digital camera: Similar to a traditional camera except that images are recorded digitally in the camera's memory rather than on film.

Digital signal: Signal that represents the presence or absence of an electronic pulse.

Digitizer: Device that can be used to trace or copy a drawing or photograph. The shape is converted to digital data that can be represented on a screen or printed on paper.

Digitizing tablet: Device that enables the user to create images using a special stylus.

Direct access storage: Form of storage that allows the user to directly access information.

Direct approach: Approach for systems implementation whereby the old system is simply abandoned for the new.

Direct entry: Form of input that does not require data to be keyed by someone sitting at a keyboard. Direct-entry devices create machine-readable data on paper or magnetic media or feed it directly into the CPU.

Direct file organization: File organization that makes use of key fields to go directly to the record being sought rather than reading records one after another.

Direct-image plotter: Plotter that creates images using heat-sensitive paper and electrically heated pins.

Directional arrow keys: Keys labeled with arrows that are used to move the cursor.

Disaster recovery plan: Plan used by large organizations describing ways to continue operations following a disaster until normal computer operations can be restored.

Discrete-word recognition system: Voice-recognition system that allows users to dictate directly into a microcomputer using a microphone.

Disk: *See* Floppy disk; Hard disk; Optical disk

Disk caching: Method of improving hard-disk performance by anticipating data needs. It requires a combination of hardware and software.

Disk drive: Input mechanism that obtains stored data and programs from a disk. It also stores data and programs on a disk.

Diskette: *See* Floppy disk

Display screen: *See* Monitor

Distributed database: Database that can be made accessible through a variety of communications networks, which allows portions of the database to be located in different places.

Document: Any kind of text material.

Documentation: Written descriptions and procedures about a program and how to use it.

Document file: File created by a word processor to save documents such as letters, research papers, and memos.

Domain code: Last part of an Internet address, which identifies the geographical description or organizational identification.

Domain name: Part of an Internet address, separated from the domain code by a dot (.), that is a reference to a particular organization.

Domain name system (DNS): Internet addressing method that assigns names and numbers to people and computers.

DOS: The standard operating system for IBM and IBM-compatible microcomputers.

Dot-matrix printer: Printer that forms characters or images by using a matrix of pins that strike an inked ribbon.

DO UNTIL structure: Loop structure in programming that appears at the end of a loop. The DO UNTIL loop means that the loop statements will be executed at least once.

DO WHILE structure: Loop structure in programming that appears at the beginning of a loop. The DO WHILE loop will keep executing as long as there is information to be processed.

Downloading: Process of transferring information from a remote computer to the computer one is using.

Draw program: Program used to help create artwork for publications. *See also* Illustration program.

Drive gate: Door covering the slot in a disk drive into which a disk is inserted.

DSS: *See* Decision support system

Dumb terminal: Terminal that can be used to input and receive data but cannot process data independently.

DVD (digital versatile disk): Similar to CD-ROMs except that more data can be packed into the same amount of space.

EBCDIC (Extended Binary Coded Decimal Interchange Code): Binary coding scheme that is a standard for minicomputers and mainframe computers.

Edit: Word processing feature that makes revising and updating easy.

EIS: *See* Executive information system

EISA: *See* Extended Industry Standard Architecture

Electronic bulletin board system (BBS): Electronically posted information on a computer that can be accessed by other computers using telephone lines.

Electronic Communications Privacy Act of 1986: Law protecting the privacy of users on public electronic-mail systems.

Electronic mail (e-mail): Similar to an electronic bulletin board, but provides confidentiality and may use special communications rather than telephone lines.

Electronic spreadsheet: *See* Spreadsheet

Electronic town: Concept that helps us visualize the convergence of electronic resources that are available to members of a community.

Electrostatic plotter: Plotter that uses electrostatic charges to create images made up of tiny dots on specially treated paper.

E-mail: *See* Electronic mail

Encrypting: Coding information so that only the user can read or otherwise use it.

End user: Person who uses microcomputers or has access to larger computers.

Energy Star: Program created by the EPA (Environmental Protection Agency) to discourage waste in the microcomputer industry.

Enter key: Key used to enter a command after it has been typed into the computer.

Enterprise computing: System in which a user on one network in an organization can access resources available throughout the organization.

Erasable optical disk: Optical disk on which the disk drive can write information and also erase and rewrite information.

Erase: Remove, as in removing obsolete electronic files from a disk.

Ergonomics: Study of human factors related to computers.

ESS: *See* Executive support system

Ethics: Standards of moral conduct.

Exception report: Report that calls attention to unusual events.

Executive information system (EIS): Sophisticated software that can draw together data from an organization's databases in meaningful patterns.

Executive support system (ESS): *See* Executive information system

Expanded memory: Special "island" of memory of up to 32 megabytes that exists outside of the DOS 640-kilobyte limit. Intended to help older microprocessors that cannot directly access memory over 1 megabyte.

Expansion board: Optional device that plugs into a slot inside the system unit. Ports on the board allow cables to be connected from the expansion board to devices outside the system unit.

Expert system: Computer program that provides advice to decision makers who would otherwise rely on human experts.

Extended Binary Coded Decimal Interchange Code: *See* EBCDIC

Extended Industry Standard Architecture (EISA): The 32-bit bus standard developed by nine manufacturers of IBM-compatible microcomputers.

Extended memory: Directly accessible memory above 1 megabyte.

External modem: Modem that stands apart from the computer and is connected by a cable to the computer's serial port. Another cable connects the modem to the telephone wall jack.

Facsimile transmission machine: *See* Fax machine

Fair Credit Reporting Act of 1970: Law prohibiting credit agencies from sharing credit information with anyone but authorized customers and giving consumers the right to review and correct their credit records.

Fax machine: Device that scans an image and sends it electronically over telephone lines to a receiving fax machine, which converts the electronic signals back to an image and recreates it on paper.

Fax modem: Special modem that enables the user to send and/or receive faxes.

Fax/modem board: Expansion board that provides the independent capabilities of a fax and a modem.

Fiber-optic cable: Special transmission cable made of glass tubes that are immune to electronic interference. Data is transmitted through fiber-optic cables in the form of pulses of light.

Field: Each column of information within a record is called a field. A field contains a set of related characters.

Filter: Program to block selected Web sites, set time limits, monitor use, and generate reports on use.

Find: In word processing, a command that allows the user to locate any character, word, or phrase in a document.

Firewall: Security hardware and software.

FireWire port: Used to connect high-speed printers and even video-cameras to system unit.

Firmware: Read-only memory.

Flat-panel monitor: Monitor that lies flat instead of standing upright.

Flexible disk: *See* Floppy disk

Floppy: *See* Floppy disk

Floppy disk: Flat, circular piece of magnetically treated mylar plastic that rotates within a jacket.

Formatting (of disk): Preparation of a disk so that it will accept data or programs in a computer. Also called initializing.

Formatting (of text): Enhancement of text by adding bold, underline, and italics, and changing type font and size and document margins.

Form-letter feature: *See* Mail merge

Formula: Instructions for calculations in a spreadsheet.

FORTRAN (FORmula TRANslation): Most widely used scientific and mathematical procedural language.

Freedom of Information Act of 1970: Law giving citizens the right to examine data about them in federal government files, except for that restricted for national security reasons.

Free-Net: Electronic community that is free not only for the members of the town but for others as well.

FTP (file transfer protocol): Internet service for transferring files.

FTP site: Computer on the Internet that allows copying of its files.

Full-duplex communication: Mode of communication in which data is transmitted back and forth at the same time.

Function: In a spreadsheet, a built-in formula that performs calculations automatically.

Function key: Key used for tasks that occur frequently, such as underlining in word processing.

Gantt chart: Chart using bars and lines to indicate the time scale of a series of tasks.

GB, G-byte: *See* Gigabyte

General ledger: Activity that produces income statements and balance sheets based on all transactions of a company.

Generations of programming languages: The five generations are machine languages, assembly languages, procedural languages, problem-oriented languages, and natural languages.

Gigabyte (GB, G-byte): Unit representing about 1 billion bytes.

Goal-seeking tool: Program tool used to find the values needed to achieve a particular end result.

Gopher: Program that helps individuals on the Internet to access other computers on the Internet.

Gopher site: Internet computer that provides menus describing its available resources and direct links to the resources.

Grammar checker: In word processing, a tool that identifies poorly worded sentences and incorrect grammar.

Graphical user interface (GUI): Special screen that allows software commands to be issued through the use of graphic symbols (icons) or pull-down menus.

Graphic suite: Group of graphic programs offered at lower cost than if purchased separately.

Green PC: Microcomputer industry concept of an environmentally friendly, low-power-consuming machine.

Grid chart: Chart that shows the relationship between input and output documents.

Group decision support system (GDSS): System used to support the collective work of a team addressing large problems.

Groupware: Software that allows two or more people on a communications network to work on the same document at the same time. *Also* called collaborative technology.

GUI: *See* Graphical user interface

Hacker: Person who gains unauthorized access to a computer system for the fun and challenge of it.

Half-duplex communication: Mode of communication in which data flows in both directions, but not simultaneously.

Handheld PC: *See* Personal digital assistant (PDA)

Hard copy: Images output on paper by a printer or plotter.

Hard disk: Enclosed disk drive that contains one or more metallic disks. A hard disk has many times the capacity of a floppy disk.

Hard-disk cartridge: Hard disk that is easily removed.

Hard-disk pack: Several platters aligned one above the other, thereby offering much greater storage capacity.

Hardware: Equipment that includes a keyboard, monitor, printer, the computer itself, and other devices.

Hashing: Program that uses mathematical operations to convert the key field's numeric value to a particular storage address.

Head crash: Occurs when the surface of the read-write head or particles on its surface contact the magnetic disk surface.

Help: A feature in most application software providing options that typically include an index, a glossary, and a search feature to locate reference information about specific commands.

Helper applications: Independent programs that can be executed by a browser. Also called add-ons.

Hierarchical database: Database in which fields or records are structured in nodes.

Hierarchical network: Network consisting of several computers linked to a central host computer. The computers linked to the host are themselves hosts to other computers or devices.

High-definition television (HDTV): All-digital television that delivers a much clearer and more detailed wide-screen picture.

History file: Created by browser to store information on Web sites visited.

Home page: Top-level or opening page of Web site.

Home PC: Specialized large-screen system with high-quality audio.

Host computer: A large centralized computer. A common way of accessing the Internet. The host computer is connected to the Internet and provides a path or connection for individuals to access the Internet.

Hot site: Special emergency facility consisting of a fully equipped computer center available to a company in the event of disaster to its computer system. *Compare* Cold site

HTML: *See* Hypertext Markup Language (HTML)

HTML editor: *See* Web authoring program

Hybrid network: *See* Hierarchical network

Hypermedia: *See* Multimedia

Hypermedia database: Database using object-oriented technology to store and link a wide range of data including graphics, animation, video, music, and voice.

Hypertext: Documents that have highlighted text that identifies links to other pages of information.

Hypertext link: On the Web, links that allow users to jump effortlessly from one computer's resources to another computer's resources.

Hypertext Markup Language (HTML): Programming language for the document files that are used to display Web pages.

Icon: Graphic symbol on a pull-down menu that represents a command.

IF-THEN-ELSE structure: Logical selection structure whereby one of two paths is followed according to IF, THEN, and ELSE statements in a program.

Illustration program: Used to modify vector images and thus create line art, 3-D models, and virtual reality. Also called draw program.

Image editor: Used to create and modify bitmap files. Also called paint program.

Image scanner: Device that identifies images on a page and automatically converts them to electronic signals that can be stored in a computer.

Index: Type of search tool that organizes documents by categories. Also called Web directories.

Index sequential file organization: Compromise between sequential and direct file organization. Records are stored sequentially, but an index is used to access a group of records directly.

Individual database: Collection of integrated records useful mainly to just one person.

Industry Standard Architecture (ISA): Bus-line standard developed for the IBM Personal Computer. It first consisted of an 8-bit-wide data path, then a 16-bit-wide data path.

Information: Data that has been processed by a computer system.

Information pusher: Program that automatically gathers information on topics of your choice and saves it on your hard disk. Also called push product and Web Broadcaster utility.

Information superhighway: Term to describe the future of communication networks and computers. *See also* Internet

Information system: Collection of hardware, software, people, data, and procedures that work together to provide information essential to running an organization.

Information worker: Employee that creates, distributes, and communicates information.

Initializing: *See* Formatting

Ink-jet plotter: Plotter that forms images by spraying droplets of ink onto paper.

Ink-jet printer: Printer that sprays small droplets of ink at high speed onto the surface of the paper.

Input device: Piece of equipment that puts data into a form a computer can process.

Insertion point: The cursor on the display screen. It shows the user where data can be entered next.

Integrated circuit: *See* Silicon chip

Integrated package: Collection of computer programs that work together and share information.

Intelligent terminal: Terminal that includes a processing unit, memory, secondary storage, communications software, and a telephone hookup or other communications link.

Interactive: Describes activity in which there is immediate communication between the user and the computer system.

Interface card: *See* Expansion board

Interlaced monitor: Monitor that creates images by scanning down the screen, skipping every other line.

Internal hard disk: Storage device consisting of one or more metallic platters sealed inside a container. Internal hard disks are installed inside the system cabinet of a microcomputer.

Internal modem: Modem that is a plug-in circuit board located inside the system unit.

Internal storage: *See* Memory

Internet: A huge computer network available to nearly everyone with a microcomputer and a means to connect to it. It is a resource for information about an infinite number of topics.

Internet service provider (ISP): Provides access to the Internet.

Internet terminal: Provides access to the Internet and displays Web pages on a standard television set. Also called Web terminal.

Interpreter: Software that converts a procedural language one statement at a time into machine language just before the statement is executed.

Intranet: Like the Internet but privately owned by an organization.

Inventory: Material or products that a company has in stock.

ISA: *See* Industry Standard Architecture

ISDN: Allows all digital communication; speed of 128,000 bps.

ISP: *See* Internet service provider

ITV (interactive TV): Cable television service that provides videos on demand, video games, interactive shopping, and an array of entertainment and informational services.

Jacket: Protective outer covering for a floppy disk.

Java: A portable programming language.

K, KB, K-byte: *See* Kilobyte

Keyboard: Input device that looks like a typewriter keyboard but has additional keys.

Key field: Group of logically related characters in a file record used for sorting purposes.

Kilobyte (K, KB, K-byte): Unit representing about 1000 bytes.

Knowledge work system (KWS): Specialized information system used to create information in a specific area of expertise.

Label: Column or row heading in a spreadsheet.

LAN: *See* Local area network

Laptop: Portable computer that weighs between 10 and 16 pounds.

Laser printer: Printer that creates dotlike images on a drum, using a laser beam light source.

LCD: *See* Liquid crystal display

Levels of programming languages: Levels used by computer professionals to describe programming languages. A lower-level language is one closer to the language the computer uses itself. A higher-level language is closer to the language humans use.

Light pen: Light-sensitive penlike device used with a special monitor to enter commands by touching the monitor with the pen.

Link: A connection to related information.

Liquid crystal display (LCD): Display consisting of liquid crystal molecules whose optical properties can be altered by an applied electric field.

List address: Internet mailing list address. Members of a mailing list communicate by sending messages to the list address.

Local area network (LAN): Network consisting of computers and other devices that are physically near each other, such as within the same building.

Local bus: Bus combining the bus-width capabilities of MCA and EISA with the ability to send video instructions at speeds to match the microprocessor.

Logic error: Error that occurs when a programmer has used an incorrect calculation or left out a programming procedure.

Logic structure: Structure that controls the logical sequence in which computer program instructions are executed. The three structures are sequence, selection, and loop.

Loop structure: Logic structure in which a process may be repeated as long as a certain condition remains true.

Lurking: Observing or reading communications from others on an Internet discussion group without participating.

Machine language: Language in which data is represented in 1s and 0s.

Magnetic-ink character recognition (MICR): Direct-entry scanning device used in banks. This technology is used to automatically read the futuristic-looking numbers on the bottom of checks.

Magnetic tape drive: Device used to read data from and store data on magnetic tape.

Magnetic tape streamer: Device that allows duplication (backup) of the data stored on a microcomputer hard disk.

Magnetic tape unit: *See* Magnetic tape drive

Mailing list: Type of discussion group available on the Internet.

Mail merge: Feature that allows the merging of different names and addresses so the same form letter can be mailed to different people.

Mainframe: Computer that can process several million program instructions per second. Large organizations rely on these room-size systems to handle large programs with lots of data.

Main memory: *See* Memory

MAN: *See* Metropolitan area network

Management information system (MIS): Computer-based information system that produces standardized reports in summarized, structured form. It is used to support middle managers.

Mark sensing: *See* Optical-character recognition

Master file: Complete file containing all records current up to the last update.

MB, M-byte: *See* Megabyte

MCA: *See* Micro Channel Architecture

Medium band: Bandwidth of special leased lines, used mainly with minicomputers and mainframe computers.

Megabyte (MB, M-byte): Unit representing 1 million bytes.

Megahertz (MHZ): Unit representing 1 million beats (cycles) per second.

Memory: Part of the microcomputer that holds data for processing, instructions for processing the data, and information (processed data) waiting to be output or sent to secondary storage.

Memory manager: In Windows, extends the capabilities of DOS to access well beyond 640 kilobytes.

Memory-resident program: Program that stays in memory all the time, until the computer is turned off.

Menu: List of commands available for manipulating data.

Metasearch program: *See* Off-line search utility

Metropolitan area network (MAN): Network linking office buildings in a city.

MHZ: *See* Megahertz

MICR: *See* Magnetic-ink character recognition

Micro Channel Architecture (MCA): Bus-line standard developed to support IBM PS/2 microcomputers. MCA bus has a 32-bit-wide data path.

Microcomputer: Small, low-cost computer designed for individual users.

Microcomputer database: *See* Individual database

Microprocessor: The central processing unit of a microcomputer. The microprocessor is contained on a single integrated circuit chip.

Microprocessor chip: The single electronic component of a microcomputer that contains the central processing unit.

Microsecond: One-millionth of a second.

Microwave communication: Communication using high-frequency radio waves that travel in straight lines through the air.

Middle-level manager: Manager dealing with control and planning. The manager implements the long-term goals of the organization.

Midrange computer: *See* Minicomputer

Minicomputer: Desk-sized machine falling in between microcomputers and mainframes in processing speed and data-storing capacity.

MIS: *See* Management information system

MO (magnetic optical) disk: Disk that uses both magnetic and optical technologies to store data.

Modem: Communications device that translates the electronic signals from a computer into electronic signals that can travel over a telephone line.

Modulation: Process of converting digital signals to analog signals.

Module: *See* Program module

Monitor: Output device like a television screen that displays data processed by the computer.

Morphing: Special effect in which one image seems to melt into another.

Motherboard: *See* System board

Mouse: Device that typically rolls on the desktop and directs the cursor on the display screen.

Multimedia: Technology that can link all sorts of media into one form of presentation.

Multimedia PC: Powerful microcomputer system with a fast microprocessor and a large hard-disk drive. A multimedia system also has a soundboard, speakers, and a CD-ROM drive.

Multiprocessing: Operating system that can effectively subdivide the CPU into separate, independent parts. This allows several users to independently run programs at the same time.

Multiprogramming: Operating system that interrupts and switches rapidly back and forth between several programs while they are running. This allows several users to run different programs seemingly at the same time.

Multitasking: Operating system that allows a single user to run several application programs at the same time.

Multiuser: Refers to an environment in which two or more users can use a computer at the same time.

National Information Highway (NIH): Term used to describe the future of communication networks and computers. *See also* Internet

National Information Infrastructure (NII): *See* National Information Highway

Natural language: Language designed to give people a more human connection with computers.

Netiquette: Etiquette for e-mail.

Network architecture: Describes how a network is arranged and how the resources are shared.

Network bridge: Connects networks of the same configuration.

Network computer: *See* Network terminal

Network database: Database with a hierarchical arrangement of nodes, except that each child node may have more than one parent node.

Network gateway: Connection by which a local area network may be linked to other local area networks or to larger networks.

Network manager: Computer professional who ensures that existing information and communication systems are operating effectively and that new ones are implemented as needed. Also responsible for meeting security and privacy requirements.

Network terminal: Low-cost alternative to intelligent terminal; relies on host computer or server for software. Also called network computer.

Newsgroup: Most popular type of Internet discussion group. Newsgroups use a special network of computers called the UseNet. Each of these computers maintains the newsgroup listing. The newsgroups are organized into major topic areas that are further subdivided into hierarchies.

Node: Any device connected to a network. Also, points in a hierarchical database connected like the branches of an upside-down tree.

Noninterlaced monitor: Monitor that creates images by scanning each line down the screen.

Nonvolatile storage: Permanent storage used to preserve data and programs.

Notebook: Portable computer weighing between 5 and 10 pounds.

Numeric keypad: The keys 0 to 9, located on separate keys adjacent to the keyboard, used for tasks principally involving numbers.

Numeric keys: *See* Numeric keypad

Object-oriented programming (OOP): Methodology in which a program is organized into objects, each containing both the data and processing operations necessary to perform a task.

Object-oriented software development: Software development approach that focuses less on the tasks and more on defining the relationships between previously defined procedures or objects.

OCR: *See* Optical-character recognition

Off-line browser: Program that automatically connects to selected Web sites, downloads HTML documents, and saves them to your hard disk. Also called pull product and Web-downloading utility.

Off-line search utility: Program that automatically submits your search request to several indices and search engines, then creates an index from received information. Also called metasearch program.

Office automation system (OAS): System designed primarily to support data workers. It focuses on managing documents, communicating, and scheduling.

OMR: *See* Optical-mark recognition

Online service provider: Provides access to Internet plus other services.

OOP: *See* Object-oriented programming

Open architecture: Microcomputer architecture allowing users to expand their systems by inserting optional devices known as expansion boards.

Operating environment: Program designed to extend the capabilities of DOS by creating an easy-to-use environment in which to work.

Operating system: Software that interacts between application software and the computer. The operating system handles such details as running programs, storing data and programs, and processing data.

Optical-character recognition (OCR): Scanning device that uses special preprinted characters, such as those printed on utility bills, that can be read by a light source and changed into machine-readable code.

Optical disk: Storage device that can hold 650 megabytes of data. Lasers are used to record and read data on the disk.

Optical-mark recognition (OMR): Device that senses the presence or absence of a mark, such as a pencil mark.

Organization chart: Chart showing the levels of management and formal lines of authority in an organization.

OS/2: The operating system developed for IBM's more powerful microcomputers.

Output device: Equipment that translates processed information from the central processing unit into a form that can be understood.

Packaged software: Programs prewritten by professional programmers that typically are offered for sale on a floppy disk.

Packet: Before a message is sent on the Internet, it is broken down into small parts called packets. Each packet is then sent separately over the Internet. At the receiving end, the packets are reassembled into the correct order.

Page: The linked information sources in a hypertext document. Any one page may contain many hypertext links to related information. *See also* Home page.

Page description language: Language that describes the shape and position of letters and graphics to the printer.

Paint program: *See* Image editor

Palmtop computer: *See* Personal digital assistant (PDA)

Parallel approach: Systems implementation in which old and new systems are operated side by side until the new one has shown it is reliable.

Parallel data transmission: Data transmission in which bits flow through separate lines simultaneously.

Parallel port: Used to connect external devices that send or receive a lot of data over a short distance. Mostly used to connect printers to system unit.

Parent node: Node one level above the node being considered in a hierarchical database or network.

Parity bit: Extra bit automatically added to a byte during keyboarding to test accuracy.

Pascal: Procedural programming language widely used on microcomputers.

Passive-matrix monitor: Monitor that creates images by scanning the entire screen.

Password: Special sequence of numbers or letters that limits access to information, such as electronic mail.

Paste: In word processing, the command that reinserts highlighted text into a document.

Payroll: Activity concerned with calculating employee paychecks.

PC card: *See* PCMCIA card

PCMCIA (Personal Computer Memory Card International Association) card: Credit card–sized expansion boards developed for portable computers.

PC/TV: The merger of microcomputers and television.

Peer-to-peer network system: Network in which nodes can act as both servers and clients. For example, one microcomputer can obtain files located on another microcomputer and can also provide files to other microcomputers.

Pen plotter: Plotter that creates plots by moving a pen or pencil over drafting paper.

Periodic report: Report generated at regular intervals.

Peripheral Component Interconnect (PCI): Bus architecture that combines the capabilities of MCA and EISA with the ability to send video instructions at speeds to match the microprocessor.

Peripheral device: Hardware that is outside of the system unit, such as a disk drive or a printer.

Personal computer: *See* Microcomputer

Personal digital assistant (PDA): A device that typically combines pen input, writing recognition, personal organizational tools, and communication capabilities in a very small package. Also called Handheld PC and palmtop computer.

Personal information manager (PIM): Software designed to help maximize personal productivity. Typically includes electronic calendars, to-do lists, address books, and notepads. Also called Desktop manager.

Personal laser printer: Inexpensive laser printer widely used by single users to produce black-and-white documents.

PERT (Program Evaluation Review Technique) chart: Chart showing the timing of a project and the relationships among its tasks. The chart identifies which tasks must be completed before others can begin.

Phased approach: Systems implementation in which the new system is implemented gradually over a period of time.

Physical security: Activity concerned with protecting hardware from possible human and natural disasters.

Pilot approach: Systems implementation in which the new system is tried out in only one part of the organization. Later it is implemented throughout the rest of the organization.

PIM: *See* Personal information manager

Pixel: Smallest unit on the screen that can be turned on and off or made different shades.

Platform scanner: Hand-held direct-entry device used to read special characters on price tags.

Plotter: Special-purpose output device for producing bar charts, maps, architectural drawings, and three-dimensional illustrations.

Plug and Play: Set of hardware and software standards developed to create operating systems, processing units, and expansion boards, as well as other devices, that are able to configure themselves.

Plug-in: Program that is automatically loaded and operates as part of a browser.

Plug-in board: *See* Expansion board

Pointer: Additional connection between parent node and child node in a hierarchical database. *See* also Cursor

Point-of-sale (POS) terminal: Terminal that consists of a keyboard, screen, and printer. It is used like a cash register.

Polling: Process whereby a host computer or file server asks each connecting device whether it has a message to send and then allows the message to be sent.

Port: Connecting socket on the outside of the system unit. Used to connect input and output devices to the system unit.

Portable language: Language that can be run on more than one kind of computer.

Portable operating system: Operating system that can be used with different types of computer systems.

POS terminal: *See* Point-of-sale (POS) terminal

PPP (point-to-point protocol): Software that allows your computer to become part of a client/server network. The provider or host computer is the server providing access to the Internet. Your computer is the client. Using special client software, your computer is able to communicate with server software running on the provider's computer and on other Internet computers.

Preliminary investigation: First phase of systems analysis and design. It involves defining the problem, suggesting alternative systems, and preparing a short report.

Presentation graphics: Graphics used to communicate a message or to persuade other people.

Primary storage: Memory that holds data and program instructions for processing the data.

Printer: Device that produces printed paper output.

Privacy: Computer ethics issue concerning the collection and use of data about individuals.

Privacy Act of 1974: Law designed to restrict the way federal agencies share information about American citizens. It prohibits federal information collected for one purpose from being used for a different purpose.

Problem-oriented languages: Languages designed to solve specific problems.

Procedural language: Language designed to express the logic that can solve problems.

Procedures: Rules or guidelines to follow when using hardware, software, and data.

Processing rights: Refers to which people have access to what kind of data.

Processor: *See* Central processing unit

Program: List of instructions for the computer to follow to process data. *See also* Software

Program analysis: *See* Program specification

Program definition: *See* Program specification

Program design: Creation of a solution using programming techniques such as top-down program design, pseudocode, flowcharts, logic structures, object-oriented programming, and CASE tools.

Program flowchart: Flowchart graphically presenting the detailed sequence of steps needed to solve a programming problem.

Program maintenance: Activity of updating software to correct errors, improve usability, standardize, and adjust to organizational changes.

Programmer: Computer professional who creates new software or revises existing software.

Programming: Six-step procedure for creating a program.

Program module: Logically related program statements.

Program specification: Programming step in which objectives, outputs, inputs, and processing requirements are determined.

Project: One-time operation composed of several tasks that must be completed during a stated period of time.

Project management software: Software that enables users to plan, schedule, and control the people, resources, and costs needed to complete a project on time.

Property: Computer ethics issue relating to who owns data and rights to software.

Proprietary database: Enormous database an organization develops to cover certain particular objects. Access to this type of database is usually offered for a fee.

Protocol: Rules for exchanging data between computers.

Prototyping: Building of a model (prototype) that can be modified before the actual system is installed. It allows users to find out right away how a change in the system can help their work.

Provider: *See* Host computer

Pseudocode: Narrative form of the logic of a computer program.

Public Gopher: Internet software that allows free access to its facilities.

Pull product: *See* Off-line browser

Purchasing: Buying of raw materials and services.

Push product: *See* Information pusher

Query: Locates specified records and displays selected fields.

Query language: Easy-to-use language understandable to most users. It is used to search and generate reports from a database.

RAIDs: *See* Redundant arrays of inexpensive disks

RAM (random access memory): Volatile storage that holds the program and data the CPU is presently processing.

Random access memory (RAM): *See* RAM (random access memory)

Read: *See* Reading data

Reader/sorter: Special-purpose machine that reads characters made of ink containing magnetized particles.

Reading data: For floppy disks, the process of taking the magnetized spots from the disk, converting them to electronic signals, and transmitting them to primary storage inside the computer.

Read-only: Refers to a disk that cannot be written on or erased by the user.

Read-only memory (ROM): *See* ROM (read-only memory)

Read-write head: Electronic head that can read data from and write data onto a disk.

Real-time processing: Processing that occurs when data is processed at the same time the transaction occurs.

Recalculation: Process of recomputing values in electronic spreadsheets automatically.

Record: Each line of information in a database is a record. A record is a collection of related fields.

Redundant arrays of inexpensive disks (RAIDs): Groups of inexpensive hard-disk drives related or grouped together using networks and special software. They improve performance by expanding external storage.

Register: High-speed staging area that holds data and instructions temporarily during processing.

Rehearsal: Feature of presentation graphics that allows you to practice and time your presentation.

Relation: Table in a relational database in which data elements are stored.

Relational database: Most flexible database organization, where data elements are stored in tables and no hierarchical structure is imposed.

Release: The number after the period in a software package. Changes in releases refer to minor changes.

Rename: Give new filename to file on a disk.

Repetitive motion injury: *See* Repetitive strain injury

Repetitive strain injury (RSI): Category of injuries resulting from fast, repetitive work that causes neck, wrist, hand, and arm pain.

Replace: In word processing, command that enables the user to search for a word and replace it with another.

Rewriteable optical disk: Similar to CD-Rs except that they can be written to many times. That is, a disk that has been written on can be erased and used over and over again.

Right to Financial Privacy Act of 1979: Law setting strict procedures that federal agencies must follow when seeking to examine customer records in banks.

Ring network: Network in which each device is connected to two other devices, forming a ring. There is no host computer, and messages are passed around the ring until they reach the correct destination.

RISC (reduced instruction set computer) chip: Powerful microprocessor chip found in workstations.

Robot: Machine used in factories and elsewhere that can be reprogrammed to do more than one task.

Robotics: Field of study concerned with developing and using robots.

ROM (read-only memory): Refers to chips that have programs built into them at the factory. The contents of such chips cannot be changed by the user.

Row: Part of the grid of a spreadsheet. Rows are labeled down the left side.

RPG (Report Program Generator): Procedural language that enables people to prepare business reports quickly and easily.

RS-232C connector: Serial port, a port set up for serial data transmission.

RSI: *See* Repetitive strain injury

Sales order processing: Activity that records the demands of customers for a company's products or services.

Satellite communication: Communication using satellites as microwave relay stations.

Save: Feature allowing you to store your work on a floppy or hard disk.

Scenario tool: Program tool that allows the user to test the effect of different combinations of data.

Screen resolution: Measure of the crispness of images and characters on a screen, usually specified in terms of the number of pixels in a row or column.

Scroll bar: Bar usually located on the right and/or bottom of the screen. It enables the user to display additional information not currently visible on the screen.

SCSI card: Small computer interface card. This card uses only one slot and can connect as many as seven devices to the system unit.

Search: In word processing, command that enables the user to find a particular term in a document.

Search operation: Activity in which a disk drive rotates a floppy disk to proper position so the read-write head can find the appropriate data on the disk.

Secondary storage: Permanent storage used to preserve programs and data, including floppy disks, hard disks, and magnetic tape.

Sector: Section shaped like a pie wedge that divides the tracks on a disk.

Security: The protection of information, hardware, and software.

Seek operation: Activity in which the access arm in a disk drive moves back and forth over the floppy disk to read data from or write data to the disk.

Selection structure: Logic structure that determines which of two paths will be followed when a decision must be made by a program.

Semiconductor: Silicon chip through which electricity flows with some resistance.

Sequence structure: Logic structure in which one program statement follows another.

Sequential access storage: Method of storage where information is stored in sequence, and all information preceding the desired information must be read first.

Sequential file organization: File organization in which records are stored physically one after another in predetermined order.

Serial data transmission: Method of transmission in which bits flow in a series, one after another.

Serial port: Used to connect external devices that send or receive data one bit at a time over a long distance. Used for mouse, keyboard, modem, and many other devices.

Server: A connection to the Internet that stores document files used to display pages.

Shared laser printer: More expensive laser printer used by a group of users to produce black-and-white documents.

Shell: Special-purpose program that allows a person to custom-build a particular kind of expert system.

Shortcut key: Key in applications for a frequently used command. They make it easier and faster to select certain commands.

Silicon chip: Tiny circuit board etched on a small square of sandlike material called silicon. Chips are mounted on carrier packages, which then plug into sockets on the system board.

Simplex communication: Mode of communication in which data travels in one direction only.

SLIP (serial line internet protocol): Internet protocol that enables your computer to become part of a client/server network. The provider or host computer is the server providing access to the Internet. Your computer is the client.

Smart card: Card about the size of a credit card containing a tiny built-in microprocessor. It can be used to hold such information as frequent flier miles.

Soft copy: Images or characters output on a monitor screen.

Software: Computer program.

Software Copyright Act of 1980: Law allowing owners of programs to make copies for backup purposes, and to modify them to make them useful, provided they are not resold or given away.

Software development: *See* Programming

Software piracy: Unauthorized copying of programs for personal gain.

Software suite: Individual application programs that are sold together as a group.

Solver tool: Program tool that allows the user to find the values needed to achieve a particular end result.

Source document: Original version of a document before any processing has been performed on it.

Spelling checker: Program used with a word processor to check the spelling of typed text against an electronic dictionary.

Spider: *See* Agent

Spike: *See* Voltage surge

Spreadsheet: Computer-produced spreadsheet based on the traditional accounting "worksheet" that has rows and columns that can be used to present and analyze data.

Star network: Network of computers or peripheral devices linked to a central computer through which all communications pass. Control is maintained by polling.

Structured programming techniques: Techniques that consist of top-down program design, pseudocode, flowcharts, and logic structures.

Structured query language (SQL): A database programming control language that allows direct communication to specialized mainframe databases.

Style sheet: In desktop publishing, a feature that enables the user to determine the basic appearance of single or multiple pages.

Subnotebook: Hand-held or pocket-size portable computer.

Subscription address: Mailing list address. To participate in a mailing list, you must first subscribe by sending an e-mail request to the mailing list subscription address.

Supercomputer: Fastest calculating device ever invented, processing billions of program instructions per second.

Super VGA, SVGA: Refers to a very high resolution standard that displays up to 256 colors.

Supervisor: Manager responsible for managing and monitoring workers. Supervisors have responsibility for operational matters.

Surge protector: Device separating the computer from the power source of the wall outlet. When a voltage surge occurs, a circuit breaker is activated, protecting the computer system.

Synchronous transmission: Method whereby data is transmitted several bytes or a block at a time.

Syntax error: Violation of the rules of whatever language a computer program is written in.

System: Collection of activities and elements designed to accomplish a goal.

System 7.5: Apple Macintosh operating system designed for the Motorola PowerPC microprocessor.

System board: Flat board that usually contains the CPU and some memory chips.

System clock: Clock that controls how fast all the operations within a computer take place.

System flowchart: Flowchart that shows the kinds of equipment used to handle the data or information flow.

System software: "Background" software that enables the application software to interact with the computer. It includes programs that help the computer manage its own internal resources.

System unit: Part of a microcomputer that contains the CPU.

Systems analysis: Determining the requirements for a new system. Data is collected about the present system, analyzed, and new requirements are determined.

Systems analysis and design: Six-phase problem-solving procedure for examining an information system and improving it.

Systems analyst: Computer professional who studies an organization's systems to determine what actions to take and how to use computer technology to assist them.

Systems audit: A systems audit compares the performance of a new system to the original design specifications to determine if the new procedures are actually improving productivity.

Systems design: Phase consisting of designing alternative systems, selecting the best system, and writing a systems design report.

Systems development: Phase consisting of developing software, acquiring hardware, and testing the new system.

Systems implementation: Process of changing from the old system to the new and training people to use it.

Systems life cycle: Phases of systems analysis and design.

Systems maintenance: Consists of a systems audit and periodic evaluation.

Tab: Feature in 3-D spreadsheet that allows you to move among multiple worksheets.

Table (in database): The list of records in a database.

Table (in word processing): Text and/or numbers arranged in row-and-column format.

Tag: Statement in Hypertext Markup Language that controls how pages are displayed and provides links.

TB, T-byte: *See* Terabyte

TCP/IP (transmission control protocol/Internet protocol): The two standard protocols for all communications on the Internet.

Technical writer: Computer professional who explains in writing how a computer program works.

Television board: Contains a TV tuner and video converter that changes the TV signal into one that can be displayed on your monitor.

Telnet: Internet service that allows you to connect to a host computer, log on to that computer, and run programs from that computer. Your microcomputer acts as a terminal.

Terabyte (TB, T-byte): Unit representing about 1 trillion bytes.

Terminal: Form of input (and output) device that consists of a keyboard, a monitor, and a communications link.

Terminal connection: Method of accessing the Internet using a high-speed modem and standard telephone lines.

Terminal network system: Network system in which processing power is centralized in one large computer, usually a mainframe. The nodes connected to this host computer are terminals with little or no processing capabilities.

Text art: *See* Word art

Thermal printer: Printer that uses heat elements to produce images on heat-sensitive paper.

Thesaurus: Program that enables the user to quickly find the right word or an alternative word by presenting an on-screen thesaurus.

3-D spreadsheet: Spreadsheet program that includes multiple worksheets.

Time-sharing system: System that allows several users to share resources in the host computer.

Toolbar: Bar located typically below the menu bar. It contains icons or graphical representations for commonly used commands.

Top-down analysis methodology: Method used to identify the top-level component of a system and break this component down into smaller components for analysis.

Top-down program design: Process of identifying the top element (module) for a program and then breaking the top element down into smaller pieces in a hierarchical fashion.

Top-level manager: Manager concerned with long-range (strategic) planning. Top-level managers supervise middle-level managers.

Topology: The configuration of a network.

Touch screen: Monitor screen that allows actions or commands to be entered by the touch of a finger.

Track: Closed, concentric ring on a disk on which data is recorded.

Tractor feed: Printer mechanism with sprockets that advance the printer paper, using holes on edges of continuous-form paper.

Transaction: Event recorded in a database.

Transaction file: File containing recent changes to records that will be used to update the master file.

Transaction processing system (TPS): System that records day-to-day transactions.

Trojan horse program: Computer crime in which instructions can be written to destroy or modify software or data.

TSR (terminate stay resident): Refers to a program that stays in the computer's memory all the time, until the computer is turned off.

Twisted pair: Copper-wire telephone line.

Typewriter keys: Keys on a keyboard that resemble the regular letters, numbers, punctuation marks, and so on, on a typewriter.

Undo: Program feature that allows the user to restore work to the way it was before the last command was selected.

Unicode: Sixteen-bit code designed to support international languages like Chinese and Japanese.

Unix: An operating system originally developed for minicomputers. It is now important because it can run on many of the more powerful microcomputers.

Uploading: Process of transferring information from the computer the user is operating to a remote computer.

Upper memory: Memory located between 640 kilobytes and 1 megabyte of RAM. Although DOS uses this area to store information about the microcomputer's hardware, it is frequently underused and can be used by application programs.

USB (universal serial port): Expected to replace serial and parallel ports.

UseNet: Special network of computers that support newsgroups.

User name: Special sequence of numbers or letters that limits access to electronic mail.

Utility program: Program that performs common repetitious tasks, such as keeping files orderly, merging, and sorting.

Value: Number contained in a cell in a spreadsheet.

Vector image: Graphics file made up of a collection of objects such as lines, rectangles, and ovals.

Version: The number before the period in a software package. Changes in version number indicate major changes.

VESA local bus (VL-bus): A bus architecture that combines the capabilities of MCA and EISA with the ability to send video instructions at speeds to match the microprocessor.

VGA (video graphics array): Circuit board that may be inserted into a microcomputer and offers up to 256 colors.

Video display: *See* Monitor

Video display terminal (VDT): *See* Monitor

Video Privacy Protection Act of 1988: Law preventing retailers from selling or disclosing video-rental records without the customer's consent or a court order.

Virtual environment: *See* Virtual reality

Virtual memory: Feature of an operating system that increases the amount of memory available to run programs.

Virtual reality: Interactive sensory equipment (headgear and gloves) that allows users to experience alternative realities to the physical world.

Virus: *See* Computer virus

Voiceband: Bandwidth of a standard telephone line.

Voice-input device: Direct-entry device that converts speech into a numeric code that can be processed by a computer.

Voice-messaging system: Computer system linked to telephones that converts human voice into digital bits and stores telephone messages in "voice mailboxes" for later retrieval.

Voice-output device: Device that makes sounds resembling human speech that are actually prerecorded vocalized sounds.

Voice-recognition system: *See* Voice-input device

Volatile storage: Temporary storage that destroys the current data when power is lost or new data is read.

Voltage surge (spike): Excess of electricity, which may destroy chips or other electronic computer components.

WAIS (wide area information server): Internet search tool that extends the search capabilities of Gopher and Veronica. A WAIS search on a topic is more thorough and provides more specific references.

WAN: *See* Wide area network

Wand reader: Special-purpose handheld device used to read OCR characters.

Web: *See* World Wide Web

Web authoring program: Word processing program for generating Web pages. Also called HTML editor; Web page editor.

Web Broadcaster utility: *See* Information pusher

Web directory: *See* Index

Web-downloading utility: *See* Off-line browser

Web page editor: *See* Web authoring program

Web site: A location on a server.

Web terminal: *See* Internet terminal

What-if analysis: Spreadsheet feature in which changing one or more numbers results in the automatic recalculation of all related formulas.

Wide area network (WAN): Countrywide network that uses microwave relays and satellites to reach users over long distances.

Windows: An operating environment that extends the capability of DOS.

Windows 95: Advanced operating system designed for today's powerful microcomputers. It does not require DOS to run.

Windows NT: An operating system designed to run on a wide range of powerful computers and microprocessors.

Wireless modem: Modem that connects to the serial port but does not connect to telephone lines. It receives through the air.

Word: Unit that describes the number of bits in a common unit of information.

Word art: Graphics enhancement that enables the user to manipulate text into various shapes in a document. Also called text art.

Word processing: Use of a computer to create, edit, save, and print documents composed of text.

Word wrap: Feature of word processing that automatically moves the cursor from the end of one line to the beginning of the next.

Workgroup: Program that allows multiple users to collaborate electronically on a spreadsheet.

Worksheet: *See* Spreadsheet

Worksheet file: File created by an electronic spreadsheet.

Workstation: More sophisticated microcomputer that can communicate with more powerful computers and sources of information.

World Wide Web (WWW, W3, the Web): Internet search tool that uses hypertext to jump from document to document and from computer to computer. The Web is accessed by browsers.

Worm: Variant on computer virus, a destructive program that fills a computer system with self-replicating information, clogging the system so that its operations are slowed or stopped.

WORM (write once, read many): Form of optical disk that allows data to be written only once but read many times without deterioration.

Write: *See* Writing data

Write once: Refers to an optical disk on which data is recorded by lasers and cannot be erased by the user.

Write-protect notch: Notch on a floppy disk used to prevent the computer from destroying data or information on the disk.

Writing data: For floppy disks, the process of taking the electronic information processed by the computer and recording it magnetically onto the disk.

WWW: *See* World Wide Web

XGA (extended graphics array): Circuit board that can be inserted into a microcomputer and offers up to 256 colors under normal circumstances and more than 65,000 colors with special equipment.

Index

Index note: The f. following a page number refers to a figure.

Illustration Credits

Courtesy of International Business Machines,Inc.: 1-3, 1-5, 1-6, 1-13, 4-2a, 4-9, 5-10, 6-14, 7-14, 12-14, YF-9
Courtesy of Apple Computer, Inc.: 1-4, 1-5, 1-17, 4-2b, 4-10, 6-9, 7-1
Courtesy of CRAY Research, Inc.: 1-8
John Greenleigh/Apple: 1-10, YF-8
Courtesy of Intel Corporation: 1-14
Bonnie Kamin: 1-15
Courtesy of USRobotics: 1-19
Courtesy of Microsoft Corporation: 2-5, 2-13, 4-5, 4-6, 4-7, 4-8, 6-3, 6-4
Courtesy of Asymetrix: 3-6
Courtesy of Lotus Development Corporation: 3-11
Andrew Sacks / Tony Stone Images: 3-14
Michael Abramson / Woodfin Camp & Associates: 3-15
Courtesy of ExSys, Inc. : 3-16
Courtesy of SRI International: 3-17
Courtesy of Interactive Pictures Corp.: 3.a
Courtesy of Sun Microsystems, Inc.: 4-11
Scott Goodwin: 5-12
Courtesy of Xircom: 5-13
Mark Richards/ PhotoEdit: 6-1
Courtesy of EPSON: 6-5
Courtesy of H.E.I., Inc.: 6-7
Courtesy of Caterpillar,Inc.: 6-8
Courtesy of Hewlett-Packard Company: 6-10, 6-16, 6-20, 6-21b, 6-25, 10-13
Courtesy of Lanier Worldwide: 6-11
Courtesy of NCR Corporation: 6-12, 6-13
Courtesy of CTX, Inc.: 6-17
Courtesy of Epson: 6-19
Courtesy of Tektronix: 6-22
Courtesy of CalComp: 6-24
Courtesy of Boise: 6-26
Courtesy of Seagate Technology Inc.: 7-6
Courtesy of SyQuest Technology: 7-7
Scott Goodwin: 7-16
Richard Laird/ FPG International: 8-2
Fred Bodin: 8-9
Courtesy of Intel Corporation: 8-10
Courtesy of CompuServ: 9-10
Spencer Grant/ Stock,Boston Inc.: 9-12
David Young/Photo Edit: 10-2
Courtesy of Canadian Airlines Intl.: 10-8
Tony Stone Images: 10-10
Steven Parks/ Tony Stone Images: 10-12
Darrell Peterson/ West Stock: 11-2, 11-11
Gary Walts/ The Image Works: 11-10
Tim Brown/Tony Stone Images: 11-12, 12-2, 12-16
Jeff Personsic/ Stock,Boston Inc.: 12-15
Courtesy of Acer: WI-2
Stacey Pickerell/ Tony Stone Images: WI-3
AFP/Bettman: WI-11
Courtesy of Pretty Good Privacy Inc.: WI-12
Tim Crosby/ Liaison International: YF-1
Courtesy of American Airlines: YF-2
Courtesy of Federal Express: YF-3
Bill Delzell: YF-4, YF-5, YF-6
Courtesy of Softbank Comdex: YF-7
Bruce Ayers/ Tony Stone Images: YF-10
Terry Vine/ Tony Stone Images: YF-11
Keith Wood/ Tony Stone Images: YF-12

Following find the Web addresses for Web sites used in our On the Web section:

Page 21: 1 http://www.internet-mall.com, *2* http://www.ipl.org, *3* http://www.yahoo.com (Text and artwork copyright " 1996 by YAHOO!, Inc. All rights reserved. YOHOO! And the YAHOO! Logo are trademarks of YAHOO!, Inc.), *4* http://www.ticketmaster.com;
page 47: 1 http://www8.zdnet.com/products/pirnuser.html,
2 http://www.microsoft.com/OfficeReference/GettingReady, *3* http://www.microsoft.com/mspowerpoint, *4* http://www.happypuppy.com; *page 69: 1* http://www.macromedia.com/software,
2 http://www.killersites.com/1-design, *3* http://www.yahoo.com, *4* http://www.shareware.com;
page 91: 1 http://macos.apple.com, *2* http://www.Microsoft.com/windows95/default.asp,
3 http://www.yahoo.com, *4* http://www.unitedmedia.com/comics;
page 113: 1 http://www.intel.com/pentiumII/home.htm, *2* http://www.pcworld.com/hardware,
3 http://www.yahoo.com, *4* http://www.wired.com/news/news/technology/index.html; *page 135: 1* http://www-nt-ok.creaf.com/sound, *2* http://www.webtv.net/corp/HTML/home.about.html (WebTV and WebTV Networks are trademarks of WebTV Networks, Inc.), *3* http://speech.apple.com,
4 http://www.teleport.com/~ilm/how_f.htm; *page 155: 1* http://www.km.philips.com/dvd,
2 http://www.iomega.com, *3* http://www.yahoo.com, *4* http://www.autoweb.com;
page 183: 1 http://www.att.com/home64, *2* http://www.direcpc.com, *3* http://www.excite.com,
4 http://www.travelocity.com; *page 203: 1* http://www.stockmaster.com (Reprinted with permission from Marketplace, Inc.), *2* http://www.stockmaster.com/sm/g/A/AAPL.html,
3 http://www.webcrawler.com, *4* http://www.musicblvd.com; *page 225: 1* http://www.cadkey.com,
2 http://www.delorme.com/products/tripmate, *3* http://www.yahoo.com,
4 http://www.abcnews.com; *page 245: 1* http://www.eatright.org,
2 http://www.urecruit.com/home.htm,
3 http://www.yahoo.com, *4* http://my.excite.com/horoscopes; *page 271:*
1 http://www.ibm.com/Java, *2* http://www.microsoft.com/activeplatform/default.asp,
3 http://www.hotbot.com/index.html,
4 http://www.weather.com/twc/homepage.twc;
page WI–22: 1 http://www.pgp.com/privacy/privacy.cgi, *2* http://www.mcafee.com,
3 http://guide.infoseek.com (Reprinted by permission, Infoseek, Ultrasmart, Ultraseek, Iseek, Quickseek, Imageseek, Ultrashop, "proof of intelligent life on the net" and the Infoseek logos are trademarks of Infoseek Corporation which may be registered in certain jurisdictions. Other trademarks shown are trademarks of their respective owners. Copyright " 1995-1997 Infoseek Corporation. All rights reserved.), *4* http://espn.sportszone.com; *page YF14:*
1 http://www.wired.com/news, *2* http://www.jobweb.org (Reprinted from JobWeb with permission of the National Association of Colleges and Employers, copyright holder.), *3* http://www.yahoo.com,
4 http://www.movielink.com/?UID:13001